Psychology *for* Higher

by

Gail Staddon
Aileen Duffy
Richard Cherrie
Jonathan Firth
Jon Aidan McDermott

Consultant Editor:
Morag Williamson

UNITY PUBLICATIONS Ltd

Unity Publications Limited
Registered Office: Sherwood House, 7 Glasgow Road, Paisley, PA1 3QS.

First published 2005.

British Library Cataloguing in Publication Data
A catalogue record for this book can be obtained from the British Library.

ISBN-13 digit: 978-0-954598-71-6
ISBN-10 digit: 0-954598-71-7

Text formatting designed by Unity Publications Ltd.
Cover designed by "impact".
Typeset by Printcare.

Acknowledgements

The authors of this book would like to thank www.allfreeclipart.com for use of the clipart of the palm tree in Chapter 1. Every effort has been made to trace and contact holders of copyright for materials used in the production of this text. However, if any material has been incorrectly acknowledged, or not acknowledged, the publishers would be pleased to correct this at the earliest available opportunity.

The authors and Unity Publications Ltd would like to extend their wholehearted thanks to Morag Williamson for her substantial contribution to the editing of this text and to Carolyn Laird for her helpful comments provided for early drafts. Also, the authors and Unity Publications Ltd would like to extend a warm thank you to Brian J. Paul at "impact", for the design of the book cover and Stephen McKeever for technical help with the formatting.

The authors would also like to make individual acknowledgements.

Gail Staddon: I would like to extend my appreciation to my students, past, present and future, for keeping alive the challenges and the rewards of my job and who make it all worthwhile; my colleagues, who so generously share their ideas and knowledge and my family, for their unquestioning love and support.

Aileen Duffy: I would like to thank Andy for all his support – and for making the odd salad!

Jonathan Firth: I wish to gratefully acknowledge the support of my family throughout this project, in particular my wife, Fiona, who has been a constant source of love and encouragement. Thanks to the editors and other writers for their professionalism and hard work and to Carolyn Laird and Morag Williamson for invaluable comments on earlier drafts.

Jon Aidan McDermott: Thanks beyond words to my support system at home, which makes it possible to do these things. My chapter is dedicated to Maureen, my wife and our children Colette, Gregory, Nicholas and wee Caitlin. I'd like to thank my brilliant friends in the NQ setting and moderation team: Marie, Morag, Aileen, Richard, Phyllis and Carolyn and also a special thanks to Lynda Malloy, Principal Nurse of the Maxillofacial unit at the Southern General Hospital in Glasgow for all her clinical knowledge and support. Very special thanks also to Marjorie Leitch for her technical wizardry and guidance.

Notes on writers

Gail Staddon is a lecturer in Psychology and Research Methodology at Forth Valley College (formerly known as Falkirk College), teaching a range of levels from introductory psychology to degree level. Gail is an experienced marker for SQA Higher Psychology examinations and Research Investigations; she also contributes to the SQA Assessment Panel for Higher Psychology and is a member of the Higher Psychology Appeals Team. Previous experience includes working as an Associate Lecturer with The Open University in Scotland and as a business trainer in the private sector.

Aileen Duffy has been teaching psychology and sociology in Scottish Further Education Colleges for 12 years. She has taught on NC, NQ, HNC/HND, A/AS level and degree courses. Currently, she lectures at Edinburgh's Telford College and as an Associate Lecturer with the Open University. She is a setter, scrutineer, external moderator and marker for SQA and has previously taught in London, Greece, Japan and China. Whilst in Israel for a year, she conducted a participant observation study on the Israeli kibbutzim.

Richard Cherrie is an experienced lecturer in Psychology at Stevenson College Edinburgh. He has taught Psychology at various academic levels: National Certificate, NQ, HN, GCSE and GCE A Level and Access to Edinburgh University. He has also been a development officer for NQ Psychology and has been involved in the NQ Psychology Review. He is an SQA marker and setter for NQ Psychology and an External Moderator for NQ Psychology and HNC/HND Social Sciences.

Jonathan Firth has taught English in Prague and Edinburgh and currently teaches Higher Psychology at Hutcheson's Grammar School in Glasgow. He is chair of the Association for the Teaching of Psychology, Scotland (ATPS) and works as a marker for the SQA.

Jon Aidan McDermott is experienced in teaching various levels of psychology for social science and occupational therapy courses. He is presently appointed as Principal Assessor for NQ Intermediate II Psychology and is a setter, marker and moderator for both HNC/HND and National Qualification psychology units. He is involved in writing learning and teaching materials for the Colleges' Open Learning Exchanges Group (Coleg) for the SQAs revised HNC/HND Social Sciences framework.

Notes on the consultant editor

Morag Williamson has taught Higher Psychology since 2000, and 'A' level Psychology for many years prior to the introduction of the Higher. She has delivered a range of Psychology courses, to a wide variety of students from introductory to postgraduate level and has survived more syllabus revisions than she cares to remember. As Psychology Subject Development Officer for the SQA NQ Review (2002-2004), she was closely involved in the design of the revised Psychology Courses. A member of the Higher examining team since 2002, she has extensive experience of curriculum development and assessment design. Currently, she teaches at West Lothian College and Linlithgow Academy, as well as at Napier University. Her areas of special interest are research methods and statistics, developmental psychology and organisational behaviour.

Contents

Chapter 1
Understanding the Individual (continued)

Chapter 2
Investigating Behaviour Part 1: Research Methods in Psychology (continued)

Chapter 2
Investigating Behaviour – Part 2: The Research Investigation 172

Chapter 3
Social Psychology (continued)

Chapter 4
Individual Differences (continued)

Preface

Higher Psychology is fun! Yes, it can be difficult too, but that just adds to the fun and this book, *Psychology for Higher*, has been designed to cater for both of these aspects. It is comprehensive and engages with even the keenest student at this level, whilst providing the clarity and fluency required to help develop study skills in even the most challenged. It is fun, too, but not in the sense that it patronises students through the use of cartoons and flashy colour plates. Rather, it is designed on the assumption that it is the *process of doing psychology* that is fun and it is this that lies at the root of the book's simple yet informative style. Psychology is a popular and ever-growing subject in schools, colleges and universities in Scotland and beyond and *Psychology for Higher* is set to become the standard text to accompany the course. Whilst aimed specifically at Higher students, the book will also appeal to the general reader seeking an accessible introduction to psychology, providing a range of 'taster' topics that they can 'dip into'.

The aims of the book necessarily follow the aims of the Higher Psychology course. Thus the general aims of *Psychology for Higher* are:

- To encourage interest in the study of psychology and to provide an essential accompaniment to classroom delivery by providing both a broad introductory overview of the discipline, as well as the opportunity to explore a selection of topics in more depth.
- To develop an understanding of psychological theories, concepts, research studies, research methods, terminology and applications.
- To develop an appreciation of the historical context in which psychology has developed as an academic discipline, thereby noting the dynamic nature of the discipline and the importance of classic and contemporary theory and research.
- To promote a critical and evaluative approach to the discipline as a science, emphasising empirical methods and methodology, the extent to which rigorously produced evidence supports theory and applications, the importance of keeping abreast of developments in the discipline and the importance of ethical considerations at all levels.

Book structure

Since the book has been designed to follow the specific requirements of Higher Psychology, it is built around the rubric followed therein. Six core 'Domains' are addressed in *Psychology for Higher*:

- Developmental Psychology.
- Cognitive Psychology.
- Physiological Psychology.

- Social Psychology.
- Psychology of Individual Differences.
- Research Methods, incorporating practical research skills.

Three core sections of the Higher Psychology course underpin the structure of the book and directly reflect the three Units in Higher Psychology.

Section 1: Understanding the Individual

Three of the six core Domains are addressed herein: Developmental Psychology, Cognitive Psychology and Physiological Psychology. The focus is on individual processes. **Three** topics are studied in total, comprising **one** specified topic from each Domain.

In the domain of Developmental Psychology, *early socialisation* is studied as a topic. In the domain of Cognitive Psychology, the topic explored is *memory* and *stress* is analysed in the domain of Physiological Psychology.

NB *Chapter 1: Understanding the Individual* covers the requirements for this Unit in the Higher Psychology course.

Section 2: Psychology: Investigating Behaviour

The single core Domain of Research Methods, including practical research skills, is addressed in the Unit. The Unit focuses on the nature of the research process, selected types of psychological research methodology, data analysis and ethical issues pertaining to psychological research. Research skills in Psychology are developed by means of instruction on how to plan, implement, log and report on the Research Investigation. NB The Research Investigation is required for external assessment of the course; internal Unit assessment focuses on the student's plan and log of their research.

Contents include:

- The cyclical nature of the research process.
- Experimental method.
- Non-experimental methods — survey, observation, case study.
- Research issues common to all methods.
- Data analysis: quantitative and qualitative data.
- Descriptive statistics.
- Correlational design and data analysis.
- Ethical issues in research.
- Planning, implementing and reporting psychological research.

NB Both *Chapter 2: Investigating Behaviour, Part 1 – Research Methods in Psychology* and *Chapter 2: Investigating Behaviour, Part 2 – The Research Investigation*, cover the requirements for this Unit in the Higher Psychology course.

Section 3: The Individual in the Social Context

In this section, **two** of the six core Domains are addressed: Social Psychology and the Psychology of Individual Differences. In line with the requirements for Unit 3 of the Higher Psychology course, the focus is on psychological processes in the context of social interaction. **Three** topics are studied: one from each of the two Domains, and one other from either Domain. In the Domain of Social Psychology, the topics prejudice, anti-social behaviour, conformity and obedience and social relationships are studied. For the domain of Psychology of Individual Differences, topics explored comprise definitions and origins of atypical behaviour, therapies for atypical behaviour and intelligence.

NB Both *Chapter 3: Social Psychology* and *Chapter 4: Individual Differences*, cover the requirements for this Unit in the Higher Psychology.

Overall, the book attempts to encourage students to engage with the complex nature of psychological processes. It is written by a highly experienced team of authors who all teach the Higher Psychology course and all of whom are involved with the course as markers for the SQA. Each author promotes the notion that, whilst psychology is a rigorous and scientific academic discipline, psychologists interpret the human mind and behaviour in different ways. They encourage readers to develop critical thinking skills of analysis, interpretation and evaluation as they would do their own students.

The general structure of the book follows that of the Higher course and, therefore, divides content into sections matching the three Units in the course. However, students should be aware that certain common themes and inter-relationships pervade topic areas, such as issues of nature and nurture, applications of psychological knowledge in everyday life, the importance of research evidence, and the ethical responsibilities of psychologists.

Finally, it is our belief that the study of Psychology is relevant to the daily lives of those who study it. As with other social sciences, psychology has particular potential to promote the development of cognitive, interpersonal, social and organisational skills. These are transferable skills of great value to studying other subjects and in wider social and professional contexts.

Good luck and happy studying!

Introduction

There is a great deal of public interest in psychology. This is reflected in the numerous television programmes, newspaper reports and magazine articles that feature psychologists and psychological issues. Whilst much of what is churned out by the popular media is best known as 'pop' or 'pseudo' psychology, academic psychology has gained prominence, too. The BBC series *Castaway 2000* featured the Scottish psychologist, Cynthia McVey, from Glasgow Caledonian University, who commented on the psychological state of the contestants. The controversial psychologist, Oliver James, regularly appears on television and in print to comment on newsworthy topical issues and psychologists regularly appear on digital channel E4's *Big Brother's Little Brother*, to 'analyse' contestants' personality and state of mind in Channel 4's popular *Big Brother* series. It seems that nowadays people want to further their understanding both of themselves and of human behaviour in general.

But what exactly is psychology? If you tell people that you are studying psychology, they are likely to ask whether you are about to analyse them! Others may say that psychology is just 'common-sense'. We all have opinions about why people behave as they do and we try to predict others' behaviour daily. In that sense, then, we are all 'armchair psychologists' – we all attempt to explain human behaviour and the workings of the mind. However, unlike common sense explanations, psychologists offer explanations derived from the scientific process of objectively analysing and evaluating evidence gained from research.

An all-encompassing and adequate single definition of psychology is very difficult to arrive at. Psychology is a very wide and diverse discipline. Most importantly, perhaps, would be some recognition that psychology attempts to be a science. As scientists, then, most psychologists limit their study to the human mind and human behaviour. This might lead us to a definition of psychology along the lines of:

'Psychology is the scientific study of the human mind and behaviour'.

Why not try some definitions of your own? You might want to decorate the walls of your classroom with posters of them to serve as reminders!

Brief history of psychology

The word, 'psychology', was first used in the sixteenth century. It is derived from the Greek terms *psyche* (mind, soul or spirit) and *logos* (discourse or study). Rudolph Goclenius (1547-1628), a Protestant theologian, published the first book that used 'Psychology' as a title in 1590. This book termed what we now refer to as the 'mind' as the *immortal, intellective soul*, which sought truth in even the most mundane events. Over the next four hundred years, Aristotelian Catholic philosophers developed the notion of the mind as an *embodied soul*, which could not exist without the body. If human essence was contained in an embodied soul, it is, therefore, understandable that it could change with development through life, be subject to emotions and be rooted in the physical world.

The French philosopher and mathematician, Rene Descartes (1596-1650), attempted to establish, from *subjectivity*, the basis of human knowledge of external reality. He described how the immortal soul could be attached to yet remain distinct from, a purely mechanical body. The immortal soul is the source of universal reason that deals with logic and mathematics. Reason is applied by the mind to gain knowledge about the world. According to Descartes, the capacity for applying reason to obtain knowledge was innate and God-given.

Descartes' ideas influenced the work of the philosopher, John Locke (1632-1704), the first British 'empiricist'. Locke, however, argued that our ability to form representations of the world is not innate, but is based on *prior experience*. He maintained that at birth the mind was a blank slate, a *tabula rasa,* on which experience made its imprint. Empiricists believed that the only source of true knowledge about the world is *sensory experience*, that is, what comes to us through our senses or what can be inferred about the relationships between sensory facts. Followers of such ideas became known as 'associationists'. They studied how ideas combine in the mind. The development of ideas on the nature of the human mind was further advanced by the Edinburgh-born philosopher, David Hume (1711-1776). In his *Treatise on Human Nature* (1739), Hume wrote about the notion of the 'self' and the nature of cause-and-effect relationships, both of which remain key concerns in contemporary psychology.

During the nineteenth century, the experimental methods were imported from the natural sciences into psychology. Wilhelm Wundt opened the first psychology laboratory in Leipzig, Germany, in 1879. By the end of the 19th century, experimental methods were applied to the study of such diverse topics as animal learning, memory, hypnosis, social interaction and child development. Wundt and his colleagues investigated the mind through 'introspection'. They recorded the structure of their own conscious mental processes under controlled conditions and this became known as 'structuralism'. Meanwhile, in the UK, psychology became a respectable academic discipline when the first British university psychology department opened at Aberdeen University in 1899.

The American psychologist, John B. Watson (1913), questioned the validity of introspection on the basis that the results could never be refuted. He maintained that psychologists should only study the measurable and observable; that is, behaviour. This shift from the study of private thoughts to observable behaviour opened the way to 'behaviourism'. The offshoot of behaviourism, 'stimulus-response psychology', studies how humans (and non-humans) respond to stimuli in the environment and, in particular, how their responses are affected by the *rewards* or *punishments* that follow these responses.

Behaviourism remained the dominant force in psychology until the late 1950s. Psychologists were influenced by the work of computer scientists when searching for the understanding of complex behaviours that could not be explained by stimulus-response psychology. As a reaction to behaviourism, psychologists became interested in the relationship between the stimulus and the response. They began to focus on 'cognition' – mental processes such as perception, attention, memory, problem-solving, reasoning and thinking. 'Cognitive psychology' views people as information processors with minds that operate in a similar way to computer programmes.

At the same time as behaviourism was evolving in the United States, the 'psychoanalytic perspective' was being developed by Sigmund Freud (1856-1939) in Europe. The basic assumption of this approach is that human behaviour and consciousness are largely determined by *unconscious motives*. Human beings are influenced by beliefs, fears and desires of which we are unaware. We are motivated by the basic instincts of sex and aggression and constantly struggle to satisfy these urges in a socially acceptable way.

The 'humanistic approach' emerged mainly in the 1950s in the United States This is a 'phenomenological approach' that focuses on *subjective experience*. It assumes that humans have the ability to choose what to do; in other words, they have free will. It rejects the notion that human behaviour is determined by external stimuli, unconscious forces or the mechanics of information processing.

The 'biological perspective' explains human behaviour by investigating chemical and electrical events occurring inside the body, particularly within the brain and nervous system. According to Darwin's theory of evolution, physical characteristics and behavioural traits emerged in evolution because they conferred an advantage on their possessor(s).

Domains

A 'domain' is a way of dividing a subject or discipline into fields of thought or action. These domains provide students with a broad introduction to psychology and an understanding of research methodology, enabling the development of practical research skills, all essential features of contemporary psychology.

'Developmental psychology' studies the emotional, social and cognitive changes that occur over an individual's lifetime, starting from conception and infancy through to adolescence, adulthood and old age. 'Cognitive psychology' focuses on mental processes such as memory, perception, thought, language and attention. 'Physiological psychology' is interested in how nerves function, how hormones affect behaviour and how the different areas of the brain are related to particular behaviours. 'Social psychology' looks at how people interact and influence each other. It investigates interpersonal relationships, group behaviour, obedience to authority, conformity, leadership and media influences. 'Psychology of Individual Differences' is the study of how people differ in terms of psychological characteristics such as intelligence, personality, aggressiveness, mental health, willingness to conform, femininity and masculinity. It examines disorders such as schizophrenia, depression and phobias, seeking explanations for the causes as well as possible methods of treatment. 'Research Methods' and the development of practical research skills stress the importance of gathering objective evidence to support or challenge theories.

Major debates in psychology

Nature and nurture

One of the most controversial and longest-running debates in psychology concerns the influence of nature and nurture – or heredity and environment – on human development. Common questions stemming from this debate might be:

- Do we inherit prejudiced attitudes from our parents or do we learn them from cultural and social norms?
- Are some people born with 'obedient' personalities or do factors pertaining to the situation compel individuals to conform?
- Is schizophrenia a genetically inherited or learned disorder?
- How much does the socialisation process contribute to gender differences in aggression?
- Do we select mates according to evolutionary principles?
- Are some people born more intelligent than others?

Behaviourists tend to emphasise the nurture side of the debate, whereas psychoanalysts stress nature. Interestingly, though, they both acknowledge the influence of childhood experiences. This illustrates that rarely is one side of the debate favoured to the entire exclusion of the other and, in fact, it is generally agreed that behaviours and abilities are influenced by the interaction of *both* nature and nurture. Most debate centres on the extent to which each side contributes.

Free will and determinism

This debate surrounds the extent to which human behaviour results from forces over which an individual has control. The 'free will' position regards people as the cause of their own actions, whereas 'determinism' holds that action is caused by environmental or biological factors. According to humanist psychologists, accurate predictions of behaviour are not possible. Behaviour cannot be determined solely by past experiences since it predominantly depends on future goals. People have self-awareness and behave deliberately and rationally in order to meet desired outcomes. For example, we might assume that you are reading these words intentionally and that you have a reason or purpose for doing so!

Notions of free will and determinism, however, are not mutually exclusive. Most modern psychologists would envisage free will and determinism as opposite extremes on a continuum. Therefore, the question to be asked is not *whether* behaviour is free or determined, but *to what extent is it* free or determined? Alternatively, the question could ask where on the continuum does behaviour lie? 'Soft determinism' stresses that the environment does determine behaviour, but only to a certain extent. 'Radical behaviourism', however, represents the extreme in environmental determinism – viewing humans as 'social robots' reacting to external stimuli.

Reductionism
This contrasts with the holistic approach taken by humanism, in that it attempts to explain complex phenomena by reducing them to combinations of simpler components. 'Physiological reductionism' reduces behaviour to neurochemical processes. 'Biological/genetic reductionism' explains behaviour solely in terms of inherited factors. 'Environmental reductionism' maintains that behaviour is simply the consequence of stimulus-response associations.

Ethics
The fundamental ethical question in psychological research is whether the end justifies the means. The British Psychological Society has provided researchers with an ethical framework within which to work. Ethical guidelines must be followed when working with human participants, including a focus on areas such as consent, deception, debriefing, withdrawal from the investigation, confidentiality and protection of participants. Likewise, there are guidelines when working with non-human subjects, such as those relating to number of animals used, type of research, species used, discomfort and pain, methods of study and laws controlling animal research.

Areas of applied psychology
Some of you will go on to university to study for a degree in psychology. After obtaining a good degree you can apply to do a whole range of postgraduate courses. For instance, *clinical psychology* training will provide you with the skills to assess people with learning difficulties, administer psychological tests to brain-damaged patients, devise rehabilitation programmes for long-term psychiatric patients,

implement programmes of therapy, become involved in community care and conduct research into the effectiveness of different treatment. Alternatively, you may prefer to study for a (postgraduate) Masters Degree in *educational psychology*, which might involve working with children and adolescents, administering psychometric tests, planning educational programmes for those with physical and mental impairments, or advising teachers and parents how to manage behavioural problems and learning difficulties. *Occupational psychologists* are involved in the selection and training of individuals for jobs, they implement programmes of industrial rehabilitation, design training schemes and advise on working conditions to maximise productivity. *Criminal (or forensic) psychologists* focus on criminal behaviour and its management, they conduct research into devising treatment programmes, crime prevention, jury selection and offender profiling.

Whatever career you are aiming for and whether or not 'knowledge of psychology' is a specified requirement in a job application, many modern employers will recognise that a qualification in psychology is a valuable element of your CV. The insight into people's behaviour that you acquire through studying psychology will be based not on hit-and-miss 'intuition' or 'gut reaction', but on knowledge of theory and scientific, objective evidence. For those of us who want to get a life outwith work – and that's most of us! – an understanding of psychology is relevant to virtually every aspect of our lives: health and wellbeing, work and leisure, spiritual life, love, family and friendships.

On behalf of all of the contributors to this book, we sincerely hope that there are many future professional psychologists among those who read these words. But for now, we wish you every success in studying for Higher Psychology. We very much hope that this book will be a useful study aid to you and we wish you every success for the future.

Chapter 1
Understanding the Individual

This Chapter relates to the SQA Higher Psychology Unit, *Understanding the Individual*, and allows you to gain an understanding of a number of key psychological processes experienced in human lives. Selected topics from 'Key Domains' of Developmental Psychology, Cognitive Psychology and Biological Psychology are addressed in this chapter, which is broken down into three different sections. Through this, you will be able to develop an understanding of the following key psychological processes: 'early socialisation', 'memory' and 'stress'. Different ways of explaining and understanding these behaviours are investigated and evaluated, as well as ways that psychological knowledge can be applied to everyday life situations and experiences.

Section summary

This Section on early socialisation will investigate:

- The domain of developmental psychology.
- The nature of attachment and its role in early socialisation.
- The nature of separation: deprivation and privation.
- The nature of parenting and child rearing styles, including cultural differences in parenting.
- The application of research relating to day care.

The domain associated with the study of early socialisation is Developmental Psychology

Developmental psychology is an area of psychology where a wide range of explanations from a number of different theoretical perspectives, is offered in an attempt to better understand the processes involved in human development. Such development takes place throughout the life cycle. This Section will identify and investigate some of the key explanations and perspectives in this important area of study.

A key focus of developmental psychology is the psychological changes that humans undergo as they grow and develop throughout their lifespan. It aims to provide an understanding of *all* stages of life development, from infancy through childhood and into adulthood and old age. The lifespan approach looks at development as a dynamic and integrated process that flows from birth to death.

Elements of development throughout the life-cycle include the continuous and progressive development of physical and motor skills, cognitive abilities, emotional development and social behaviour. These categories are explained in more detail in the **Table 1.1**.

Although presented as separate entities in Table 1.1, the categories often overlap and are interdependent. For example, changes in cognitive ability go hand in hand with emotional developments. The development of physical and motor skills impacts on social behaviour. The rise to prominence of the lifespan approach in developmental psychology has been, however, relatively recent.

The traditional emphasis in this area of psychology concentrated on child cognitive development, where changes are rapid and dramatic. Perhaps the most influential contribution to this area has been made by the Swiss scientist, or, more accurately, 'genetic epistemologist', Jean Piaget (1896-1980). Piaget worked in the area relating to the theory of knowledge and how knowledge grows and develops. He proposed that children actively construct their own view of the world that is rational to them. This view of the world changes and develops as the child grows older and matures into adulthood.

Table 1.1

	Elements of Development
Physical and motor skills	We all undergo the same basic physical development at approximately the same time in our lives. Physical changes occur and bodily processes alter as we grow through childhood, into adolescence, adulthood and old age. Our ability to perform different motor skills changes alongside our physical development. These changes impact on our social and emotional behaviour.
Cognitive abilities	Cognitive abilities are our intellectual abilities that develop and change throughout life. In particular, they concentrate on the ability to think and reason. Cognitive processes that are investigated include perception, attention, language memory and thinking/ problem solving.
Emotional development	Our emotional development includes the type of attachments we form with other people, our identity, or how we perceive ourselves in relation to others, our personality and temperament.
Social Behaviour	The social behaviour we display develops as we grow older. Areas of interest of social behaviour include how we learn to be social beings, how we are raised as children, our moral development, the effect that our peers have on our behaviour, the effect that other groups have on us, etc.

Piaget's theory of cognitive development suggests that children go through a series of distinct stages, as outlined in **Table 1.2**. From birth onwards children develop increasingly more sophisticated ways of thinking. As young children their understanding of the world is quite different from that of an adult. As they grow older, children are able to understand more difficult concepts until they finally achieve the ability to reason and think about abstract concepts.

A brief summary of Piaget's stages of cognitive development is given in **Table 1.2**.

Table 1.2

Stage	Approx. age	Characteristics displayed by child
1. Sensorimotor	0-2 years	An infant makes sense of the world through motor activities, touching and feeling, and by using their senses. They understand only the 'here and now' - what is in front of them that they can see, feel, hear, taste, smell. They have no anticipation of the future or thought about the past. Eventually, infants develop an understanding of 'object permanence', which is the belief that objects still exist even when they are not visible.
2. Preoperational	2-7 years	From around the age of 2 years a child begins to understand that objects can be represented through images and language. For example, the word 'ball' means the round object they play with; a picture of a car indicates a real car. At this age children are 'egocentric', which means that they only see things from their own viewpoint. An example of this is if a child looks in a hand mirror and sees her/himself, then you look in the mirror and they assume you will see them, rather than yourself. They are only able to focus on one feature of the environment, ignoring others however important they may be ('centration').
3. Concrete operational	7-11 years	By the age of around 7 years children are able to understand other people's points of view. They begin to develop logical thought processes, but they need to handle and manipulate actual objects to solve a problem. They are able to conserve number, shape, weight and volume.
4. Formal operational	11+ years	In this stage children are now able to reason and think about abstract concepts. They can systematically test out several ideas, thinking about each possible solution until a problem is solved. They develop their own ideas and beliefs. Thinking becomes more adult in nature.

In contrast to this exclusive focus on childhood development, Erik Erikson (1902-1994) attempted to develop an overall lifespan approach that investigated development not only in children and adolescents, but *all* stages of adulthood through to what was formerly known as 'old-age'. This type of approach views adulthood as consisting of a series of stages that are marked by age-group and by certain life events, or 'milestones', such as marriage, becoming a parent, retirement, bereavement and death.

Erikson was strongly influenced by the work of the founder of the psychoanalytic approach, Sigmund Freud (1856-1939). In fact, he studied alongside Freud's daughter, Anna, who worked mostly with older children and adolescents. Erikson (1963) emphasised the importance of people's social relationships with others. He proposed that development follows a sequence of stages throughout life. Each stage is marked by a 'crisis' that the individual must try to resolve. In working through the particular crisis, either a favourable or an unfavourable result is achieved and this result determines how successfully the person develops through the lifecycle. A favourable result occurs when the person successfully overcomes, or resolves, the crisis and an unfavourable result is experienced when they are unable to do so. The individual who is unable to satisfactorily resolve a particular crisis will experience psychological problems and subsequent progress will be adversely affected. These crises and possible favourable or unfavourable outcomes are listed in the **Table 1.3**.

Within the context of a discussion on socialisation, it is important to discuss the 'nature-nurture' debate. The nature-nurture debate is a debate that occurs throughout most areas in psychology. It is something you are likely to come across many times in your studies. Developmental psychology looks at the various influences that affect babies, children and adults, as they develop and mature. There are factors such as parents, friends and peer groups that make up the environmental influences ('nurture') that affect development. Biological factors such as genetic influences and physiological changes ('nature') are also considered within the premise of developmental psychology. **Box 1.1** provides further explanation of this debate.

Box 1.1

The Nature-Nurture Debate

Some psychologists believe that we are influenced in our behaviour by hereditary factors. This is the 'nature' side of the debate and these psychologists are called 'nativists'. Nativists believe that we are born with a pre-programmed blueprint for behaviour; the environment is seen as having little or no influence on what we do.

Other psychologists believe that our behaviour is influenced by factors in our environment and through the process of learning. They are known as 'empiricists' and form the 'nurture' side of the debate. Empiricists believe that we are born with minds that resemble a blank slate (a *tabula rasa*) since all behaviour is learned through subsequent experience and interactions with the environment.

Table 1.3

Erikson's Lifespan Stages of Development

Age	Life Crisis	Favourable result	Unfavourable result
0-1 year	***Trust v. Mistrust*** Children need secure and stable care in order to develop feelings of security.	Develop trust in the environment and hope for the future.	Develop insecurity, suspicion and fear of the future.
2-3 years	***Autonomy v. Shame and doubt*** Children seek a feeling of independence from their parents. Parental discipline should not be too harsh or unbending.	Develop self-esteem and a sense of independence.	Develop feelings of doubt in ability to cope.
4-5 years	***Initiative v. Guilt*** Exploration of environment, planning activities.	Develop the ability to plan and carry out activities.	Develop feelings of guilt and fear of punishment.
6-11 years	***Industry v. Inferiority*** Acquisition of knowledge and skills.	Develop a sense of ability and achievement. Gain confidence in being able to make things.	Develop feelings of inadequacy and inferiority.
12-18 years (Adolescence)	***Identity v. Confusion*** The search for a realistic identity.	Develop a strong personal identity.	Lack of integrated identity. Confusion over who they are.
20-40 years (Young Adulthood)	***Intimacy v. Isolation*** Search for deep and lasting personal relationships.	Develop an ability to love and show commitment to others.	Feelings of isolation, only experience superficial relationships with others.
40-64 years (Middle Adulthood)	***Generativity v. Stagnation*** Aim to be creative and productive in life and make a contribution to society.	Develop feelings of care and concern for others in society.	Too concerned about self. Feelings of boredom.
65+ years (Late Adulthood)	***Integrity v. Despair*** Evaluation and review of accomplishments in life.	A sense of satisfaction with what has been achieved in life is gained. An acceptance of death.	Regret is felt over missed opportunities. Fear of death.

Early socialisation and the role and nature of attachment

The particular focus of this chapter is to study 'early socialisation'. 'Attachment' is the term given to the two-way emotional bond that develops between a child and the primary caregiver. We will look at why attachments are so important to a child's early socialisation and how attachments develop.

The effects of separation – a breach of the attachment – will be investigated. This is an area of psychology that has particular relevance to contemporary society where, in many homes, parents go out to work and children are looked after by other people, perhaps in a day care nursery, or by a childminder. Attitudes towards the raising of children vary by culture and so cross-cultural studies offer different explanations and ideas about attachment. For example, *styles* of parenting and child-rearing are thought to affect socialisation patterns and these will also be discussed.

Theories of attachment

Attachments are usually formed between a child and the primary caregiver, who, in Western societies has traditionally been the mother. Each forms an attachment to the other. This relationship is not exclusive, however, as a child is also likely to form attachments to others with whom they have close contact. Maurer and Maurer (1989) suggest that the formation of an attachment occurs due to the nature and extent of interactions between the child and attachment figure and not merely because they spend time together.

What is attachment?

Maccoby (1980) investigated the parent and child relationship and described four characteristics that identified the bond of attachment:

1. The child will seek to be close to the primary caregiver, especially when stressed.
2. The child will show distress when separated from the primary caregiver.
3. The child will show pleasure when reunited with the primary caregiver.
4. The behaviour of the child is generally targeted towards the primary caregiver.

One of the most important and influential theorists in the field of attachment is child psychologist, John Bowlby (1907-1990), whose work revolutionised the way that psychologists think about the bond that develops between a child and its mother. Bowlby was a supporter of the psychoanalytic theories proposed by Sigmund Freud. (See **Box 1.2** for further details.)

Box 1.2

Freud's Psychoanalytic View

The Psychoanalytic view of attachment grew from the work of Sigmund Freud (1856-1939). Freud believed that all humans possess an inborn drive and desire for physical pleasure. He proposed that our personalities are made up of three parts, the 'id', the 'ego' and the 'superego'. An instinctive and primitive part of our personality, the 'id', is in place from birth. The id is governed by the 'pleasure principle' that demands immediate satisfaction in its desires. In infants the demands of the id manifest themselves in a desire to be fed, looked after and to feel warm and secure. An infant will, according to Freud, develop an emotional attachment to the person who fulfils these desires and thus satisfies the demands of the child's id, what is often termed 'cupboard-love'. In most cases this person is the child's mother.

The attachment to a caring and attentive mother will develop into a relationship that, Freud claimed, will be unique in the child's life and will last throughout the child's life. This special bond between mother and child lays down an exemplar model for the child's later emotional relationships. The strength of the attachment between child and mother will determine the future emotional well-being of the child and the success of the child's future relationships. Infants who do not form a satisfactory and secure attachment with their mother will, according to Freud, be unlikely to be able to form relationships successfully either in later childhood or as an adult.

The psychoanalytic explanation of the nature of attachment and why it occurs has been criticised by some because it is unable to be scientifically researched. It uses abstract concepts such as the 'id' and the 'pleasure principle', concepts that cannot be objectively observed or measured. However, many others claim that psychoanalytic theory provides insightful and inspired explanations of human behaviour. Bowlby, himself, was a psychoanalytic psychologist even though he felt that Freudian theory failed to adequately explain the extreme emotional distress experienced by the infant during separation.

Bowlby conducted research into the effects of deprivation and privation (for explanations of these terms see the 'Definitions' in **Box 1.3**). He aimed to discover what effect *deprivation* and *privation* have on psychological development from childhood into adulthood and on psychological health generally. Theories of the effects of deprivation and privation will be discussed later in this Chapter.

Bowlby proposed that a child would need to develop a single, primary attachment in order to facilitate healthy psychological development. This primary attachment would ideally be formed with the child's mother, or, at least, a 'mother figure'. Bowlby called this attachment process 'monotropy', which he defined as 'turning towards one person.' He was influenced by the ethological approach, which studies the natural behaviour of animals, and claimed there was a 'critical' or 'sensitive' period in the formation of attachments in all animals, including humans, which lasted from birth to when the child was 3 years of age. If no single, primary attachment forms in this period, then future psychological maturation is affected – 'mother love in infancy and childhood is as important for mental health as are vitamins and proteins for physical health' (Bowlby, 1951).

Box 1.3

Definitions: Deprivation and Privation

Deprivation When a child is separated from its attachment figure. This can occur through temporary separation such as would be the case if a child's mother were to go away for a short while. Deprivation can also occur as a result of permanent separation such as that experienced on the death of or abandonment by the mother. The important point is that there can be significant consequences when attachments have been formed and are subsequently disrupted.

Privation A situation where no attachments have been formed, perhaps through isolation, or inadequate care.

For Bowlby, the desire to form attachments is an innate capacity in the caregiver and infant that has evolved in the human species. The forming of attachment bonds is genetically 'adaptive' behaviour in that it helps humans to survive and reproduce. Adults are likely to have an inborn tendency to form attachments with their offspring in order to secure the survival of their genes in the next generation. This 'offer' of attachment on the part of the adult is taken up by human infants since they are physically dependent on adults to feed them, look after them and protect them from harm. To have these needs met, infants must be able to attract the attention of others and Bowlby claims that newborn babies are innately equipped to do this by crying, smiling, 'rooting' and sucking. If this care is not provided then the infant will not survive and therefore those infants who do not form successful attachments are less likely to survive and later reproduce (Bowlby, 1969). Forming attachments may also help to develop social and emotional relationships as children grow and mature.

How attachments develop

Most researchers agree that attachment develops in a series of stages, as indicated in **Diagram 1.1**, below.

Diagram 1.1

Four Stages of Attachment

Stage 1 - the 'pre-attachment' stage, which occurs from birth to around 2 months.
In this stage babies react in the same manner to all objects, whether they are animate or inanimate. For example, a baby would react the same way to a parent as they would to a toy. They do not show recognition of individual people and are as easily comforted by a stranger as by a parent. Towards the latter part of this stage infants begin to recognise familiar faces, voices and smells. They begin to develop a preference for being with people.

Stage 2 - the 'attachment in the making' stage, which lasts from 2 months to 7 months.
In this stage infants become much more sociable and enjoy being with people. They are able to recognise familiar individuals and are better comforted by someone they are familiar with than a stranger. However, they do not get anxious if they are with strangers.

Stage 3 - the 'specific attachment' stage, which occurs from the age 7 months on.
Attachment is beginning to develop and the infant demonstrates distress when separated from his primary carer. This behaviour is called 'separation protest'. This distress can occur if the carer leaves the room the child is in, or even when the child is laid down in a cot. The infant shows delight when the primary carer returns, or lifts them up and they are most easily comforted by this person. They have formed what is called a 'specific attachment'. At this time the infant begins to display anxiety if picked up or even approached by a stranger.

Stage 4 - the 'multiple attachment' stage, which occurs from around 8 months.
Once an initial attachment is formed with the primary carer, an infant goes on to form additional attachments with other people. The number of attachments that are formed very much depends on the number of consistent and enduring relationships the infant has. There is some debate as to whether these additional attachments are as strong as that with the primary carer, or of a lesser intensity.

More recent research questions the assumption that, in Stage 1 (**Diagram 1.1**), infants do not recognise familiar faces. Bushnell (1989) found that infants of less than one day old would look longer at their mother's face than they would at another female. Reacting in this way to their mother's face may encourage interaction between the infant and the mother and thus aid the development of the attachment bond.

Bowlby proposed that the primary caregiver is almost always the child's mother, who is also the main provider of emotional and physical care. Other highly influential researchers in the field of attachment, such as Rudolph Schaffer and Peggy Emerson (1964), found that this is not necessarily the case.

Box 1.4

Research: Schaffer and Emerson's Glasgow Infants (1964)

In 1964, Schaffer and Emerson studied 60 infants in Glasgow for a period from birth to one year old. They revisited the children again at age 18 months.

Schaffer and Emerson found that 60 per cent of the children formed their primary attachment with their mother, but a substantial number, 40 per cent, formed their primary attachment with someone else, their father, older brother or sister, or a grandparent.

Schaffer and Emerson discovered that the primary attachment is not necessarily formed with the person who mainly looks after the child's physical needs, nor is it necessarily with the person who spends most time with the child. The main attachment appears to be formed with the person who interacts with and responds to the child the most, and who provides stimulation for the child to respond to. The babies, therefore, actively choose those with whom they form attachments.

Schaffer and Emerson found that most infants in their study had formed only one main attachment by the age of 7 months, but most of the children (87 per cent) had more than one attachment by the age of 18 months. During the first year of life, a child rapidly learns the skills of interaction with others and develops unique 'interactional synchronies' between themselves and their attachment figure(s).

Schaffer and Emerson's findings have been supported by subsequent research carried out in different countries and different cultures. An example can be found in the work of Mary Ainsworth who studied infants from a tribe in Uganda in 1967. She found that the babies in her study developed primary attachments with their mothers by around the age of 6 months and demonstrated anxiety with strangers by around the age of 9 months. The infants tended to be looked after by other adults in the tribe as well as by their mothers. She found that, similarly to Schaffer and Emerson's study, the infants developed multiple attachments with the people who were around them. Other similar findings have been found in cultures where caring for a child is shared beyond the mother alone (Fox, 1977; Ainsworth, 1964; Tronick, 1992).

There is still, however, some debate on whether the primary attachment, typically formed with the mother, remains stronger than other attachments that may be formed.

So, why might the process of forming attachments be so important to child development? Bowlby and other researchers such as Ainsworth (1978) agree that the nature of attachments formed in infancy will have a bearing on the child's development and on the formation of future relationships that develop in later life. Moreover, Bowlby (1973) developed the idea that the relationship a child has with its primary caregiver will provide a model for all future relationships. He called this the 'internal working model'. By this, Bowlby suggested that a child builds up a representation in his or her mind of the type of relationships they have with the significant people in their lives. These representations contain memories of the interactions the child has had with their attachment figures and the representations are laid down as cognitive structures or 'schemas'. The child then uses these as reference points for future interactions with people, in order to predict how people might behave in particular contexts, for example, and to plan appropriate responses.

Obviously, not all attachments are the same and studies have been carried out to discover the effects on a child of what is known as 'secure' and 'insecure' attachments. Mary Ainsworth carried out research into this, the results of which suggested that three types of attachment are variously formed (see **Box 1.5** below).

Analysis of the responses made by the child allows the researchers to determine the type of attachment the child has formed with the caregiver. Both the type of attachment that develops and the effects that occur as a result of it, may be enduring and can influence responses throughout the child's entire lifetime. The types of attachment identified by Ainsworth's study and a number of other supporting studies are discussed below.

Secure attachment' ('Type B')

A 'secure attachment' ('Type B') is demonstrated by the following incidences:

- When the caregiver is present, the infant plays happily with toys and explores the environment.
- When the child shows some distress if the caregiver goes away and goes to the caregiver when they return in order to be comforted.

- When the child chooses to be with the caregiver rather than with the stranger.

Box 1.5

Research: Ainsworth's 'Strange Situation' (1978)

Ainsworth (1978) developed an experimental technique called the 'Strange Situation'. It aims to assess the attachment relationship between an infant and its primary caregiver. The infant participants are usually 12-18 months old and usually the primary caregiver is the child's mother.

A structured observation takes place in an unfamiliar environment where the participants can be watched by researchers to assess behaviours. The room contains toys for the child to play with. Over a period of time a number of events take place that are intended to be increasingly stressful for the child. Two variables are manipulated:

1. The child being separated from the primary caregiver
2. A stranger being present.

Initially the caregiver sits in the room and watches the child playing with the toys and exploring the room. After a few minutes a stranger enters and talks to the caregiver before playing with the infant. The caregiver then quietly leaves the room for a few minutes.

While the caregiver is out of the room the stranger talks to the infant and plays with the toys. The caregiver then returns and the stranger leaves the room. The caregiver greets the infant, comforting and soothing as necessary. The caregiver then says goodbye and leaves the room again.

Now the infant is left alone in the room for a few minutes before the stranger returns and talks and plays with the infant. (If the infant becomes too distressed at being left alone this period is cut short.) After another few minutes the caregiver returns to the room and picks up the infant. The stranger then leaves.

The whole procedure takes just over 20 minutes.

There are several measures used to assess the type of attachment that exists between the child and the caregiver. These include:

- How the infant reacts to being separated from their caregiver.
- How the infant reacts to being reunited with their caregiver.
- How the infant reacts to a stranger being in the room.
- How willing the infant is to explore the unfamiliar environment when in the contexts of being on their own, when with the primary caregiver and when with a stranger.

Notably, most researchers agree that secure attachments, as evidenced above, develop if the caregiver responds sensitively to the child and is consistent in that response, which runs contrary to old-fashioned child-rearing notions of 'spare the rod, spoil the child'.

In later childhood securely attached children would be at ease with social interactions, confident at school and able to deal with challenging situations (Lewis *et al*, 1984). In adulthood, they would find it relatively easy to form close relationships with others and be comfortable with the idea of depending on other people and in being depended upon (Hazan and Shaver, 1987).

Insecure/avoidant attachment ('Type A')
An 'insecure/avoidant attachment' ('Type A') is demonstrated by the following:

- When the infant largely ignores the caregiver and pays little attention when the caregiver leaves the room.
- When, on returning, the child pays little attention to the caregiver and the caregiver tends to show little interest in the child.
- When distressed, the child shows no preference in being comforted by a stranger or the caregiver.

In a study conducted in 1989, Browne found there was a link between infant maltreatment or abuse and the development of insecure-avoidant attachment. In one study, 70 per cent of babies who had been maltreated were found to have developed insecure-avoidant attachments with their parents. Ainsworth (1978) found mothers of babies who were classified as insecure-avoidant ('Type A') tended to be relatively cold and displayed rejection towards their babies. They were also generally unresponsive to the babies' social signals.

In childhood, insecurely attached ('avoidant') children may show a tendency to avoid social interactions. Behavioural problems may occur and there may be a tendency towards bullying other children. As an adult, there may be difficulty in trusting others or being able to depend on other people. An avoidant adult may feel uncomfortable being overly intimate with a partner and resist getting too close (Hazan and Shaver, 1987).

Insecure attachment (resistant/ambivalent) ('Type C')
An 'insecure attachment (resistant/ambivalent)' ('Type C') is demonstrated as follows:

- If the infant is distressed when the caregiver leaves the room and, although goes to the caregiver when they return, struggles and is difficult to comfort. The child may show anger towards the caregiver for going away. The child tends not to explore the environment very much as they tend to stay close to the caregiver. The caregiver behaves in an inconsistent way towards the child, too, sometimes being angry or ignoring the child, other times being responsive and sensitive to the child's needs. Strangers tend to be ignored by the child and any attempt by the stranger to comfort the child when distressed meets with resistance

Ainsworth (1978) found that mothers of insecure-resistant ('Type C') babies were inconsistent in their response to their child. On some occasions the mothers responded to their child's social signals but at other times ignored them.

A child who has developed insecure attachments of the resistant type is likely to both desire and yet reject contact with other children. They tend to lack confidence and self-esteem and be dependent on the teacher at school for help and attention. They may also become the victims of bullying and subsequently withdraw from social interactions with others. As an adult they are liable to be overly possessive and need constant reassurance from their partners and may scare them off. 'Resistant' adults worry that their partners do not really love them and may not want to stay with them (Hazan and Shaver, 1987).

Most subsequent research on attachment employed Ainsworth's 'three types model' of attachment. However, in 1986, Main and Solomon suggested that a fourth type be recognised. In the studies they carried out, they found that a small number of infants appeared to be disorganised and disoriented during the research procedure. Thereafter, they classified these infants as demonstrating what they called 'Type D' – 'Disorganised and Disoriented' behaviour. 'Type D' infants were sometimes wary of the stranger and at other times wary of the mother. The infant's movements and reactions were curtailed or incomplete and they did not seem to have any ability to cope with the stresses of the 'Strange Situation'. Carlson *et al* (1989) suggested that 'Type D' infants were likely to have been raised in an abusive home where the regime was highly stressful and inconsistent. While the infant has an instinctive desire to seek to be close to their caregiver, the child becomes confused and wary due to previous ill treatment and rejection.

Attachment theorists claim that the formation and type of childhood attachments is crucial due to the fact that it impacts on later childhood and adult life. One example would be that Hazan and Shaver (1987) propose that romantic love between adults operates as an attachment process and reflects the style of attachment formed in childhood. These attachment styles differ by culture (see **Box 1.6**).

Box 1.6

Cultural Differences in the Types of Attachment Formed

Different cultures have different norms and expectations of bringing up children. There have been various studies across the world using the 'Strange Situation' structured observation. In traditional Japanese culture, for example, great emphasis is placed on developing close family relationships and inter-dependency, laying the foundations for secure attachments to be formed.

By contrast, in Western countries such as the USA, more emphasis is placed on encouraging a child to become independent and self-reliant and so North American children may be more likely to manifest an avoidant-type attachment that fosters independence from the caregiver. Overall, though, in all the countries studied the most common type of attachment found has been 'Type B' (secure) attachment.

It is important to note that the findings from cross-cultural studies assume that all infants experience the same levels of anxiety at separation. This is clearly not the case.

In Japan and other Oriental cultures, children are very rarely separated from their primary caregiver for the first few years of their lives and the process of being separated during the study may be so unusual that the reactions of the infant cannot be put down to 'separation anxiety' alone. Of particular note with regards to the studies, is that the Japanese parents did not allow their child to cry for any length of time.

This created a difference in the standard procedure when carrying out the 'Strange Situation' research, which had the effect of virtually negating any direct comparisons with findings from other cultures (Takahashi, 1990).

By contrast, in Western cultures infants tend to spend more time physically separated from their caregivers and later, as children, are actively encouraged to develop independence. Of course, no culture is unilateral in the style of parenting it adopts.

Within any culture there will be variations in child-rearing practices.

Grossmann and Grossmann (1991) carried out the 'Strange Situation' research in Germany. They found that German infants were more likely to be classified as insecurely attached rather than securely attached. This anomaly was thought to be due to the German cultural norm of maintaining some distance in the interpersonal relationships between parents and children. German infants, therefore, may be less likely to seek to be close to their parents in a stressful situation and would therefore, by default, be classified as insecurely attached. Overall, cross-cultural findings may present an oversimplified view of attachment.

Multiple attachments

Schaffer and Emerson (1964) demonstrated that most children form attachments with a number of family members such as their mother, father, brothers and sisters as well as grandparents. Bowlby argued that infants need one attachment bond that is stronger than all others – 'monotropy', meaning 'turning towards one person'. Other researchers, such as Lamb (1981), argue that children need a variety of attachment bonds that satisfy their needs. The anxiety and distress a child may feel from being separated from its primary caregiver can be lessened by the presence of others to whom they have formed attachments. Forming multiple attachments means that a child is not dependent on one caregiver. Cultural differences in child rearing may account for different patterns of attachment in different societies throughout the world.

Paternal attachments

Until recently the role that fathers play in the upbringing of children has been generally overlooked and it was assumed that the child's mother provided the main parenting responsibilities. Bowlby saw the main role of a child's father as that of supporting the mother economically and materially in order to allow her to devote her time to caring for the child. By additionally providing emotional support to the mother, a contented and loving atmosphere is created where the child can thrive (Bowlby, 1953).

In more recent years family life has changed and many fathers now tend to become more involved in child-rearing than previously. More mothers now have careers or a financial need to return to work after their child is born. Frankenhauser *et al* (1991) carried out studies on families where the mother worked and found that the fathers took more responsibility for caring for their children than Bowlby had found in earlier years.

There would appear to be no naturalistic difference between men and women when it comes to parenting ability in the form of child rearing. The main caring role, however, is still predominantly held by the mother, who generally does more of the domestic and child-rearing tasks (Lamb, 1977).

In the *UK 2000 Time Use Survey* carried out for the Office for National Statistics (ONS), it was found that women spent an average of around three hours a day on housework (excluding shopping and childcare) as compared with an average of 1 hour 40 minutes for men. Two in five men did no ironing or laundry. Women spent longer on childcare per day than men. Lamb (1977) also found that the type of interactions that occurred between a father and child were qualitatively different. Fathers tended to play with their children in a more lively and boisterous way than the mother does; they spoke to the children in a more adult manner and did not have such close physical contact as the mothers did. Perhaps because of such differences, boys between 15 and 24 months actually showed a preference for their father's company. Lamb (1977) also found that infants show few differences in the types of attachment shown to fathers and mothers, although when both parents are present, infants seem to overtly display stronger attachment to the mother. Interestingly, one of the difficulties in conducting research in this area is that there are still very few families where the father is the primary carer.

Alternative approaches to attachment theory – behaviourism

So far we have focused on a broadly psychoanalytic perspective on attachment. The 'Behaviourist' perspective offers an alternative approach.

Behaviourist theories attempt to explain attachment by the use of 'learning theory'. A fundamental principle of the behaviourist approach is that learning takes place though conditioning. There are two types of conditioning that are used by Behaviourists to explain the process of learning – these are 'classical conditioning' and 'operant conditioning'.

Classical conditioning

Classical conditioning occurs when a reflex response becomes associated with a stimulus not normally directly associated with it. A 'reflex', or uncontrolled, response is any response that occurs automatically following the presentations of an identifiable stimulus, or 'trigger'. Examples of reflex responses are feeling sudden fear when faced with significant threat or salivating at the smell or sight of food. Reflex responses are involuntary; we have no control over them occurring. When a reflex response becomes associated with a stimulus that is not the usual trigger stimulus then classical conditioning can occur.

Ivan Pavlov (1849-1936) conducted important experimental research into how animals and humans can learn through classical conditioning, as indicated in **Box 1.7**.

Box 1.7

Classical Conditioning - Pavlov's Dogs

Pavlov noticed that if dogs were presented with food (a stimulus that causes a natural, that is, 'unconditioned' or automatic response) they salivated. This inspired Pavlov to investigate whether the dogs could be conditioned, or taught, to respond to an *unrelated* stimulus such as a bell.

In the learning phase, Pavlov accompanied the presenting of food to the dogs with the ringing of a bell, what he called the 'conditioned stimulus'. Very quickly the dogs learned to associate the bell with food and began to salivate in response to the ringing of the bell. The response had now become a learned response and was therefore labelled the 'conditioned response'. Even when the bell was rung and no food was forthcoming, the dogs still salivated. They had learned, through what Pavlov called 'classical conditioning', to associate the bell with food.

Diagram 1.2 provides a useful graphical summary of classical conditioning.

Diagram 1.2

Classical Conditioning - Pavlov's Dogs

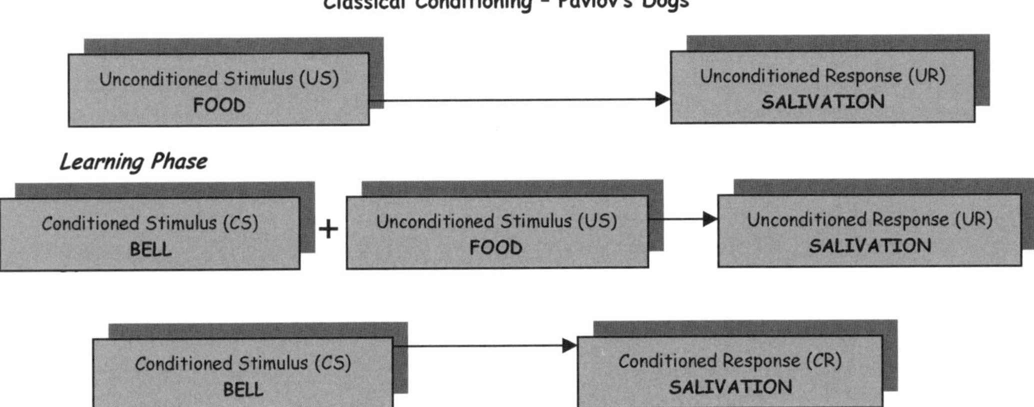

Pavlov's theories can be applied to explain how and why an infant forms an attachment with the primary caregiver.

If an infant is presented with food (Unconditioned Stimulus, US), then the infant feels comfort and pleasure (Unconditioned Response, UR). The mother (Conditioned Stimulus, CS) is associated with providing the source of food, (US) that gives rise to comfort and pleasure (UR). The mother (CS) then creates a feeling of comfort and pleasure (CR) in the infant. **Diagram 1.3** illustrates this further.

Diagram 1.3

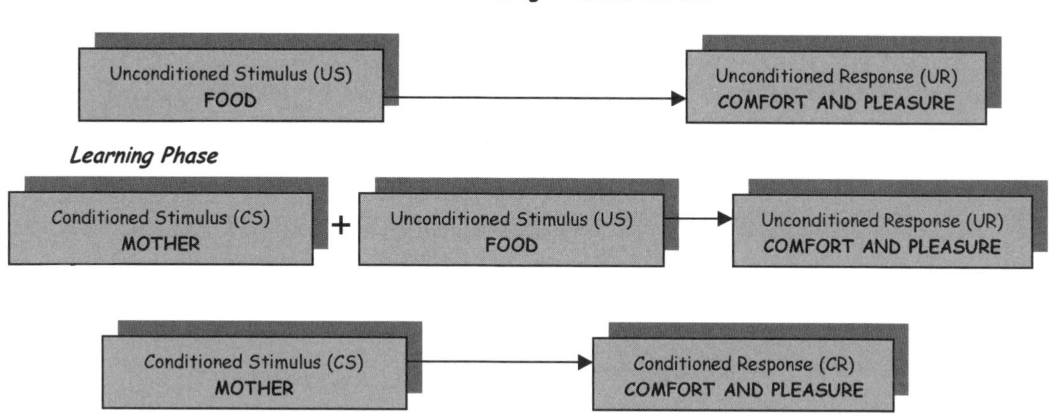

Operant conditioning

Not all learning can be attributed to classical conditioning, since not everything is learned through a reflex or natural response. Through experimental research, Burrhus Skinner (1904-1990) developed another theory of learning called 'operant conditioning'. This type of learning occurs where behaviour is followed by a consequence (see **Box 1.8**).

Dollard and Miller (1950) used the principles of operant conditioning to explain the process of attachment. They suggested that when an infant is hungry s/he is motivated to relieve the discomfort. A feeling of pleasure results when the infant is eventually fed, which then constitutes a reward. The person providing the food (usually the mother) is associated with this rewarding feeling of pleasure and of avoiding the discomfort of hunger and the infant becomes attached to them as a source of pleasure and comfort.

The mother, or primary caregiver, also learns attachment through operant conditioning. When the mother feeds the infant she is positively reinforced by the infant's reaction, in the form of smiling, for example. Alternatively, she is negatively reinforced by the motivation that the child will stop crying when provided with food.

A major weakness of the development of attachment through learning theory has been found by Schaffer and Emerson (1964), whose study we looked at earlier in this Section. In that study, it was found that infants do not always form a primary attachment with the person who usually feeds and looks after them. Such findings run contrary to the behaviourist theory of how attachment bonds are formed.

Box 1.8

Operant Conditioning - the 'Skinner Box' Experiment

Skinner placed a rat into a box (the 'Skinner Box') where a lever, when pressed, delivered a pellet of food. As the rat explored the box, it eventually pressed the lever and was presented with a pellet of food. The rat was then drawn to this area of the box and eventually pressed the lever again, whereby another pellet of food appeared. Very quickly the rat learned that when it pressed the lever, a pellet of food was delivered. The food acted as a reward or 'reinforcer' and encouraged the behaviour (pressing the lever) to be repeated. Skinner therefore theorized that if behaviour is rewarded or 'reinforced' then it is likely to be repeated. This prediction forms part of Skinner's theory of operant conditioning called 'positive reinforcement'.

Another aspect of operant conditioning is 'negative reinforcement'. This takes place when an unpleasant event occurs and the individual reacts to stop the occurrence of the unpleasantness. This was demonstrated in another experiment with the rat in the Skinner box. Here, Skinner found that if an electric current was passed through the floor of the box the rat found the effects unpleasant. The only way to switch off the current was to press the lever. The rat soon discovered that pressing the lever stopped the unpleasant electric current and so was motivated to increase the behaviour of pressing the lever.

Thus, if a reinforcer is present, whether positive or negative, then the behaviour it is connected with will be maintained or even increased.

Skinner also investigated the effects of punishment. The rat in the Skinner box discovered that pressing the lever produced a shock of electricity. This was unpleasant for the rat and acted as a 'punishment'. The behaviour of pressing the lever now decreased following the effect of punishment. Therefore, punishment causes a type of behaviour to decrease.

Further evidence against the behaviourist explanation of attachment can be found in the classic research carried out by Harry Harlow in the late 1950s. Harlow (1959) believed that the main reason for attachment formation is the provision of comfort and security rather than food. He tested his theory with an experiment using rhesus monkeys. This experiment is discussed in detail in **Box 1.9**.

Box 1.9

Research: Harlow's Rhesus Monkeys (1959)

Harlow (1959) separated eight newborn rhesus monkeys from their mothers and isolated them in individual cages. In each cage there were two frames made out of wire mesh that were designed to emulate a 'mother figure'. One of these wire frame 'substitute mothers' was covered in soft towelling material, while the other was left as a plain wire frame.

Four of the rhesus monkeys were provided with milk from a feeding bottle attached to the bare wire frame 'mother'. Four of the monkeys were provided with milk from a bottle attached to the cloth covered 'mother'. Both groups of monkeys drank the same quantity of milk and they all gained weight at a comparable rate. However, the monkeys who were fed by the bottle attached to the bare wire frame 'mother' only approached the figure when they wished to feed. Most of the time they spent clinging to the soft cloth of the towelling covered frame. If anxious, the monkeys all ran to the cloth covered frame 'mother' and clung to it seeking comfort and security.

Interestingly, the infant monkeys formed an 'attachment' to the soft and comforting cloth covered frame 'mother' whether or not food was provided. Harlow theorised that it was the feeling of comfort and security that led to attachments being formed and not the provision of food. He also found that the 'attachment' that the infant monkeys formed for their wire mesh 'mothers' was not sufficient for them to develop proper social relationships. As they matured the monkeys were unable to form typical social relationships and they were often either indifferent or aggressive towards other monkeys. They had difficulty in forming bonds with a mate and in caring for their own offspring (who were conceived through artificial insemination after natural mating failed).

Harlow's research questioned the basis of behaviourist learning theories and their explanations of how and why attachments are formed. He did demonstrate that the cloth covered 'mother' was the one that the infant monkeys turned to for the comfort and security associated with regular attachments, but rather than this leading to healthy psychological development, the monkeys developed dysfunctional social relationships. The cloth mother was unable to provide a template for behaviour that a normal rhesus monkey mother would, indicating that there must be some social element required in order to develop normally.

In a later study in 1970, Harlow and Suomi found that infant monkeys who played socially with other young monkeys for one hour a day grew up normally and were able to form the social relationships that the monkeys from the first experiment lacked.

Harlow's experimental studies were, and still are, very influential. However they have been criticised as being ethically and morally suspect and they would very likely break the 'Code of Conduct' that has been set up by the British Psychological Society (BPS) to protect the participants in psychological research, whether human or animal, from any physical or emotional harm. (The 'BPS Code of Conduct' can be found on their website at: www.bps.org.uk.)

The fact that Harlow established his theories on the basis of the behaviour of rhesus monkeys makes it questionable as to whether the same findings can be assumed to be applicable to humans.

Social learning theory

Albert Bandura developed a theory of social learning, which he used as a basis for explaining attachment. He demonstrated that learning can occur through observing and imitating the behaviour of other people. Forming attachments to mothers or primary caregivers can, according to Bandura (1965), provide the child with a 'role model' for future behaviour. If the role model is loving, responsive and caring then the child will be likely to copy this behaviour and learn to behave in a similar fashion as they mature. Bandura's theory gains support from Harlow's findings on the importance of learning behaviour from a role model. The infant monkeys in Harlow's study were unable to develop the necessary social behaviours to facilitate successful relationships in adult life.

Box 1.10

Summary of Three Theories of Attachment

Evolutionary approach This theory proposes that attachment is developed as a means to aid survival. Animals, including humans, are genetically programmed to give out signals that encourage those around them, in particular the mother, to care for them and respond to their needs. The infant then forms a bond with this caregiver and learns from the relationship how to behave and respond socially to others and, in adult life, how to care for their own offspring. A mother is motivated to care for her infant in order to ensure the continuation of her genes in that infant and in turn to further her genetic legacy in future generations.

Psychoanalytic approach The caregiver satisfies the demands of the infant's 'id' that works on the 'pleasure principle', demanding satisfaction. The care, food, comfort and security provided to the infant by the caregiver creates a feeling of pleasure in the infant.

Behaviourist approach An infant learns attachment by a process of conditioning, or by observing and imitating the caregiver. They associate the caregiver with the supply of food, comfort and security and with reducing feelings of discomfort. The infant learns to associate the provision of these benefits with the caregiver and so forms a bond of attachment with them.

Summary of the current theoretical position Recent theoretical views take the wider context of a person's early socialisation into account. Rather than focus only on the attachment 'pair', recognition is made of the influences of the family as a system, as well as the society and culture in which they live. The role of the attachment process is regarded as very influential in the child's overall emotional and social development. Parents' experiences of 'bonding' are also being researched, and the 'two-way' nature of attachment relationships is increasingly being recognised.

The nature of separation

In normal circumstances a child forms attachments with one or more people who are motivated to look after that child and ensure its comfort and security into adult life.

Researchers suggest that this bond of attachment is essential, or at least very important, for the emotional and social development of the child throughout childhood and into adulthood. However, what happens if this process is disrupted or fails altogether? In this Section we will investigate research into the effects of deprivation and privation and how they can affect psychological and social development.

According to Bowlby, it is vital for an infant to develop a bond of attachment with its mother, or primary caregiver. Without attachment bonds a child is likely to suffer serious repercussions and experience problems in forming close relationships in adult life, he claims. Bowlby used the term 'maternal deprivation' for either the failure to form an attachment bond in infancy, or for the loss of the person with whom the attachment has been formed.

Deprivation

Bowlby believed that the role a mother, or a mother figure, plays provides the basis of all our future relationships. In the course of his work in London during the 1930s Bowlby studied case histories of some of the boys he met during his work in the London Child Guidance Clinic. In his first piece of empirical research, Bowlby attempted to demonstrate the importance of the links between a person's later behaviour and their history of maternal deprivation.

Box 1.11

Research: Bowlby's 'Forty-four Juvenile Thieves' (1944)

In 1944, Bowlby's research, 'Forty-four Juvenile Thieves', collected data from 88 boys who had been referred to the London Child Guidance Clinic. Forty-four of these boys were referred to the clinic for stealing. Bowlby referred to this group as the 'thieves'. From this group of 44 'thieves', fourteen were classified by Bowlby as 'affectionless psychopaths' by which he meant that they showed little sense of responsibility and showed no remorse or guilt for their crimes. The data from the 44 'thieves' were compared to a second group of 44 other boys who had been referred to the clinic because of emotional problems, but who had not committed any crime, nor shown any form of antisocial behaviour.

Bowlby interviewed the boys and their families in order to construct a history of their early lives. He found that 86 per cent of the 'affectionless psychopaths' (12 out of the 14) had experienced separation from their mothers at an early age. None of the second group of 44 boys (who had not committed any crime) had undergone any separation.

Bowlby claimed that his findings supported his theory of maternal deprivation and that early separation from the attachment figure may cause psychological and emotional problems later.

There are criticisms of Bowlby's research:

- The sample of participants was small and not representative of the general population.
- The information from the boys and their families was collected retrospectively and so was reliant on memory, which may be unreliable and inaccurate.
- The length of time that some of the boys had been separated from their mothers was actually quite short and so unlikely to be the source of major problems.
- Bowlby diagnosed the 'affectionless psychopaths' himself and so may not have been truly objective. However, there may be ethical implications of attaching such labels.
- The findings that link early separation from a primary caregiver with 'affectionless psychopathy' are correlational, this means that they may be linked but it cannot be said that one 'causes' the other. Bowlby suggested that separation from an attachment figure causes antisocial behaviours.
- This assumption cannot be made from the findings of the research. All that can be said is that there may be a 'link' between separation from an attachment figure and later delinquent behaviour, but not that separation 'causes' the delinquency.

In a review of Bowlby's work carried out in 1981, Michael Rutter generally supported Bowlby's theories but suggested that Bowlby's assumption that separation causes antisocial behaviours was flawed. Rutter felt that the link between separation and antisocial behaviours may occur because factors that cause separation to occur (such as unsound family relationships, or poor living conditions) also contribute to the likelihood of delinquent behaviour. Rutter proposed that it is the events leading up to separation that have more effect on later behaviour than the actual separation itself.

In 1976, Rutter and his colleagues carried out a study of 2000 boys aged between 9 and 12 years, some living in London, others on the Isle of Wight. The researchers interviewed the boys and their families in order to determine the effects of different types of separation. Rutter wanted to find out if there is a difference in outcome when the separation is due to illness or death, and when it is due to some event that results from a discordant build up within the family, such as conflict, divorce, or addiction to drink or drugs.

Rutter found that the children who had experienced a discordant family life prior to separation from their mother were four times more likely to exhibit delinquent behaviour later than those children who had undergone separation because of the illness or death of the mother. The findings supported Rutter's theory that it is a discordant family life that causes antisocial behaviours, rather than the act of separation in itself.

Again, though, we can see some criticisms of Rutter's research as similar to those we found with Bowlby's work. First, the data were collected retrospectively so we have the problem of unreliable and inaccurate memory and secondly the findings are correlational so although there may be a link between discordant family life and antisocial behaviour, no assumption can be made that the former causes the latter. Also, from an ethical perspective, there may be complications in working with families with the problems mentioned.

The process of separation

Bowlby established a research unit looking into the effects of separation. He recruited James Robertson to help him with his studies of children who were separated from their primary caregivers through hospitalisation (either the child being hospitalised, or the caregiver) and children who were sent to live in an institution. Robertson and Bowlby (1952) produced a model that suggests there are three stages that children go through in their reaction to separation from their primary caregiver. They called this the 'protest-despair-detachment model' (PDD), which can be seen in Diagram 1.4.

Diagram 1.4

The first reaction a child shows when separated from their mother/primary carer is **Protest**. This is demonstrated by the child crying and being distraught, possibly panicking, when their mother does not return. They are likely to call out for their mother but they can be comforted by others. This reaction can last for a few hours or possibly up to a week.

The next reaction is **Despair** which is shown when the child becomes disinterested in what is going on around them. They become apathetic and do not try to seek comfort from others. Instead they may try some form of self-comfort such as rocking, or sucking their thumb.

The final stage is **Detachment** that may occur after a prolonged separation. Detachment is demonstrated when the child appears to cope better with the separation from their mother. They may respond to other people and show interest in their surroundings, however, the child is likely to be detached emotionally from those around them and, when their mother or primary carer does return the child is likely to be cold and unresponsive towards the mother, possibly being angry and rejecting their mother's attempts to comfort them.

Nowadays, it is quite usual for parents to stay with a child who is hospitalised and there are generally few restrictions on parents visiting a child in hospital. A few decades ago this was generally not the case and medical practitioners thought that all that children needed was to be cared for physically. No thought was given to preparing children for being separated from their caregivers and being in an unfamiliar and sometimes frightening new environment. Parental visits to the child in hospital were also very strictly limited.

Robertson and Robertson (1971) were instrumental in changing this viewpoint. They discovered that if children are well prepared for a separation they adjust and cope much better than if no preparation is made. If a child is familiarised with their prospective surroundings beforehand and the separation is spoken about with the child then the child seems to cope well. Above all, the child's distress is reduced if a 'mother substitute' is available, to whom the child can direct their attachment behaviours. On the other hand, where no preparation is made and there is no substitute attachment figure available, a child is likely to react in the manner suggested by the PDD model created by Robertson and Bowlby.

Parental death

Bowlby linked the response to the death of an attachment figure as similar to that outlined in the 'despair' stage of the PDD model that he and his colleague Robertson devised in 1952.

Studies carried out with participants who had suffered the early death of their mothers showed that there is a higher incidence of depression in people who have suffered such bereavement. The participant group studied demonstrated twice the normal rate of depression and anxiety. Researchers found the rate of depression is particularly high in people who were less than 6 years old when their mother died (Bifulco *et al*, 1992).

The type of care the child receives after the death can lessen the detrimental effects of the death of a parent on a young child. Good quality care offering comfort and security can help the child better come to terms with the death. Bowlby (1953) proposed that a child should be allowed to grieve in his/her own way rather ignore or gloss over it.

Divorce

Divorce is much more common in today's society than it was even a few decades ago. The effect that divorce has on children varies greatly, although Schaffer (1996) found that no matter how old a child is, they are nearly all affected by the divorce of their parents in some negative way. Boys in particular are adversely affected. These effects may be short-term as most children seem to be able to eventually cope with their parents splitting up. How much the divorce affects a child depends on a variety of factors:

- The extent to which contact is maintained with the parent who does not have custody of the children.
- The type of lifestyle the remaining lone-parent family maintains.
- Whether the parent with whom the child lives remarries and, if so, the structure of the new 'step-family'.

(Source: Hetherington and Stanley-Hagan, 1999)

Hetherington and Stanley-Hagan (1999) found certain effects in their study of how children adjust to the divorce of their parents. Some of these effects are listed below. They found that:

- Higher incidents of delinquent or antisocial behaviour.
- Higher levels of psychological problems in childhood and adolescence.
- Lower levels of self-esteem.
- Lower levels of academic achievement.
- Evidence of 'growing up' earlier. Events such as leaving home, living with a partner or getting married, having children, occurring earlier than normal.
- Greater incidence of depression.
- More frequent changes of job.
- Lower socio-economic status.
- Family relationships less close in adulthood.

These findings are based on correlated data that may link divorce with these behaviours and tendencies, but divorce cannot be said to be the cause of them directly. Other factors must also be considered. Perhaps parents who are going to be divorced may display differences in the way they bring up their children. Any conflict in the home before the divorce or separation occurs may be detrimental on the child. The level of conflict following a divorce may also have an effect on the child. Recent research shows that children from conflict-ridden homes suffer less, in the long term, if their parents divorce. Negative effects on children are also reduced if they are able to continue good relationships with both parents, and where the parent with custody has adequate income, as well as social support from friends and relatives (Hetherington *et al*, 1998).

This Section has looked at a variety of studies, and a variety of the effects of separation. There is no simple unambiguous relationship between separation and the effect it has on a child. Many factors have to be taken into account. It is often the type of life the child experiences *before* a separation that has more effect on the child rather than the separation itself.

Box 1.12

Evaluation - the Work of John Bowlby

The work of John Bowlby has given rise to almost half a century of controversy and debate. The importance that Bowlby placed on the mother-child bond has led to some feminists proposing that, according to his theories, mothers can be blamed for many social and political failings in a society. Mothers could become scapegoats for later problems in a person's life if the mother is anything less than perfect. It has been suggested that Bowlby's theories are too simplistic as they do not take into account the complex and unique lives that children lead.

There is no doubt though that Bowlby's work has had, and still does have, an enormous effect on how psychologists regard attachment. He raised awareness of children's emotional needs, which had previously been largely ignored by researchers and policy-makers. Researchers still continue to investigate Bowlby's theories and to refine and develop his work, rather than to reject it outright.

Privation

Unlike deprivation, where a child who has formed an attachment bond is then separated from its primary caregiver, 'privation' occurs when a child fails to form any attachment bonds due to adverse environmental circumstances. There can be several reasons why this bonding process does not occur and we will investigate two of these: children who were brought up in institutions and case studies of children who were abandoned or locked away by their parents and so isolated from society.

As we saw with deprivation, the long-term effects of separation from the attachment figure can be harmful. With privation the effects are more extreme and often irreversible. The work of Harry Harlow with rhesus monkeys indicated that growing up without an attachment figure to act as a role model can have a very harmful effect on relationships in later life. Some tragic case studies where children have grown up without an attachment figure indicate that a similar effect is shown in humans.

There are two main methods that have been used in order to study the effects of privation. **Diagram 1.5** provides further details.

Diagram 1.5

Case Studies, Natural Experiments and Longitudinal Studies

Case studies are research studies which are carried out on a particular individual participant who, for some reason, warrants close investigative research. The case studies usually run for a lengthy period of time sometimes lasting for many years.

Strengths: Lots of valuable and in-depth 'qualitative' information is gathered about the individual and the effects of their experiences.

Weaknesses: Whilst case studies are very useful in providing richly detailed information, it must be remembered that they only apply to that individual and the insights gained may not be applicable to other people.

Natural experiments are scientifically based studies that take advantage of an already occurring event. The researcher does not manipulate the setting in any way, so it is ecologically valid (like 'real-life') but uses the existing set up in order to provide the basis for their experiment.

In the studies we will look at a number of children were assessed and monitored several times over a period of many years in order to determine the effects of their early lives on their later maturation, development and behaviour.

Strengths: The studies are more scientifically based than case studies and have high ecological validity allowing data to be generalised to a wider population

Weaknesses: In a longitudinal study it is difficult to maintain contact with all the participants over the period of the study. The later failure to gather data from a number of original participants may affect the reliability of the findings overall.

Longitudinal studies are studies that take place over a period of time, sometimes many years. The participants are revisited a number of times and their progress monitored.

Some children, for whatever reason, spend their early lives in care, living in institutions such as orphanages. In some of these institutions, the care is of a high quality and the children are well cared for, in others it is the opposite, the quality of care is poor and the children experience little contact with others. Refer to **Box 1.13** for further discussion on low quality care in institutions.

Box 1.13

Research: Dennis' 'Low Quality' Care in Institutions (1973)

Dennis (1973) carried out a longitudinal study of children who were raised in an orphanage in Beirut, Lebanon. The children were put into the orphanage shortly after they were born and were looked after by people who had also lived their lives in the orphanage. The caregivers fed, changed, bathed and dressed the children but did not play or speak with the children. The infants were put into their cots and left all day. Older children who could walk were put into playpens and left all day with only a ball to play with.

Dennis assessed the infants shortly after they arrived at the orphanage, at two months old and they seemed to be normally developed for their age. He then reassessed them after one year and found that their development was well behind what it should have been. The children only showed the ability to perform tasks expected of someone half their age.

When the children reached the age of 6 years the boys and girls were separated and sent to different institutions. The girls' institution followed similar lines to the previous orphanage, there was little stimulation, and little care and attention was paid to them. Dennis assessed the girls' IQ (intelligence quotient, a measure of intellectual ability) and it was half of what is considered normal. The girls showed little ability to read or write.

The institution the boys were sent to was an improvement on the orphanage. The boys were taken on trips and were able to experience more stimulating and varied environments than the girls. They were trained for jobs and came into contact with a wider variety of adults who interacted with them. Dennis found at the age of 16 years, although the boys' average IQ score was lower than normal, it was higher than that of the girls, and was in the range that would allow them to function in society.

Several of the children were adopted from the orphanage and Dennis assessed these children in comparison to those who stayed in institutional care. He found that the children who had been adopted before the age of two years had normal IQ scores by the time they were around 5 years of age. The children who were adopted after the age of two, but before they left the orphanage at 6 years of age, attained IQ levels only slightly lower than what is considered normal. (The normal level of IQ is taken to be a score of 100.)

Dennis's study suggests that the effects of privation on a child depend on the environment they are raised in. If the environment is stimulating and rich, a child may grow up to be intellectually normal. If an environment is lacking in stimulation, a child is more likely to suffer in their cognitive development.

In 1989, Hodges and Tizard investigated institutions that offered high quality care. **Box 1.14** discusses high quality institutional care.

Box 1.14

Research: Hodges and Tizard - 'High Quality' Institutional Care

Hodges and Tizard carried out a longitudinal study of 65 children who had been put into the care of an institution in the UK. Hodges and Tizard compared these children with a group of children of similar age who were raised at home.

The institutionalised children in the study were all less than 4 months old when they were placed in care. The residential nursery provided high quality care with toys and books for the children to play with and the staff gave the children lots of attention. However, the policy in the institution was that caregivers should explicitly not form attachments with the children in their care. There was a high turnover of caregivers and by the age of 4 around 50 different caregivers had cared for the children. Consequently, the children had little opportunity to form any bonds with the people who cared for them.

Most of the children in the institution had, by the age of 8 years, been adopted or had returned home to their natural families. Hodges and Tizard assessed the children at various ages, at 4 years, 8 years, and 16 years.

At the age of 4 years all the children were found to be within the normal range for cognitive development and their language skills were also comparable with that expected of children of the same age. By 8 years of age, most of the adopted children had formed close relationships and attachments to their adoptive parents, who were motivated to build a good relationship with a much-wanted child.

Fewer of the children who returned to their natural families managed to form close attachments. The natural parents were generally less sure about their child's return to the family and there remained the financial problems and difficult circumstances that had precipitated the sending of the child to the institution in the first place.

Although the adopted children generally seemed to settle better in their new homes, both the adopted children and those children who returned to their natural families displayed behavioural problems outside the home. Teachers of the institutionalised children from both adopted families and those returned to their natural families reported that the children displayed problem behaviours. These problems consisted of attention-seeking, disobedience, and trouble in forming peer relationships.

By the age of 16 years a similar pattern was repeated. The children who were adopted generally had close, loving relationships with their adoptive parents. The children who returned to their biological parents generally had poor relationships with their families. Teachers still reported that both groups of adopted and restored children displayed behavioural problems similar to those mentioned previously.

Conclusions on the institutional care studies

These two important and revealing studies show that the quality of care given to children raised in an institutional setting plays a major role in their social, emotional and cognitive development. They showed that attachments can be made after infancy but, despite this, there do seem to be some lasting effects of privation that may be manifested in behavioural problems. However, not all the children showed lasting effects, so the effects of privation may be mitigated by individual differences and may not be inevitable given a stimulating environment and enough love, attention and interaction with others.

Isolated children

Case studies of isolated children provide richly detailed data about the effects of severe privation. There have been many stories throughout history about children who have been discovered after years of living in unbelievably deprived conditions away from human contact, comfort and security. We will look at *three* case studies (**Box 1.15**, **Box 1.16** and **Box 1.17**) that investigated the effects of such trauma.

Box 1.15

Research: Case Study 1 - the Story of Genie

Genie was found in 1970 in California when she was aged 13 years. She had been isolated in a small room and had not been spoken to by anyone since infancy. Her father apparently hated children. A previous daughter was put into the garage because the father could not stand the baby's crying. The baby girl died of pneumonia at two and a half months old. A second child, a boy, died from choking only a few days after he was born. A third child, also a boy, was rescued by his grandmother when he was three years old and he is still alive. The grandmother was killed by a truck shortly after the fourth child, Genie, was born.

Genie lived in isolation in a small room, naked, sitting on a potty and restrained by a harness. She often went hungry. At night, if her parents remembered to move her, she was put into a 'cot' that had wire sides and a cover overhead. If Genie cried or made any noise her father beat her. The father never spoke to Genie and the only communication between them was through him growling or barking at her. Genie's mother was terrified of the father. Genie's brother (who had been rescued by the grandmother and returned to live with the family after her death) was also terrified of the father and obeyed the father's instructions not to speak to Genie.

Eventually, after a violent argument Genie's mother ran away from the family home, taking Genie with her. They went to the welfare office where the mother asked for help. Genie was sent to the Los Angeles Children's Hospital for tests. Both her parents were charged with child abuse, although the charges against her mother were later dropped as it was recognised that she, too, was a victim of the father's cruelty. The father later shot and killed himself.

Genie's case caused great interest among psychologists, neurologists, linguists and other researchers interested in child development. They were interested to know what Genie's mental capabilities were at the time she was found, and how she would go on to develop.

Genie has been the subject of many journal articles and books, she was repeatedly tested and observed and much research has been sparked as a result of discoveries made in Genie's case.

When she first arrived in the hospital, Genie was very malnourished, incontinent, was unable to walk properly due to her limbs being squashed up in her confinement. She did not know how to chew solid food as she had only been given baby food and milk to eat. She made almost no noise. Tests that measure social maturity showed Genie to be at the level expected of a one year old child. Genie was 13 years old.

Genie first started to speak in one-word utterances, then two words. Despite many years of learning at special schools and with speech therapists Genie never managed to speak normally. She failed to grasp the basic grammatical principles necessary for language fluency. Genie's IQ was tested using special tests where verbal skills are not required. The level of her IQ increased from 38 in 1971 up to 74 in 1977.

In 1978, Genie's mother was, once again, appointed her legal guardian, and very shortly afterwards the mother withdrew Genie from all further investigative research.. She filed a law suit against the hospital and against her primary researcher, with whom Genie had built up a trusting relationship, charging them with using Genie's case for 'prestige and profit'. The mother charged the therapists and researchers with subjecting Genie to 'unreasonable and outrageous' testing not designed to treat Genie but to exploit her case for economic gain. Genie's on-going intellectual and language development came to an abrupt halt (Curtiss, 1977).

Box 1.16

Research: *Case Study 2* - the Story of the 'Monkey Boy'

Following the civil war in Uganda, John Ssebunya disappeared from his home at the age of four or five. He was discovered in 1998 living with a group of vervet monkeys in the trees. The 'monkey boy' as he was dubbed, was malnourished and covered in scars from crawling and from climbing trees. He was looked after by a Ugandan couple who run an organisation for Ugandan orphans.

John lived with the family and they have helped him to learn to speak and gain some of the skills necessary for living in society. He learned to eventually trust the people who looked after him. He plays football and travelled to the United States of America to play with the Ugandan Soccer Team in the Special Olympics. He also sings with a choir.

However, John, at the age of 14 years in 1999, could not read or write and his language skills were not fluent. His social behaviour was, at times, inappropriate for someone of his age.

It has been impossible to conclusively determine whether John's developmental problems were caused by his time spent away from human society and being deprived of an attachment figure.

(Sources: 'The Scotsman', October 1999 and the BBC 'Living Proof Documentary', October 1999)

Box 1.17

Research: Case Study 3 - the Story of the Czech Twins

Identical twin boys, Andrei and Vanya, were born in Czechoslovakia in 1960. Their mother died shortly after their birth and the boys were looked after by the social service for the first year of their lives. They then spent six months being fostered by an aunt. During this first eighteen months the boys appeared to develop normally. Eventually, at the age of one and a half, the twins went to live with their father and his new wife.

Their father was of low intelligence and the household income was meagre. The father spent most of the time away from home trying to earn money. The new stepmother did not like the boys and was cruel to them. Andrei and Vanya were put into a small, unheated room where they spent the next five and a half years. The only time they came out of the room was to be sent into the cellar as a punishment. The boys were often beaten by their stepmother and were deprived of proper food, exercise and any human interaction, other than what they developed between themselves.

The twin boys were discovered at the age of seven years. They could hardly walk as they suffered from rickets (a condition that results in a softening of the bones and inadequate bone growth. It is caused by a lack of vitamin D in the diet and through lack of sunshine that forms vitamin D in the skin). They had the appearance of children half their age and could barely communicate other than through gestures. The boys were very frightened of the world around them. Their IQ level was estimated to be 40, less than half the normal level. The doctors at the hospital where they were initially sent predicted that the twin boys would suffer permanent physical and mental handicap.

Andrei and Vanya were placed in a residential home until, at the age of 8 years, they went to live with two sisters who gave them a loving and caring home. The boys underwent a programme of physical remediation and started at a school for children with severe learning disabilities. They put on weight and learned to walk and talk. They soon were sent to a mainstream primary school and then on to secondary school. Their language ability, emotional development and intellectual capabilities eventually caught up with that of their peers around the age of 14 years. Their IQ at this stage was measured and found to be normal at 100. After leaving school Andrei and Vanya trained in electronics, got married and had children. They are now reported to be in secure and loving relationships and are well adjusted and intellectually able. One is a computer technician; the other is a technical training instructor (Koluchova, 1976).

Box 1.18

Wild Child - the Story of Feral Children

Dr. Bruce Perry is a clinical neuroscientist who founded the Child Trauma Academy in the United States of America (www.childtrauma.org). He has conducted clinical research on the behavioural, emotional, social and physiological effects of neglect and trauma in children. The author of over 200 journal articles, various book chapters and a regular contributor on American television and radio, Dr. Perry is a recognised authority on the effects of neglect and maltreatment in children. Dr. Perry speaks about children who have suffered severe privation and isolation:

> 'We should look at these children, not with pity, but with awe. They have this kernel of humanity that will not be crushed. You can't imagine what these children go through, being raised in a cage, in a dark room, nobody talking to you, nobody telling you you're special, nothing. It's fascinating that you could go through something like that and that you would still be willing, after what human beings have done to you, to put your hand out and touch another person.'

(Quote taken from 'Wild Child - the story of Feral Children', Channel 4 Television, December 2003, reproduced with kind permission from Dr. Perry.)

Whilst these case studies provide rich and important insights into children who have suffered from severe privation and the effects of isolation there are problems associated with the information and data that is obtained.

- The number of cases reported is very few and of those that are reported even fewer are well researched and well documented.
- Each case is individual and children are affected in different ways, so comparisons cannot be made to allow an overall picture of the effects of privation.
- The children who show signs of poor cognitive development may have had those problems from birth. There is no way of knowing whether the lack of mental capability is a result of their privation, or if it was always present.

However, conclusions have been drawn that give some insight into the effects of privation and isolation on children's development.

- A child's normal cognitive, emotional, physiological and social development can be severely restricted when that child has undergone extreme isolation, has suffered a lack of care and a lack of stimulation and has not had the benefit of normal social relationships.

- The effects of isolation and privation on a child may not be irreversible, they can regain a level of normal developmental achievement and go on to lead normal lives, as shown with Andrei and Vanya, the Czech twin boys who went on to lead normal and fulfilling lives following their five and a half years of severe privation.
- Bowlby claimed that the first 2 to 3 years were a 'critical period' in a child's life. If a child was denied emotional care during this period then, he claimed, permanent harm was almost inevitable. Some studies of isolated children, such as the Czech twins researched by Koluchova in 1976, challenge this claim and show that good recovery, in respect of socialisation and language is possible even after many years of deprivation. Other researchers, such as Hodges and Tizard in 1989, support Bowlby's critical period hypothesis finding that there were some permanent effects on children following early privation. Overall it may be preferable to think of there being a 'sensitive period' in a child's life, when emotional care is seen as *very important*, rather than a 'critical period' when emotional care is deemed *vital.*

Parenting styles

Most researchers agree that parents play a significant role in the way children develop their sense of identity and how they learn to cope with the problems they encounter in childhood and, indeed, in adult life too. The style of parenting that is adopted in bringing up a child has been shown to influence that child's self-esteem and confidence and many other characteristics and behaviours. Parents also act as role models enabling children to learn the skills of parenting that they in turn will be likely to use when they become parents themselves.

Research has been carried out into the way that parents behave and it has been proposed that there are three main types of parenting styles. These are: 'authoritarian', 'democratic' and 'permissive' styles. These styles are based on the research of Diana Baumrind that took place in the 1960s and which was updated by her in 1996.

Authoritarian style: Authoritarian parents expect their children to obey their rules without question and they feel no necessity to explain the reasons for their rules. They are very strict and have many rules for the children to follow. The children are not allowed to question the rules, nor are they allowed to have their own opinions. This parenting style is rigid and unbending and, because the children are expected to obey without question, they do not learn to think for themselves. Subsequently, as the children grow up, they will often be less confident and lack independence. As teenagers the children will often become rebellious.

Permissive style: In contrast to the authoritarian style parents, the permissive-style parent has very few rules and those rules that do exist are frequently not enforced. Children are left to their own devices and allowed to do what they wish. Parents give in to a child's demands. Children raised in the permissive style often display difficulties in socialising with others. They are used to getting their own way and tend to be somewhat selfish in their attitudes to others. Baumrind found that parents who adopted the permissive approach were likely to have been raised by parents with the other extreme way of parenting, the authoritarian style, and had adopted the permissive style as a reaction to their own overly strict upbringing.

Democratic style: Democratic-style parents still have rules within the household, but rather than expecting the blind obedience of the authoritarian style, the democratic parents discuss and explain the rules with their children. Democratic style parents expect disciplined behaviour from their children but they also explain the reasons for their expectations. Children are given more choices and learn to make decisions for themselves. A child's opinion is listened to and treated with respect by democratic parents and, because children brought up in this style are able to make decisions, and also make mistakes that they can learn from, they generally grow up with higher self-esteem and are more independent and self-confident. They tend to be more responsible than their authoritarian-raised peers.

Although these three styles are very distinct, in real life parents may switch between styles, depending on other factors such as stress levels and external influences. However, Baumrind suggests that most parents have a greater tendency towards one dominant style.

Although Baumrind's research has been highly influential with professionals in the field of family issues, she has been criticised by other researchers. Harris (1998) proposes that children are, in fact, influenced not so much by parenting styles but rather by their peers, and by their genetic make-up. Harris questioned Baumrind's research as it only studied one child in each family and no investigation was made to see if the parents treated other children in the family in the same way.

Baumrind mainly studied white, middle-class, Anglo-American families. Critics suggest that different cultures would favour different parenting styles depending on the community influences of their own culture. For example, Asian or African based cultures would tend to adopt a more controlling style of parenting. The predominant community culture would have more impact on a child than the style of parenting they were raised in. It is also suggested that Baumrind's findings were based on an unrepresentative sample, giving a false understanding of the influence that a particular parenting style has on a child's behaviour.

The development of parenting skills

In this Section we have seen the importance of parenting behaviour in helping children develop emotionally, socially and intellectually. The quality of parenting or care that a child experiences impacts on the type of attachment that develops, whether secure or insecure. If a child's parents/caregivers are warm, sensitive and responsive, then that child is more likely to develop secure attachments and go on in later life to be at ease socially, to be confident and able to cope with life. Insensitive parenting can lead to children developing insecure attachments and developing problems later that can include behavioural problems, bullying, lack of trust in others and difficulty in maintaining relationships with a partner (Ainsworth, 1978).

For most people, becoming a parent is an extremely important life event, and they are expected to demonstrate parental behaviours without any formal 'training'. How do parents learn the necessary skills for raising children? A survey carried out for the National Family and Parenting Institute found that many parents felt they needed help, but were unsure of where to get it (www.nfpi.org).

One view is that we are pre-programmed to raise our children in the most effective way to improve their chances of survival and thus carry on our genes into the next generation, and beyond. This is called the evolutionary view and it suggests that parenting behaviour is adaptive and innate.

'Social learning theory' (SLT) suggests an alternative view; that we learn parenting skills by watching and imitating our own parents and other influential people in our lives. An individual's experiences of how they were treated as a child by their parents/caregivers will strongly influence how they go on to treat their own children.

SLT also suggests that the media can play a part in the development and learning of parenting skills. There are frequent magazine articles, newspaper reports and television programmes relating to parenting and child-rearing. The 'soaps', such as *Eastenders*, *Coronation Street* and *River City*, depict various types of family life in which many millions of us share each week.

Box 1.19

Research: National Family and Parenting Institute

In 1999, the market research company MORI conducted a survey for the National Family and Parenting Institute. They interviewed 2,059 adults in Great Britain about their views on parenting. The survey found that:

> 'There is surprising unanimity between parents and non-parents, men and women, younger and older people about what matters in raising children. Upbringing is seen as a key determinant in forming the attitudes to parenting and the behaviour of individual parents. But natural instinct and the individual needs of the child are seen as playing a significant part in influencing parents' attitudes and behaviour. Loving care, time spent with children and so-called 'positive parenting' is seen as the key requirements of parents, in their turn.'

(Source: National Family and Parenting Institute, 2000, www.nfpi.org)

Different cultures have different ways of raising children. Generally speaking, Western cultures are more lenient with their children than Eastern cultures. For example, strict discipline is seen in Japan and Korea as a sign that parents love and care for their children, whereas in the UK and America being overly strict is often seen as being less affectionate. Cross-cultural differences in child-rearing practices should be considered in terms of their effectiveness in preparing the child to adapt to their own particular culture. Further discussion of cross-cultural practices is considered in relation to day-care at the end of this Section.

A degree of cross-cultural agreement over appropriate ways of treating children is, however, evident in the United Nations Convention on the Rights of the Child (1989), which includes the right not to be separated from parents (unless this would be in the child's best interests), and the provision of assistance and guidance for parents in child rearing.

While many people experience good parenting throughout their own childhood and are able to learn the skills to be successful parents, some do not. Yet many people who have had negative experiences in their upbringing do go on to provide good parenting for their own children. In today's society parents and prospective parents are offered support to enable them to learn the skills necessary to be effective in their parenting. Various organisations and government initiatives have arisen that aim to give support to those that need or want it: Mother and Toddler Groups; Buddying programmes; Home-Start; the National Family and Parenting Institute; Parentline

Scotland (provided by Children 1st); Sure Start Programme; the Home Office 'Supporting Families'. (Website addresses are provided at the end of this book.)

Box 1.20

Activity - Classroom Debate on Parenting Skills

Hold a class debate on the following topic:

'Parenting skills should be part of the school curriculum for everyone'.

Application

When Bowlby proposed his theory of maternal deprivation in the 1950s, he suggested that if a child was separated from its primary caregiver then that child would suffer harm. Bowlby argued that placing a child in day care, especially a young child of less than 30 months old, would likely be detrimental to the child. The implications of Bowlby's theories were that mothers should stay at home to look after their children. At the time far fewer mothers went out to work while their children were young than is the norm in today's society.

Day care for children, even young babies, is now a quite usual occurrence as mothers return to work following the births of their children. Nowadays, we expect childcare facilities to be provided much more than they were a few decades ago. Most local authorities provide their communities with pre-school nurseries and day care facilities. This topic area has been the subject of recent research much of which questions the ideas proposed by Bowlby.

Schaffer (1998) suggests that day care may actually be beneficial for children as an addition to a positive environment at home. Of course, the day care provision must be of a high standard. Schaffer suggests that two important factors need to be taken into account when assessing whether the quality of day care provision is acceptable and likely to benefit the child. Day care needs to provide consistent and quality care. Schaffer suggests this can be achieved by providing:

- Sufficient stimulation for the child, such as the provision of suitable and appropriate toys and books.
- High levels of interaction, especially verbal interaction, between the caregivers and the children.

- Sensitive emotional care for the children. The caregivers should be sensitive towards the emotional needs of the children.
- Consistency is achieved by allowing the children to develop relationships with the staff. A low staff turnover in institutional care is one of the key factors in achieving this. Ideally each child should be able to develop links with one main member of staff who should be responsible for that child.
- Establishing routines for the children helps in maintaining consistency.

Children can be as securely attached to their primary caregivers if they attend day care as those who stay at home. Children who demonstrate less secure attachments to their primary caregivers may benefit more from attending day care as long as the care is of high quality. In some cases, therefore, day care can be advantageous for a child. The key is that the day care should be of high quality.

Most studies seem to agree that if the quality of day care is of an acceptable level, and is consistent, then children generally do not suffer in their developmental progress if they attend day care. High quality day care can be beneficial for a child's cognitive and social development.

A child's social development can, with good quality day care provision, be enhanced through their interactions with other children and with the day care staff. Children can become more independent and able to cope with new situations. They generally develop better social skills and learn to interact better with others than those children who do not attend day care. Of course, the key again is that the day care is of a high quality (Schaffer 1998).

Cultural differences

The focus of what is considered important in providing quality day care is different in different cultures. Japanese culture, for example, promotes group integration and co-operation and generally encourages children to be part of a group. Western ideals, like those of the United States, promote independence and self-sufficiency (Tobin *et al*, 1989).

The accepted norms and values of each culture influence the provision of day care for children within that culture. More cross-cultural research is needed, however, to determine universal characteristics of what constitutes high quality day care.

Memory

Section summary

This Section on memory will investigate:

- The domain of Cognitive Psychology.
- The nature of memory.
- Models of memory.
- Theories of forgetting.
- Application of memory improvement techniques to study and exam skills.

The domain associated with the study of memory is Cognitive Psychology

Cognitive psychologists believe that if behaviour is to be fully understood the internal workings of a person's mind must be studied: these include processes such as memory, thinking and how we perceive things. The cognitive viewpoint is in distinct contrast to the psychoanalytic view, which emphasises how our unconscious mind and emotions play a large role in affecting our behaviour. The unconscious mind is that part of our mind that is not readily accessible to us, but that contains our basic urges and instincts and our repressed memories. The cognitive view is also in contrast with the behaviourist view that concentrates on external events and their effects on our behaviour, rather than our thoughts and feelings.

Cognitive Psychology emphasises the importance of studying internal mental processes, what goes on in a person's mind, as a means of understanding behaviour. Cognitive psychologists study these mental processes, called 'mediators', in order to understand why we behave as we do. Mediators include:

- **P**erception – how we make sense of the world through using our senses: sight, smell, sound, taste, touch.
- **A**ttention – our ability to focus on important information coming into our brains and disregarding that which we consider unimportant.

- **L**anguage – the ability to transmit and receive information through an agreed set of symbols.
- **M**emory – the acquisition, storage and retrieval of knowledge.
- **T**hinking – the mental manipulation of thoughts, ideas, memories.

Diagram 1.6

(Source: www.allfreeclipart.com)

Tip: The mediators can be remembered by using a mnemonic - the first letters of the mediators spell out **PALM T**(ree).

The human mind, according to cognitive psychology, is like a computer and our internal mental processes are organised in a systematic and logical way. Cognitive psychology has developed since the 1950s, alongside the development of the modern computer. Like a computer processing information, the brain takes in information, processes it through mediators, and a response occurs. The 'information-processing' approach is the dominant view in cognitive psychology today.

This Section will concentrate on one of the mediators, memory, which has been, and continues to be, studied extensively.

Psychologists have been studying memory since psychology began more than 100 years ago. In 1885, Hermann Ebbinghaus created a series of experiments that investigated learning and forgetting, as discussed in **Box 1.21**.

Box 1.21

Research: Ebbinghaus' Nonsense Syllables (1885)

Using himself as the subject, Ebbinghaus attempted to learn a series of nonsense syllables (like POV and GUZ) and then recall them. He found that after a delay 10 or 20 minutes, memory loss was very rapid but then it levelled off, so that delays of several hours, or even days, made very little difference to the remaining syllables that he remembered.

Ebbinghaus's research was very systematic and he tried to be rigorously scientific. Using nonsense syllables meant that his recall was unaffected by previous knowledge. However, his work has been criticised because using the nonsense syllables and being based in a laboratory meant that his research was 'not ecologically valid' that means it was not like real life. Also, because Ebbinghaus used himself as the subject, his findings should not be assumed to be the same in the wider population.

Box 1.22

Activity – What Makes You Who You Are?

Take a few minutes to think about what makes you who you are. Jot down some of your ideas.

Now think about how you would do this activity if you had no memory to call on.

Memory is essential to us and trying to imagine what life would be like without it is impossible. Without memory we would not know who we are; we would not know what we have done in the past; we would not be able to function in the present without knowledge from our past. We would not be able to plan anything, understand anything or learn anything.

Our memories are used to process enormous amounts of information of various types and forms. We use our memories to store images, sounds, smells, the feel of something, the taste of things, words, meanings and so on. Our memories involve the taking in of information, the storing of information and the retrieval of information when needed.

To understand memory, we need to look at how it is structured, how we put information into memory, how we store it, and how we can retrieve it later. As you may know from bitter experience in exams, being unable to retrieve information that is stored in our brains can be very frustrating! We will also look at other 'models' of memory that have been proposed by researchers and the criticisms have been made about them.

The nature of memory

In order to study memory we first need to understand a few key terms that are used by researchers to explain how memory works.

- **Stages** – there are thought to be three stages that information has to go through if it is to be remembered and become a memory. These stages are:

  (i) **Encoding**: This is the input stage where information enters the memory system and is coded in some way. This coding may be *visual* – how it looks, *acoustic* – how it sounds, *semantic* – what it means.

  (ii) **Storage**: The storage stage organises and holds information in the memory system. It is similar to how we put information we are storing in a computer into files.

  (iii) **Retrieval**: Once information is stored it is only going to be useful if we can later get access to it again. Storing information in a computer file is only useful if we know where that file is and can open it up again to access the information stored there. The retrieval stage is being able to remember or recall information that is in our memory.

In order to successfully remember something the information must be correctly encoded, stored appropriately, and be accessible later. If any of these stages fail then the information will be lost.

- **Capacity** refers to how much information can be stored.
- **Duration** is how long information can be held in a particular store.
- **Encoding** is how the information is coded in a particular store. There are various methods of encoding information. It can be encoded acoustically or visually or semantically. Other encoding methods, such as smell, may also occur. Can you remember a particular smell from your childhood? Perhaps the smell of home baking? What is your favourite smell?

Models of memory

Multi-store model of memory

A very influential model of memory was proposed by Atkinson and Shiffrin in 1968 and their ideas have been used by other theorists who have tried to understand how memory is structured. It is worth mentioning though, that not every memory researcher agrees with Atkinson and Shiffrin's model and we will investigate other ideas of how memory is structured later on in the chapter.

Atkinson and Shiffrin developed their 'Multi-store Model of Memory' (**Diagram 1.7**, below) to try to explain how information flows through the memory system in distinct stages.

Diagram 1.7

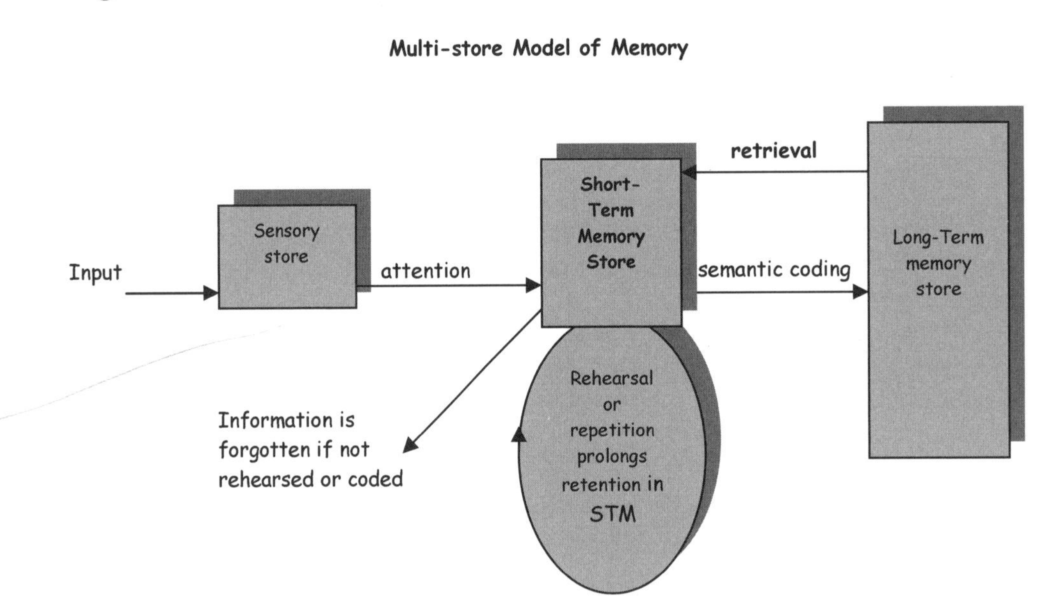

The first stage is sensory memory, where information is assessed according to which of the senses (sight, sound, smell, taste and touch) the information enters through. Information is held in sensory memory for only a very brief time, approximately 1-2 seconds, before it is either passed on to the next stage, or is lost through decay. Most research has focussed on the visual process and the auditory process.

Stop and think for a moment about all the information that is entering your mind via your senses. You may feel warm, or cool, or just right. Perhaps you can hear noises from around you, or smell your dinner cooking. Our senses are constantly bombarded with information, most of which we do not need to process and so that information is lost through decay. Information that is processed by us paying attention to it gets passed on to the next stage that is 'short-term memory' (STM).

STM Duration

The STM store is limited in its capacity to process and store information. Information is constantly flowing into STM and, because of the limited capacity here, it can be quickly displaced. Atkinson and Shiffrin believed that information in STM is lost within about 30 seconds. (See **Box 1.23**.)

Box 1.23

Research: STM - Brown and Peterson

In 1959, two researchers, Brown and Peterson, attempted to discover how long information can be held in STM. To test the duration of STM they presented participants with sets of three consonants, called consonant trigrams, such as NFW, GPV. The participants were then asked to count backwards in threes from a number given by the researchers. This technique (now called the Brown-Peterson technique) prevented participants from rehearsing or thinking about the letters. After set intervals varying between 3 and 18 seconds the participants were asked to recall the trigrams. Results showed that information was forgotten very rapidly and after 18 seconds only 10 per cent of trigrams could be remembered.

This, and other studies since, shows that information disappears from STM within a few seconds if rehearsal does not take place or if people do not make a conscious attempt to retain the information.

STM capacity

Important research by George Miller (1956) concluded that the STM capacity was 'the magic number 7, plus or minus two'. He found that most people can hold between 5 and 9 pieces of information in their STM. Find out your STM capacity by doing the activity in **Box 1.24**, below.

Box 1.24

Activity - find out your STM Capacity

You can find out what your STM capacity is by doing the following test, called a 'digit span test'.

1 6 7
4 2 9 4
2 7 4 9 1
8 6 9 7 2 0
4 9 0 6 2 9 7
9 3 6 1 8 4 3 4
8 0 5 2 0 5 7 2 6
0 7 4 7 2 4 1 0 6 5
4 6 0 3 1 7 0 5 8 3 9
1 0 6 6 1 9 4 5 9 1 1

Read each horizontal row of numbers out loud to yourself, one row at a time. Once you have read a row out loud, cover up the numbers and repeat them, then check if you have got them correct. Continue onto the next row, and the next, until you make a mistake. Your STM capacity is how many numbers you can remember correctly. How do you compare to the magic number 7 (+ or - 2)?

The capacity of STM, however, is for 7(+ or -2) pieces of information. Miller also found that by 'chunking' pieces of information together, each 'chunk' counts as one item of information. A 'chunk' is a meaningful unit. For example, if we take the last row of numbers from the digit span test and split them into three 'chunks' of numbers we get:

1066 – 1945 – 9/11

This is much easier to remember than the whole sequence of numbers individually. Effectively we have made up four 'chunks' of numbers, which is well within the limits of our STM capacity. Think about how you tell someone your telephone number, you are likely to split it into 'chunks' automatically, which will help them to remember it more easily.

We have seen that STM has a limited capacity and a limited duration. Information is lost through decay or through being displaced by new information coming in. We can keep information in STM for longer if we repeat it to ourselves, which is called 'rehearsal'. An example of this is when we look up a telephone number in the directory and then say it over and over to ourselves while we put the directory back on the shelf and then dial the number into the phone. Once we have dialled the number we no longer need to keep the number in our STM so it is allowed to decay or be displaced by new information. Rehearsal may, or may not, cause information to be transferred into 'long-term memory' (LTM).

STM encoding

Evidence from Conrad (1964) has shown that most of the encoding that is done in STM is done acoustically; we tend to remember a telephone number by saying it, either out loud or in our heads. We do not usually think of the visual shape of the numbers that are written in the directory. **Box 1.25** refers to this.

Box 1.25

Research: Conrad's SMT Test (1964)

Conrad used random groups of consonants from the list:

B, C, F, M, N, P, S, T, V, X.

Six letters were shown to participants by rapidly flashing them onto a screen.

Participants were required to write the string of six letters down as they appeared, but the speed at which they were presented on the screen was too fast for the participants to keep up so they had to rely on their STM.

Conrad noted the errors the participants made and found that the majority of wrong letters were substitutions of a letter with a similar sound. For example 'B' was substituted for 'P', and 'F' was substituted for 'S'.

This study indicates that even when we see letters written down we transfer them to STM acoustically.

Long-term memory (LTM)

The final stage of Atkinson and Shiffrin's model is the 'long-term memory' (LTM) store. Here is stored our knowledge, information about our lives, beliefs, understanding, people we know, places we are familiar with, skills we have learned and so much more. Unlike STM, which has limited capacity and limited duration, LTM is thought to be unlimited in capacity and unlimited in duration. Information stored in LTM can last a lifetime. LTM is a much larger and much more complex store than STM. LTM constantly revises information and modifies it as we gather new and updated facts.

Glanzer and Cunitz (1966) developed research that demonstrates the distinction between short-term memory and long-term memory. They investigated the effect of the order in which material is presented and how this impacts on remembering. When participants are presented with a list of words, they are more likely to remember the first few words and the last few words, but will likely forget the words in the middle of the list. This is known as the 'serial position effect'. Recalling words at the beginning of a list is called the 'primacy effect'. The recall of words at the end of the list is called the 'recency effect'. This research presents evidence that there are *two* memory stores. The words at the beginning of the list are recalled from the LTM store (having been transferred there as a result of rehearsal), while the words at the end of the list are recalled from the STM. The words in the middle of the list are lost as they have not been rehearsed and have not been retained in STM.

Capacity in LTM

So far, no one has managed to determine the capacity of LTM. Most researchers agree that there is no limit to the capacity of LTM. We always seem to be able to learn more without the loss of previous knowledge (although some students would disagree at times when they think their brains can take in no more information!).

Because of the huge capacity of LTM it requires a highly organised structure in order to allow us to retrieve information when we require it. Research suggests that we organise information in LTM 'semantically'. That is, we apply understanding and meaning to the information in order to store it appropriately. However, we also use visual coding techniques when required, for example when remembering faces, or imagining taking a visual tour through our home. Acoustic coding allows us to remember noises such as fire-engine sirens, and the ring tone of our mobiles. Perhaps you have also experienced certain smells that bring back memories of childhood.

Box 1.26

Different kinds of LTM

Semantic memory relates to words and meanings.

Episodic memory is used to remember what we did last week or a special event that occurred some years ago.

Procedural memory enables us to remember how to tie our shoelaces, or how to swim; 'declarative' memory enables us to remember facts and figures, such as 'the square of the hypotenuse is equal to the sum of the square of the other two sides' (how to find the length of the sides of a right-angled triangle!).

Evaluation of the multi-store model of memory

Strengths: There is considerable evidence for the existence of the three memory stores (sensory store, short term store and long term store) with each store differing in its capacity, duration and encoding capabilities. The multi-store model provides a simple, yet effective, framework for understanding memory. Research evidence supporting the multi-store model has been carried out through the use of 'positron emission tomography' (PET), which scans the brain and allows a view of the region of the brain that is being used during a task. Beardsley (1997) found that when short-term memory is required for a task the pre-frontal cortex is activated. A task requiring LTM activates the part of the brain called the hippocampus. Other supporting research comes from detailed case studies of a man, HM, who had the hippocampus removed from his brain following a tumour. HM was able to still perform tasks requiring STM but was unable to lay down any long-term memories following his operation (Milner, 1966).

Weaknesses: It is the simplicity of the multi-store model that accounts for its weaknesses. Although the sensory store is acknowledged to have five separate stores within it to account for the five senses, the other two stores (STM and LTM) are seen as singular stores. For example, the LTM store is shown as a single store for all types of memory. The model does not take into account that there may be different types of memories such as the memories we have for past events (episodic memories) and the memories we have for doing things like riding a bike or tying our shoelaces ('procedural memories').

The multi-store model sees LTM as a place where knowledge is passively stored until it is needed, whereas there is some evidence to show that the LTM is much more active in the whole memory system than Atkinson and Shiffrin describe.

Craik and Lockhart (1972) questioned the multi-store model's reliance on simple rehearsal to get information to stay in LTM. They believed that it is the type of rehearsal that is important. They made a distinction between what they called 'maintenance rehearsal', which is simply repeating a piece of information without any other processing and does not lead to long-term memories being created and 'elaborative rehearsal', which involves a much deeper processing of the information, using some form of evaluation or analysis. Only elaborative rehearsal leads to long-term memories being established.

Craik and Lockhart suggested that there were several levels of processing, from shallow to deep, and the level at which processing occurs determines how well it is remembered.

Diagram 1.8

Levels of Processing

Shallow processing is simply coding the information in terms of either its visual appearance, such as whether the words is written in CAPITALS or perhaps in *italics,* or coding the information in terms of its acoustic properties, such as whether the voice is soft or loud. At a slightly deeper level information can be processed by analysing its sound properties. Does this word rhyme with that word?

Deep processing incorporates some semantic understanding, or thinking, about what the information means. Craik and Lockhart proposed that information would be much better remembered if there is an understanding of what it means, than if no thought is given to its meaning.

Diagram 1.9

Processing words by appearance, sound and meaning.

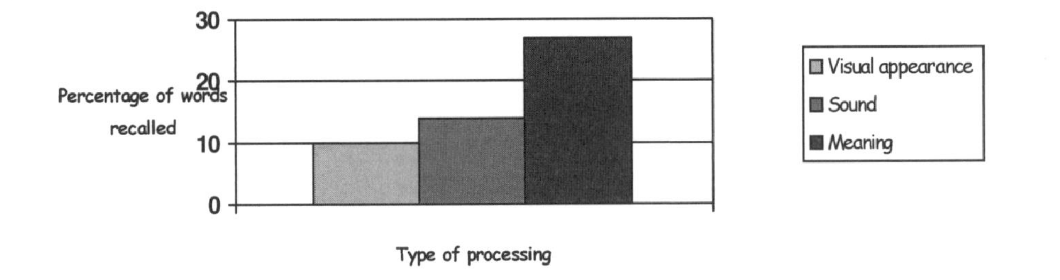

(Source: Craik, F.I.M. and Lockhart, R.S. (1972) 'Levels of processing: A framework for memory research', *Journal of Verbal Learning and Verbal Behaviour*, Vol. 11, pp. 671-684.)

Box 1.27

Activity: Processing Questions

1. Which of the following words are in **bold italics**?

bird
cake
bicycle
rain
football
lipstick

This activity requires shallow level processing. You are only required to visually compare the appearance of the words.

2. Which of the following words rhymes with 'ring'?

apple
thing
banana
spring
sing
telephone

This activity requires slightly deeper levels of processing. You are required to think about the sound of the word.

3. Which of the following words are types of bird?

flamingo
sapphire
seagull
ebony
puffin
toucan

This activity requires deep levels of processing. You need to think about what each word means in order to decide whether or not it is a type of bird.

Refer back to **Diagram 1.9** to see Craik and Lockhart's (1972) results when they carried out an experiment similar to that in the above activity.

Working memory model

Following criticism that the multi-store model was too simplistic in its concepts of STM and LTM as separate stores, Alan Baddeley and Graham Hitch (1974) devised a new model of memory, the 'working memory model'. This new model took a more active view of memory, in contrast to the passive storage system of the multi-store model. Baddeley and Hitch concentrated on short-term memory and argued that the multi-store model portrayed STM far too simplistically. They believed that STM is much more elaborate in how it works and they proposed the working memory model to depict their ideas.

Diagram 1.10

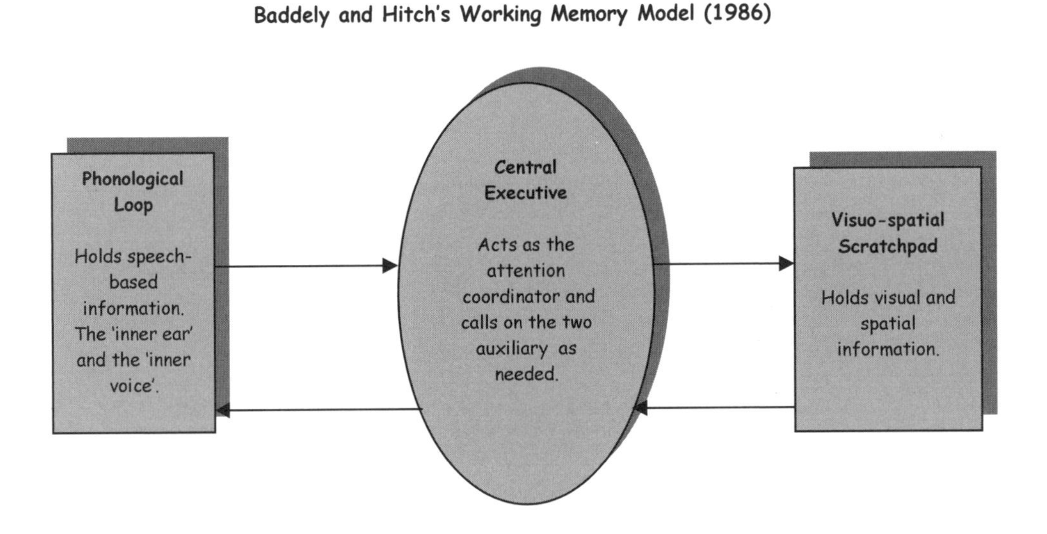

The working memory model suggests that we have separate stores for processing different types of information:

- **Central executive**: This decides what information should be attended to and what should not. It is thought to be involved in demanding mental activities, such as decision-making, planning and problem-solving. The 'central executive' is flexible and deals with both visual and auditory stimuli. It calls on the other components of the model, the auxiliary, or 'slave' systems made up of the 'phonological loop' and the 'visuo-spatial scratchpad', when they are required to process information. The central executive co-ordinates attention and performance. It has a limited capacity and cannot deal with too many things at once.

- **The phonological loop**: Sometimes called the 'phonological-articulatory loop', this is made up of two parts. The phonological store holds spoken words for approximately two seconds and acts like an 'inner ear'. The other part of the 'phonological loop' is the 'articulatory' process that converts written words or planned speech into sound before they enter the loop. This acts like an 'inner voice'.
- **The visuo-spatial scratchpad**: Sometimes called the 'visuo-spatial sketchpad', this deals with visual and spatial information. Visual information accounts for what things look like, while spatial information accounts for how things relate to each other in terms of position, distance, form and size. The 'visuo-spatial scratchpad' is used to analyse and manipulate visual and spatial information and it is involved in the perception of movement. This acts like an 'inner eye'.

Baddeley *et al* (1975) demonstrated that people remember short words better in STM than long words. They found that the length of a word affects the capacity of STM and that it is harder to remember long words like 'simultaneous' and 'representative' than short words like 'love' or 'harm'. Baddeley proposed that because the phonological loop only holds information for around two seconds, long words, which take longer to say, take up more of the available storage than short words. Short words can be rehearsed within the two seconds available in the phonological loop, whereas long words take too long to say and there is not time for repetition.

Box 1.28

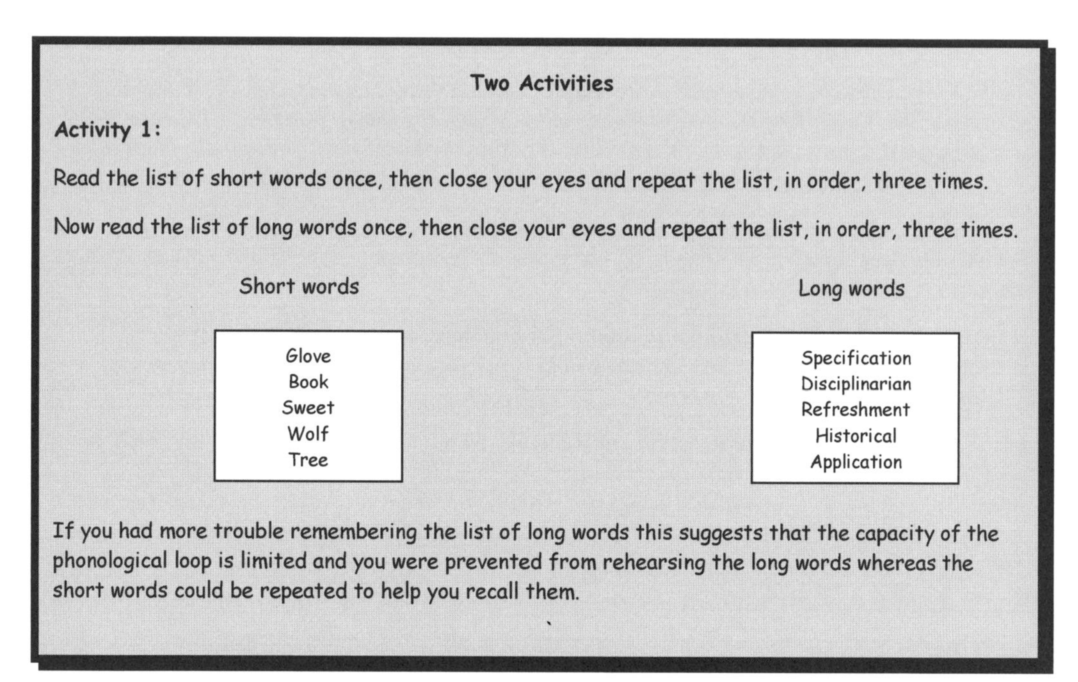
Two Activities

Activity 1:

Read the list of short words once, then close your eyes and repeat the list, in order, three times.

Now read the list of long words once, then close your eyes and repeat the list, in order, three times.

Short words	Long words
Glove	Specification
Book	Disciplinarian
Sweet	Refreshment
Wolf	Historical
Tree	Application

If you had more trouble remembering the list of long words this suggests that the capacity of the phonological loop is limited and you were prevented from rehearsing the long words whereas the short words could be repeated to help you recall them.

Activity 2:

In order to get a feel for how the working memory operates, Alan Baddeley (1997) suggests doing this exercise.

How many windows are there in your house? (Stop and work out the number before continuing.)

Most people will conjure up a mental image of their house and, looking at it either from the outside, or taking a tour of the rooms inside, will count the number of windows from the image created in your memory.

The visual image is processed by the visuo-spatial scratchpad and you can wander around the house, inside or out, looking at the windows in your imagination.

Counting the number of windows uses the phonological loop as you keep a check on the number as you go round.

The whole procedure is supervised by the central executive that assigns the tasks to the appropriate slave system (phonological loop or visuo-spatial scratchpad) and then recognises when the task is finished.

Check out **Box 1.29** for further research on the working memory model.

Box 1.29

Research: Hitch and Baddely on the 'Central Executive' (1976)

In 1976, Hitch and Baddeley carried out research that investigated the capacity of the central executive. They gave participants two tasks to carry out simultaneously. The first task consisted of analysing whether a statement was true or false (e.g. the participant was told that 'B is followed by A', they were then asked to analyse whether 'AB' was true or false). This task utilised the central executive.

Participants were asked to perform an additional task at the same time as carrying out task 1. They were asked to do ONE of the following:

- Say 'the, the, the' repeatedly (that utilised the articulatory loop).
- State random numbers (that utilised both the central executive AND the articulatory loop).
- No additional task.

Hitch and Baddeley found that when using only the articulatory loop for task 2 ('the, the, the'), or when no additional task was performed, the time taken to perform task 1 (using the central executive) was the same. However, when using both the central executive and the articulatory loop in task 2 (random numbers), performing the first task, which also utilised the central executive, took longer.

The results show that using the central executive to perform two tasks at the same time causes problems, but using different components, such as the central executive and the articulatory loop, at the same time creates no such difficulty. It appears then that the central executive is limited in its capacity.

Evaluation of the working memory model

Strengths: The working memory model convincingly explains how a range of different tasks can be dealt with, such as spatial processing, understanding written information, problem-solving, verbal reasoning. The model can be demonstrated using real-life tasks and is supported by many research findings. The role of a central executive in the overseeing of tasks is logical and appealing given the usage of several different sub-systems.

Weaknesses: Although appealing in its logic, the role of the central executive has never been fully explained or fully defined and so remains rather vague. Baddeley and Hitch claim that the central executive has limited capacity, yet no research has defined exactly what that capacity is, or how the central executive actually operates.

Theories of forgetting

Although it is assumed that LTM has an unlimited capacity, obviously we do forget things. An important part of studying memory is how and why we forget things. Some psychologists believe that forgetting is not due to information being lost, but is caused by a failure to access and retrieve the information. There are several theories that try to explain why we forget things stored in both STM and LTM.

Forgetting in short-term memory

We have seen that the short-term memory store is very limited in its capacity and in the length of time information can be held in STM without rehearsal or repetition. It is these factors that are thought most likely to account for forgetting in short-term memory.

Displacement

As we have already discovered, the capacity of STM is limited to seven pieces of information (plus or minus two) (Miller, 1956). Displacement theory provides the simple explanation that forgetting occurs in STM when the capacity is reached and new information coming into STM pushes out, or 'displaces', the information that is already there.

Research carried out by Waugh and Norman (1965) and by Shallice (1967) used a technique called the 'serial probe technique' to investigate forgetting in STM. A series of numbers is presented to participants and after the list is completed the researcher tells the participants which number is the 'probe' number. Participants then have to recall the number that came after the probe number in the list.

Box 1.30

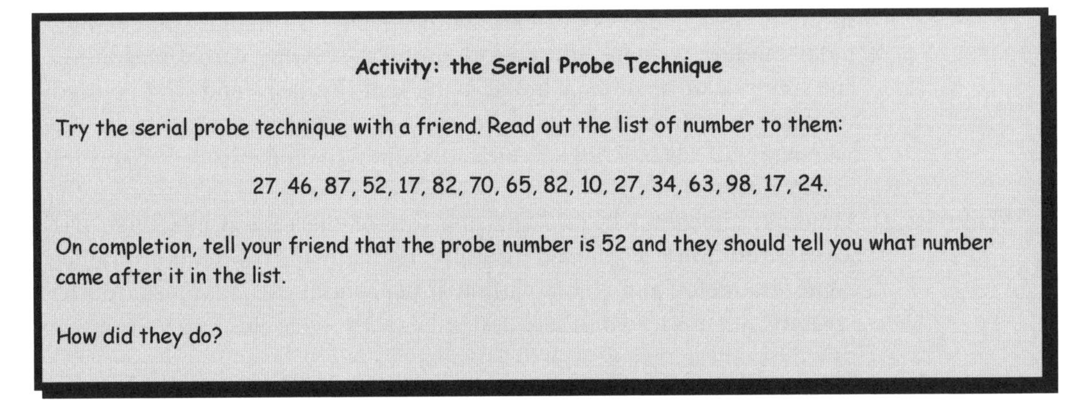

Waugh and Norman (1965) found that if the probe number was in the first part of the list, then participant's recall of the following number was poor, with less than 20 per cent. If the probe number was towards the end of the list then recall was much better, with over 80 per cent.

These findings support the theory that displacement occurs in STM as the later numbers displaced the earlier numbers from STM.

Decay

This occurs when the duration of time that information can be retained in STM is exceeded. The length of time information can be held in STM has been shown to be less than 30 seconds. The Brown-Peterson technique shows that when rehearsal is prevented, forgetting through decay occurs very quickly, within around 20 seconds.

Forgetting in long-term memory

According to most researchers, the long-term memory store is unlimited in its capacity and in the length of time it can hold information. If this is true, then why do we still forget things from our long-term memories? If forgetting is not due to decay or displacement then other factors must influence our memories. There are several possible reasons for forgetting in LTM. Some theorists propose that we do not forget things as such, but fail to access them or retrieve them from the store.

Below are some of the theories of why we forget information from LTM.

Trace decay

This theory suggests that the reason we forget things from our long-term memory store is that memories fade away over time. When a memory is laid down, it is thought that some structural event occurs in the brain, such as a pattern of neurons firing. This structural change, if not compounded through regular use, is fragile and susceptible to interference. Some psychologists think that the structural pattern or 'trace', caused in our brain by information, knowledge and skills will, if not used for a long time, eventually fade from our memory. This is called 'trace decay'. However, there is little evidence to support this theory as most of us can clearly remember particular events that occurred many years ago, such as the first day at school, or a particular family holiday. Some older people can easily recall events from their youth, yet are hazy about recent events. We are also able to perform skills that we learned in childhood even though we have not done them for many years, such as riding a bike or skipping. Some skills appear to be very robust over time. Other types of skill seem less robust.

In 1985, McKenna and Glendon researched the effects of forgetting in LTM through trace decay. They studied 215 workers who had learned the skills of cardiac resuscitation. Performance of their skills was tested over periods ranging from three months to three years after the training took place. McKenna and Glendon (1985) found that many of the skills learned were forgotten within a three-month period and were almost completely forgotten after three years.

Other findings, however, show that other types of skill are much more able to stand the test of time. Fleischman and Parker (1962) tested the skills learned when participants were trained to fly in a flight simulator. The skills were assessed over a period of between 9 months and two years after the initial learning phase. They found that the participants were able to fly the simulator with as much skill as when they first learned. No decay occurred in the long-term memory store.

The findings of both these studies suggest that skills requiring a continuous flow of actions, such as riding a bike, or flying a plane, where one action leads on to another, are more likely to be retained in LTM. Skills that require more involvement of knowledge and understanding, as well as motor skills, are less able to be maintained over time. Baddeley (1999) suggests that these more complex skills need to be frequently used if they are to be accurately maintained in LTM.

Trace decay may play a part in some aspects of forgetting in LTM, but it is generally not regarded as a major factor in why we forget.

Interference

Interference is said to influence forgetting when another event occurs either before or after a particular event and disrupts the memories of that specific event in LTM.

There are *two* types of interference that influence our memories.

1. **Retroactive interference**: This is when new information disrupts the memory of old information. An example of this would be when your friend changes her telephone number. You soon learn the new number and 'forget' the old one.
2. **Proactive interference**: This occurs when an old memory interferes with new information. You may find you dial your friend's old telephone number by mistake long after it has changed.

Box 1.31

Baddeley and Hitch's Rugby Player Recall (1977)

To test the idea of interference affecting long-term memory, Baddeley and Hitch (1977) conducted research into the recall of fixtures played by rugby players over a season. Some players had played in all the matches, while others had missed some matches due to injury or illness. The time period (the rugby playing season) was the same for all, but the number of games was different for each player. Players were asked to recall the fixtures they had played in.

If decay theory had an effect on memory, all the participants would tend to forget a similar number of fixtures played. If interference occurred then the players who had played more games would be expected to forget more than the players who only played some of the games.

Baddeley and Hitch were able to investigate whether forgetting occurred due to the amount of time elapsed (decay theory) or because of the number of games played (interference theory). They found that the more games a player had taken part in, the more fixtures they forgot. The findings support the idea that interference affects our memories.

There is compelling evidence to suggest that interference does have an effect on our memory. We do seem to forget when old, or new, information interferes with the memory. The more similar the interfering information is to the memory, the more likely it is to have an impact.

However, some research has shown that 'forgotten' memories can resurface later indicating that the problem was not a memory loss, but a failure to access and retrieve the memory at the required time.

Another problem with interference theory is that much of the research has been carried out in a laboratory situation that is not 'ecologically valid' or not like real-life. Whether the same results would occur in a real-life setting is uncertain.

Retrieval failure

We have seen that sometimes we are unable to access a memory that is stored in our long-term memory. 'Retrieval failure' occurs when we are unable to access a stored memory at a particular time when it is required. You have probably experienced the feeling that you know something, but just cannot bring it to mind. That is an example of retrieval failure.

In order to retrieve information from memory, certain requirements need to be met. The information has to be stored in the memory; we cannot expect to remember information that has not actually been stored! This is called 'availability'. Second, the information that is available needs to be retrievable. This is called 'accessibility'.

There is evidence to suggest that information is more likely to be retrieved from memory if appropriate retrieval cues are present. Research carried out by Tulving (1974) provides evidence that if the same factors, or cues, are in place when information is to be recalled as when it was first encoded in memory, then that recall will be made easier. If such cues are not available, then cue-dependent forgetting may occur.

Retrieval cues may be based on different situations found in the environment in which the information was first learned. Retrieval cues may be dependent on *where* the information is coded or retrieved (context dependent). They may be dependent on the *physical or emotional state* of the person when the information is coded or retrieved (state dependent).

Context dependent retrieval

External factors, such as the setting or situation in which information is encoded or retrieved, may be important for retrieval to take place. Forgetting is more likely to occur when, for example, the place where recall occurs is different from the place where the information was learned or encoded.

Have you ever revisited a place from your childhood and, while there, recalled events that you thought you had since forgotten? This is an example of 'context-dependency'. You had forgotten the information until the appropriate cues were re-established.

Box 1.32

Godden and Baddeley - Deep Sea Divers (1975)

In 1975, an experiment carried out by Godden and Baddeley demonstrated the importance of the setting when retrieval takes place. They asked groups of deep-sea divers to learn lists of words. One group learned the words while underwater; another group learned the words while on land.

The groups were then asked to recall the words either in the same setting as they had learned them (e.g. learned underwater, recalled underwater), or in the opposite setting (e.g. learned underwater, recalled on land).

The results showed that when the setting was the same for learning and recall, the participants recalled more words than they did when the setting was different for learning and recall. Forgetting occurred due to the absence of context cues.

NB Using the suggestion that we can recall information better when the external factors are the same as when we learned it can play an important part in helping students to recall information in an exam situation. You can find details of how to use the ideas in the 'applications' Section of this Chapter.

State-dependent retrieval

Research suggests that if a person's internal state, that is, their physical or psychological state, is the same or similar when recalling information as it was when learning the information then recall is improved. Goodwin *et al* (1969) found that if participants learned information when they were drunk, they were more likely to recall it when they were drunk again rather than when they were sober.

Studies that investigated recall in terms of the mood the participants were in when learning information, and when they recalled information, found some evidence that a similar mood helped in recall. The effect was more evident in a real-life setting than in an experimental laboratory setting. However, care should be taken in interpreting these findings as they are not particularly strong or convincing (Bower, 1981; Ucros, 1989).

The evidence for cue-dependent forgetting is compelling. It has been collected from both strictly controlled laboratory experiments and from real-life settings. Forgetting is more likely when context and state are altered between learning and recall. Recall is more likely if the context and state cues are the same when learning and recalling.

Motivated forgetting

Sometimes we lay down memories in our long-term store that we would rather not remember. Forgetting information because we do not want to remember it is called 'motivated forgetting' and is generally explained through the theories of Sigmund Freud and psychoanalytic theory.

Repression

Freud theorised that the conscious mind protects itself from remembering traumatic memories by repressing the information in the unconscious part of the mind. These repressed memories are not available to the conscious mind and are effectively locked away in the unconscious. However, Freud believed that repressed traumas would affect our behaviour in some way even though we are not aware of their effect and could account for psychological problems occurring.

There have been many cases recently where evidence has been uncovered of repressed memories of child sexual abuse. Repressed memories are very difficult to recover and can be difficult to verify when they are. The person remembering may encounter severe emotional problems and suffer great distress. In cases of child sexual abuse remembered in adult life, problems can occur as there is often no independent witness to confirm the remembered information. However, there have been cases where repressed memories of sexual abuse in childhood have led to successful prosecutions of the perpetrators many years after the events took place.

Unfortunately, there have also been instances where so-called repressed memories have been 'uncovered', yet they have turned out to be false memories. False information can easily be 'planted' into a person's memory and they can believe that what they think they remember is actually true. It is important, of course, not to discourage the reporting of abuse by genuine victims.

Elizabeth Loftus is a very influential researcher into memory and has spent many years studying the concept of false memories. One such study, carried out in 1993, involved a boy wrongly telling his 14 year-old younger brother about a time when the younger brother was lost in a shopping centre at the age of five. The younger brother was convinced that the event actually occurred and within a couple of weeks he started to 'remember' details about the event. He claimed to remember how he felt at the time, the people who had helped him, and the names of the shops in the centre.

When the younger boy was told that the event had not really happened he continued to claim he could remember details and took some convincing that the memory was false.

Evidence shows that while repressed memories do exist, false memories can also be formed. It is essential, therefore, that these memories are thoroughly and carefully investigated and independent support be found to verify the information.

Suppression
Unlike repression, which is the unconscious forgetting of unpleasant and distressing memories, suppression is the conscious and deliberate forgetting of information. If we want to forget something that causes us distress, we can literally 'put it out of our minds'. If you have, for example, failed your first driving test because you could not reverse the car round the corner and completely mucked-up the whole procedure, and you then go to sit the test again, you can deliberately push the memory of the first attempt out of your mind – and hopefully pass the test!

Applications of memory improvement techniques to study/exam skills
There has been a huge amount of research carried out in the field of memory. Many of the findings of this research can be used in our everyday lives to understand how our memories work and how we can improve our ability to remember. Students can particularly benefit from techniques to enhance memory.

Listed below (and in **Boxes 1.33**, **1.34**, **1.35** and **Diagram 1.11**) are several applications of memory research that have been, or can be, incorporated into everyday life and can help with study and exam skills. These are particularly relevant to students.

Box 1.33

Mnenomics

The use of simple terms to help us remember longer and more complex pieces of information.

Perhaps you know the saying, 'Richard Of York Gave Battle In Vain', that helps us remember the colours of the rainbow, or spectrum, in the correct order. Red, Orange, Yellow, Green, Blue, Indigo, Violet?

Another example of a mnemonic was used at the beginning of the Section when discussing the mediators used to process information in the brain. Can you remember what the mediators are using the mnemonic PALM Tree?

Mnemonic techniques

Other mnemonic techniques can also be useful. If you want to remember the number of days in each month recite the rhyme: 'Thirty days has September, April, June and dull November, all the rest have thirty-one, excepting February alone, which has but twenty-eight days clear and twenty-nine in each leap year'.

Making up your own mnemonics using the first letters of what you want to remember, or making up a rhyme, are useful ways of aiding recall. Sometimes the sillier the rhyme, the better the information will be remembered!

Elaborative rehearsal

In 1975, Craik and Tulving suggested that not only is memory dependent on the level of processing carried out, whether shallow or deep, but it is also dependent on how complex or elaborate that processing is. Processing information semantically can help produce memories, but by carrying out complex semantic processing we can improve our memories even further.

Box 1.34

Elaborative Rehearsal

Craik and Tulving (1975) developed the idea the more complex the processing of information was, the stronger the memory it would create. To test this idea they came up with an experiment using simple and complex sentences. Participants were given sentences with one word missing. They were asked to decide whether a target word would fit the space.

Some sentences were simple, such as:

'He ironed the......................' (Target word 'shirt')

Other sentences were complex, such as:

'The pale blue car smashed into a brick wall and broke its........' (Target word 'headlamp')

Craik and Tulving found that when the sentences were presented later to participants, but without the target word, the participants recalled the target words from the complex sentences twice as often as they could recall the target words from the simple sentences. Craik and Tulving proposed that their findings indicated that things are much better remembered when deep processing has taken place.

We can use the idea of elaborative rehearsal when learning information, or when revising for an exam. One way to process information more elaborately and create meaningful associations, is to think about how the information can be meaningful to you in a personal way and by adding your own 'cues' to it. You might think about how the information relates to you now, or to things you have done in the past, or how it relates to your goals for the future. By linking new information to personal memories already stored, you will create what are called 'mental hooks' and you will have a better chance of recalling the important information when it is needed.

Box 1.35

Visual Imagery - the Use of Imagery to Aid Memory

Creating mental pictures helps to enhance recall. If you wanted to remember what 'displacement' is, you could conjure up a mental image of a bookshelf packed full of books. If you add another book to the shelf, the book at the other end will fall off. Displacement in STM works in the same way, new information added into short-term memory will squeeze out an older piece of information.

Spider diagrams and pictorial notes
A variation on visual imagery has been used very effectively around the world by students and, indeed, many people who need to remember lots of information. 'Spider diagrams' and 'pictorial notes' are particularly effective methods of using pictures and diagrams to aid memory. (See **Diagram 1.11** for a 'mind map'/spider diagram'.)

Tony Buzan has written many books on the techniques of 'mind mapping'. The idea is that a personalised diagram is created using the topic requiring attention as a central image. The main themes of the topic radiate out from the central image, a bit like the branches of a tree. Each branch comprises a key image or a key word printed on the branch line and each branch is coloured differently. From each of these branches other related topics radiate out. Images and pictures are added to personalize the diagram and to further help the information to be processed deeply (Buzan, 1993).

Diagram 1.11

Spider Diagram/'Mind Mapping'

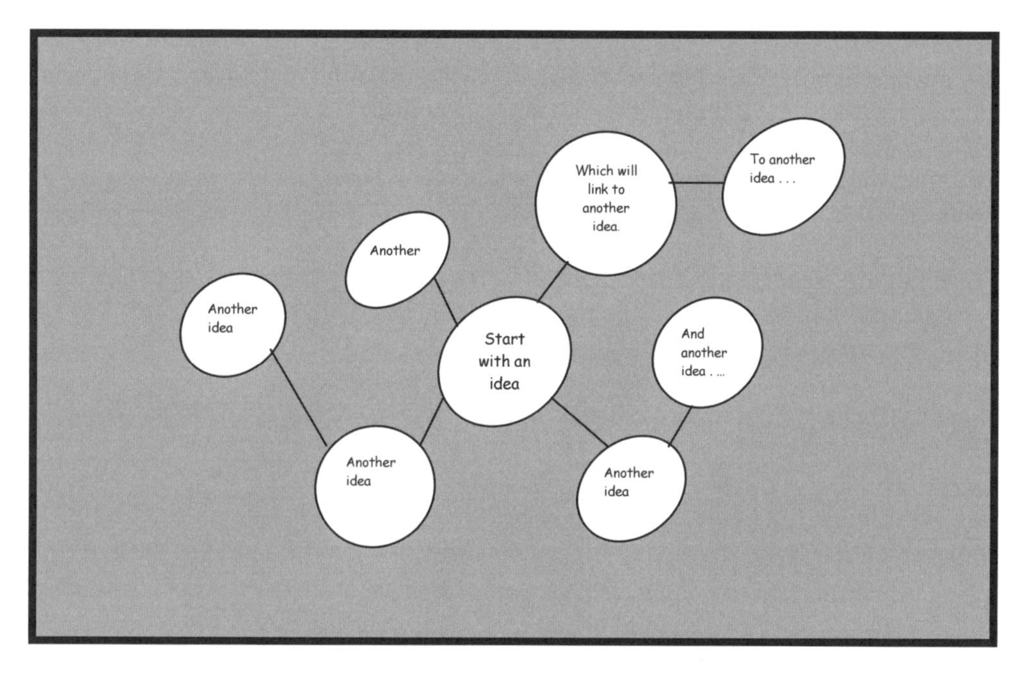

Cue dependency

We have seen how the retrieval of information can be aided by re-creating the context in which the information was learned. This idea can be used by students in an exam situation.

Although the actual place cannot be revisited, conjuring up a mental image of where the information was learned can often help to trigger the necessary memory. Smith (1979) found that recall can be improved if the original learning setting is imagined when recall is required.

If you revise different subjects in different places you can use the mental image of the appropriate place to help you remember the information when you are in your exam. Perhaps you revise Psychology in the dining room? You can picture yourself sitting in the dining room when you need to recall the information learned there. History could be revised in your local library and so on.

Alternatively, you could create a separate context for different subjects by using your sense of smell. Put some lemon oil on a hanky when you are studying Psychology and then take a hanky with lemon oil on it into the Psychology exam. You could use peppermint while learning and revising History and so on.

Memory and sleep

Maquet (2000) suggested that one of the functions of sleep and dreaming is to help 'lay down' memories. He found that many areas of the brain that are activated during mental processing are the same as those activated during the period of sleep when we dream (REM – rapid eye movement – sleep). He theorised that REM sleep is important in memory processing, probably helping to strengthening memories. REM sleep, *after* a learning episode, helps the information to be learned and remembered.

These findings suggest that for students it is important to get good nights sleep *after* a revision session in order to help consolidate learning, and establish it in LTM for recall when needed.

So, after you have revised for your exams, make sure you get a good nights' sleep!

Box 1.36

Hints for Successful Exams

An understanding of how memory works can be useful when you are studying and revising for exams. Some specific hints may help you to prepare better and cope with exams successfully.

As we have seen, if you learn information in a detailed way is much more likely to be remembered then if it is only processed in shallow form. This might seem like stating the obvious, but the more you understand information and transfer it into your own words, perhaps using mnemonics or rhymes, or mental images to help, then recalling it will be much easier. Thinking about the meaning of what you are learning, as suggested by Craik and Lockhart, helps deep processing to take place.

Devising pictorial images or creating Mind Maps after each class or each revision session helps in processing and recall. Linking information together so that one thing directly leads to another is also a useful way of storing information. Mind Maps provide a framework for linking, using images and colour too.

Stress

Section summary

This Section on stress will investigate:

- The domain of Physiological Psychology, also called biological psychology.
- What is stress?
- The biological processes that our bodies go through when we are stressed.
- How our natural reaction to threat, as a short term response, can helps us.
- How we can suffer adverse heath effects when stress is prolonged.
- The sources of stress in our everyday lives and how different people react in different ways.
- Applications of different stress reduction strategies and their effectiveness in reducing adverse effects.

The domain associated with the study of stress is Physiological Psychology (otherwise known as biological psychology)

Physiological psychologists believe that our behaviour is governed by our biology, which includes our hormonal, bio-chemical and genetic make-up. They propose that our physiological (bodily) and psychological behaviour is determined by our physiological make-up. Many of the beliefs of this domain of psychology are based on the work of Charles Darwin.

Charles Darwin (1809-1882)

Much of our fundamental understanding about biological processes has been influenced by the work of Charles Darwin. Darwin was a British naturalist whose theories caused great controversy at the time he published his major work, The Origin of Species, in 1859, when he denounced the strictly religious-based viewpoint of the time; that God created Man in his own image. Darwin proposed that all animals, including humans, have evolved to their present state through a gradual and opportunistic process he called 'natural selection'.

Darwin proposed the idea of the 'survival of the fittest', where animals whose genes are most 'fit' for their environment survive and reproduce. Animals that do not have the characteristics necessary to survive in their environment will die, and so will not pass on their genes.

As humans, our children resemble us, a process Darwin termed 'like begets like'. We inherit 50 per cent of our genes from our mother and 50 per cent of our genes from our father. New characteristics can, therefore, be formed by 'genetic recombination', by the combining of the two sets of genes. Those characteristics that are advantageous to our survival and reproduction are passed on to our offspring. Another method of changing genetic characteristics is through 'genetic mutation'. Mutation occurs when there is an imperfect copying of genetic material and a variation in characteristics results. Mostly, genetic mutations are not advantageous and they die out. However, sometimes they create an advantageous characteristic and can be passed on through reproduction and become part of the evolutionary process.

Darwin's work was, at the time, revolutionary. It led to a belief that many psychologists still embrace today; that, by studying animal behaviour, we can develop insights into human behaviour. That belief is maintained in physiological psychology.

The biological approach to psychology is strictly scientific in its research and, in particular, investigates the functions of the brain and the nervous system in influencing our thoughts, feelings and behaviours. The domain also looks at the influence of genetic factors on our behaviours and investigates how some human behaviour's may have adapted to aid our evolutionary development.

The role of the brain and the nervous system in influencing thoughts, feelings and behaviour

In order to respond to information from the environment our nervous system must react to messages it collects from throughout our bodies. The nervous system is an integrated structure that can be broken down into different sections. It is made up of a 'central nervous system' (CNS) consisting of the brain and the spinal cord, and a 'peripheral nervous system' (PNS) that is made up of the remainder of the system of nerves from the periphery. **Diagram 1.12**, below, shows the way the nervous system is divided into subsections that work together to allow our bodies to respond appropriately to external stimuli.

Diagram 1.12

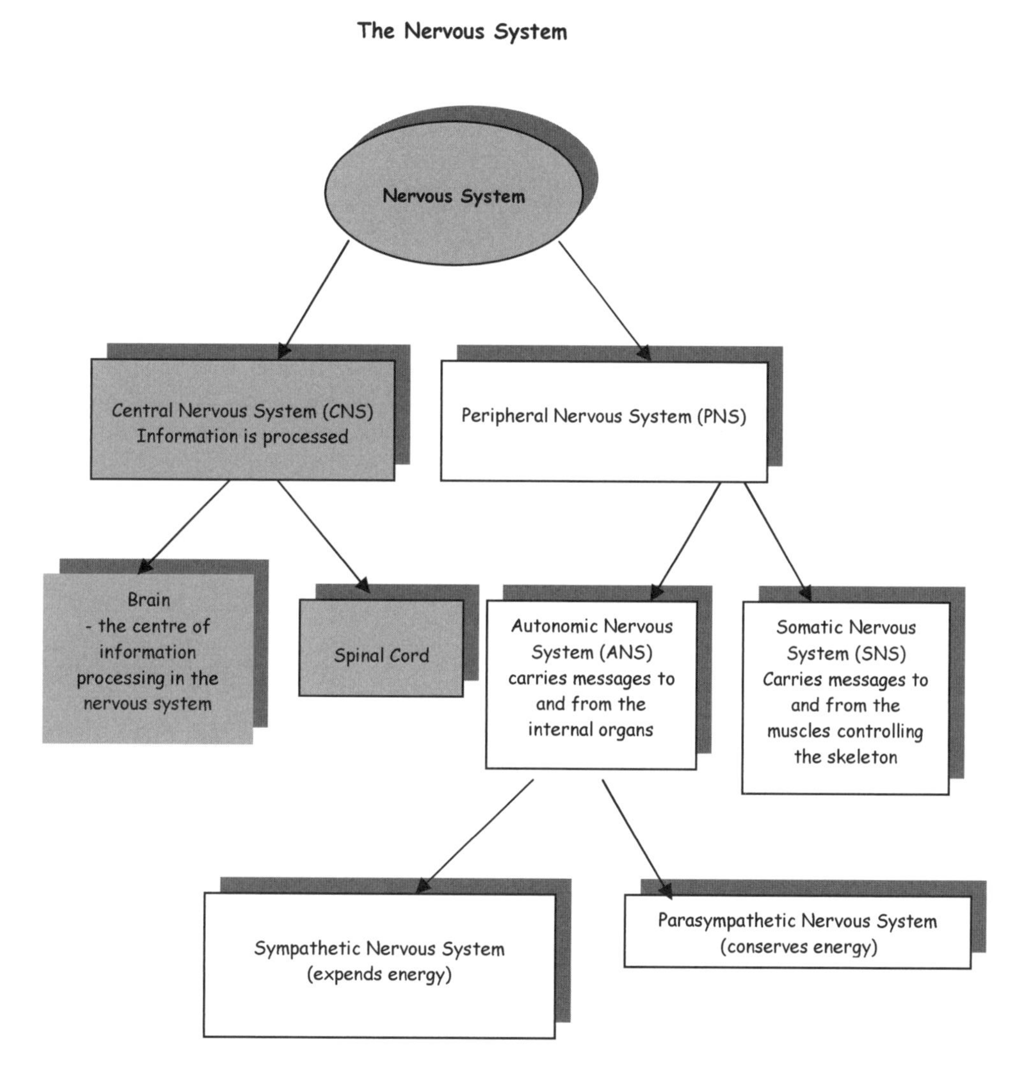

Information is gathered from the external world using our five senses – sight, sound, smell, touch and taste. The information is processed in the central nervous system (in particular by the brain) using our memories of past experiences and our knowledge in order to make sense of the information. The information is organised and interpreted and decisions are made on how to respond to the information. The brain sends out the appropriate signals to the body's organs, muscles and glands in order to instigate the responses. These responses can be physical movements such as running, speaking, moving limbs, or they can be internal bodily reactions, such as an increase in heart rate, dilation or contraction of the pupils in our eyes.

Neurons

In order for information to be transmitted throughout the nervous system, the body has a complex network of neurons. Neurons are responsible for carrying information throughout the whole body and there are estimated to be over 10 billion neurons in the brain alone. Our whole body relies on neurons to pass information between different areas.

Neurons are made up of dendrites that receive the signal information from the previous neuron and pass it on through the cell body, containing the nucleus. The signal, an electrical impulse, passes down through the axon that is protected by the myelin sheath. This sheath of fatty material protects and insulates the axon, allowing the signal to pass through quickly. The electrical impulses leave the neuron via the terminal buttons. They cross a gap that exists between every neuron and its neighbour called the 'synapse' or 'synaptic gap', and on to the next neuron in the chain. The signal is carried across the synapse by chemicals called neurotransmitters.

There are three types of neuron, each carrying out different functions, as indicated in **Diagram 1.13**.

Diagram 1.13

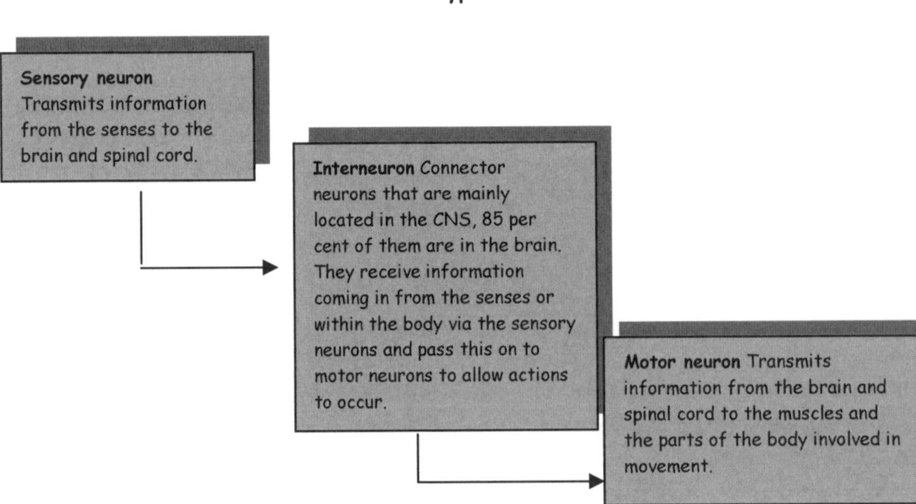

Physiological psychology is the area of psychology most closely related to the natural sciences such as biology, chemistry and physics. It falls firmly on the 'nature' side of the nature-nurture debate, by advocating that if our physiology is determined by adapting to the environment through evolution, then our behaviour will also be adaptive and is, therefore, genetically influenced.

What is stress?

The term, 'stress', is used in physics and, in particular, in mechanics. It refers to the force that places tension, or strain, on an object.

Imagine a metal bar with a weight hanging from the middle. The bar is put under 'stress' and, depending on how heavy the weight is relative to the metal bar, the bar may bend or break. The object causing the stress, or tension, is called a 'stressor'. See **Diagram 1.14**.

Diagram 1.14

Stress and Stressors

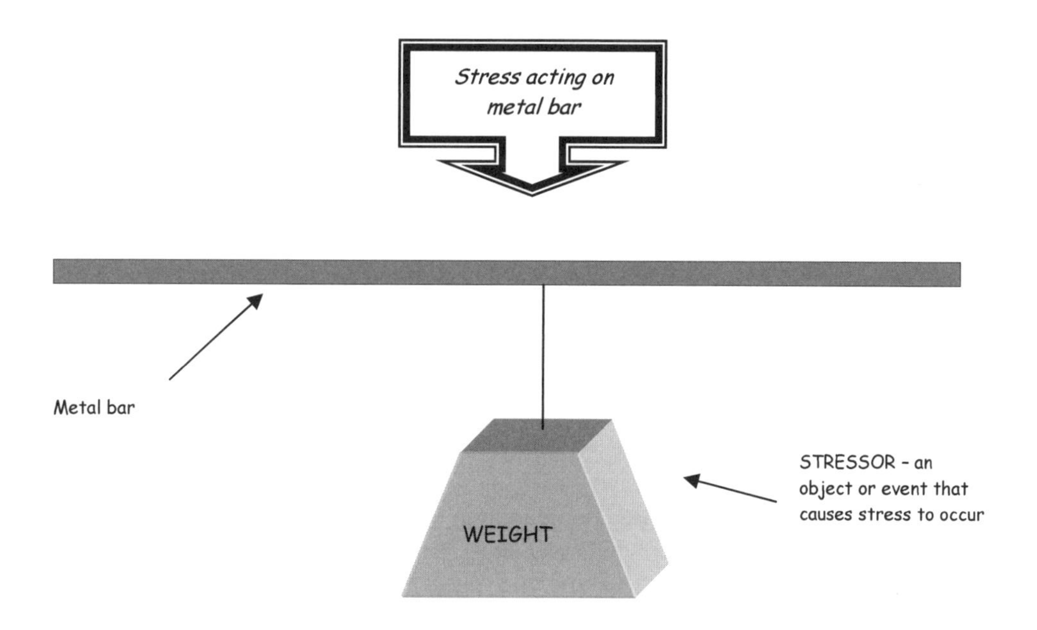

In psychology, stress can be seen as a similar process. It is a force that causes a strain on a person. Stressors can be things such as taking exams, arguments, too much work, too little work, divorce, bereavement, etc. Any force that we perceive as a threat can be termed a stressor.

If a threat is perceived the 'fight or flight' response is triggered.

The 'fight or flight' response
When we feel threatened our sympathetic nervous system is triggered and our body immediately goes into life-saving, emergency mode, preparing us either to fight the threat, or to run from it. Our body is primed and ready for action.

In the short-term, the response of the sympathetic nervous system to threat is healthy and normal. It is adaptive; we might need it to save our lives. Once the threat is passed the parasympathetic nervous system is triggered and our bodies relax and return to normal. **Diagram 1.15** provides further detail.

Diagram 1.15

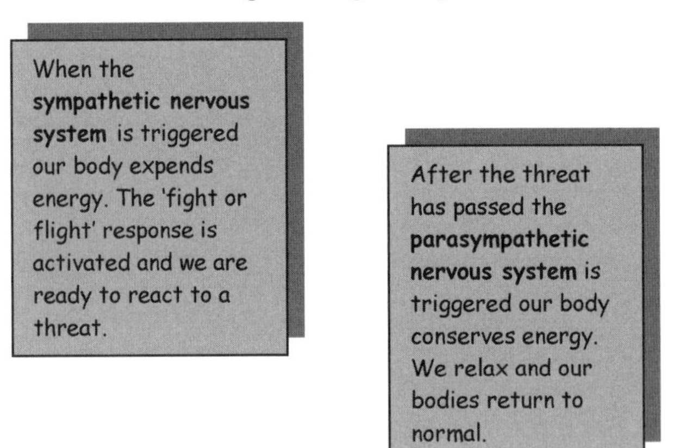

Let us look at what happens to our bodies when we are under threat. Imagine that you are walking along the road when you see a truck heading towards you out of control. Your body reacts swiftly to allow you to respond by either running to get out of danger, or fighting whatever is threatening you. (In this case, you would hopefully choose the former!)

The reaction to threat causes certain physiological (bodily) responses to occur. The 'fight or flight' response to threats triggers a number of possible responses, as indicated in **Diagram 1.16**.

Diagram 1.16

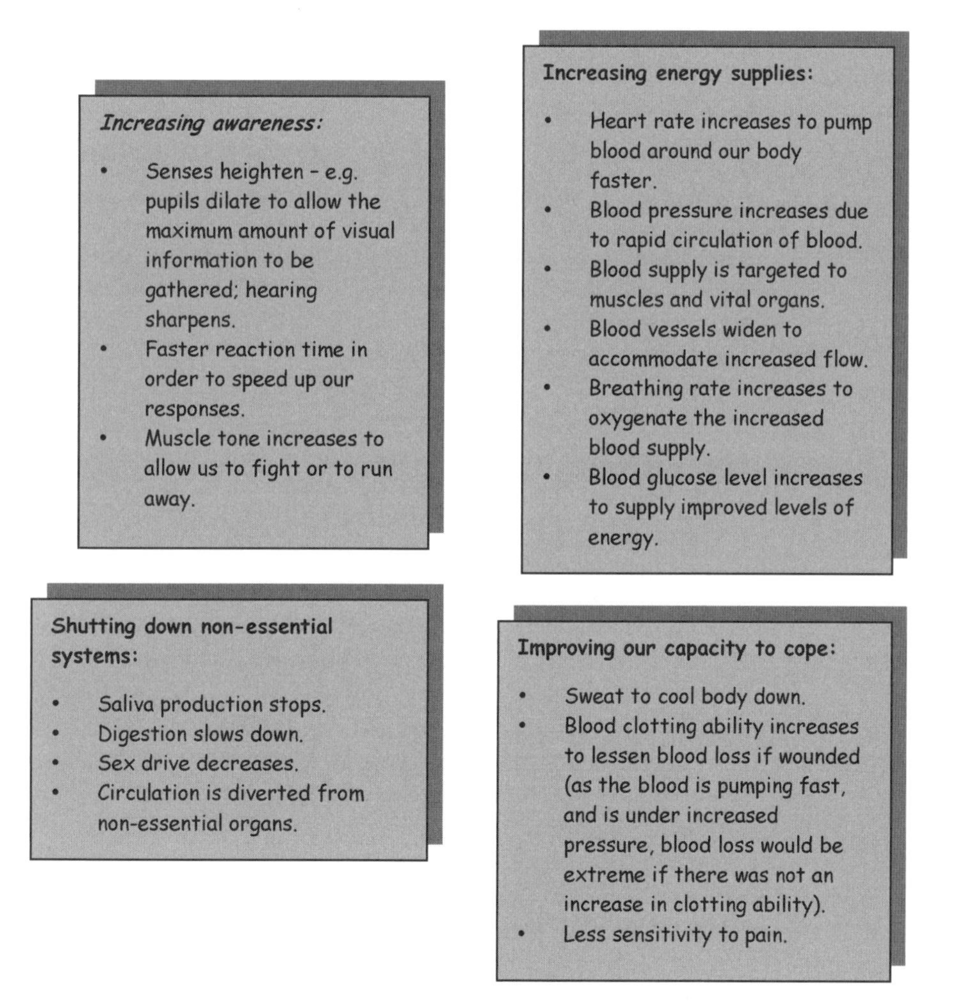

These responses to threat are vital for survival. They are normal and healthy and allow us to function effectively and to deal with immediate threats. They are short-term responses to short-term threats. However, as we shall see, the stress response can be harmful if prolonged.

General adaptation syndrome (GAS)

Hans Selye introduced stress as a psychological concept in the 1950s. Selye made detailed and comprehensive studies of the effects of stress on the body.

Using animals (mainly rats) in an experimental laboratory, Selye investigated the effects of a variety of stressors such as injections and surgical procedures, temperature extremes, physical restraint, enforced exercise and others. Selye found that no matter what the stressor was, the bodily reaction to it was the same. The results of his research led Selye to develop a model of stress called the 'General Adaptation Syndrome' (GAS). Selye proposed three main stages in his model of stress.

Alarm stage: The first stage is the 'alarm stage', when the body prepares itself for a rapid response. The ANS receives information from the body that causes the sympathetic nervous system to be activated. The 'fight or flight response' is triggered. If the stressor passes quickly and the body has successfully reacted to the stressor then the parasympathetic nervous system will be activated and the body will relax and return to normal.

Resistance stage: If the stress continues, then the next stage sees some decline in the initial extreme response. The sympathetic nervous system still keeps the body in a state of readiness and levels of adrenaline remain high. The adrenaline is not dissipated as it would be after a physical response of fighting or running from the stressor. High levels of adrenaline cause the body's immune system to be less effective than normal and it is less able to ward off attack from bacteria and viruses.

Exhaustion stage: By the third stage, if the individual has been unable to get rid of the stressor, the body's stores have been used up and the there are very few resources left to fight any more attacks. Severe and irreversible health problems may occur, such as heart disease, high blood pressure, stomach ulcers and other digestive problems. The body's defence mechanisms are exhausted. In extreme cases the result can be death.

In 1991, Cohen *et al* injected healthy participants with either a harmless salt solution or the common cold virus. The participants completed a detailed stress questionnaire that gave an indication of the level of stress they were experiencing in their lives. Nearly all the participants who were injected with the cold virus showed symptoms of infection; however, only around 30 per cent of these actually developed a cold. The researchers discovered that the higher the level of stress recorded from the stress questionnaire, the more likely the individual was to develop cold symptoms. These findings support Selye's expectations of the 'resistance stage' of the GAS.

The three stages of the GAS are *not* inevitable. Most people will deal with a stressor in the first stage (alarm stage) or the second stage (resistance stage) and the body returns to normal. Only in the third stage (exhaustion stage) are the responses likely to be irreversible.

Gender appears to make a difference to the stress response. Women appear to react to stress much more strongly than men, but their response return to normal more quickly than men's responses (Frankenhauser, 1983). This difference in response may be the cause of differences in the types of illnesses experienced by men and women as a result of stress. Men have a higher incidence of cardio-vascular disease, a direct result of long-term stress.

Evaluation of the GAS
Strengths

- The GAS was developed as a result of extensive and scientifically based research in the carefully controlled environment of a research laboratory.
- It has been very influential in the field of stress and has subsequently led to much research being carried out.
- The GAS established a link between the psychological reaction to stress and physical responses of the body in term of illness and disease.

Weaknesses

- The use of animals in his experimentation may mean that Selye's findings may not be applicable to humans.
- Selye did not take into account any differences there may be in how an individual responds to a stressful situation. The General Adaptation Syndrome model proposes a 'general' response. People differ in what they find stressful, and in how they respond to stress.
- Selye assumed that the level of physiological response is the same whatever the stressor might be. Cox (1978) has found that this is not the case and people bodily responses differ depending on the type of stressor they are experiencing.

Transactional model of stress
There are *three* main ways of looking at stress:

1. Stress can be viewed as an *external force*, acting on the individual.
2. Stress can be viewed as an *internal reaction*, physical or psychological, to a stressor.

3. Stress can be viewed as a transaction between how an individual perceives the demands placed on them and their perceived ability to cope with those demands.

The transactional model of stress is the most popular approach currently used to study stress. The most important aspect of this model is the individual's perception of the *stressor* in relation to their perception of their own *ability* to cope. Some people may get very stressed about exams; the perceived demands an exam makes on them are greater than their perceived ability to cope. Other people of similar intellectual ability do not get stressed about exams; they perceive that they are able to cope with the demands the exam places on them.

Sometimes our bodies respond to things that we perceive as threats, but these threats last for a more considerable length of time. They may occur as a result of the changed nature of modern life compared to our evolutionary past. The parasympathetic nervous system is not activated and our bodies remain on 'high alert' with the continued activation of the sympathetic nervous system. This is when stress occurs. It is the long-term response to a long-term threat.

Longer-term stress response

We all need some degree of stress to function properly; to perform to our full capability. However, it is when our bodies perceive that we are under prolonged or extensive threat that problems occur and when the 'fight or flight' response is triggered at inappropriate times and is not switched off.

Look back to the table of responses to short-term threat and think how we may feel when the body is on high alert to threat for an extended period of time.

Look at **Diagram 1.17**. Can you identify any of these symptoms as those that you feel when you are 'stressed'? Recognising and identifying your own symptoms of stress will go a long way in helping you to overcome the debilitating effects it can cause.

Diagram 1.17

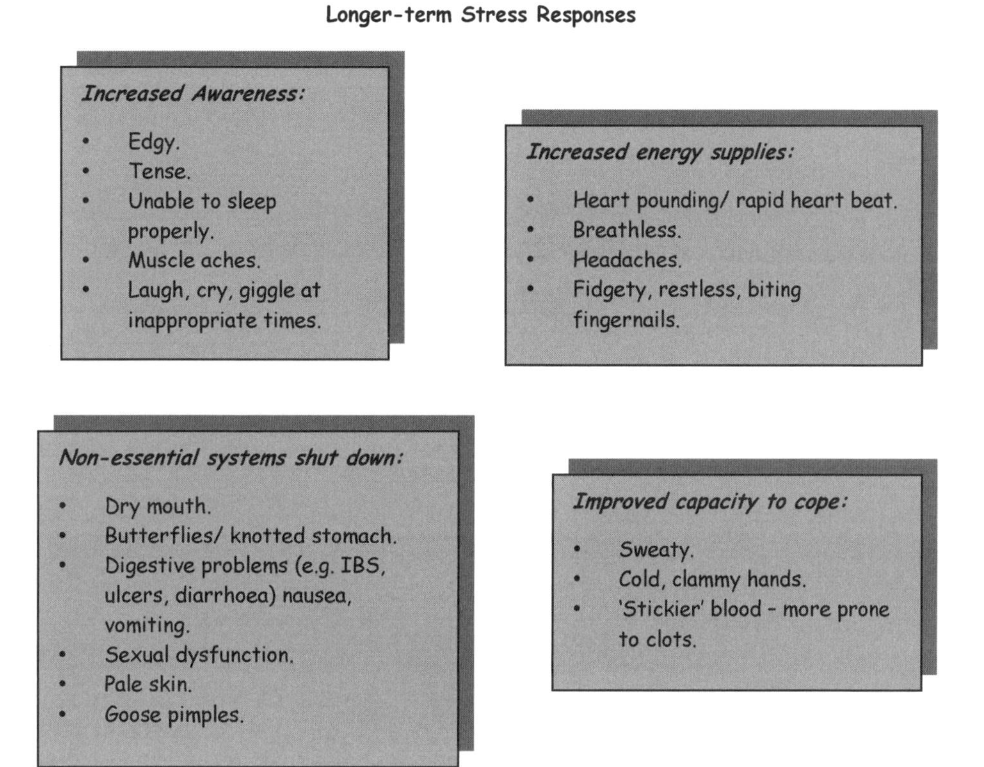

Box 1.37

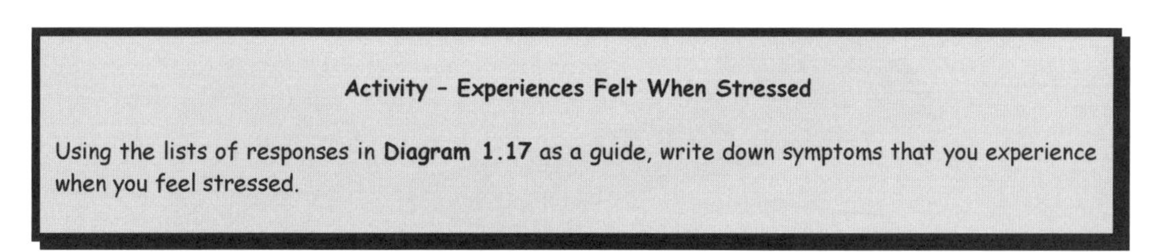

Activity - Experiences Felt When Stressed

Using the lists of responses in **Diagram 1.17** as a guide, write down symptoms that you experience when you feel stressed.

According to the transactional model, stress can be defined as a mismatch between perceived demands and our perceived ability to cope. It is a balance between how we view demands and how we think we can cope with those demands that determines whether we feel no stress, a healthy stress, or debilitating stress.

Diagram 1.18

Healthy and Unhealthy Stress

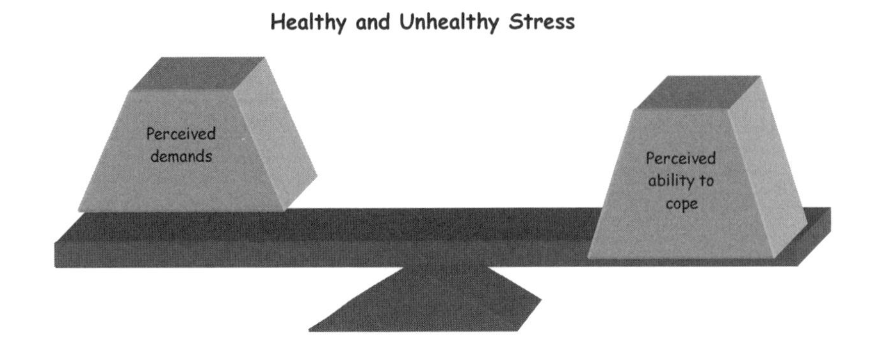

A healthy balance between perceived demands and perceived ability to cope allows us to work at optimum capacity.

Unhealthy stress occurs when we feel we cannot cope and the perceived demands far outweigh our perceived ability to cope.

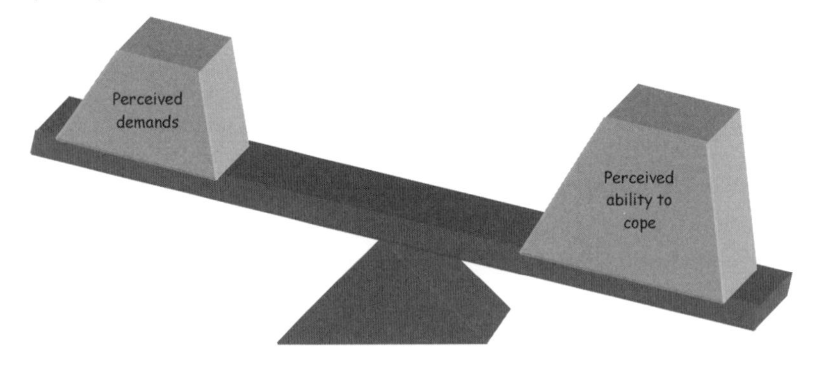

Unhealthy stress can also occur when we feel we are not being challenged enough, *when our perceived ability to cope exceeds the demands that are placed on us.*

The 'transactional model' of stress suggests that whether someone experiences stress or not depends on their perception of the event, or stressor, and their perception of how able they are to cope. Potential sources of stress include any events or circumstances that an individual experiences in their lives. Events such as bereavement, divorce, the breaking up of relationships and exams are all obvious potential sources of stress, but other less obvious events can also be a source of stress. Happy events, such as holidays and Christmas, can also be sources of stress to some people.

An important point to remember is that an event is not simply a source of stress waiting to happen. Only if the individual experiencing the event perceives that event as a source of stress, and thinks they are unable to cope with it, will it become stressful.

Social, occupational and environmental sources of stress

Sources of stress can come from all around us in our everyday lives. As we have seen, a stressor can be anything that causes a strain on an individual. We can experience stress from a variety of sources, which can be seen in **Diagram 1.19**.

Diagram 1.19

Social, occupational and environmental sources of stress

Social factors

Stress may be the result of conflict or unpleasant interactions with others. If we experience conflict with the people we are close to: parents, children, work colleagues, school friends, lovers, for example we may suffer a stress response. Any relationship we have with other people could be a potential source of stress if things are not going well in the relationship.

Occupational factors

Situations we experience throughout our lives, such as work, school, college, driving, shopping can influence levels of stress. Any 'occupation' we participate in can potentially be a source of stress. Perhaps you have experienced stress when working at a computer and it will not perform as you want it to, or it 'loses' data, or is too slow.

Environmental factors

Features in our environment can also act as stressors. If you work in a particularly noisy place you may well experience stress. High temperatures are also seen as influencing levels of stress.

Workplace stress

Workplace stress is a topic that has been researched extensively. Stress is a major factor in contributing to days lost through absence or illness. In 2002, 1 in 5 men were reported to have visited their doctor because of stress (DTI and *Management Today* survey, 2002). It is, therefore, an important topic of research from both an employee's viewpoint, where maintaining good health is a primary concern and from an employer's viewpoint, where maintaining a healthy work force increases productivity and performance and helps to improve employer/worker relations.

All jobs involve some levels of stress at least some of the time. The field of psychology that concentrates on investigating and applying research into sources of stress in the work environment is known as 'occupational psychology' and is one of the fastest growing fields in the discipline. Every workplace has potential sources of stress and every workplace is different, but there are some potential sources of stress that are found in most workplaces.

Workload

The number of people who work long hours seems to be increasing according to a government survey carried out in 2002. A DTI and *Management Today* survey found that 1 in 6 workers surveyed in 2002 worked over 60 hours a week compared to 1 in 8 in 2000. One in 8 women now work 60 hours or more a week, which is more than twice the number in 2000. The majority of the people who work long hours are young people. Working long hours also has an impact on the next source of stress.

Home-work interface

With many people working long hours and many homes where both partners work, there is an increasing potential for stress in the conflict between responsibilities at work and responsibilities at home.

Job insecurity

The trend in recent years has been to move away from long term security, where jobs were often seen as being secure for the working life of the employee, towards shorter term contracts and more frequent job changes. Although changing jobs can be stimulating and energising, stress can also occur.

Role ambiguity

If the requirements of your role at work are unclear there is a major potential for stress to occur. It is essential to get clear guidelines as to what your role entails and the expectations of that role.

Lack of control

The feeling that you are not in control of your work, that it is dictated by someone else, is a major factor in stress.

Opportunities

Many jobs offer little in the way of career progression and people may find themselves stuck at the same level with little or no opportunity to move forward. They feel little incentive to give their best in their work. The only way they can progress in their career is to move jobs – that can itself be a cause of stress.

Colleagues

How well you get on with your supervisors, your subordinates and those on the same level as you can be potential sources of stress.

Environment

The work environment is important. Lack of suitable or appropriate space, the layout of the work-space, lighting, temperature and any environmental factor can be a potential source of stress.

In 1967, the researchers, Holmes and Rahe, investigated factors that contribute to stress in our lives and attempted to quantify a number of these to produce a rating scale. Holmes and Rahe wanted to measure the levels of stress associated with particular events that occur in our lives and investigate whether people who experienced a high level score will be more prone to stress related illness than those who have lower scores. (See **Box 1.38**.)

Box 1.38

Research: Holmes and Rahe's 'Social Readjustment Rating Scale' (SRRS)

In 1967, Holmes and Rahe developed what was to become the most well known scale that is used to measure the level of stress an individual is experiencing. They called their scale the 'social readjustment rating scale'.

Holmes and Rahe based their scale on important and significant changes that occur in life, called 'life events'. These life events cause changes in a person's life and disrupt their normal everyday existence. Events that are seen as enjoyable are included as well as those that are upsetting or unpleasant.

Holmes and Rahe investigated around 5,000 medical records of people who had experienced illness. They discovered that, in many cases, the patients had undergone important life changes in the months prior to illness being diagnosed.

They selected a number of these 'life events' and asked a group of 394 people to rate them in relation to the amount of 'social readjustment' each event would need.

The results enabled Holmes and Rahe to create a table of life events, each with a score. An individual's stress score is the total of the scores for all the life events they have experienced over a set period of time (usually either one or two years).

Holmes and Rahe proposed that high score would increase the likelihood of a stress related illness.

Value	Life event	Value
1	Death of spouse	100
2	Divorce	73
3	Marital separation	65
4	Jail term	63
5	Death of close family member	63
6	Personal injury or illness	53
7	Marriage	50
8	Being fired from work	47
9	Marital reconciliation	45
10	Retirement	45
11	Change in health of family member	44
12	Pregnancy	40
13	Sex difficulties	39
14	Gain of new family member	39
15	Business readjustment	39
16	Change in financial state	38
17	Death of a close friend	37
18	Change to different line of work	36
19	Change in number of arguments with spouse	35
20	Mortgage or loan over £60,000	31
21	Foreclosure of mortgage or loan	30
22	Change in responsibilities at work	29
23	Son or daughter leaving home	29
24	Trouble with in-laws	29
25	Outstanding personal achievement	28
26	Wife begins or stops work	26
27	Begin or end school	26
28	Change in living conditions	25
29	Revision of personal habits	24
30	Trouble with boss	23
31	Change in work hours or conditions	20
32	Change in residence	20
33	Change in schools	20
34	Change in recreation	19
35	Change in church activities	19
36	Change in social activities	18
37	Mortgage or loan less than £60,000	17
38	Change in sleeping habits	16
39	Change in number of family get-togethers	15
41	Vacation	13
42	Christmas	12
43	Minor violations of the law	11

To calculate an individual's stress score over a given period of time (usually one or two years) the values of the life events experienced by the individual during that period are added together.

The total is the life change score and is used to indicate whether that person has a greater or lesser likelihood of suffering from a stress induced illness in the near future.

Holmes and Rahe proposed that a score of 150 or more would increase the chances of stress related problems by 30 per cent; a score of 300 or more increased this likelihood to 50 per cent.

(Adapted from Holmes, T.H. and Rahe, R.H. (1967) 'The social readjustment rating scale', 'Journal of Psychosomatic Research,' Vol.11, pp. 213-218.)

Although studies do indicate that there may be a significant relationship between a high life event score and stress related health problems, the level of relationship, or correlation, is relatively small (a maximum correlation of around 0.3). These findings suggest that although there may be a relationship between stress and health, the relationship is not very strong.

Evaluation of the SRRS

- The values that the scales propose are arbitrary and relative. What affects one person a great deal will affect other people very little. The background leading up to an event may also affect the level of stress experienced. For example if a husband/wife has been very ill for some time and has been suffering, then their death may be seen as a release from that suffering and this may cause a different level of stress than a spouse who has died unexpectedly and suddenly. Overall, the SRRS does not cater for individual differences in responses to life events.
- The relationship found between the SRRS score and health is a correlational relationship, and as such, no element of cause can be attributed. One cannot be said to cause the other. Other factors need to be considered.
- The SRRS scale makes no distinction between positive and negative events and assumes that both contribute to stress levels. There is no evidence given by Holmes and Rahe to support this assumption.
- Any form of self-report where individuals carry out their own rating is very unreliable and subjective. This lack of objectivity may influence the reliability of the scale.

Correlational relationships

A 'correlational relationship' is when two variables are related; as one variable increases the other variable increases, or as one increases the other decreases. However, although a relationship may exist, one variable cannot be said to *cause* a change in the other.

A simple example that demonstrates a correlational relationship is the relationship between rainfall and the number of umbrellas that are put up. As the amount of rain increases, the number of open umbrellas increases, but if you place a furled umbrella outside in the rain, the rain does not cause it to open – it needs other factors to do that.

So, although a correlational relationship may exist between two variables, no causation can be inferred between them.

Although there are a number of criticisms of the SRRS proposed by Holmes and Rahe, it has had a major impact on research into stress by indicating that life events can influence health.

Other researchers have suggested that it is not so much the major life events that impact on our levels of stress, but instead it is the daily hassles that affect us more. Lazarus (1966) suggested that small daily problems build up until we feel we cannot cope. DeLongis *et al* (1982) found that daily hassles were a better predictor of ill health than major life events. They also suggested that the effects of hassles could be offset by what he called 'uplifts'.

Box 1.39

Key terms

Hassles
Daily problems and upsets that may cause stress. They can include events like: being caught up in traffic jams, arguments with a partner/parent/child, electrical items not working properly, car not starting, etc.

Uplifts
Positive daily events that make us feel good. They can include things like: being paid a compliment, getting on well with partner/parents/children, doing well at school or work, losing some weight, etc.

DeLongis *et al* (1982) found that hassles scores gave a higher correlation with ill health than the SRRS score. A higher correlation indicates that the relationship is stronger - but, as with all correlations, no causal element can be inferred.

Individual differences in susceptibility to stress

Not everyone reacts to stress in the same way – and something that may cause a lot of stress to one person, may have little or no effect on another. Each person responds to a potentially stressful situation in a different way. It is not so much the situation itself, or the individual, but the interaction between the two that triggers the stress response. It is the judgement, or perception, that a person makes about the demands of the situation and their ability to cope with those demands.

Some people have an 'internal locus of control', whereby they feel they are responsible for what happens to them in their lives – whether good or bad. When things go well they feel good about themselves, if things go wrong they feel bad, but have the sense that they are in control of their own lives. These individuals generally cope better with stress as they feel they can influence what happens to them and take measures to counteract the influences of stress.

Other people have an 'external locus of control' and believe that things happen to them rather than them controlling their lives. If things go wrong then someone or something else is to blame. If things go right then it is just fate or good luck. These individuals do not cope so well with stress. They are very passive in their response, believing that whatever they do will have little effect, so they might just as well accept things as they are. This lack of perceived control can increase the levels of stress.

Although much of the research into stress tends to generalize findings as being applicable to everyone, there are obviously major differences in how individuals cope with stress. The transactional model of stress does account for individual perception of stressors and individual ability to cope. However, the SRRS assumes we all react to major life events in much the same way.

Personality is one factor that can have a strong influence on whether or not a person suffers stress. One of the most important and influential pieces of research in the field of stress was published by Friedman and Rosenman in 1974. They studied the behaviour patterns of patients who suffered from coronary heart disease (CHD) and found that certain behaviours were exhibited by these patients. Men who did not exhibit these behaviours were less than half as likely to get CHD as those who did.

Friedman and Rosenman called the different personality types 'Type A' and 'Type B'.

Diagram 1.20

Friedman and Rosenan's 'Type A' and 'Type B' Personality Types

'Type A' personalities are likely to be: ambitious, impatient, irritable and aggressive. They speak quickly and frequently use gestures to enhance what they are saying. They tend to interrupt others while they are speaking. They appear 'driven' and are anxious to meet deadlines often doing several things at one time and constantly working against the clock. 'Type A' personalities are highly competitive in all aspects of their lives, work and leisure. Often 'Type A' people are very successful in their work and so they tend to be encouraged in their responses by their employers.

'Type B' personalities are easy-going and do not appear to be 'driven'. Although 'Type B' people may be as ambitious as 'Type A', they do not allow their ambitions to dominate their lives. They enjoy their family and friends and their social lives. Generally their choices of leisure activities are less competitive than those chosen by 'Type A' people. 'Type B' people will play for the fun of playing - not just to win.

Box 1.40

Research: Friedman and Rosenan's 'Type A' and 'Type B' Personality Types

Friedman and Rosenman (1974) carried out a longitudinal study of a self-selected sample of 3200 healthy middle-aged men from California, over a period of $8\frac{1}{2}$ years. They aimed to discover if 'Type A' individuals (who demonstrated a high-stress personality) were more likely to develop coronary heart disease (CHD) than the more relaxed personality 'Type B' participants.

Using structured interviews and observation, Friedman and Rosenman initially assessed the men's personality type and their health status. Their personality type was determined by levels of competitiveness, impatience and hostility.

Participants were classified as:

Type A1 (fully 'Type A')
Type A2 (not fully 'Type A')
Type X (equal amounts of 'Type A' and 'Type B')
Type B (fully 'Type B')

The follow up study $8\frac{1}{2}$ years later recorded the incidence of CHD in the participants. A correlational analysis was carried out to determine if a relationship existed between 'Type A' and 'Type B' participants and CHD.

Friedman and Rosenman found that people who demonstrated 'Type A' behaviour patterns were more than twice as likely to develop CHD than 'Type B' personalities. Overall, there were 257 incidences of CHD among the 3200 participants. Of these 70 per cent had been classified as 'Type A'. A moderate, but significant correlation was found between personality type and CHD.

Friedman and Rosenman concluded that 'Type A' behaviour increases the likelihood of the person experiencing stress, this then increases the likelihood of physiological reaction to stress and, in turn, the likelihood of suffering from coronary heart disease.

Later studies support the idea that 'Type A' personality traits do seem to be a factor in CHD but that they are not a reliable *predictor* of CHD developing. What may be a crucial factor is the level of hostility demonstrated by some people. Hostility is one of the identified traits of a 'Type A' personality and this may have influenced the results found by Freidman and Rosenman.

Studies of male law students showed that those with high hostility levels, measured by a personality test, were five times more likely to die before the age of 50 years. (Barefoot *et al*, 1989). People who are particularly vulnerable to heart problems are those who repress their high levels of hostility rather than expressing it in some way.

Various programmes have been developed to help people who appear to be vulnerable to CHD. These programmes are designed to increase awareness of the effects of stress and hostility and demonstrate how to cope with them. Cognitive-behavioural techniques are designed to help the individual to recognise those situations in which they become angry or stressed and analyse the reasons for the problems occurring. They are then taught to develop techniques, often using role-play, to help them think about how to cope with the situations (the 'cognitive aspect') and how to overcome their reactions through relaxation (the 'behavioural aspect').

Cultural differences

There are cultural differences in the sources of stress. Thankfully, in Scotland and in the rest of the UK, we do not generally have to worry about finding food and water to keep us alive, but these are major stressors for people in some countries of the world. Likewise, someone living in an underdeveloped Third World country may not worry about whether they can afford to go on holiday to Florida or not. Again, we come down to the idea that it is the individual's perception of the stressor that causes stress to occur or not.

Some researchers have criticised scales such as the SRRS and the Hassles and Uplifts scale because they are biased towards the cultures to which they relate. Events that cause stress in one culture may not exist in another. It is also recognised that people who live in ethnic minority communities within the UK or in the United States may face stressors that others do not come across. Anderson (1991) identified stressors faced by some African-Americans that mainstream white Americans do not generally face. These include racism, poor living conditions, overcrowding, daily conflict in becoming assimilated into the American culture and the barriers they face in trying to do so.

Gender differences

Surveys have indicated that where both partners in a household have full-time jobs, it is generally still the female who takes most of the responsibility for child-rearing and household tasks. The *UK 2000 Time Use Survey* found that women spend an average of around three hours a day on housework compared with an average for men of 1 hour 40 minutes. This figure does not include time spent on shopping and childcare. They found that two in five men do no ironing or laundry (Office for National Statistics, 2000). Studies have shown that women who have children and who hold down full time jobs show more instances of ill-health than women who work full time and who do not have children.

Sources of stress may differ between men and women but there is no evidence to suggest that *levels* of stress are any different between the genders. However, it does seem that generally men show greater levels of physiological arousal when stressed than women do. Where there are similar levels of stress reported between men and women, men seem to experience higher levels of adrenaline and greater rises in blood pressure levels than women (Frankenhauser *et al*, 1976; Stoney *et al*, 1990).

Women often have stronger social support networks than men and these support networks can play a large part in coping with stress. Another factor that helps offset the effects of stress is exercise. It has been found that men generally take more physical exercise than women. Both these factors will be investigated further in the applications section of this chapter.

When stress becomes a long-term, prolonged problem it is likely to be an important factor in diseases such as:

- Coronary heart disease, strokes, thrombosis.
- High blood pressure.
- Asthma.
- Migraine.

- Diabetes.
- Ulcers.
- Insomnia.
- Depression.

Box 1.41

Activity – Linking Problems and Diseases to the Symptoms of the Body's Response to Stress

Can you link the problems and diseases listed here to the symptoms of the body's response to stress?

Can you link them to the general adaptation syndrome (GAS) effects on the immune system?

All of the conditions listed above can be linked to the effects of the long-term stress response. We have seen the effect on the human body when the sympathetic nervous system is triggered. We go into 'fight or flight' mode. When this reaction is not 'switched off' problems can occur. Our bodies react to stress/threat by increasing blood circulation and blood pressure that has, in the long-term, an adverse effect on the cardiovascular system, increasing the likelihood of heart disease, high blood pressure, migraine headaches and strokes. Our breathing rate increases to oxygenate our blood, but in the long-term this can lead to breathing problems, including asthma. An increase in glucose levels helps to increase our energy supplies, but as a long-term response it can lead to diabetes. The 'fight or flight' response causes our blood to become thicker and stickier, which is useful in helping reduce blood loss in the event of wounding, but in the long-term it gives rise to an increased susceptibility to blood clots and thromboses. Our digestive processes are not needed if we are trying to escape from a threat and so they are shut down, but long-term this can cause digestive system problems such as irritable bowel syndrome (IBS) and ulcers. Our heightened senses can, in the long-term cause us to lose sleep because we are too aware and primed for action. In the long-term many of these normal reactions to threat, which are vital in the short-term, can add to feelings of general malaise and possibly, depression.

In relation to the 'general adaptation syndrome', the harmful conditions listed can begin to manifest themselves during the 'resistance stage', when the body's immune system is less effective than it should be and is less able to ward off viruses and bacterial infection. By the 'exhaustion stage' of the GAS the body is no longer able to fight off attacks from viruses etc. The body's defence mechanisms are exhausted. It is then that severe health problems such as heart disease and high blood pressure can occur (Selye, 1956).

Applications of stress research

Once we have identified sources of stress and the effect it has on us, it is possible to develop stress reduction strategies that will actively counter the harmful effects of long term stress. Stress may be reduced by tackling *either* the external stressors, *or* the internal processes, *or* both.

There is no single panacea for stress. Stress is an individual response to different situations. Recognising your own triggers, your own responses, and working with your body's own rhythms, you can use a variety of techniques and strategies to help yourself to deal with stress.

There are *three* key areas of our lives where stress hits hardest:

1. Personal/home life.
2. School/work/care.
3. Financial.

Stress seems to be contagious, if we are affected badly by stress in one area of our lives it can seep into the other areas.

Dr Vivien Swanson of the University of Stirling specialises in investigating the stress problems caused by the demands between work and home, called the 'home-work interface'.

In one research study into occupational stress and family life that concentrated on comparing the experiences of male and female doctors, Swanson *et al* (1998) found that male doctors experienced pressures from home because of their perceived expectation that they should be the breadwinner in the family. They felt pressure on a professional level due to the perceived expectation that their home life should not affect their working life. Male doctors also said that while they would like to play a bigger role in bringing up their children, there was little opportunity for male doctors to work part-time.

Female doctors experienced 'constant guilt feelings about neglecting family' and felt there was pressure on them not to take time off work for pregnancy or children's illness. One female consultant stated that she felt that she was 'viewed as a second-rate parent and a second-rate doctor – you can't win' (Swanson, 2004).

Some people attempt to counteract stress in one area of their lives by resorting to drinking, using drugs, extreme levels of physical exercise, sleeping too much, being aggressive to those close to them or other extreme activities. These are maladaptive strategies. Although in the short term these methods may dull the effects of stress, eventually they inevitably increase stress in the other areas of life and result in negative effects, some of which may be disastrous.

Fortunately, there are various techniques to reduce stress in more positive ways. Some techniques target the physiological effects of stress and attempt to reduce these effects. They attempt to treat the physical symptoms of stress. Other strategies try to help the person deal with the situation that causes stress, using psychological techniques to cope with or lessen the negative effects of stress. In this Section, we will identify and evaluate several stress reduction techniques that use either physiological or psychological techniques.

Physiological strategies

'Drug therapies' involve the use of medically prescribed drugs to help combat stress. It is a commonplace method of tackling stress in our society. The types of drugs most commonly prescribed by doctors to treat the symptoms of stress are called benzodiazepines. You may have heard of these drugs by their trade names: Valium, Librium, Ativan, Halcion? These drugs slow down the activity in the brain and central nervous system. Neuron activity is slowed reducing anxiety and helping the individual to relax.

Other drugs, such as beta-blockers, help relieve stress by inhibiting the sympathetic nervous system directly. The sympathetic nervous system, as we saw at the start of this chapter, is activated when we perceive we are under threat. By reducing the response of the sympathetic nervous system, beta-blockers reduce the negative consequences of stress.

Evaluation

Drugs can be very effective in helping to relieve the negative symptoms of stress. They require no other input from the stress sufferer other than actually taking the drugs as prescribed. However, drugs can be addictive and it is therefore advisable to take them only in the short-term. As soon as you stop taking the drugs though, their effectiveness ceases, so if the problem still persists then the individual is left requiring more drugs, or some other method of stress management. Drugs help combat the negative effects of stress but do not tackle the underlying causes of stress.

Box 1.42

Research: Holroyd *et al* On the Effectiveness of Behavioural and Pharmacological Therapies for Chronic Tension Headache (2001)

Holroyd *et al* (2001) carried out an 8-month trial to investigate the effectiveness of behavioural and pharmacological therapies for chronic tension headache. They studied 203 adults who averaged 26 chronic tension headaches a month. Participants were randomly assigned to one of four treatments:

- Tricyclic anti-depression medication (the main type of drug therapy used for tension headaches at the time).
- Placebo.
- Stress-management therapy plus placebo.
- Stress-management therapy plus anti-depression medication.

Participants recorded headache activity, the use of analgesics, the use of the study medication (if any) and the level of disability caused by the headaches. They used self-report techniques in a daily diary.

Holroyd and his colleagues found that three of the four treatments (tricyclic drugs alone, stress management plus tricyclics, and stress management plus placebo) reduced the amount of chronic tension headaches, as well as reducing the use of analgesia and the level of disability caused by the headaches. The combined drug and behavioural therapy (tricyclics plus stress management) produced a significant reduction of over 50 per cent in the amount of headache activity for more participants than either stress-management therapy alone, or drug therapy alone. Participants who took the placebo did not report any reduction in the amount of headache activity they experienced.

The study provided the first evidence that chronic tension headaches respond to behavioural therapy to the same degree as drug therapy alone. The most effective method was a combined use of stress-management therapy plus anti-depression medication.

Biofeedback

'Biofeedback' is a fairly new technique where external devices are used to help a person monitor their own body responses that are triggered during stress. Using biofeedback we can learn when we are overly stressed and when to use relaxation techniques. We can then consciously help our bodies regain and maintain control.

A wide variety of biofeedback equipment is available to monitor information about the ANS responses that are triggered at times of stress. These responses include raised blood pressure that can be checked using blood pressure monitors and increased heart rate that can be checked using heart-rate monitors.

Bio-dots are another simple, but effective, form of biofeedback. They are a small, self-adhesive temperature sensitive dots that are stuck onto the skin on the inner surface of the wrist. Bio dots work by detecting minute changes in skin temperature and changing colour accordingly. When you are tense and stressed blood vessels constrict, reducing the blood flow and lowering the temperature of the skin. When you are relaxed the blood circulates more easily near the skin surface and the skin becomes warmer.

Once feedback is obtained from the body the individual can then use relaxation techniques that reduce the effect of the sympathetic nervous system and, in turn, activates the parasympathetic system that reduces heart rate, reduces blood pressure, raises the surface temperature of the skin and counteracts all other physiological symptoms of stress.

Evaluation

Biofeedback has been shown to be an effective and non-invasive method of counteracting the effects of stress. It allows the individual to deal with the symptoms of stress without the use of drugs. It also gives them the ability to achieve a long-lasting control over the adverse symptoms of stress. However, the method still only treats the symptoms of stress and not the underlying cause. Special equipment such as blood pressure and heart rate monitors can be expensive.

Physical exercise

Physical exercise provides an outlet for the physical effects of the stress response. Through exercise the body can 'get rid of' the excess energy and heightened awareness that being stressed causes. It may work by de-activating the sympathetic response: the brain gets the message that the threat is over. Physical exercise can be a very effective and cheap method of relieving the effects of stress.

Relaxation

Relaxation takes many forms. Progressive muscle relaxation is where each area of the body is relaxed in turn starting from the toes, up through the feet and ankles, calves.......and on up to the face and scalp. Other examples of relaxation occur while meditating, doing yoga, or sitting quietly. During relaxation breathing is controlled and heart rate and blood pressure are lowered. One of the easiest methods of relaxation is deep breathing. It can be done whenever you can find a few minutes when stress threatens to get the better of you, even in the middle of an exam if necessary!

In 1975, the Lancet reported a study designed to evaluate the difference between yoga relaxation methods with biofeedback, and general relaxation methods. Thirty-four participants who suffered from high blood pressure were assigned to one of two groups. One group undertook yoga relaxation techniques with biofeedback; the other group used relaxation techniques alone. Both groups experienced some reduction in blood pressure, but the group using yoga relaxation with biofeedback showed a highly significant reduction of 16 points over the relaxation only group.

As we have seen already, stress takes its toll on breathing among many other things. Being stressed means our breathing becomes short and shallow, it means you take in less oxygen and more carbon dioxide.

Box 1.43

Activity - Exercise in Stress Relief

Try this: Sit relaxed with your spine straight and your shoulders back, but loose and low, to allow your lungs to expand. Rest your hands on the arm of your chair, or in your lap. Put your feet flat on the floor.

Breathe in slowly through your nose. As you inhale you should think about your abdomen slowly inflating like a balloon. Feel it swelling.

Now breathe out slowly through your nose. Pull in and tighten up your abdominal muscles as you squeeze all the air out of your lungs.

Carry on breathing in deeply, being conscious of your abdomen inflating and deflating. Establish a rhythm that is natural and comfortable for you.

If you try this, even for just a few minutes, whenever you are feeling tense you will find it really works. It is free - and does not even take much time - but pays great dividends!

Whoever said that *laughter* is the best medicine knew what they were talking about! Humour and taking time out for a good laugh does actually benefit you. It eases mental tension, aids concentration, and enhances creativity. Smiling relaxes many of the facial muscles and actually improves the blood supply to the brain. So, have a good laugh whenever you can – but perhaps not in the middle of an exam!

Dr Lee Berk and his colleagues at Loma Linda University in California have spent many years studying the effects of laughter on the immune system. They have found that laughing lowers blood pressure, reduces stress hormones, relaxes tense muscles, and improves levels of infection and disease-fighting antibodies. Laughter also triggers the release of endorphins that produce general feelings of well-being (Berk *et al*, 1989).

Also, stress can be counteracted by developing an anti-stress regime. Eating healthily, moderate exercise, and relaxation are very effective in controlling stress symptoms. Learning to recognise your own early stress symptoms can help you to tackle stress before it becomes a major issue. Any regime must, of course, fit in easily to your daily schedule and be fun. Forcing yourself to do anything you don't find enjoyable will be counter-productive.

Psychological strategies

Cognitive strategies

Cognitive strategies towards coping with stress allow the individual to change the way they think about stressors that they may have no control over, such as stress in the workplace. Cognitive techniques attempt to change a person's *perception* of the stressor, and their *perception* of how well they are able to cope.

Meichenbaum (1985) developed a cognitive technique called 'stress inoculation training' (SIT). Inoculations against infectious diseases work by introducing a small dose of the disease into the body so that the body develops antibodies and can then fight off a full attack from the disease. SIT works in a similar way by introducing stressors to the individual as problems to be solved and the individual is taught how to break down the stressor into manageable pieces so it can be tackled effectively.

A variety of appropriate coping skills (such as time management, assertiveness skills, relaxation, positive thinking, social skills, etc.) are taught through role-play in a controlled and safe setting before they are put into practice in real life. The skills cover both cognitive and behavioural techniques. They teach the individual to think in a different way about stressors, and they also teach them new behaviours through rewarding appropriate behaviour. The individual is then given opportunities to practice their new skills in different situations that are made increasingly stressful.

Evaluation

SIT deals with the causes of stress not just the symptoms. Individuals learn techniques tailored to their own needs that can help them deal with stress and stressors throughout their lives. SIT has been found to be an effective method of stress management. The training for SIT, however, is very time consuming and costly. It requires a high level of motivation on the part of the individual undergoing the training.

Assertiveness

Assertiveness is a method of standing up for your own rights and expressing your needs, wants, opinions, feelings and beliefs in a direct, honest and appropriate way. Being assertive also means respecting the rights of others, and listening to their views, needs, opinions, etc. Individuals learn to ask for what they want without being overly aggressive or overly passive. Assertiveness can be a highly effective technique that can counteract stress by allowing individuals to increase their perception of being able to cope and of being in control of situations.

Individual coping strategies

The individual who is experiencing stress can learn coping strategies that allow them to feel more in control of their reactions.

Psychoanalytic psychology suggests that we use defence mechanisms in order to help us cope with problems, anxieties and stress that we do not wish to face up to. First suggested by the founder of psychoanalytic psychology, Sigmund Freud, defence mechanisms are thought to protect the 'ego' from the demands of the 'id' or the 'superego'. We do not, however, have any conscious control over our defence mechanisms.

Freud proposed that our personalities are made up of three parts, the id, the ego and the superego. The id is an instinctive and primitive part of our personality and is in place from birth. The id is governed by the 'pleasure principle' that demands immediate satisfaction in its desires, seeking pleasure and avoiding pain. The ego operates on the 'reality principle' and attempts to control the demands of the id until an appropriate time or place occur. The superego is the moral part of our personality that imposes what is right and proper and what is wrong and unacceptable, it works on the 'morality principle'. The ego acts as a balance between the demands of the id and the superego and protects itself from their demands by using defence mechanisms.

Defence mechanisms include:

- ***Denial***: If a situation is too painful to face, an individual may refuse to accept that it exists and deny there is anything amiss.
- ***Displacement***: If you cannot express your negative feelings towards a person directly, you may redirect these feelings on to another person or object.
- ***Repression***: If a situation is too painful or frightening Freud believed that we push the memory out of the conscious mind into the unconscious mind where it is not readily available to us.

These are just a few of the defence mechanisms that Freud suggested we unconsciously use to help us cope with anxiety and problems. Defence mechanisms involve the distortion of reality and, while giving some relief by avoiding the problems, they do not offer any attempt to solve them and may be harmful in the long term.

In contrast to the distorted reality of defence mechanisms, Grasha (1983) described ways of using coping mechanisms as conscious ways of adapting to stress in a positive and constructive way.

Grasha described eight major coping mechanisms for dealing with stress:

Objectivity
The separation of one thought from another thought, or our feelings from our thoughts. This allows us to gain a better understanding of how we think and feel and to make an objective evaluation of our actions.

Logical analysis
The systematic analysis of our problems in order to find explanations and, based on the realities of the situation, make plans to solve them.

Concentration
The ability to set aside any disturbing thoughts and feelings we may have in order to concentrate on the task.

Empathy
The ability to sense how other people are feeling so that our interactions with them take account of their feelings.

Playfulness
The ability to use our past ideas, feelings and behaviours in a suitable manner in order to enhance the solution of the problem and add enjoyment to life.

Tolerance of ambiguity
The ability to function in situations where either we, or others, cannot make clear choices because the situation is so complicated.

Suppression
The ability to consciously forget about, or hold back, thoughts and feelings until we are in an appropriate time or situation to express them.

Sublimation
The channelling of anxiety in socially desirable ways so that it is positive and constructive.

Control
The ability to have control over our thoughts and feelings, and to have some control of the situation.

Positive thinking
Positive thinking is designed to combat negative, self-defeating thoughts that we often use to talk ourselves out of achieving what we could achieve. By looking at

'problems' as challenges, we turn our negative outlook into a positive one. We can learn from challenges, we feel good when we rise to a challenge and succeed. By thinking positively we can change our whole outlook on life and think 'I can and I will' rather than 'I can't and I won't'. This technique takes time and practice, but by changing our attitudes into positive rather than negative, we can go a long way to combating the negative perception that we are unable to cope with stressors.

Emotion-focussed coping attempts to reduce the negative thought patterns that generally accompany stress. However, problem-focussed coping seems to be more effective.

Social strategies and support

Social support is the term given to the network of friends and relatives who are available to support us when we are stressed. Brown and Harris (1978) found that social isolation is a factor in causing depression, and social support can be beneficial in protecting us from the psychological effects of stress. There are three main areas where social support can help:

Emotional support

Emotional support helps us by raising our self-esteem and encouraging us to believe we can cope with the stressful situation. We feel comforted and reassured.

Practical support

Practical support benefits us by helping in practical ways, such as a friend helping us to study for an exam, or someone taking our children to the park to allow us to catch up on necessary jobs around the house.

Giving advice

Friends and relatives can also help by *giving advice* on how to deal with a situation. Sometimes it is difficult to see solutions to our own problems and another person's perspective can help us solve a particular problem or see an alternative way of dealing with it.

As well as our own support networks, there are also various specialist support groups that can help us to deal with particular problems, for example: Relate, the Samaritans and Gamblers Anonymous.

Correlational studies have demonstrated that there are links between greater numbers of friends and lower levels of stress. There are gender differences in the effectiveness of support networks. It has been found that men generally have larger social networks than women but women use their social support networks more effectively (Ratcliffe-Crain and Baum, 1990).

Organisational stress-reduction strategies

As we saw previously stress in the workplace is a major contributor to ill health and days lost in productivity. Some companies and some managers equate maximum productivity with pressure. The message they send out is that work always comes before personal commitments. An individual needs to decide if the experience, money or prestige is worth the cost in terms of their health and personal life. Some companies are now much more attuned to the problems that stress causes amongst the workforce and employ specialist stress consultants, offering time-management courses, 'employee assistance programmes' and similar, in order to help reduce the negative effects of stress in the workplace. There is evidence of improved productivity where work stress has been tackled by employers.

Time management

One of the main causes of stress in our lives, at work or at school or college, is the feeling we have too much to do and too little time to do it. Time pressures can make us feel we are constantly battling to get things done. Detailed below you will find a practical activity designed to help you think about how well you organise your time. Is your time management effective, or do you waste time on less important tasks when you should be concentrating on the more important ones? One area where you could use the ideas is in planning your revision strategies for your exams.

By using time management techniques and by setting priorities you can help reduce stress levels.

Diagram 1.21

Activity: Time Management

	Analysis: How well do I spend my time?	Strategy: What will I do to improve?
Do I use my time efficiently? How do I waste time?		
What or who distracts me from work?		
Do I need to plan out my time: - for the year? - for the term? - for the week? - for the day?		
Do I waste time getting started?		
Do I make the most of spare moments?		
Do I find time passes and I don't know where it has gone?		

Think about your college/school workload (or your exam timetable). Split your tasks into A, B, and C tasks:

- 'A' tasks are the very important, top priority tasks that can only be carried out properly by you. These tasks cannot be delegated.
- 'B' tasks are of average importance, they could be left for a short while.
- 'C' tasks are less important but still need to be done eventually. Perhaps they could be delegated to someone else.

What often happens is that time is wasted on 'C' tasks while the really important 'A' tasks are neglected. We put off doing the more demanding tasks for ones that we feel more comfortable doing.

You will probably be aware of when, during the day, you are at your most alert and able to deal with more demanding work, and when you feel less able. Our bodies work on a natural rhythm, called the circadian rhythm, which spans approximately a 24-hour period. There is a time to sleep, and a time to work, a time when our metabolism is at its peak and when it is at its lowest, a time when we can work most efficiently and think clearly, a time when we really need to rest and recover from the demands of the day.

Think about when you feel at your brightest, and when you want to slow down. You may feel brightest in the morning, and slowest around 3 or 4 pm, or vice versa. By becoming aware of your own body's rhythms you can use your peak times to tackle more demanding tasks, and the troughs to do more routine or mundane tasks – or even rest!

By using this information about your body's rhythms you can target the 'A' task list for your most alert and productive times, and allow yourself to do the routine, less demanding tasks when your body feels the need to relax more.

This technique does take practice and it does take time. It is worth investigating your body rhythms, and breaking down your tasks into levels of importance. The time you spend may seem to compound your problem of LACK of time – but it will pay dividends in the long run by managing your time more effectively, working with your body's natural rhythms, and, ultimately, reducing your stress levels.

Chapter 2
Investigating Behaviour Part 1: Research Methods in Psychology

Section summary

This Section on research methods will investigate:

- The domain of research methods.
- The methods of data collection in research.
- The scientific nature of psychology versus 'common sense'.
- The research process.

Introduction to the domain of research methods

The research methods

In this Section you will be introduced to *four* of the main methods of data collection used in psychology research: experiments; surveys; observations and case studies.

Common sense versus scientific psychology

In our everyday lives we continually try and make sense of why people behave as they do. In order to do so, we often use 'common sense' explanations.

Psychologists and other social scientists tend to view such explanations as subjective, based on personal opinion and often ill informed. They seek to develop social scientific explanations that aim to be objective, systematically constructed and evaluated and not based on personal opinion. By way of example, a popular explanation of why young people display aggressive behaviour is because they watch a lot of violent programmes on television – an idea that is prevalent in the popular media and among the general public. Such a view has been shown to be subjective, biased and ill informed.

Psychology differs from common sense explanations in that it uses research methods to generate data. Instead of trying to prove a singular point of view at the outset to research, psychologists attempt to remain objective and so a number of possible outcomes are investigated. Social science researchers attempt to be objective; that is, impartial and unbiased. They are obliged to accept the results of their research even if the results do not support the ideas that the psychologist had before carrying out the study. This is the basis of scientific research and what differentiates it from common sense explanations.

Psychological knowledge is based on scientific theories and explanations and deals with a wide range of areas such as: the possible long-term effects of infant separation from the 'mother figure', how memory operates, why we forget things and whether there is a relationship between individual stress and personal health. These theories have been tested through research involving the use of a variety of research methods of investigation: experiments, the technique of correlation, surveys – questionnaires and interviews, observations, and case studies

The research process

The stages involved in scientific research are often referred to as the 'research process'. You can see an illustration of what is involved in **Diagram 2/1.1**.

Diagram 2/1.1

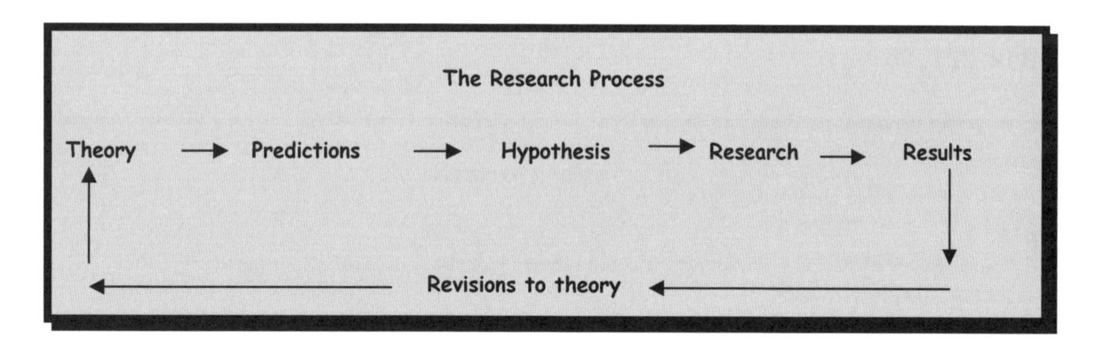

The psychologist attempts to produce a 'theory' as to why something occurs. For example, why do we remember some things and not others? A psychologist who gives a possible rational and scientific explanation of why this happens has produced a *theory* of memory.

Using the theory constructed, the researcher attempts to make more specific predictions. This means that the researcher attempts to predict likely behavioural outcomes given particular circumstances, i.e. what will or will not happen. Such a prediction leads to a 'hypothesis' – a statement of what is expected to happen.

The researcher is now ready to begin to test the hypothesis. Will the hypothesis be supported or rejected by the 'data' – the information that is gathered from the 'real world'?

To test the hypotheses, a variety of 'research methods' and techniques are used. For example, psychologists use experiments, surveys (including questionnaires and interviews) observations and case studies.

When the researcher has gathered and analysed the data, the 'results' are then examined to see if they support the hypothesis or not. Statistical techniques are used to decide if this is the case. If the hypothesis is rejected, the researcher will then make revisions to (or abandon) the theory. The whole process may then start afresh.

It should be noted that the research process means that 'new' data is always being collected, and that the various psychological theories used to explain psychological processes, are constantly being changed and refined.

To illustrate the research process, let us take the example of 'memory'. Concentrate on trying to follow and understand the underlying logic of the research process as described.

Box 2/1.1

The Research Process

STEP 1:
A simple **theory** of memory functioning: 'People tend to have better recall of information if they repeat or rehearse things'.

STEP 2:
Make a **prediction**, formulated as a hypothesis: 'Participants will recall more of what they have learned if, as part of the learning process, they repeat it five times rather than once'.

STEP 3:
Research to test the hypothesis: 'The hypothesis will be tested by laboratory experiment'.

STEP 4:
Results found: 'It may be that repetition/rehearsal is seen to have no effect on recall'.

STEP 5:
Revise theory: 'The theory would have to be developed so that it took into account factors other than rehearsal'.

The sequence of stages followed in the example is typical of that followed by all scientists, including psychologists, in what is referred to as the *research process*. It is this process of enquiry that makes psychology scientific and not whether the psychologist wears a lab coat or works in a science faculty of a university. You will notice that there is no end to the process, as the new revised theory will lead to new predictions and hypotheses. The research process is cyclical; it is never ending and is, therefore, forever open to critique and amendment.

The experimental method

Section summary

This Section on research methods will investigate:

- The experimental method.
- Causes and effects.
- Variables.
- Operationalising variables.
- Experimental conditions.
- Allocation to conditions.
- Types of experiments.
- Extraneous variables.
- Hypothesis testing.
- Experimental design.
- Correlational design and data analysis.

Causes and effects

We will begin by looking at the experiment, the main research method used by psychologists. A central concern of any experiment is that it tries to establish what psychologists call a cause – effect relationship. This is sometimes referred to as 'causality'.

It is because of this that the experimental research method is generally acknowledged as being the most useful research method. Other research methods may give some indication that one thing causes another, but they do not systematically test the relationship in the way that the experimental method does.

Diagram 2/1.2

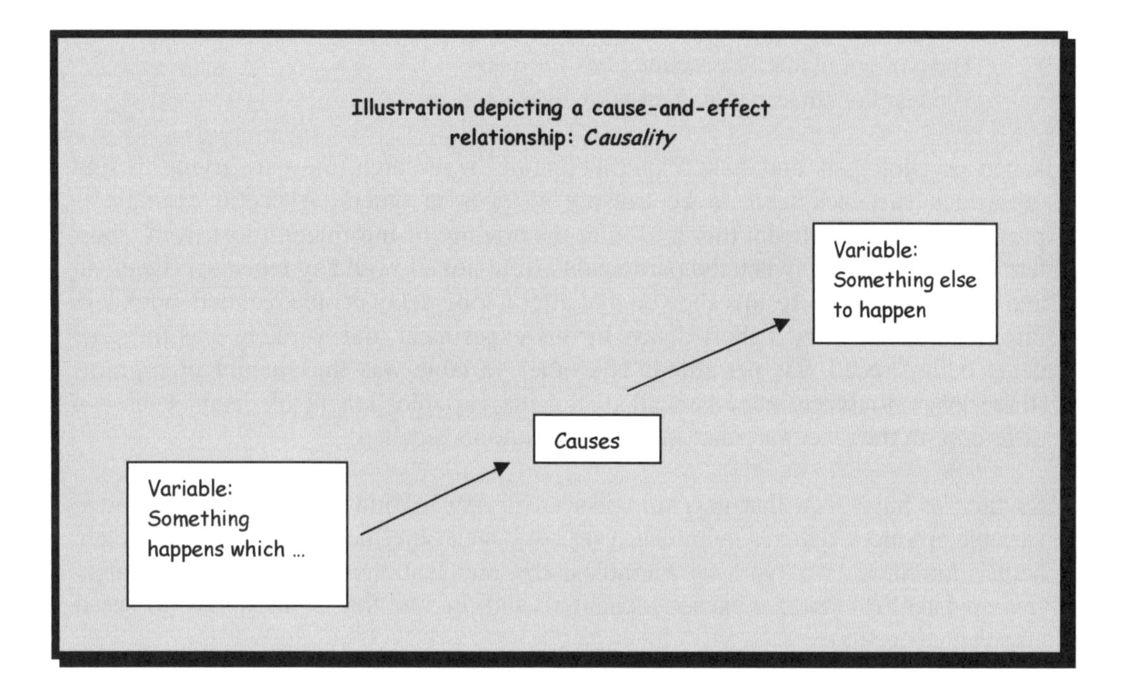

When psychologists attempt to investigate causal factors behind human and non-human behaviour they are mindful that behaviour is often caused by a number of factors; that is, behaviour is determined by *multi-causal* factors. Also, some factors that are assumed to be causal are, in fact, spurious; (that is, not directly linked) or even accidental. If a person takes a painkiller and their headache goes away, can they be certain that the painkiller caused the pain to go away? Of course, it is possible that the headache would have gone away anyway, for some other reason, such as the passage of time, or that the taking of the pill had produced a *placebo* effect – the very thought that the pill would remove the headache, produced the effect in reality. Experiments in psychology must be very carefully designed and controlled if they are to stand any chance of being able to detect what causes what.

Variables

Any phenomenon or feature in people or the environment that is subject to change and manipulation is called a variable. Psychologists use the concept of variable to refer to 'something' that may cause another 'thing' to happen. For example, if an experiment seeks to investigate whether level of stress affects aggression, then the stress level and incidences of acts of aggression can be viewed as the variables.

Other examples of variables are:

- The type or quality of attachment between child and parent.
- The amount of study someone does for a test.
- The level of stress people feel in an examination.

When psychologists undertake experimentation in research, they are trying to find out which variables seem to be causing changes in others. A useful example is provided in an experiment that looked at the amount of information lost from 'short term memory' (STM) when the participants were not allowed any rehearsal (Peterson and Peterson, 1959). Results showed that after a long delay people recalled much less information than after a short delay. In this experiment, one variable was the time delay before recall was permitted. The other variable was the amount of trigrams (three letter nonsense words) recalled. So, the variable 'length of delay' caused a difference in the other variable, 'number of trigrams recalled'.

So far, we have seen that psychologists are trying to find out if a change in one variable produces changes in another variable – a cause-effect relationship. There are names for these two types of variables, the one that the researcher deliberately 'manipulates' (to see if it causes a change), and the one that is measured (to see if any change occurs).

The variable that the researcher manipulates is called the 'independent variable' (IV). The researcher then tries to see what effect, if any, this has on the other variable, the 'dependent variable' (DV). Thus, **Diagram 2/1.2** (above) illustrates a cause-and-effect relationship. Therefore, 'causality' becomes a cause-and-effect relationship: causality – (IV) *causes* measurable changes in the DV.

Let us consider an example. We might suppose that if we trained people in a memory technique, such as mnemonics – this is when new material to be remembered is integrated into existing memory they would be better at remembering things than people who have had no training in memory techniques. In such an experiment, the independent variable (IV) would be the training in the technique, or no training. The dependent variable (DV) would be the number of words correctly recalled from a list of words.

Box 2/1.2

Activity - Working With Variables

1. What is the name of the variable that the researcher manipulates?
2. What is the name of the variable that the researcher measures?
3. For each of the following experiments, identify the independent variable (IV) and the dependent variable:

HINT: it is sometimes easier to identify the DV first, as this is always what is measured, i.e. the 'results':

a) An experimenter is interested in the effects of television violence on the aggressive behaviour of viewers. Some participants are exposed to television programmes that depict violence. Other participants are shown television programmes containing no violence. The amount of amount of aggression shown by each group of participants is then recorded.
b) Kiecolt-Glaser *et al* (1995) undertook an experiment into the effects of stress on the immune system. They did this by looking at how quickly wounds healed. There were 26 female volunteers aged between 47-81 years. Thirteen of the women were currently looking after relatives who were experiencing senile dementia. The other 13 women were not. All the participants were given a small wound.
c) Craik and Tulving (1975) undertook an experiment to investigate the levels of processing model of memory. They gave participants sentences that varied in terms of their complexity. They found that sentences that focused on the meaning of a word led to better recall than those focused on the sound of a word. This suggests that memory can be improved if processing takes place at deeper levels - in terms of meaning.

(The answers are at the end of the Chapter.)

Operationalising variables

Once experimental psychologists have decided on what the variables are and which one should act as the IV and which as the DV, they then go through a process called 'operationalisation'.

The variables psychologists are interested in, such as violence or stress, are often very broad, and can be open to several interpretations. To operationalise a variable means to specify these variables in such a way that they can be accurately measured. The level of 'violence on television' may be operationalised as the number of people who are killed in the first half hour of a programme. A DV such as 'memory recall' could be operationalised as 'the number of words recalled in 60 seconds'.

Let us take a further example. Suppose a social psychologist was interested in the extent to which drivers conform to the Highway Code. The assumption 'young male drivers will conform less than older female drivers', might inform the formulation of a hypothesis. The next stage would be to operationalise what is meant by 'young' and 'older' with the result, perhaps, that a more specific measurement of age is adopted, perhaps using age brackets as in '17-30 years', for example. The term, 'conform', would also have to be defined in a form that is measurable. An example might be how often drivers travelled through a red traffic light.

As can be seen the process of operationalising can be quite complex. However, it is essential to be so thorough in an attempt to gather data that is objective.

Experimental conditions

Once we have operationalised the Independent Variable (IV) and the Dependent Variable (DV), we can then begin to manipulate the IV. This means that the researcher is *deliberately* changing the values or levels of the IV. A simple experiment might consist of two parts, one with a certain value of the IV and one with a different value of the IV. This could mean that something is present in one part of the experiment, and absent in the other. These two parts are known as 'experimental conditions'.

In the example relating to memory used above, psychologists can vary whether or not mnemonics are used to aid learning. Mnemonics would be included in one condition (which could be called 'Condition A'), but they would be absent in the other ('Condition B'). Once this has been done, the researcher is then interested in seeing if the changes to the IV have produced any changes in the DV. The researcher records the level of the DV – in this case, recall – pertaining to the different conditions for comparison.

If the change in the DV is the result only of the change in the IV, then the researchers can say that they have found what causes the changes to happen. They have demonstrated causality.

This is a very simple experiment, but it nevertheless illustrates the logic of the experiment. The manipulation of the IV into 'Conditions A' and 'B' (i.e. presence or absence of the mnemonic technique) allows comparison between the two sets of recall scores, i.e. the DV. If the memory technique were effective, we would expect recall to be better among the participants in 'Condition A'.

There are also experiments where researchers are interested in more than two conditions of the independent variable. For example, psychologists might be interested in seeing if the number of hours spent studying influences exam grades and not simply looking to see if there is a causal relationship between studying and exam grades. This can be seen in **Table 2/1.1**.

Table 2/1.1

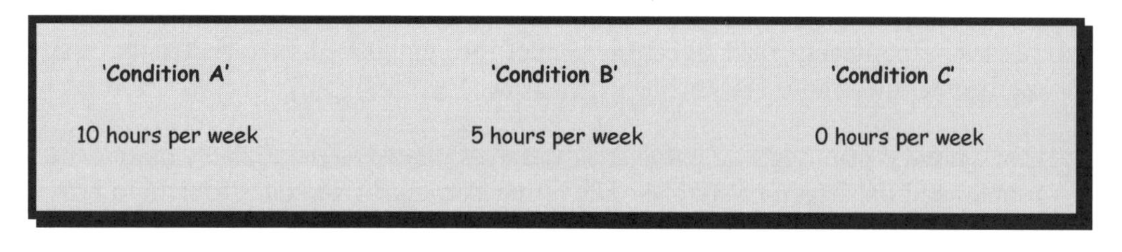

'Condition A'	'Condition B'	'Condition C'
10 hours per week	5 hours per week	0 hours per week

Thus, with three or more 'levels' of an IV, three or more experimental conditions are used. It would be too convenient to refer to all that occurs in an experiment as 'conditions of an experiment'. It should be clear, however, that the term, 'condition', has a specific technical meaning in the context of an experiment.

Extraneous variables

If when we find a difference in the DV we wish to attempt to determine cause – and – effect, we have to ensure that the IV is the only variable undergoing change. It could be that as we change the IV other variables are also changing. An experimenter has to be very careful that other variables are not responsible for the changes in the DV. Such variables are called 'extraneous variables'. These must be controlled; otherwise the researcher cannot measure the effect of the independent variable on the dependent variable. What does the term controlled mean here? This refers to the idea that everything in the conditions must be kept the same (as far as possible) except for the *one* thing that is manipulated, i.e. the IV. If control is not achieved, the dependent variable may be affected in a systematic way. When they do so, they are referred to as 'confounding variables', as they confuse the cause-effect relationship and confound attempts to state logically that the change in the IV causes the change in the DV.

For example, in the above example of memory technique and recall ability, it may be that the participants in 'Condition A' (mnemonic technique) show better recall than those in 'Condition B' (*no* mnemonic technique), but we cannot be automatically certain that this is solely due to the use of mnemonics. It may be that due to the need to devise the mnemonics, these participants spent longer learning the material than those in 'Condition B'. Study time may have become a confounding variable – one that researchers would have to control by giving both groups exactly the same amount of time.

There are many things that can vary, and not all of them can be predicted or controlled. It could be that a participant in 'Condition B' (*no* mnemonics) has a heavy cold, and another may have an exam immediately after the experiment is finished. Some noisy traffic might go past during the experiment, affecting people's concentration. The effect of these variables on the results is known as 'random error', that is, a degree of inaccuracy in the data that the researcher gets. Even in a well-designed experiment, random error cannot be eliminated. Exceptionally, the experimenter may choose to stop the experiment.

There are three main types of extraneous variables: *participant* variables, *situational* variables and *investigator* variables. The term, 'participant variables', refers to how participants' performances in an experiment might be influenced by any differences between them. There are many such variables for example, personality, intelligence, individual motivation to take part in the experiment and age.

The term, 'situational variables', refers to the actual setting of the experiment, which could, if overlooked, influence the performance of the participants. These include the heating, lighting conditions, the time of the day, and many others. These could also include the instructions given to the participants and the actual experimental procedures. For all of these things, care must be taken to ensure that these variables are held constant over the different conditions in the experiment.

The last category of extraneous variables is 'researcher ('investigator') variables'. This refers to the attributes of the researcher, for example, their personality, age, ethnicity or gender. Sometimes these cannot be controlled, but, again, they should be kept constant between conditions.

Box 2/1.3

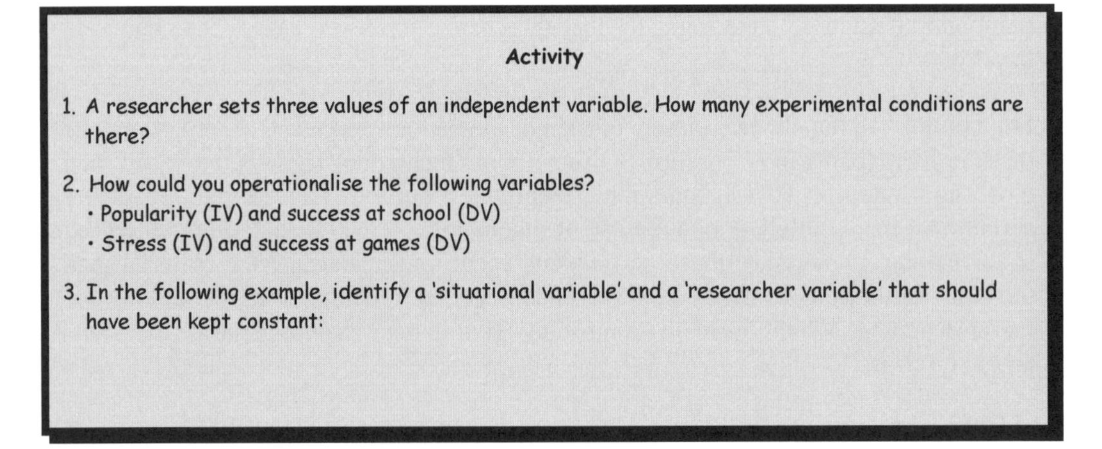

Activity

1. A researcher sets three values of an independent variable. How many experimental conditions are there?
2. How could you operationalise the following variables?
   - Popularity (IV) and success at school (DV)
   - Stress (IV) and success at games (DV)
3. In the following example, identify a 'situational variable' and a 'researcher variable' that should have been kept constant:

Alfonso, Jean and Jane are 20-year old students investigating gender differences in IQ estimates, and each of them selects two participants – Jean chooses her brother and sister, and Alfonso selects his mother and father, as does Jane. Each asks these participants to estimate their own IQ. Alfonso asks this question at home; the others ask the question when out shopping. The group thus obtain six scores (or two sets of data) – three from male participants and three from female participants

(Answers are at the end of the Chapter.)

We have looked above at some of the key features of the experimental method, a method that seeks to establish whether there is a *cause-and-effect* relationship between two *variables* – the IV and the DV. To do this, we have to *operationalise* these variables – define them so that they can be measured. The different values of the IV determine the different *conditions* of an experiment. However, care has to be taken to ensure that it is the IV and not an extraneous variable that is affecting the DV.

We will now consider another essential feature of experiments: hypothesis testing.

Testing hypotheses

The hypothesis stage is crucial to the construction of successful experiments. This is a statement that a researcher makes when research first begins, in an attempt to predict what might occur. Any hypothesis should fulfill *three* criteria:

1. It should predict that a difference would occur between the IV conditions.
2. It should be a precise statement that contains the 'independent' and 'dependent' variables (in their 'operationalised' form).
3. It should be open to being disproved or refuted. The philosopher, Karl Popper, said that a statement is not scientific if it cannot in principle be proved wrong, or 'falsified'.

When psychologists conduct experiments, they test component parts of a theory by suggesting an 'experimental (or 'alternative') hypothesis' and then setting up certain circumstances in order to test the hypothesis.

It should be noted that *all* experiments have experimental hypotheses, and there are two types: a 'one tailed experimental hypothesis' and a 'two-tailed experimental hypothesis'. The former is sometimes known as a 'directional hypothesis' and the latter as a 'non-directional hypothesis'.

Table 2/1.2

Experimental Hypotheses

One-tailed = directional

Two-tailed = non-directional

A two-tailed experimental hypothesis for the mnemonic experiment mentioned above would state that the IV will produce changes in the DV (see **Table 2/1.2** above). There will be a difference in the scores between 'Condition A' and 'Condition B' – it does not state whether the scores will be higher or lower in a specific condition, it simply states that there *will be* a difference.

A one tailed experimental hypothesis predicts that there will be a difference between 'Condition A' and 'Condition B'. It also states the direction that the difference takes, for example, 'higher' or 'lower'.

The other possible outcome would be that there is no difference between 'Condition A' and 'Condition B'. Researchers also include this as a prediction. This is called the 'null hypothesis', which states that the IV will not have an effect on the DV and any difference observed *between the conditions* is due to factors such as chance, spurious, or extraneous, variables. Note, however, that a *difference in DV scores* would imply that the IV has affected the DV.

In the memory experiment, it may be that participants in 'Condition A' – those who have used mnemonics – do produce better recall results than 'Condition B' – who have not used mnemonics, but these results have been produced by chance and not because of the use of the mnemonics in 'Condition A'.

As with the experimental hypothesis, every experiment has a null hypothesis. Although it always says much the same thing – there will be no difference between the conditions, and that any changes in the DV are due to chance – this hypothesis is very important for experimentation and scientific research in general. Research can never 'prove' that an idea is 'true', but we should in principle be able to show that it is 'false'.

As mentioned above, Karl Popper (1959) argued that a 'good' scientific theory should be open to testing to see whether the claim can be proven to be false. This is ideally what psychologists and all scientific researchers should be doing. Once researchers have gathered and analysed the data, they must make a decision as to whether to accept or reject the null hypothesis. If they reject the null hypothesis, then, by definition, they accept the experimental hypothesis and vice versa.

Experimental design

The next thing the psychologist must decide is how to allocate the participants to the experimental conditions. This is what is referred to as the 'experimental design'.

There are *two* main experimental designs: 'repeated measures' and 'independent measures'. These relate to whether participants take part in just *one* condition of an experiment, or, if the same people do both, *all* conditions.

In the mnemonics experiment, the researcher must decide whether to disperse the participants across the different conditions: 'Condition A' (trained in mnemonics) and 'Condition B' (*no* training in mnemonics). We could allocate one group of participants to 'Condition A' and allocate another (different) group of participants to 'Condition B'. A design where we have groups of different participants in each of the experimental conditions is called an 'independent measures design', because it compares data that has been generated by two different and independent groups of participants. Independent measures are sometimes called a 'between-groups' design.

The researcher could instead use a 'repeated measures design'. This would involve comparing the recall ability of the *same* participants. The researcher could measure each participant's recall performance before they have been trained in using mnemonics ('Condition B') and after they have been trained in and used mnemonics ('Condition A'). The same participants perform in each of the experimental conditions. This experimental design is called a repeated measures design because any changes in the DV are taken from each participant, in both, or all, conditions. It should *not* be confused with repeating an experiment, a process known as 'replication' (see below). Unlike the independent measures design, repeated measures involve comparing two sets of data from the same participants. This is sometimes called a 'within-groups' design.

A simplified 'repeated measures design' would show the participant allocation as depicted in **Table 2/1.3**.

Table 2/1.3

A Repeated measures design		
Participant Number	'Condition A'	'Condition B'
P1	2	1
P2	2	1
P3	2	1
P4	2	1

In the mnemonics experiment, we have used two conditions of the IV – 'Condition A' and 'Condition B'. A simplified independent groups design would show the participant allocation as follows (see **Table 2/1.4**). Note: 'P' stands for participant. Thus, P(1) is participant '1' and P(a) is participant 'a' – these are different participants.

Table 2/1.4

An Independent Groups Design	
'Condition A'	'Condition B'
P(1)	P(a)
P(2)	P(b)
P(3)	P(c)
P(4)	P(d)

How do researchers decide which design to use? Each has its advantages and disadvantages. They also differ in the extent to which they control for confounding variables. Sometimes, however, there is no choice.

Repeated measures – advantages and disadvantages

The main advantage of this experimental design is that the issue of participant variables does not apply, since all the participants are exposed to all the conditions of the experiment. Participant variables cannot be said to influence the DV. Given this, the researcher will require fewer participants.

While this source of bias may be reduced, another arises in the form of what is known as 'order effects'. This is where, for example, participants are affected by having done one of the experimental conditions. For example, performance may be enhanced due to participants becoming more accustomed to the experimental task. Alternatively, there could be a decrease in participant's performance due to lack of motivation, fatigue, or becoming bored with the experimental task. Participants are also more likely to guess the aim of the experiment. This is known as 'demand characteristics' (see Section 4, below).

The researcher will also have to generate more experimental materials. In the mnemonics experiment, the same material cannot be used in both conditions. For example, if we used lists of words to be recalled, they would have to different ones in each condition. However, they would have to be similar enough to be compared and for the experiment they would be presumed to be equivalent in, for example, the extent to which participants were familiar with them.

Psychologists attempt to overcome the problem of order effects by 'counterbalancing'. One way of doing this is to get half of the participants to undertake 'Condition A' first and 'Condition B' second. The remaining half of the participants takes 'Condition B' first and 'Condition A' second. Since this spells 'ABBA', it is often known as the abba design (any association with the highly popular Swedish pop group of the same name is purely coincidental!) This is an attempt to balance the order by which the participants are tested in the conditions allocated. Order effects still exist, but they impact on both conditions equally. Factors, such as *fatigue* or *boredom* or *practice* are balanced out, since if they influence the DV, they do so equally in both conditions.

Independent measures – advantages and disadvantages
This design uses a completely separate group of participants for each condition. An advantage of doing so is that order effects are not an issue. Since each participant completes one condition, only they have no opportunity to practice and therefore there is no reason why conditions should differ by how bored or fatigued participants are.

It is sometimes vital to have two separate groups of participants. This would be especially true when an experiment involves some degree of deception, as people are unlikely to be deceived twice in the same way!

If the mnemonics experiment, using an independent measures design, showed that those who used the technique of mnemonics did better than those who did not, we could say that this is due to the use of the mnemonics. However, it could be that the participants with a better memory by chance were placed in 'Condition A'. If so, then there has been bias in the allocation of participants (Ps) to conditions. In short, the advantage of the repeated measures design – using the same participants – is the disadvantage of independent measures – the possible existence of 'participant variables': personality, intelligence, age, individual motivation to take part in the experiment, for example.

Can researchers do anything to minimise this problem? It would not be possible to eliminate all possible participant variables, but what can be done is to try and make sure that any such variables are spread across all the experimental conditions. For example, those with 'better' memories should be spread across the conditions.

Often researchers choose to 'match' the participants in one condition with similar individuals in the other. Each would have to be assessed in terms of memory ability before the experiment began. Then each would be 'matched' with another participant of similar ability. This is what psychologists call a 'matched pairs design' or, alternatively, 'matched groups design'. (See **Table 2/1.5**.)

Table 2/1.5

Matched Pairs Design

Condition A		Condition B
P(1)	MATCHED	P(a)
P(2)	MATCHED	P(b)
P(3)	MATCHED	P(c)
P(4)	MATCHED	P(d)

This type of experimental design provides all the advantages of the independent groups design, but allows better comparisons to be made between the two groups. However, it cannot achieve the same extent of control as the repeated measures design – no matter how similar the pair, they cannot be as similar as being compared to yourself! It is also very difficult to exactly match participants. Psychologists must know what to match for, but it is not always clear what confounding variables there might be. Two participants might score very closely on a memory test, but be very different in personality. One common situation where psychologists have used this design is with identical ('monozygotic') twins.

Allocation to conditions in independent measures and matched pairs designs
Finally, researchers must decide which participants take part in which condition. In a well-designed experiment, this will be done randomly in an attempt to prevent researcher bias in the allocation of participants to groups.

The essential principle whenever one is randomizing, is that any person or item should always have an equal chance of being selected. This means that if we are trying to place participants into 'Condition A' and 'Condition B' of an experiment, such as the mnemonics experiment, the chances of any individual being selected for either one of the conditions must be equal. A common way of doing this is by using what are called tables of 'random numbers'.

In a matched-pairs design, the allocation is not entirely random, but the choice of which of the two participants in the pair did which condition could be decided randomly.

Sometimes it is not possible to allocate participants to conditions randomly. This could be due to an inherent quality or trait in the participant that pre-determines the condition that they are allocated. For example, Levy (1976) tested left-handers' and right-handers' preferences for complex pictures, and found that right-handers preferred pictures with the centre of interest oriented towards the right, while left-handers showed no preference either way. In such research, participants could not be randomly allocated; left-handers necessarily were allocated one condition ('Condition A') and right-handers the other condition ('Condition B'). When the IV is an attribute of the participant in this way, and participants cannot be randomly allocated, the design is known as a quasi-experiment. Quasi means 'as if' or 'almost' – the lack of randomisation means that a quasi experiment is not a 'true' experiment, but it is similar in most ways (O'Conner, 2004). 'Quasi-experiments' are always associated with independent groups or matched pairs design. Other attributes that might constitute the IV of a study, and therefore make random allocation impossible, are participants' age, intelligence level and their sex. These are also known as 'naturally occurring variables'.

Above we have looked at the various styles of experimental designs that psychologists use. We will now look at the various types of experiments that use these designs.

Types of experiment

We have so far been looking at experiments in terms of design, or internal structure. It should, however, be noted that there is a variety of types of experiment including 'laboratory experiments', 'field experiments', and 'quasi' and 'natural experiments'.

Laboratory experiments

This type of experiment is conducted in a 'laboratory' – a place with controlled conditions. The reason for these controlled conditions is to minimise the effects of situational variables such as noise and other distractions, as discussed above.

The laboratory experiment attempts to control for effects of extraneous variables and thereby record accurate measurement of any changes in the DV. It is the high degree of control that allows psychologists to be able to say that changes in the IV have produced changes in the DV. We have already seen that participant and situational variables must be controlled. Another variable that should be controlled is the relationship between the participant and the researcher. As is the case in all areas of psychology, there is disagreement over the extent to which laboratory experiments have 'internal validity'. An experiment has internal validity, if it successfully measures what it is intended to measure. For example, Orne and Holland (1968) argue that Milgram's (1968) classic 'Obedience' experiments were not internally valid, as participants may have realised that Milgram was deceiving them, and that no actual harm was occurring to the 'learner'. Therefore, this raises the issue of whether participants perceive the artificial environment of the laboratory differently and change their behaviour accordingly.

This is a common criticism of the effectiveness of laboratory experiments and is known as 'ecological validity' – 'the degree to which the behaviour of the subjects in the laboratory corresponds to their behaviour in the natural environment' (Breakwell *et al*, 1995: 221). For example, Asch (1956) found a high level of conformity in a laboratory study, with participants going along with the aggregate feelings of the group, despite personal convictions that the group response to the question set was clearly wrong. Although this mode of behaviour is of interest in itself, it does not necessarily indicate levels of conformity in 'real life', since participants are aware that the context is artificial.

Field experiment and natural experiments

One way of attempting to increase the ecological validity of the experimental method would be for them to take place in the participants' 'normal' environment. These are called 'field' or 'natural experiments'. Such methods lay claim to high ecological validity, since they record behaviour as it occurs in everyday life. However, a consequence of this is that they have limited control over the effects of situational variables, thereby decreasing the degree of certainty over whether it is the IV alone that is responsible for any change in the DV. A further difficulty is that of replication, due to the varying uncontrolled situational variables in varying contexts.

Important differences exist in how these experiments are conducted. The field experiment involves manipulation of an IV, and measurement of a DV as is the case for laboratory experiments. In a natural experiment, however, the difference in IV is naturally occurring rather than being deliberately manipulated by the researcher. Examples of naturally occurring differences in IV might be employees who have undergone specific training and those who have not, or students in paid employment and those who are not. In such cases, the researcher uses an IV from everyday life and measures related effects on DV. As such, it could be argued that this method has high ecological validity, but is not a true experiment. The researcher is not directly manipulating the IV. Moreover, there is even less likelihood of the situation occurring again in its entirety than with field experiments, replication, generalisation of results and prediction are made very difficult. Nevertheless, natural experiments have been used with a degree of success in psychology, particularly in relation to the study of attachment.

Demand characteristics

Since the focus of research in psychology is on human behaviour, problems arise when subjects' awareness that their behaviour is under investigation impacts on how they behave. For example, participants may use certain 'cues' from the experimental situation as a guide to the behaviour that they believe is expected of them (Orne, 1962). These cues are known as 'demand characteristics'.

An experiment undertaken by Orne and Scheibe (1964) demonstrated the influence of demand characteristics. Using an 'independent groups design' one group of participants was introduced to a number of cues, which increased their expectation that they would suffer stress during the experiment. One such stressor arose from the fact that this group were asked to sign a form that would release the researcher from any legal liability for consequences of running of the experiment. This potential stressor was not introduced to the other group. It was found that the first group experienced higher levels of stress regardless of the IV. It was concluded, therefore, that they had behaved in the way they thought the experiment demanded. These demand characteristics had become confounding variables.

'Experimenter effects' may influence demand characteristics. This occurs where experimenters themselves unintentionally influence participants' behaviour, perhaps by giving unconscious hints about whether they are expected to do well or badly. Even personal characteristics of experimenters, for example, their personality, age, gender and ethnicity, impact on the behaviour of participants.

Participants, too, can influence the results of an investigation. Participants who know that they are under investigation may worry about their level of performance; that is, they experience 'evaluation apprehension'. Participants want to make a good impression when doing something, or when being watched by someone they may respect or admire, and will often try to behave in ways they think are appropriate. This is referred to as the 'social desirability effect'.

A further participant effect is known as the 'Hawthorne effect', because it was first identified at the Hawthorne plant of the Western Electric Company in the United States (Roethlisberger and Dickson, 1939). In a study carried out by George Elton Mayo and colleagues between 1924 and 1932, the researchers were interested in factors that influence how hard people work, and had assumed that it would depend on the immediate work environment of employees, such as lighting and heating. They systematically manipulated a variety of these 'environmental variables', but no matter what they did, the chosen participants continued to work equally hard. The researchers concluded that the main causal variable was the fact that the employees felt special that they were chosen by the researchers to take part in the experiment. As the IV was the environmental conditions, this participant variable was in fact a confounding variable. Despite this, the findings were important for social science research and our understanding of participants' behaviour.

Given the huge impact that such variables can have on the results of any research investigation, can researchers do anything to try to, if not eliminate, at least reduce, their effects?

We have already looked at some of the ways to control such confounding variables as order effects by means of counterbalancing, and participant individual differences by means of random allocation. To attempt an elimination of demand characteristics, and experimenter effects, researchers use what they call 'single and double blind control', and 'deception'. We will see that the last method of eliminating potential extraneous variables leads to ethical concerns.

Demand characteristics can certainly be reduced if participants are not aware of which of the experimental conditions they are operating under. This would reduce the likelihood of them being able to guess what the aim of the experiment might be. Researchers refer to this as 'single-blind control'. For example, if the research investigation is about the development of a new pill, which it is hypothesised will reduce high blood pressure, the participants will not know whether they are in the condition receiving the pill, or whether they are in the condition receiving a placebo – for example, a sugar pill. This kind of control does not rule out experimenter effects, however.

A 'double-blind control' is where neither the participant nor the person who administers the experiment knows the hypothesis or which condition participants belong to. This control procedure attempts to deal with demand characteristics and experimenter effects. The researcher will be unable to reveal anything to the participants, either consciously or unconsciously, as they do not know what the outcome of the experiment is expected to be.

'Deception' involves keeping the aim of the experiment from participants. Again, it should be noted that although participants may not be accurate in their ideas about the purpose of the experiment, this may impact on behaviour. Perhaps the only way around this particular problem would be to carry out experiments without informing those under investigation. This now tends to be forbidden for ethical reasons (see Section 4 of this Chapter).

Evaluation
We have seen that a variety of attempts have been used by psychologists to attempt to control demand characteristics, experimenter effects and participant effects. It is probably safe to say that these variables will never be entirely eliminated. The best that researchers can hope for is that any likely effects have been considered and controlled for as far as possible. The possibility of demand characteristics or experimenter effects confounding the results should always be considered when data are analysed.

Correlation design and data analysis

There are many cases when researchers wish to study two variables, but cannot manipulate one and measure the other, as would be the case in the experimental method. For example, psychologists may wish to look at the effects of stress on illness, but it would be unethical and impractical to subject participants to long-term stress. Instead, psychologists could choose to study the relationship between two variables, non-experimentally by obtaining the necessary information from sources such as questionnaires, surveys or national statistics. Data gleaned from such methods are often termed correlational and are analysed and interpreted using correlational techniques.

Correlation relies on quantitative data, which simply means numbers. It is a statistical technique that measures the strength of relationship between two or more variables (rather than IV and DV, which are called co-variables). The purpose is to see whether there is a trend or pattern between the variables; if changes in one variable are related to changes in the other variable.

This may sound familiar. What then is the difference between this and an experiment? As mentioned above, a key feature of experiments is to attempt to establish a cause–effect relationship. It is very important to appreciate that when researchers speak about correlation and the relationship between variables, they are *not* speaking about a causal relationship between the co-variables.

This is because in some circumstances it may not be possible to undertake experimentation, due to practical or ethical considerations. In this case, there can be no manipulation or control of variables in order to establish any cause–effect relation. We cannot say that changes in one variable cause changes in the other since, for example, the reverse could be the case, or a third factor could cause both variables to change, or the result could be a complete coincidence. We may find a correlational link between levels of stress and levels of illness and, although it might seem that the stress was causing the illness, it would be unscientific to do so. All that we can say is that there may be an *association* between the two variables. This association may in fact coincide with results from other research, such as is the case between stress and health, but may actually be spurious and accidental as would be the case with an association between number of storks hatching in mainland Europe and birth rate in Britain.

Another possible interpretation of an apparent relationship between two variables is that a third variable may be impacting. For example, when mid-flight in an airplane, the association between fastening a seat belt on the appearance of the seat belt sign and the occurrence of air turbulence may give the impression that putting on the seat belt, or being prompted to do so, caused the bumpiness associated with air turbulence. However, a third variable, the movement of air and its impact on the movement of the plane is the cause of the bumpiness in this example and, indeed the switching on of the seat belt sign and our response to it.

Types of correlation

There are *two* types of correlation. A ‘positive’ correlation exists where the variables rise and fall together in direct relationship and a ‘negative’ correlation exists where as one variable rises, the other falls and vice versa. This association in terms of movement of variables is known as the ‘direction’ of correlation. Researchers are also interested in what they refer to as the ‘strength’ of a correlation, which is commonly represented by a numerical value ranging between the values 0.00 and +1.00 for positive correlation and between 0.00 and -1.00 for negative correlation. These numerical values are what are known as ‘correlation coefficients’. A correlation coefficient indicates the ‘strength’ of correlation.

Thus, correlation coefficients can be visually represented by mapping the value as a point on a **Diagram 2/1.3**.

Diagram 2/1.3

The Relationship between 'Strength' and 'Direction' in Correlation

-1.00 ------------------------------------ 0.00 ---------------------------------- +1.00

There is a correspondence between the numerical values ('strength') and the 'direction' of a correlation:

Perfect negative	negative	zero	positive	Perfect positive

-1.00 --------------------------------------- 0.00 ---------------------------------- +1.00

As is the case with experimentation, researchers using the correlational technique develop hypotheses – 'correlational hypotheses' – in an attempt to predict a relationship/association between two or more variables. Like experimental hypotheses, they can be 'directional correlational hypothesis' and 'non-directional correlational hypothesis'. A directional hypothesis states that there will a *positive* correlation between Variable A and Variable B or that there will be a *negative* correlation between Variable A and Variable B. A non-directional hypothesis simply states that there *will be* a correlation between Variable A and Variable B.

Unlike experimental hypotheses that predict changes to a variable, correlational hypotheses predict associations or 'similarity'. Let us look at some examples of correlational hypotheses.

'Non-directional correlational hypothesis':

- There will be a correlation between the number of hours of study and examination grade.

'Directional correlational hypotheses':

- There will be a positive correlation between the number of hours of study and examination grade.
- There will be a negative correlation between the number of miles driven and the amount of petrol left.

As is the case with experimentation, it is the 'null hypothesis' that is tested.

'Non-directional correlational ('null') hypothesis':

- There will be no correlation between the number of hours of study and examination grade.

'Directional correlational (null) hypotheses':

- There will be no positive correlation between the number of hours of study and examination grade.
- There will be no negative correlation between the number of miles driven and the amount of petrol left.

Correlations are usually illustrated by 'scattergrams' (also known as 'scattergraphs' or 'scatter diagrams'). The scattergram provides for graphic illustration of correlational association between two variables ('co-variables'). There are two axes: a vertical x-axis and a horizontal y-axis. One variable is mapped on the x-axis and the other variable on the y-axis. Plotting the related values of the two variables produces the points on the graph. The measurements are related in the sense that they usually come from the same participant.

For example, the researcher might predict that if a pupil is proficient at reading they may be equally proficient at spelling. They then might give five participants a reading test, followed by a spelling test. This might produce the following data:

Table 2/1.6

Data relating to Participants' Reading and Spelling Test Scores

Participant score	Reading test score	Spelling test
P1	8	5
P2	4	6
P3	9	8
P4	3	7
P5	6	7

Plotted on a scattergram, the data in **Table 2/1.6** translates into the following diagram (**Diagram 1.4**).

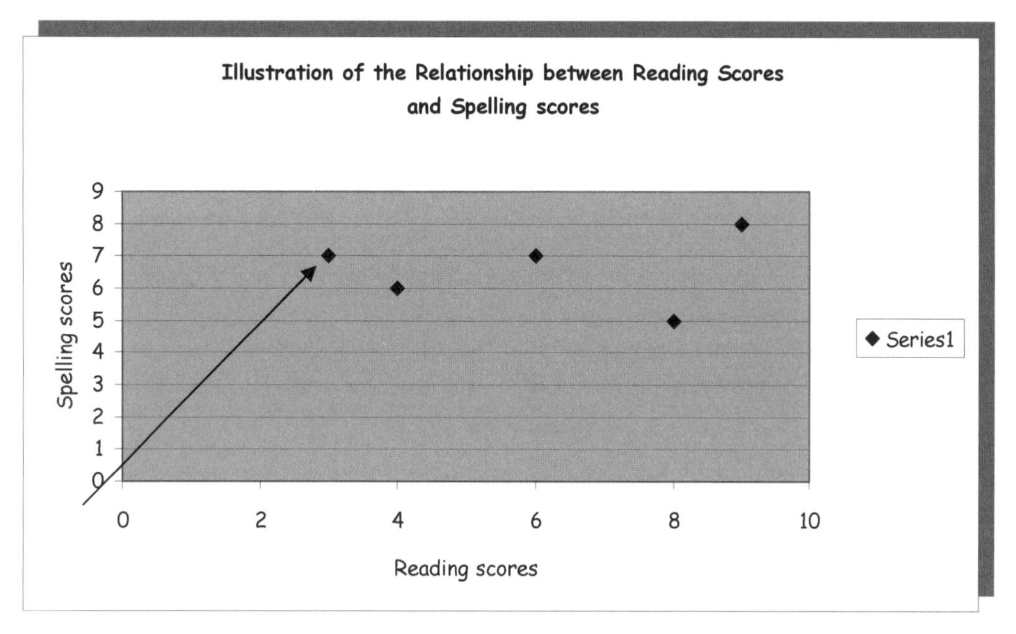

Each point on the scattergram represents a pair of scores. For example, the point indicated by the arrow, represents a spelling score of 7 and a reading score of 3. These are the scores achieved by participant number 4. The other scores are obtained in the same way – each represents a participant's level on each variable (in this case, their score on each test).

The way that the scattergrams look gives us a quick visual summary of the relationship between the variables in terms of direction and strength. If the points appear spread randomly across the scattergram with no obvious pattern or direction, we could assume that there is no relationship between the variables. This is called a 'zero ('no strength') correlation'. The correlation coefficient in this case would, in numerical form, be 0.00. An example is shown below in **Diagram 2/1.5**, where co-variable A represents IQ scores and co-variable B represents shoe size.

Diagram 2/1.5

Illustration of the Relationship between Shoe Size and IQ: a Zero Correlation = 0.00

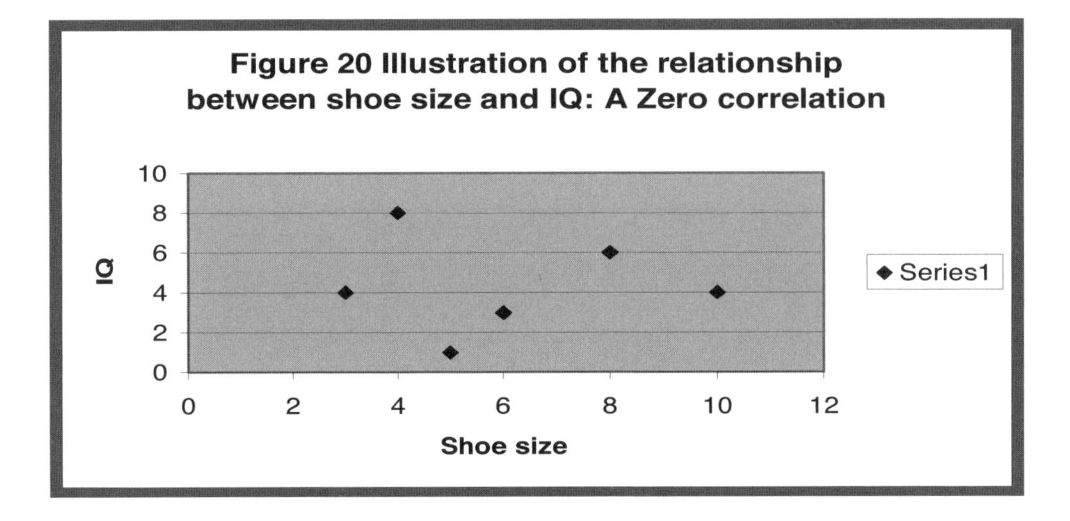

If a scattergram shows a straight line it represents an exact one-to-one relationship between the pairs of scores. The pattern obtained might be as indicated in **Diagram 2/1.6**.

Diagram 2/1.6

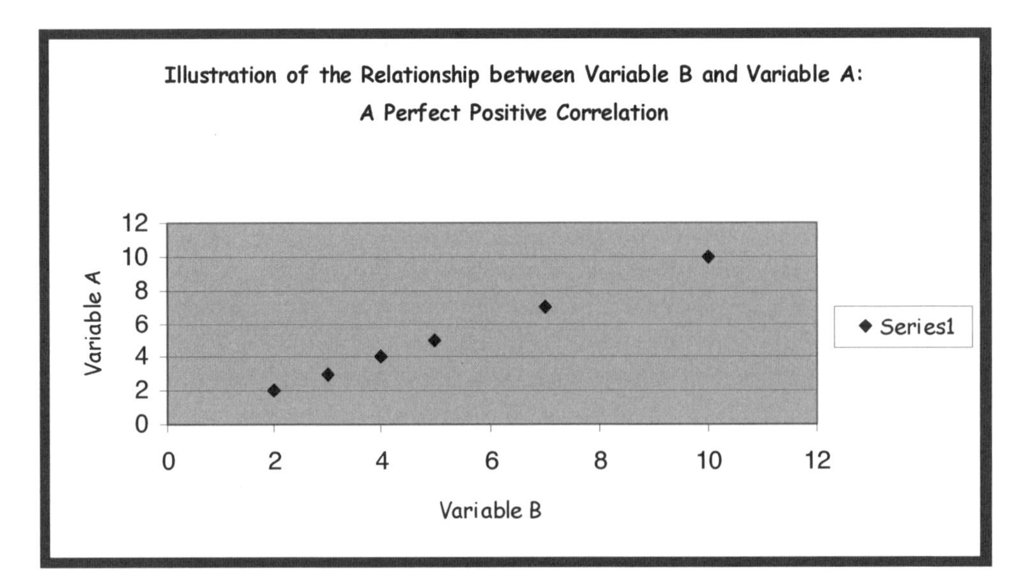

Diagram 2/1.6 indicates a positive direction, which is a very strong one – a correlation coefficient = +1.00.

A situation where each of the scores on one variable is high, but the scores on each of the corresponding variables are low by the same amount produces what is known as a 'perfect negative correlation', as illustrated in **Diagram 2/1.7**.

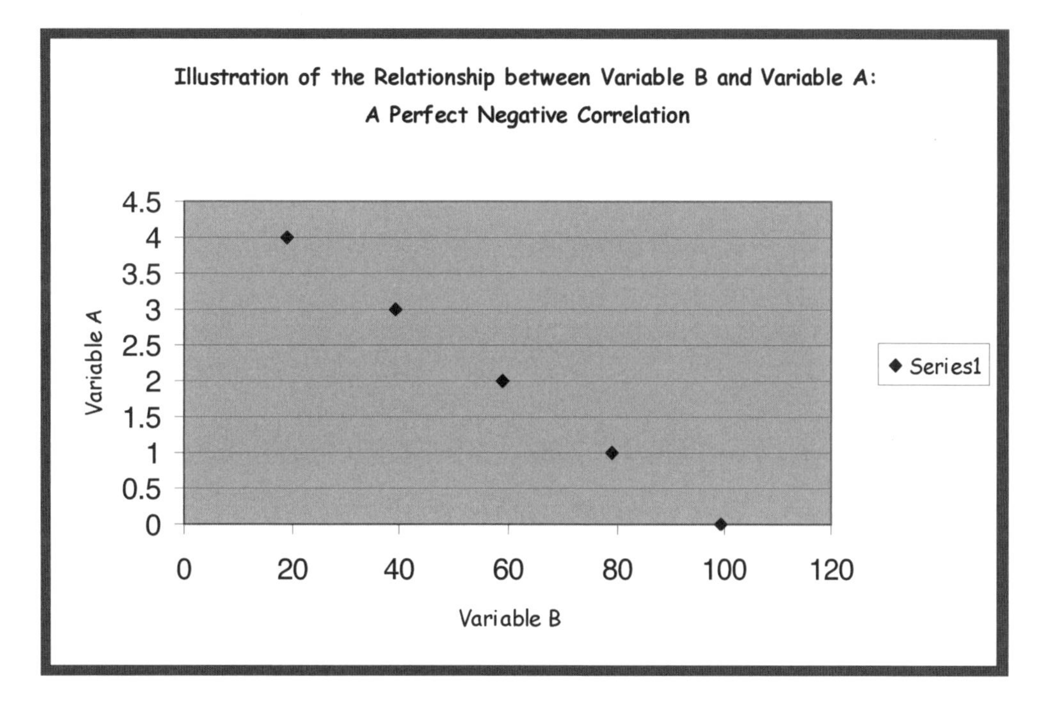

Diagram 2/1.7 indicates a negative direction, which is a very strong one – a correlation coefficient = -1.00.

Another way of describing a perfect negative correlation (direction) is to say that there is an *inverse relationship* between variable A and variable B. That is, when one variable increases by a certain amount, the other decreases by the same amount. An example of this type of relationship might be if an aircraft on the runway has a full load of fuel, then the further it progresses through the flight the less fuel will be left in its fuel tanks.

With regard to the study of human behaviour, however, researchers very rarely encounter perfect correlations since humans tend not to behave in automated and mechanical ways. A scattergram representing human behaviour, therefore, is much more likely to show more moderate direction for positive and negative correlation:

Diagram 2/1.8

Illustration of the Relationship between IQ and Chastisement

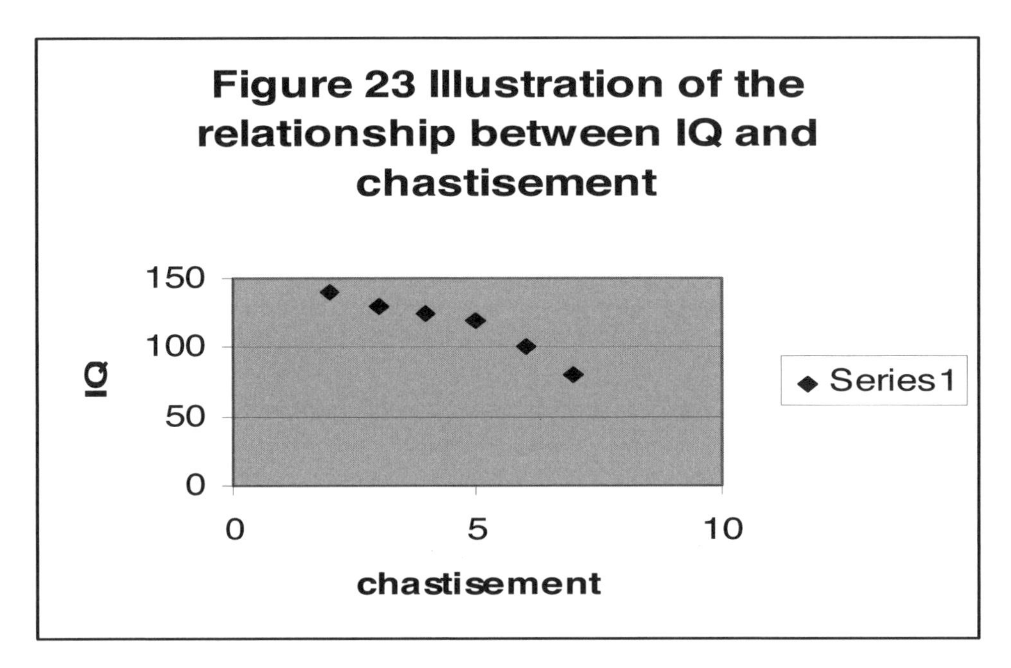

Diagram 2/1.8 indicates a correlation of -0.88. (Note: this numerical value is an estimate. The only way that we can know the exact value of a correlation coefficient is to calculate it by using an appropriate statistical formula.)

Similarly, the relationship between variable B and variable A: is shown in **Diagram 2/1.9**, which is a positive correlation – a correlation of +0.75. (Note: this numerical value is an estimate. The only way that we can know the exact value of a correlation coefficient is to calculate it by using an appropriate statistical formula.)

Diagram 2/1.9

Illustration of the Relationship between IQ and Praise: a Positive Correlation

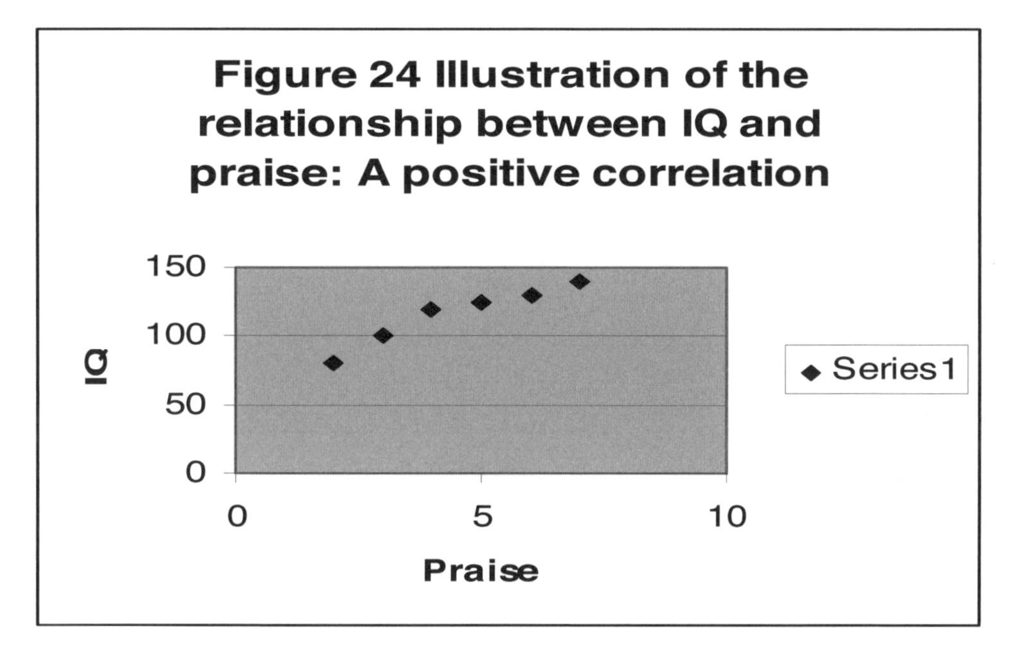

As can be seen from looking at **Diagram 2/1.5** to **Diagram 2/1.9**, a negative correlation occurs when a high score on one variable tends to associate with a low score on the other. Scores on such a scattergram would generally spread from the top left down to the bottom right. A positive correlation means that high scores on one variable tend to be associated with high scores on the other variable. Remember, this has nothing to do with cause. We are not saying that a high score on, for example, variable A, causes a high score on variable B. Scores on such a scattergram will be seen to be spread generally from the bottom left of the diagram to the top right.

It should also be noted that it is often the case when plotting scattergrams that some points lie away from most of the others, as indicated in the figure below. This point is known as an ‘outlier’ and is indicative of the fact that anomalies occur in human behaviour.

Diagram 2/1.10

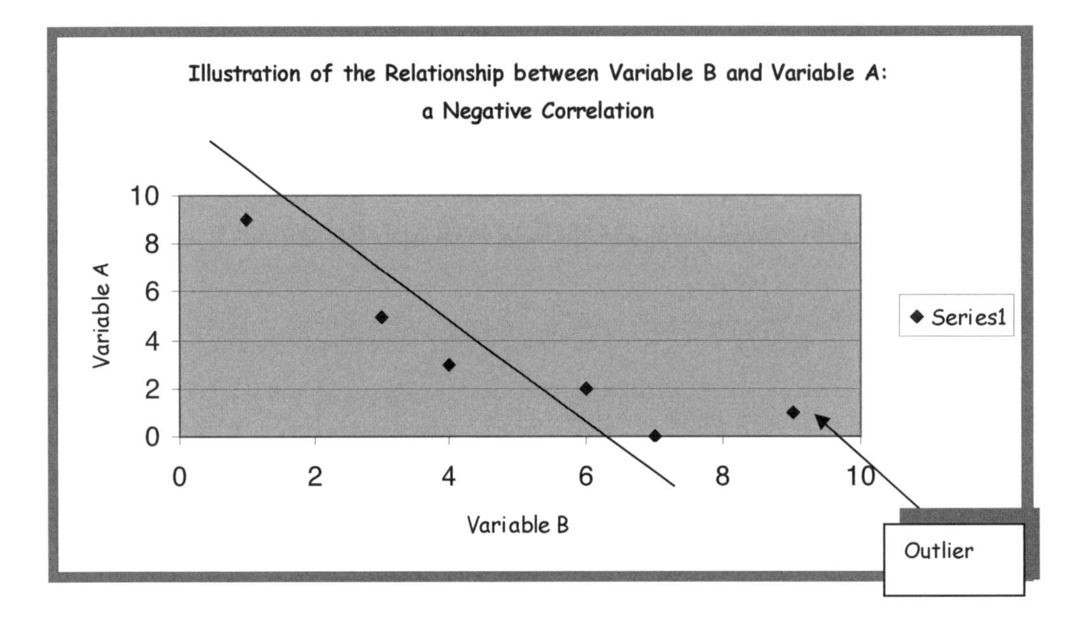

Also, researchers may or may not draw a line on the scattergram, which would be known as 'the line of best fit'. This provides a summary of the correlation and its position can be calculated on a computer by taking the shortest possible distance between the highest and lowest points. It may be that several points fall on this line but this is not always the case. The distance the points as a group lie away from the line indicates the strength of the correlation. The closer the points are to the line, the *stronger* the correlation, the greater the numerical value of a correlation coefficient would be. If all of the points lie on the line, this is the strongest possible correlation, known as a perfect correlation.

As we have seen, scattergrams are a visual indication of the *strength* of a correlation. It should be noted, however, that scattergrams provide visual representation of 'descriptive' statistics and, therefore, are usually supplemented with 'inferential statistics'. In other words, statistics that test the *significance* of the relationship.

Evaluation of correlational designs

- Although correlational designs are often used in psychology to assess possible association between variables, psychologists usually employ a number of additional methods and techniques to find out more about the relationship between the co-variables than just association.

- Correlation is, therefore, most useful to researchers in that it assesses the 'direction' (positive or negative) and 'strength' of any relationship between two or more variables and thereby indicates whether further investigation should be taken into the nature of the relationship shown. Strong correlations would suggest that further investigation is appropriate, whereas 'zero' correlations (0.00) indicate that variables are entirely unrelated and unworthy of further investigation.
- Correlations also enable psychologists to estimate the likely changes in one variable of changes in the associated variable.
- Correlation is often used simply because it is more practical to collect data in this way than by experimentation. Correlation may also be the only way in which researchers can ethically investigate a topic.
- The main disadvantage of correlations is that they *do not* assess causality. As stated above, an association between two variables does not indicate that one causes the other. Changes in the two variables may be caused by a third unknown variable. It may be possible to identify the precise nature of the relationship, but only through further research.

Box 2/1.4

Activity

Look at the data below. It shows the number of assignments that students completed over the year, and the mark they achieved in their examination.

Student	No. of assignments	Exam mark achieved (per cent)
1	13	73
2	4	47
3	14	13
4	13	70
5	6	57
6	5	30

Questions:

Draw a scattergram by computer (e.g. in Excel) or on graph paper for the above data. Remember to label the axes and title the graph.

1. Is there a relationship between the two variables?
2. If there is a relationship, is it in a positive or negative direction?
3. From the scattergram, estimate if the relationship is a strong or weak one.
4. Explain why you think it is strong or weak.
5. What is the name for that mark achieved by student 3?

The non-experimental methods

Having looked at the experimental method and the technique of correlation we will now look at a variety of additional research methods, which are categorised as 'non-experimental methods'. We begin with looking at surveys, questionnaires and interviews.

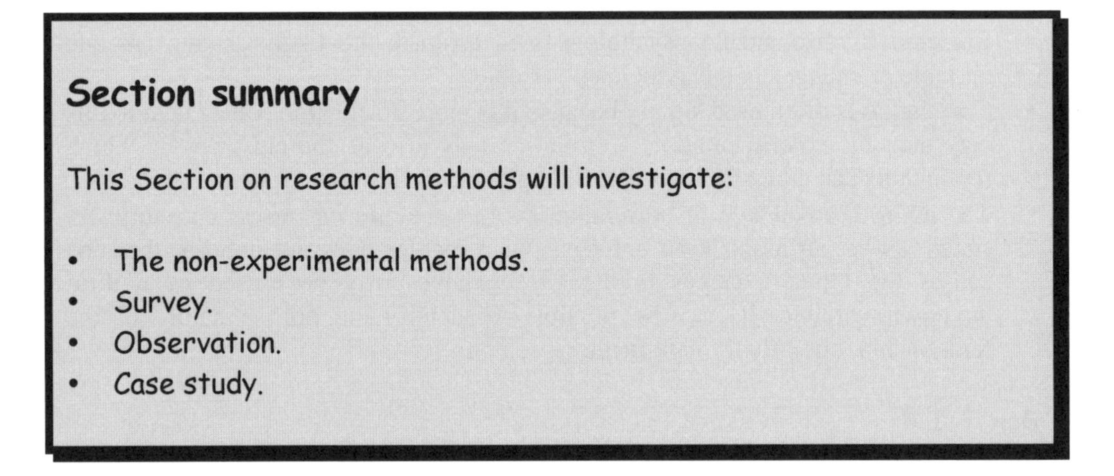

Section summary

This Section on research methods will investigate:

- The non-experimental methods.
- Survey.
- Observation.
- Case study.

Surveys and interviews

The 'survey' method of data collection may include the use of questionnaires and interviews in order to obtain information from people. There are a number of steps in conducting a survey as depicted in **Diagram 2/1.11** below.

A 'survey' can be descriptive or explanatory. 'Descriptive surveys' describe the features of the population under investigation, for example, the amount of households in the UK that have a home computer, or which popular magazines are purchased by young people aged 17-19 years.

'Explanatory surveys' may seek to test an hypothesis or provide explanations for relationships between variables. For example, researchers may attempt to identify and explain any relationship between personal income and voting behaviour.

Surveys using the questionnaire method typically involve collecting a large amount of data from a lot of people. It is, therefore, important to identify the target population and researchers will usually take measures to ensure that the sample of participants surveyed is *representative* (see below). Data can be collected over any area, but are usually gathered in a short period of time and only provide a snapshot of behaviour or characteristics at that time. The data are normally 'quantitative' – numerical – and are standardised by asking all participants the same questions.

Diagram 2/1.11

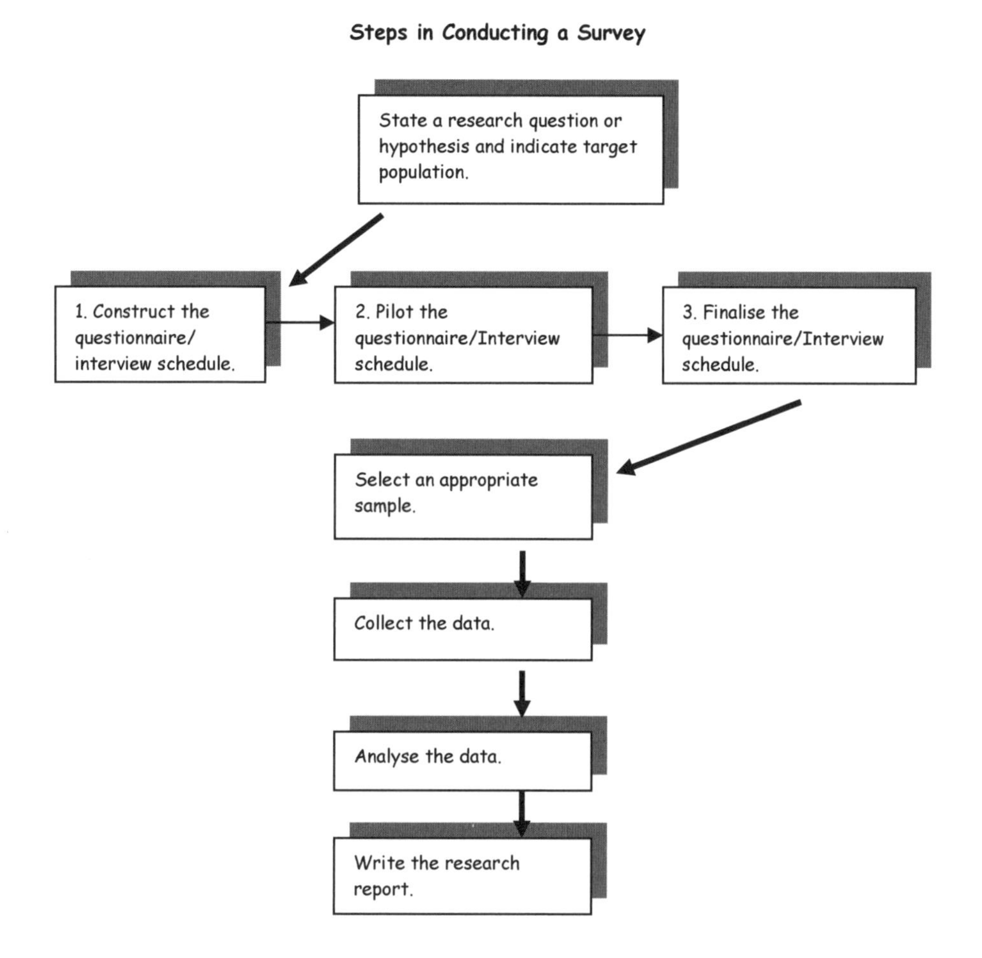

Researchers obtain a representative sample by following a series of stages. First, they find a relevant population. They then try to get what is called a 'sample frame'. This is usually a fully comprehensive list of peoples' names in the relevant population.

However, even in such sampling frames as the Electoral Register there are omissions that can seriously distort the sample. Indeed, the only fully comprehensive and representative sample is the Census, as it records all the members of the population in the UK. Notwithstanding these problems of sampling, once representative sampling has been achieved, generalisation is possible. An example of this is when pollsters predict the winner of political elections from relatively small samples.

Designing the questions to be used in the questionnaire is also very important. Considerable care needs to be exercised in order to avoid using the following:

- Leading, or biased, questions.
- Unwarranted assumptions, e.g. assuming that all participants in Scotland will be Scottish or that all children will have two parents in the household.
- Double-barrelled questions – two questions in one, e.g. 'Are you happy with the present education system or do you want it changed?'
- Strong/emotive language, e.g. 'Do you believe that criminals are nasty, evil, people?'

As is the case with experiments, variables in a survey need to be operationalised *before* they can be manipulated or measured. If, for example, researchers wished to measure racism, they would have to come up with an operational definition that would allow that concept to be measured.

Once the variables have been defined, the questions to be posed in the questionnaire are designed.

Closed questions require set answers like 'yes', 'no', 'don't know' and so on and responses are coded in order to calculate measurements accurately. Further depth or elaboration on responses can be obtained by asking more 'open' questions that use prompts such as 'please explain your answer'. These questions are difficult to codify specifically, although they can be placed in general categories such as 'positive/negative' responses or 'in agreement/disagreement' with the proposition contained in the closed question. Many questionnaires will be a mixture of closed and open questions.

Other issues relating to the design of questionnaires should also be considered by researchers. They are illustrated below, in **Diagram 2/1.12** on design issues.

Administering surveys
Researchers have to decide how they are going to give the questionnaires to respondents. This can be done in four main ways: face-to-face, over the telephone, by post, or over the Internet.

Postal surveys
This is a questionnaire, which is sent to respondents through the mail. This is useful if the researcher wishes to gather data from respondents from different parts of the country. A problem with this type of questionnaire is the low response rate. Rarely do researchers achieve a response rate of 50 per cent or above. This impacts on how data can be interpreted. Results may be biased in the sense that there may be

differences between those respondents who have returned the questionnaire, and those who have not.

Diagram 2/1.12

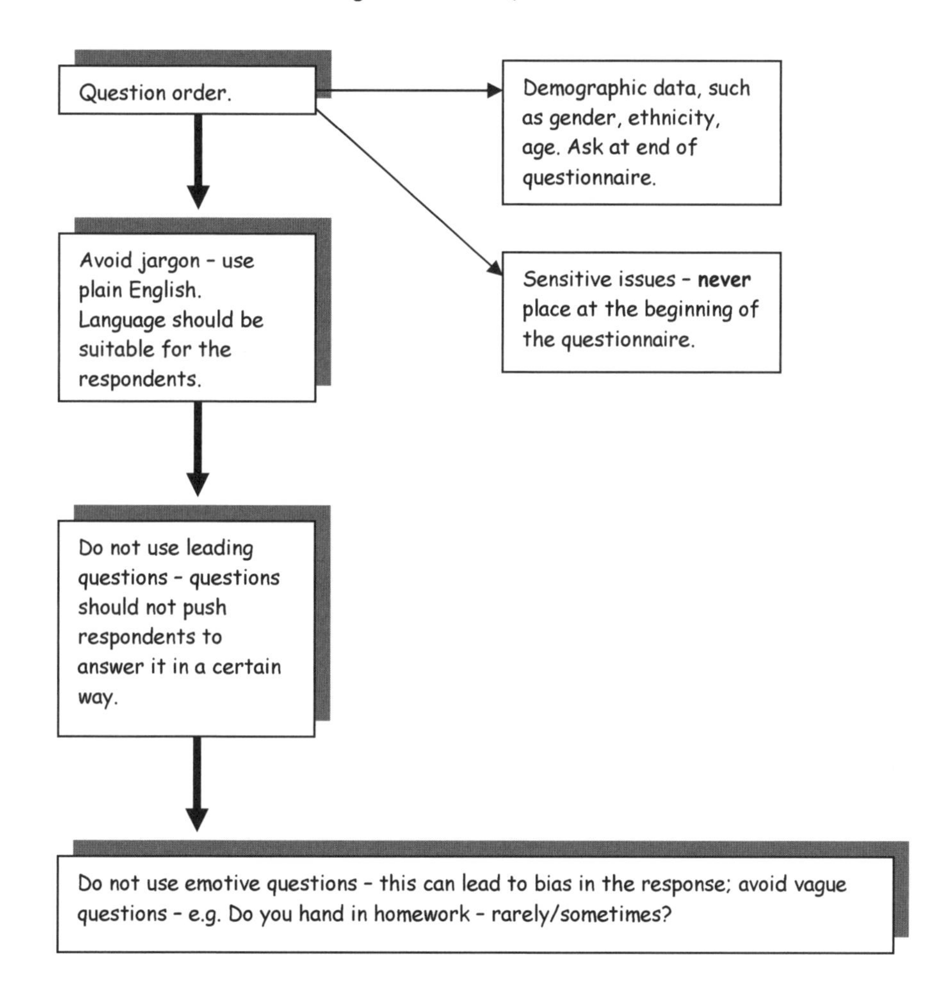

An evaluation of the advantages and disadvantages of using questionnaires as a data gathering technique is summarised below in **Diagram 2/1.13** and **Diagram 2/1.14**.

Diagram 2/1.13

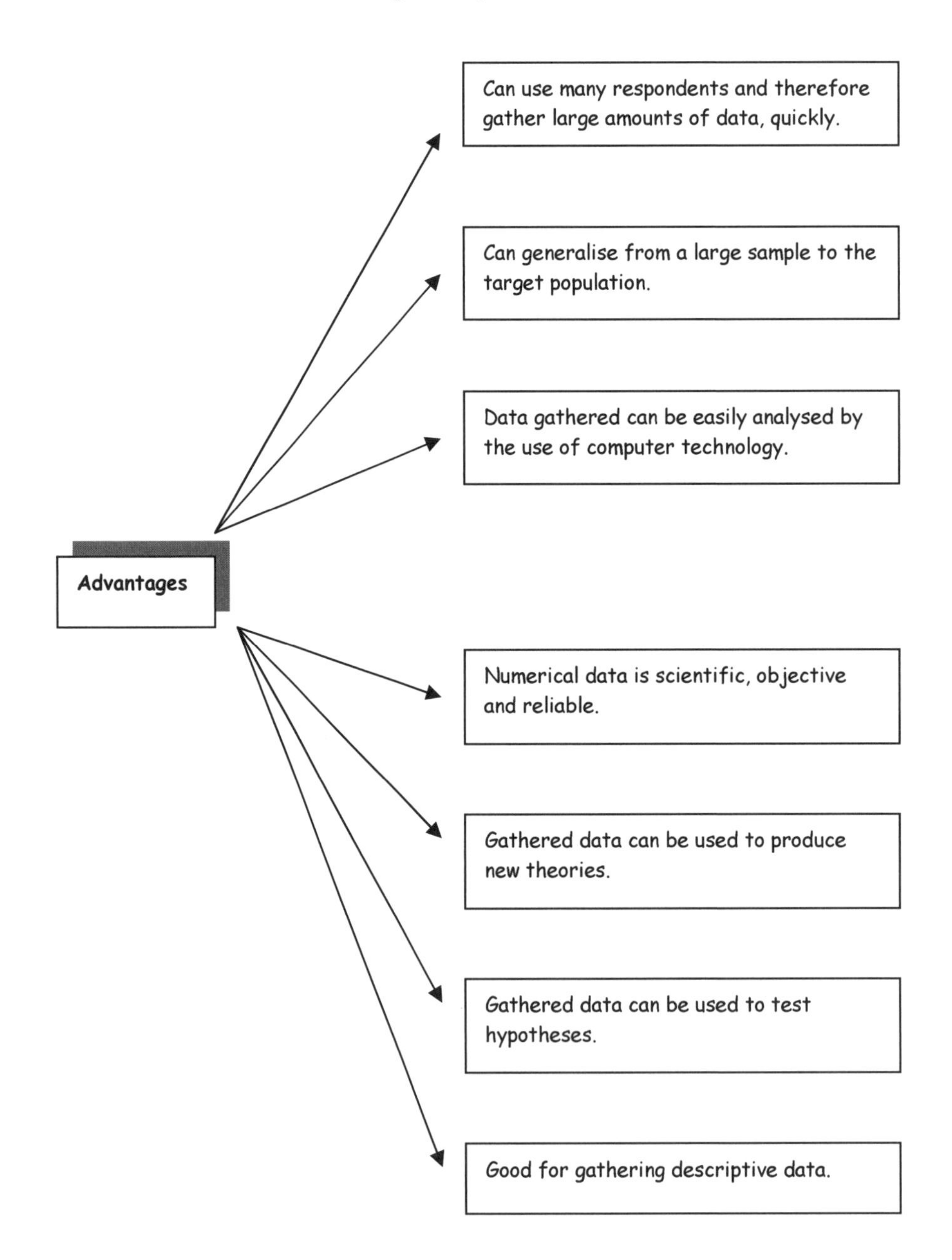

Diagram 2/1.14

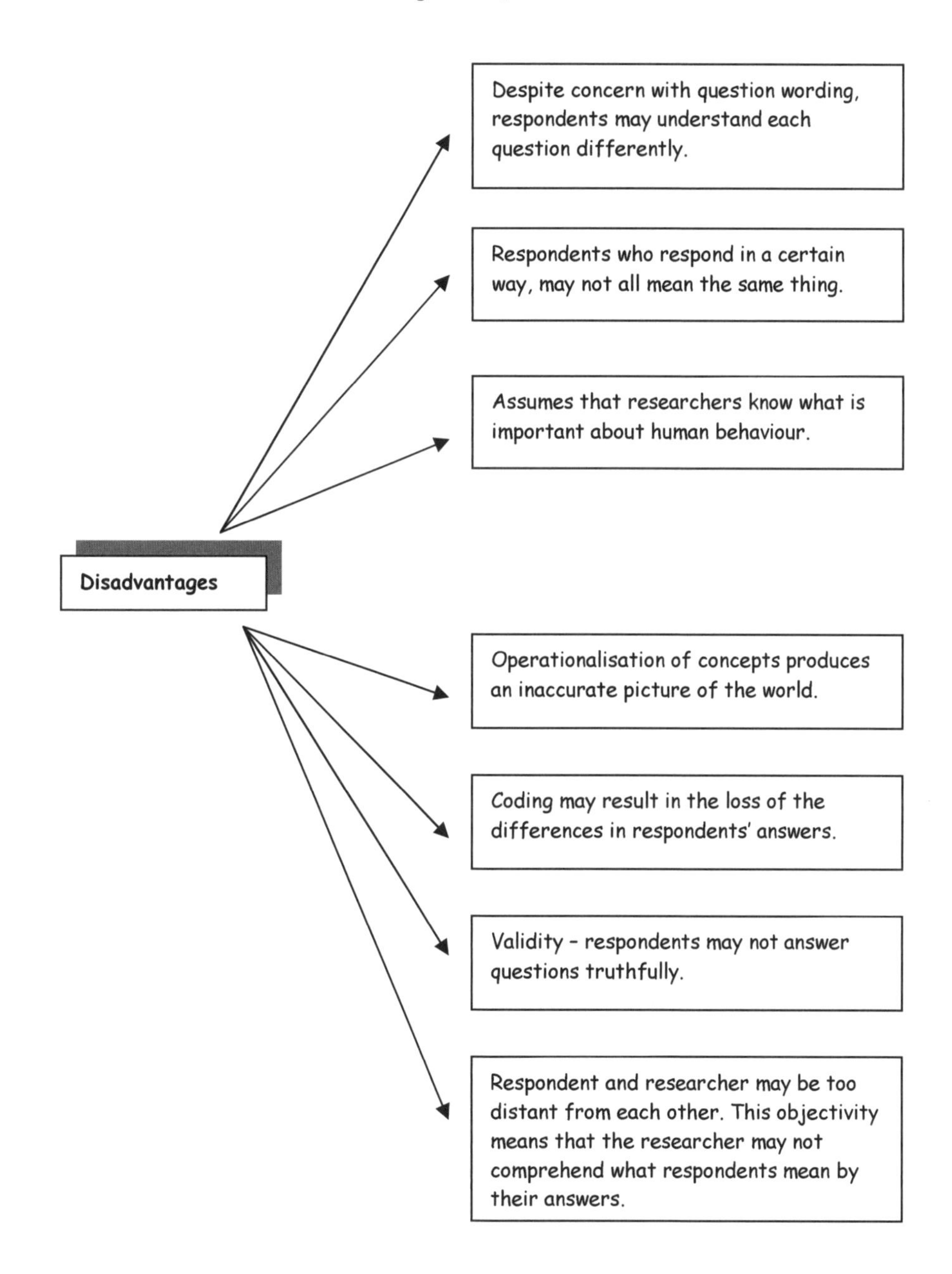

Telephone surveys

Market research organisations often use this technique. It is very likely that they will not get a representative sample. Consequently, psychologists would tend not to use this method of administering questionnaires.

Internet surveys

The Internet is useful in that it provides a cheap, paperless way of administering a survey, and can, theoretically at least, reach respondents all over the world. However, it is limited in that the researcher will have limited control over who completes the survey. This might lead to a non-representative sample, especially as the Internet is used more by the young than the old, and by those who are financially better off. If, however, the target population of the study was, for example, young professionals, this may not present a problem.

Interviews

A technique often associated with the survey method is the 'interview'. In social surveys, the most common method of gathering data is by personal interviewing. The term, 'interview', is a broad term, but the most common type used in surveys is the 'formal interview'. This is where set questions are asked of a number of respondents and answers are recorded similarly. Interviewers are trained to follow the researcher's instructions relating to, for example, the order in which the questions are asked. The recording of responses depends on the type of questions being asked; that is, whether open or closed questions. Formal interviews are also known as 'structured interviews'.

Researchers may also use 'informal' or 'unstructured interviews'. This is where the interviewer may deviate from the set questions, alter the sequence in which they are asked, or change the wording of the questions to fit the context. In very informal interviews, there may be no set questions, but, rather a number of key points that provide a rough guide to the interviewer. In practice, psychologists tend to use interviews that blend the formal and informal approaches, as **Diagram 2/1.15** illustrates.

Diagram 2/1.15

Illustration of various types of interview

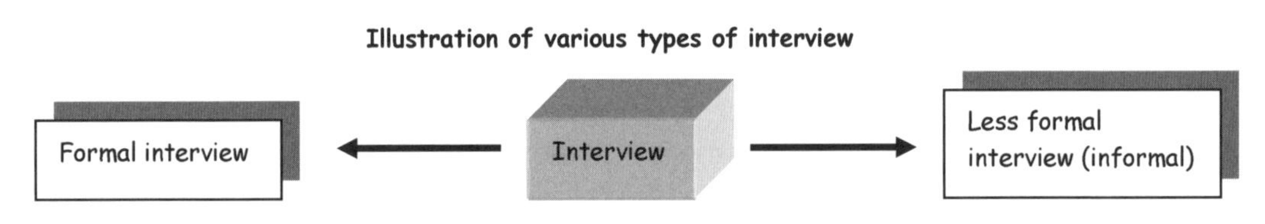

The main strength of formal interviewing is that since all respondents are asked exactly the same questions in the same order, the researcher can be reasonably sure that respondent's answers are comparable. As such, all the answers can be added together to get an idea of what the respondents in general are saying. This type of interview produces 'quantitative' data. Another benefit of using the structured interview is that the interviewer is able to help the interviewee respond fully to questions.

The interviewer can also intervene if the interviewee does not understand a question. As with experimentation, however, the very presence of the interviewer may influence the responses of the respondent. This is known as 'interviewer bias'. The researcher may influence respondents through, for example, their age, gender, or ethnicity.

Informal interviews are useful as the conversation may develop naturally and there is more scope for the development of rapport between interviewer and interviewee. The interviewer would, however, have to be careful that the required areas are covered and may from time to time have to bring the conversation back to the subject under investigation. Informal interviews provide more enriched, 'deeper', answers from respondents but, consequently, the 'qualitative' data they produce are more difficult to analyse.

In other words, answers obtained from informal interviews are *more* valid, but *less* reliable. The opposite is true of formal interviews; that is, they are *more* reliable but *less* valid. (See **Diagram 2/1.16**, below, for an illustrative example.)

As could be expected from subjective self-report data, responses in interviews may be neither reliable nor valid. Respondents may lie, exaggerate, be inaccurate, or answer in accordance with what the interviewer wants, or expects, to hear.

Observation

All research involves observation to some extent. In fact it is often everyday observations of human behaviour that inspire researchers as to what to study. Our attention here though is on the observational method as the main means of obtaining information in non-experimental research.

Diagram 2/1.16

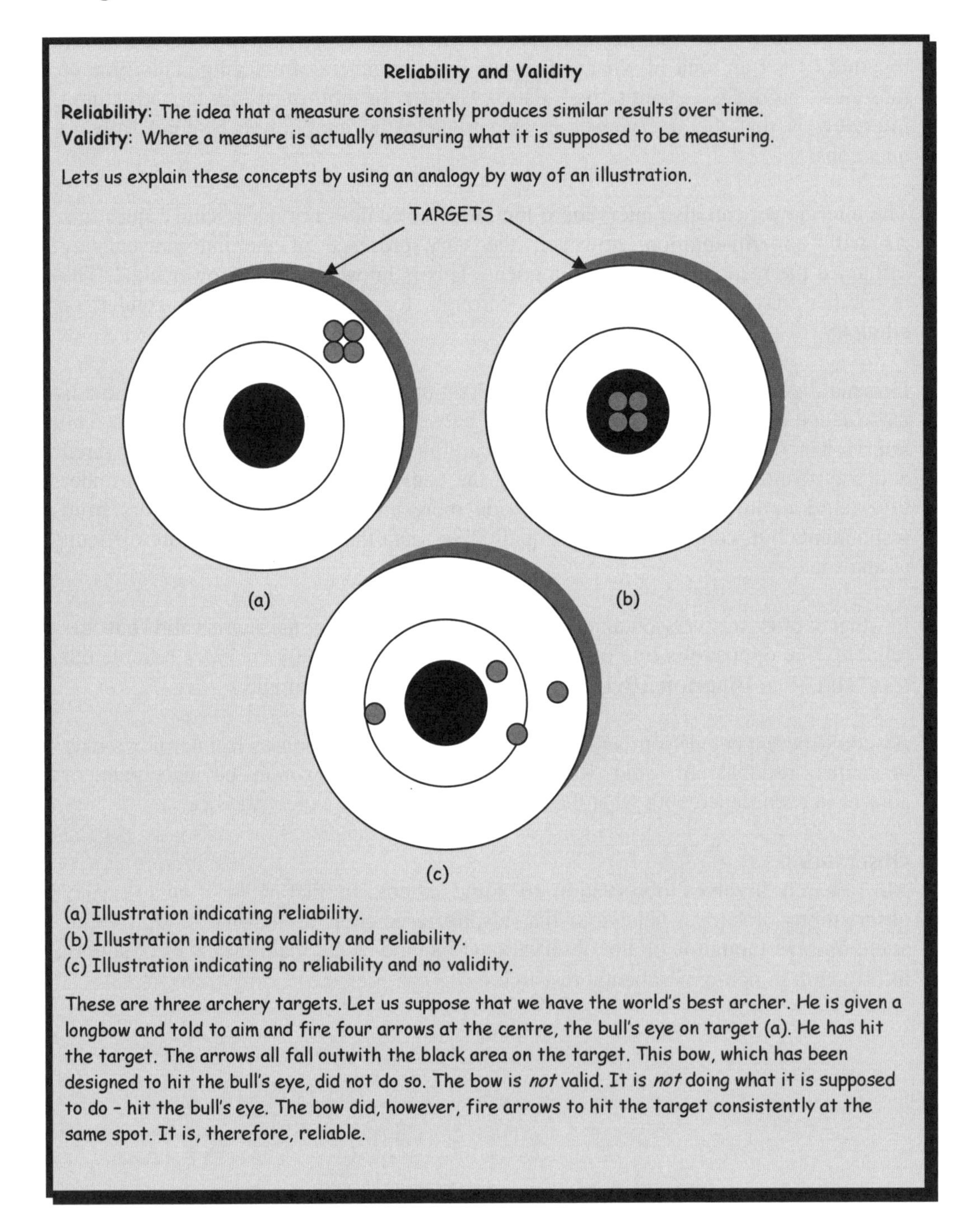

Reliability and Validity

Reliability: The idea that a measure consistently produces similar results over time.
Validity: Where a measure is actually measuring what it is supposed to be measuring.

Lets us explain these concepts by using an analogy by way of an illustration.

(a) Illustration indicating reliability.
(b) Illustration indicating validity and reliability.
(c) Illustration indicating no reliability and no validity.

These are three archery targets. Let us suppose that we have the world's best archer. He is given a longbow and told to aim and fire four arrows at the centre, the bull's eye on target (a). He has hit the target. The arrows all fall outwith the black area on the target. This bow, which has been designed to hit the bull's eye, did not do so. The bow is *not* valid. It is *not* doing what it is supposed to do - hit the bull's eye. The bow did, however, fire arrows to hit the target consistently at the same spot. It is, therefore, reliable.

The archer then tries a different bow. As before, he aims and fires, this time at target (b). This time all four arrows hit the bull's eye. This bow is much better. It has done what it is supposed to do - hit the bull's eye. It *is* valid. It *is* also reliable, that is, it is **consistently** hitting the bull's eye. Therefore, if the bow is valid it must be also reliable.

Archery target (c) demonstrates that this bow and arrow is neither reliable *nor* valid. Neither is doing what they have been designed to do. Even worse, they are *not* consistent either.

To view the above in relation to psychology, reliability refers to the idea that a measure gives results that are consistent time after time. Validity is where a measure is actually measuring what it says it is measuring.

One way to look at the method of observation is to look at a number of key features associated with it.

Setting

The setting refers to where the observation is to take place. As with experiments, this could be a laboratory of some type, or it could be the participant's everyday environment such as home or work. As we saw in relation to experiments, discussion of levels of ecological validity is relevant here also. Researchers must choose between the control over situational variables in a laboratory that enhances internal validity and the greater ecological validity of the natural environment, but detracts from the ability to have a high level of internal validity.

Structured observation

If the researcher wishes to collect quantitative data, a 'structured ('systematic') observation' will be used. For example, if the researcher wishes to investigate 'disruptive' behaviour in the classroom, behaviour will be categorised by observers using what is referred to as an 'observation schedule' of behavioural categories. This is really a *checklist* of a variety of categories of behaviour, such as 'chatting' and 'passing notes in class'. The observer devises the checklist before research begins and simply ticks the appropriate category each time the behaviour is observed in practice.

In order to interpret results, the researcher will have 'operationalised' the behaviour categories. In the above example, 'chatting' in the classroom may be defined as talking during a lesson, which involves at least two participants for at least 30 seconds without significant pauses.

The *checklist* referred to above might look something like the example given in **Table 2/1.7**, below.

Table 2/1.7

An Example of an Observation Schedule

Participant	Chatting	Number of times occurred	Passing notes	Number of times occurred
1				
2				
3				
*				
*				
*				

The observers will need to be trained in the use of the observation schedule, to ensure that they adequately and consistently record the desired information. Thus, 'observer reliability' is ensured. If more than one observer is used, it is important that all observers record the behaviour similarly, thus producing 'inter-observer reliability'. The degree of such consistency can be measured using correlation.

Perhaps the main weakness of using structured observation relates to the use of the observation schedule since, as indicated in the example in **Table 2/1.7**, the observer only records behaviour that falls into the specified categories, thus precluding the recording of other, potentially important, behaviour. In order to limit the possibility of this occurring, a pilot observation would be conducted to establish appropriate categories of behaviour.

Also, since it is the researchers who interpret the behaviour, the participants have no opportunity to say why they behaved in the way they did. We cannot get an insight how the participants saw what they did or why they did it. If this information is important to the researcher they are more likely to use 'participant observation'.

Participant observation

Participant observation, as the name suggests, involves the participation of the observer in the situation under investigation. This method focuses on gathering qualitative, in-depth, information from the experience of the observer and other participants and does not use observation schedules or pre-specified categories of behaviour.

This ensures that observers are able to gather a much wider variety of data and a common feature of this approach is that there tends to be a merging of data gathering and data analysis. The data obtained by the researcher is interpreted and then more data is gathered to help illuminate the early findings. In this approach, the researcher lives or works in the observed setting.

Before beginning participant observation, the researcher has to decide how they are going to approach the group they are interested in and whether the research will be 'overt' – openly declared to the group that the observer is a researcher – or 'covert' – where the researcher does *not* reveal their true identity. A problem associated with the former is that people may act differently (see demand characteristics). In the latter case, there are ethical problems attached to integrating with a group and observing them under false pretences, regardless of the fact that the method can be highly effective in gauging 'real life' behaviour (see Section 4 on ethics in research).

A middle ground is sometimes found by informing participants that one of the group members is a researcher, but withholding the hypothesis and the fact that he/she is a psychologist. Even in the case of overt participant observation, 'observer effects' can be reduced by the full participation of the observer in group activities, dress codes and conversations.

Diagram 2/1.17

Participant Observation: Overt and Covert

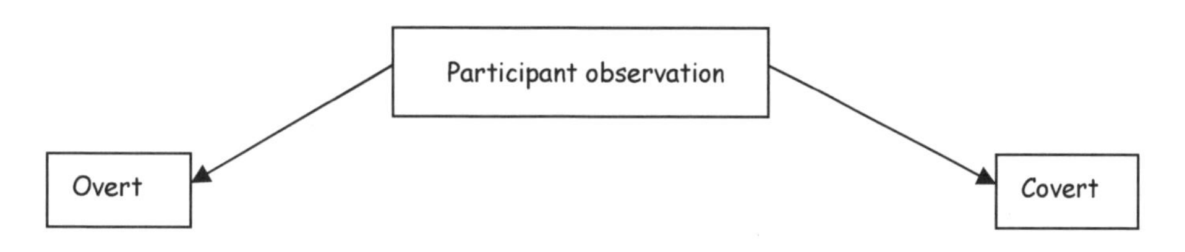

A classic example of covert participant observation was Rosenhan's (1973) study of life in a psychiatric hospital, in which Rosenhan and several other observers secured admission to the hospital by faking symptoms of mental illness. Generally, researchers using this method tend to gather data based on informal interviews, notes that they have taken, and their own interpretations of their situation. Many participant observation studies combine a variety of methods. For example, they may use in-depth interviews, or even set up field experiments.

A significant advantage of participant observation is that given the fact that the researcher is close to the setting of the research, there is a tendency not to miss any 'important' behaviour. The proximity of the researcher in relation to the participants makes for a more intimate, or 'empathic', understanding of meanings and intentions attached to modes of behaviour. The researchers will have a clearer idea of why participants behaved the way that they did.

Such proximity, however, can compromise observer impartiality and so participant observers have to be careful to strike a balance between being distant and aloof from other participants and so personally involved as to impact on their observations, judgements, or interpretation of results.

Involvement of observer
The degree of involvement of participant observers varies widely. At the lowest level of involvement the observer would neither interact with or be seen by the participants. Observation in this case could be conducted through a one-way mirror or television camera, somewhat similar to how contestants are observed in Channel Four's popular *Big Brother* 'reality TV' programme. The next level of involvement would be where the observer interacts with participants, but where she/he is not a member of the group. The greatest level of involvement is where the observer is a full participant observer. In the latter case, the recording of data is problematic as it would be difficult to do so whilst operating as a full group member. One way to get round this might be to take on a role in the group that enables them to do so. For example, an educational psychologist conducting research might take on the role of a classroom helper. Observations could then be recorded under the guise of doing ordinary paperwork. Alternatively, participant observers have to simply rely on memory and record information as soon as it is possible to do so, which may cast doubt on the accuracy of the information recalled.

Disclosure
As mentioned above, 'observer effects' may occur when it is disclosed to participants that they are under observation. An obvious way then to avoid this methodological problem would be not to disclose this information. This, however, raises ethical issues and whilst modern research practice would be to always seek consent from participants to conduct and publish the results of research, the question remains over *when* to do so. As always there will be extreme examples to consider, but these are useful in helping setting the parameters to the debate. For example, if a researcher was observing general crowd behaviour at a large sporting occasion, it would generally be agreed that seeking consent from all crowd members would be impractical and unnecessary due to the amount of participants and the fact that they would be behaving in a 'naturally occurring' environment. If, however, the researcher wished to covertly video individual fans reactions to, say, the deliberately racist chants of a nearby researcher posing as a fellow fan, disclosure would be necessary since an individual can be clearly identified. The latter example is useful in

that it illustrates the difference between journalistic 'research' and the scientific research undertaken by psychologists. Journalists often do not disclose their true identity in such situations and often air results without the consent of 'participants'. Psychologists would consider this unethical. In general, if at all possible, modern researchers should acquire consent from participants to publish the findings of the research, debrief them when the observation has been completed and apologise and/or make recompense for any inconvenience caused.

There is also the issue that participants may have disclosed much more information to an individual whom they thought was a full member of the group than they would do to a researcher. Researchers may, in this case, guarantee participant anonymity when publishing results and present results to participants for their scrutiny and permission to use, before any report is placed in the public domain.

Again, as is the case with all research methods, there is the inevitable trade-off between the methodological advantages gained by minimal disclosure and the ethical considerations over doing so. In terms of methodological competence, if the researcher is somewhat detached from the group, she/he can be more objective, but may not be able to adequately comprehend the participant's behaviour. On the other hand, the 'full participant' researcher may have to face the problem of 'going native'; that is, their level of participation as a group member may cloud their judgement and perspective as an observer.

Case study

The one remaining non-experimental technique used in research to consider here is the 'case study'. This is a research *strategy*, as opposed to a research method and usually takes the form of an in-depth study of an individual or small group of individuals, over a significant period of time. Various research methods, for example, participant observation as used by Rosenhan (1973), form components of wider case studies.

Case studies, therefore, are often compiled from several individual pieces of research over a period of time. As such, any individual case study may include the use of a variety of examples of research and research methods. Whichever research methods are used, there is still the same emphasis on rigour. Some researchers regard the case study as a 'soft' approach – in that 'no one is harmed in the process' – but one that generates meaningful qualitative data; others see it as an unscientific approach since little numerical data is gathered. Perhaps the greatest weakness of the case study, however, is that it lacks reliability and validity. Results and processes are not easily repeated in other contexts, thereby seriously diminishing the potential for generalising results. In fact, though, the case study method was never designed to allow generalisation and proponents claim that attempting to do so is undesirable in any case, since behaviour is often influenced by social context.

One of the main benefits of the case study research strategy is the potential for the creation of new hypotheses, which can then be tested by methods such as experimentation. The strategy has become well established in psychology and notable examples include Thigpen and Cleckley's (1954) study of 'multiple personalities, Koluchova's (1976) study of severe deprivation in young children and Freud's famous case study of Anna O, which allowed Freud to trace the relationship between physical symptoms and psychological traumas in her early life.

Conducting research in psychology

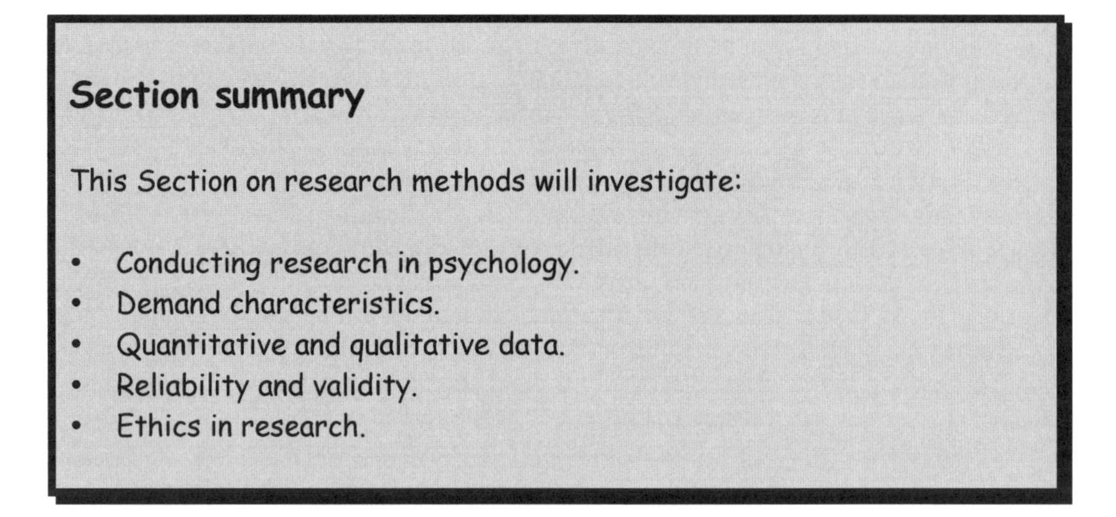

Quantitative and qualitative data

Having looked at the various research methods and strategies used by psychologists, we will now look at some of the practical issues involved in using them. This involves looking in particular at the research process and the distinction between quantitative and qualitative data, the relationship between the type of data and research method used and issues of reliability and validity in relation to data type. The importance of considering ethical issues in research, briefly referred to above, will be explored in greater detail as a topic in its own right.

As noted above, psychology makes use of a variety of research methods that all have as a central aim the collecting and subsequent analysis of relevant data. The data collected can be categorized by *type* and there are essentially two types of data – 'quantitative' and 'qualitative'.

'Quantitative' data consist of numerical measurements, or, put simply, quantities. These might be things such as reaction times, amount of alcohol drunk by 18-year olds, or score on an IQ test. Such data are clear-cut and objective, and can be used as the basis of statistical techniques.

'Qualitative' data are non numerical and are usually written or spoken and often provide a more in-depth, detailed, account of behaviour. They may be derived from sources such as people's written opinions, descriptions of observed behaviour, or answers to interview questions.

It is tempting to use the similarity to the words 'quantity' and 'quality' to assume that quantitative data means *more* data and qualitative data means higher *quality* data. It would be better, however, to think of quantitative data as referring to quantities such as amounts or numbers and qualitative data as referring to qualities such as information about a person. Indeed, quantitative data may in fact present much more concisely, since numbers can easily be summarised and averaged.

Quantitative and qualitative data – research examples

Quantitative data

Raye *et al* (1970) hypothesised that there was relationship between the number of 'critical life events' and physical illness. Their subsequent research found a positive correlation of 0.118. The use of quantitative data in this example enables the researchers to demonstrate an apparent link between 'critical life events' and illness and to further hypothesise that the link may be stress-related. This numerical technique can also be graphically illustrated, which in this case, might take the form of a scattergram (see Section 2 for a number of examples of scattergrams).

Qualitative data

Freud (1963) provides a classic case study referred to above. Freud notes the character Dora as experiencing violent coughing and problems with her breathing. As might be expected, perhaps, Freud believed that these symptoms were due to a problem Dora had with her sexuality and the particular experiences she had in early childhood. The intensive study provided detailed qualitative data, since Freud diligently wrote details of Dora's verbal descriptions and made no attempt to quantify them.

Reliability and validity in relation to data type

An important consideration when choosing the type of data to pursue is the extent to which the data will enhance the method's 'reliability' and 'validity', as detailed earlier in this Chapter.

Research methods that generate quantitative data are considered by many psychologists to have high levels of reliability. This focus on reliability, however, often overlooks the fact that these methods also achieve validity. Nevertheless, research methods that focus on the generation of quantitative data, such as the laboratory experiment, do allow for successful replication of results (reliability) since they gather numerical data that can be compared with results of repeated attempts to examine the hypothesis. The particular experimental method adopted could be described as reliable if it produced similar results when repeated. By doing so, however, it is possible that the data gathered may lose validity – it ceases to measure what it is supposed to measure.

It is research methods that generate qualitative data that make the greatest claim to validity. In fact, this is the only claim made by researchers using these methods as no claim to reliability is appropriate with such methods. Rather, the aim of obtaining qualitative data is to elicit a detailed understanding of the behaviour under investigation in the form of in-depth, personalized and in that sense unique data. Such specific information allows researchers to claim high levels of validity for this type of research.

It should be noted that these two types of data are in fact complementary and are often used together in research. Each method acts as a check on the other and together they give a more accurate analysis of behaviour. Methods that generate qualitative data are often used as the starting point when conducting research and are then followed by the use of methods that generate quantitative data, such as experimentation. It is also the case that we cannot easily categorise methods of research by the type of data they generate. The relationship between research method and type of data generated is best represented on a continuum as **Table 2/1.7** illustrates.

Relationship between Research Method and Type of Data

Quantitative data ———————————— Qualitative data

Experiments
Correlation
Surveys
Non-participant observation
Unstructured interview
Participant observation

It should be noted that a method commonly known for generating quantitative data, such as the survey, may actually produce some qualitative data and observation may produce either, or both. The choice of focus on type of data effectively depends often on a number of factors, such as the aims of the research, the topic or phenomena under investigation, the rationale behind the research project, who is funding it and why and how the results are to be used. It is not as simple, therefore, to say that any one research method makes exclusive use of quantitative or qualitative data.

Guidelines on ethical research

A variety of influences have contributed to an increased concern among researchers over ethical issues in recent years. The notion of 'ethical research' is associated with what should be generally considered as acceptable and/or 'good conduct when investigating human and non-human behaviour. In psychology, the concept of ethics is very important. Ethical principles have been established in the United Kingdom by the British Psychological Society (BPS) to ensure the protection of human and non-human participants in psychological research and in general to consider the possible impact of any research on wider society. This could include the consequences of research that might be considered socially sensitive as would be the case with, for example, research into 'racial' difference.

Psychologists, including students of psychology like you, must be concerned about the likelihood of any research causing harm or discomfort to participants or others. These concerns must be incorporated into your understanding of psychological research.

We will consider the issue of ethics in general in psychology and in relation to each of the research methods we have discussed above. As you read through this material, it is strongly recommended that you look at *A Code of Conduct for Psychologists* by the British Psychological Society (BPS, 2000). Your teacher/lecturer may have a copy, or you could visit the BPS website at www.bps.org.uk to view the *Code*.

If you are conducting your own research, you should be familiar with the *ATP Guide to Ethics for Teachers and Students of Psychology at Pre-degree Level*, from the Association for the Teaching of Psychology (ATP). As this *Guide* makes clear, research by students must show even more stringent ethical control than real-life research, particularly in relation to deception and the use of participants younger than 16 years of age.

Of equal importance, is The British Psychological Society's (BPS) *Code of Conduct*, which states that psychologists should establish the highest ethical standards, ensure scientific integrity and protect participants when engaging in human and non-human research. All practicing psychologists should be particularly concerned with four areas: *competence*, *obtaining consent*, *confidentiality* and *personal conduct*. This is illustrated in **Diagram 2/1.18**, below.

Diagram 2/1.18

'Code of Conduct' of the BPS

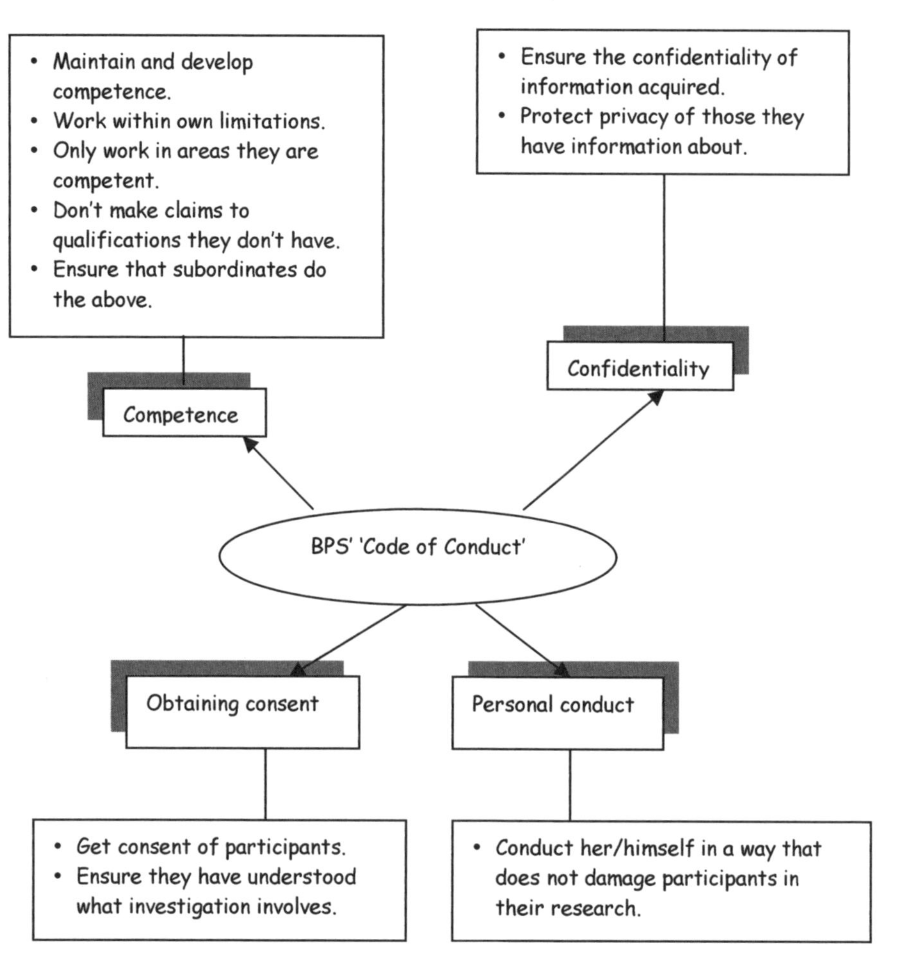

(Adapted from *A Code of Conduct for Psychologists* by the British Psychological Society, BPS, 2000.)

The British Psychological Society also issues particular guidelines indicating how research with human participants should be conducted. This guideline contains a number of areas of concern. The main areas are illustrated below in **Diagram 2/1.19**.

Diagram 2/1.19

BPS 'Ethical Principles for Conducting Psychological Research with Human Beings'

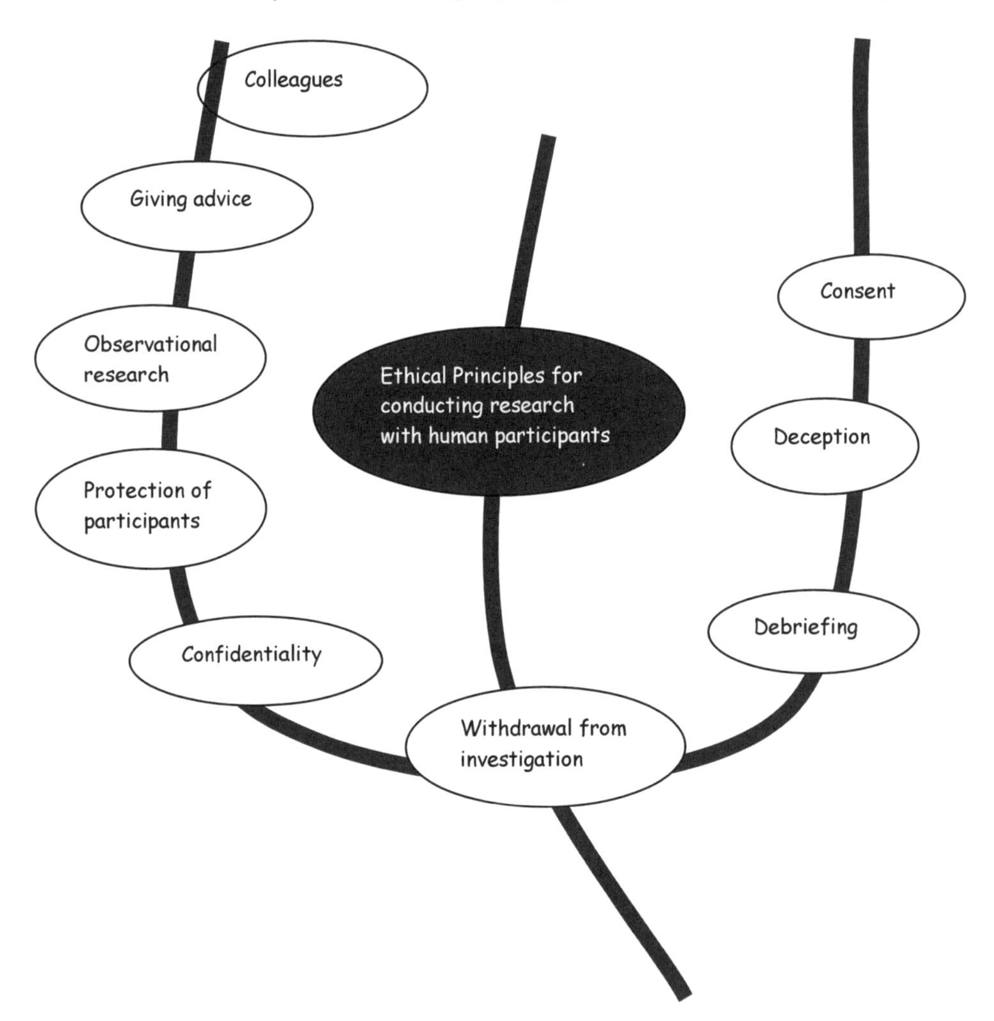

There must be mutual respect between researchers and participants. The guidelines outline the conditions under which psychological research is acceptable. All BPS members and those under its supervision should abide by the principles and be aware of the legal implications of alleged misconduct.

Researchers must always consider the ethical implications and psychological consequences for the participants and should recognise possible impacts of their research on participants from a range of ethnic and social backgrounds, and ages.

Consent
If at all possible, participants should be told of the objectives of the research. In particular, they should be informed of anything that might influence their decision to participate. If full disclosure of the purpose of the research is not possible, the researcher must provide additional safeguards to protect participant's welfare and dignity. If the research involves children or participants who have impairments that limit their understanding to the extent they cannot give their real consent, consent should be sought from parents or from those *in loco parentis*.

Deception
Researchers should not withhold information or mislead participants if they are likely to show unease when debriefed. If there is any doubt, the researchers should consult with others who share the social and cultural background of the participants as to the likelihood of misappropriate conduct. Researchers should also consult ethics committees or experienced colleagues. Intentional deception about the purpose and nature of the research should always be avoided and the misleading of participants should be avoided if without extremely strong scientific or medical justification.

Debriefing
Researchers should provide participants with comprehensive and comprehensible information with regard to the research. They should discuss the participant's experience of the research in order to detect any unforeseen negative effects or misconceptions and amend future research accordingly. The practice of debriefing does not provide justification for any unethical practices that may take place during the research, either intentionally or otherwise.

Withdrawal from investigation
Researchers should stress to participants that they retain the right to withdraw from the research at any time. This is irrespective of any payment or inducement that has been offered. Participants can even withdraw after the research has been conducted and ask the researcher to destroy or disregard data pertaining to their involvement.

Confidentiality
Information obtained about a participant during the research should be considered confidential unless otherwise agreed in advance. Use of information is also subject to the Data Protection Act. The anonymity of participants should as far as possible be guaranteed and where not possible, participants should be warned of this prior to their agreement to participate.

Protection of participants
Participants must be protected from physical and mental harm during the research. The risk of harm to the participants should be no greater that that encountered in their daily lives and participants should be consulted over any potential risk factors that may arise during research and advised of any action they should take to avoid or contain risk.

Observational research
Research based on observation must respect the privacy and psychological well-being of participants. Unless researchers obtain permission otherwise, observation is only acceptable in contexts considered appropriate according to local cultural values.

Giving advice
If in the process of research an issue pertaining to the health of participants' psychological or physical well-being comes to light, participants should be informed of this and advised on how to proceed. If the researcher is not qualified to offer assistance, advice should be imparted or facilitated on where and how appropriate advice can be obtained.

Colleagues
Researchers share the responsibility for the ethical treatment of participants with their collaborators, assistants, students, and employees. Any researcher who is aware that another psychologist is conducting research that is not following ethical principles, should encourage that researcher to re-evaluate the research.

(Adapted from the BPS' *Ethical Principles for Conducting Research with Human Participants.*)

Ethics and research methods
Having looked briefly at the guiding principles on ethics in psychological research, let us now turn and look at the issue of ethics in relation to the specific research methods used in psychology. We will as we proceed illustrate some of the more important research studies that have in some way failed to adhere to certain ethical guidelines and have thereby, through their popularity for other aspects, highlighted concerns, which, in turn, have been instrumental in the development of current ethical guidelines in psychology.

Experimentation
The conduct of experimentation with human participants has raised many ethical issues. In the earlier stages of the development of psychology as an academic disciple, psychologists saw themselves as scientists in pursuit of 'truth', where the ends of research justified the means. There were many studies relating to the effects

of drugs, or the effects of electric shocks on participants that would be considered unethical to contemporary psychologists. Nowadays, any form of experimentation that might cause pain or distress to participants is debarred.

As we have seen, there are cases where an element of deception is necessary to access adequate data in an experiment. In such cases, however, researchers must ensure that any deception is limited only to that which is strictly necessary for the purposes of the experiment, not long lasting in its experience and effects and results only used on securing participants' consent. Similarly and in order to avoid the impact of demand characteristics, it is normal not to give participants full information about aims and hypotheses before they do the experiment. However, it is now standard to also debrief participants, explaining all procedures and the reason for them, at the end of the data-gathering stage of the experiment.

Certain 'classic' experiments in psychology have highlighted the need for ethical guidelines following the widespread public criticism of methods adopted in them. In experiments such as those conducted by Milgram (1974), Piliavin *et al* (1969) and Latane and Darley (1968), had the participants known the real aims of the study, their behaviour would undoubtedly have been different.

Regarding the protection of participants, experiments involving children are particularly susceptible to criticism for causing stress to the participants, or for having a detrimental effect on their development. Even studies that apparently have a positive effect on child participants, such as that undertaken by Rosenthal and Jacobson (1966), which labelled a randomly selected 20 per cent of children in a school as having superior intelligence, could be criticised for potentially harming the other children who were not afforded the label. For these reasons, experimentation on children should be undertaken with great care and only by suitably qualified professional researchers. In the Higher Psychology course, you will be advised to ensure that all of your participants are over 16 years of age.

Correlation

The main concern over correlational research is the way(s) in which research may be interpreted and used. This arises from the fact that this technique is commonly used instead of experiments in areas that may be very socially sensitive. As we have seen, correlation *does not* show causality and a cause-effect relationship cannot be inferred even from a strong correlation. However, not everyone is aware of this and political groups with a race-hate agenda could interpret research that showed a correlation between a person's race and their likelihood to commit a crime as being a causal relationship. Think about this yourself; do you think such research should be permitted?

Most people are not professionally trained psychologists and journalists or the public at large can easily misinterpret correlational research. Causality must *not* be inferred from correlation.

Observation

As mentioned above, the need for consent can cause a problem, as people behave differently if they know they are being observed. Nevertheless, it is totally unacceptable to covertly observe people in private – it would invade their privacy, and if they do not know they are being studied, they cannot exercise their right to withdraw from the study.

Survey

It is essential that complete confidentiality be guaranteed on a survey as people have the right to privacy with regard to their thoughts and opinions. Numbering questionnaires rather than using names can do this. As well as the ethical imperative to do so, confidentiality is important methodologically, in order to get accurate answers to interviews and questionnaires. Participants might be less willing to tell the truth if their name is on the questionnaire.

Case study

The issue of the protection of participants is also important here. Case studies provide detailed personal information. It is very important that the identity of participants is protected and this is often done through the use of the participant's initials in the publication (as in the case of HM in memory research, see Chapter 1) or a false name. Researchers should also be aware that participants might disclose problems that they the researchers are not qualified to deal with. They should be prepared to provide or recommend appropriate support.

Answers to Activities

Activity 1 - Box 2/1.2

1. The variable that the experimenter manipulates is the independent variable.
2. The name of the variable that the experimenter measures is the dependent variable.
3. (a) The IV is the presence or absence of violent scenes in television programmes. The DV is the amount of aggression that is shown by the participants.
3. (b) The IV is whether or not women experienced stress, as they were caring for elderly relatives who were experiencing senile dementia. The dependent variable (DV) is the time taken for the wound to heal.
3. (c) The IV is: the complexity of sentences. Those sentences that focused on meaning produced better recall, than those that focussed on the sound of a word. The DV was the number of sentences recalled.

Activity 2 - Box 2/1.3

1. There will be three experimental conditions.
2. The variables can be operationalised as follows:
   - Popularity (IV) - the number of people who attend your birthday party.
   - Success at school (DV) - the number of Higher Grades you achieve at school.
   - Stress (IV) - the number of times you are absent from PT during a term
   - Success at games (DV) - the number of times you have been selected to play for your school during a term.
3. Situational variable: where the researcher asks the participants to estimate their IQ.
   - Researcher variable: the sex of the researcher.

Chapter 2
Investigating Behaviour – Part 2: The Research Investigation

Section summary

This Section is a guide to planning the Research Investigation, carrying out the research and analysing the data and will cover the following:

- What is the Research Investigation?
- Research topics and background reading.
- Planning the research investigation.
- Keeping a research log.
- Obtaining a sample of participants.
- Gathering the data.
- Ethical considerations.
- Analysing the data.

Planning and conducting the Research Investigation

What is the Research Investigation?

The Research Investigation (RI) is the project component of the *Investigating Behaviour* Unit in the Higher Psychology course. It involves planning and conducting a psychology experiment or study and completing a *research report* in the standard scientific style. The aim of this part of the course is to develop research and report-writing skills. The Investigation should give you a feel for the exciting process of research from the initial development of an idea, perhaps as part of a small team, through to putting your results and conclusions down on paper in the form of a scientific report. You will have the opportunity to put into practice some of the research methods you are learning about in Part 1 of this Chapter. Through conducting the RI, you may also gain a deeper understanding of what is involved on a much larger scale in published research.

Whilst the process of conducting and writing up the investigation can take several weeks, the actual data collection stage may be over in a day! Research requires careful planning and your materials may also take some time to prepare. Once you have collected the data, you need to perform some analysis of the data, such as calculating the arithmetic average of a group of scores and producing graphs.

Throughout the research process you should be maintaining a practical portfolio, which will include a research plan and an ongoing progress log. Your collected raw data and calculations will also be included in this portfolio, which will be assessed internally by your teacher/lecturer and will constitute the equivalent of a National Assessment Bank (NAB) assessment for Outcome 3 – 'Demonstrate practical research skills in the implementation of a psychological research investigation', for this Unit of the Higher. You should also be continuously drafting out your RI report or 'write-up' as far as possible (except in the case of students who are doing 'Investigating Behaviour' as a stand-alone unit, who should only produce the plan and log of the Investigation).

While your teacher or lecturer will assess your research plan and log and may be able to help you with your RI report draft, the final version of the report is sent to the Scottish Qualifications Authority (SQA) to be marked externally. It is worth 20 per cent of the overall grade for the Higher Psychology external exam. You should refer to SQA documents about the Research Investigation, in particular the *Research Investigation Guidelines* and *Research Investigation Brief*, the latter of which specifies the research topics and is changed from year to year.

Diagram 2/2.1

A flow chart of steps in the Research Investigation (RI)

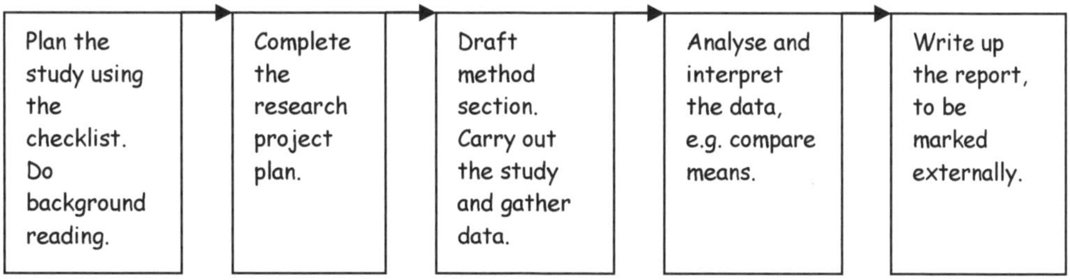

Plan the study using the checklist. Do background reading.	→	Complete the research project plan.	→	Draft method section. Carry out the study and gather data.	→	Analyse and interpret the data, e.g. compare means.	→	Write up the report, to be marked externally.

Remember: throughout the research process, you should log (record) each stage

Research topics and background reading

The topic for each RI must come from the *Research Investigation Brief* ('RI Brief') provided annually by the SQA. Each topic is related to one of the topics of the Higher Psychology course, for example, *memory*. Some of these will require an experiment, but for non-experimental studies such as surveys, it will be particularly important to look carefully in advance at how the RI should be written up (see next Section) and still be rigorous when analysing the data.

Throughout any piece of work of this nature and especially at the beginning, a researcher should try to find out about other research that has been conducted in similar areas. The SQAs information on RI topics will give a starting point by briefly summarising the research background. The best place to start your own background reading is with a general text on the topic, such as the relevant chapter of this textbook.

Of course, it is necessary to go beyond one book in doing background research. One of the simplest ways of finding further reading is to make a note, as you read, of research studies which seem relevant to your RI topic and look up these references at the back of the book. You can then search for these topics in other books or on the internet. For example, if your topic involved the use of imagery to improve the memory, you might come across a study by Gordon Bower of Stanford University that showed that making mental images of words leads to more successful recall than simply trying to memorise them, especially if the images are unusual (Bower, 1972). To find out more about this from other books, you could then look up the name 'Bower' in the index. Try to find some recent references (i.e. within the past 10-15 years), as it sometimes happens that older sources become discredited.

Students who have read widely tend to do better in the 'Introduction' section of a report. Make use of this textbook, but also dip into other books, such as more specialist books on the topics (see the 'Further reading' section at the end of this textbook). The Internet can also be a useful source, but obviously there is no guarantee of quality. When using the Internet to find sources, give preference to URLs with the ending 'ac.uk', or '.edu', which indicate university websites. Alternatively, use other reputable sources such as the *Encyclopaedia Britannica*. Be very careful about taking information from non-academic sources. Such sources may provide useful ideas, but could also mislead and present out of date, biased, or even incorrect information. Do not treat information from such sites as fact, but rather as opinion. Of course, you can always try consulting your teacher or lecturer for further guidance on what websites may or may not be useful.

Planning the Research Investigation

A research investigation plan and log will be awarded a mark out of 20, which constitutes half of the internal assessment for this Unit. At least 12 marks are required to pass this element. (Make use of the SQAs plan and log template available at http://www.sqa.org.uk.)

The quality of planning and the care taken over designing the experiment will often make the difference between a good investigation and a bad one. Planning well is especially important when several people are working together. Teamwork is one of the most enjoyable, but also one of the most challenging aspects of research. Working collaboratively and allowing ideas to develop in discussion can be exciting. It also presents significant demands – coordinating group members and ensuring that you are aware of each other's ideas, but avoiding copying sections of each other's work, which can be done inadvertently as well as deliberately.

The SQA has recommended that groups for the Psychology Research Investigation should comprise *no more than four members*. Whilst it is acceptable to work in a pair or group to plan and to collect data, the plan/log and the written report *must* be done individually and partners' reports must not include sections of text that are identical. Even though group members' results sections will include the same data, each member should submit their own analysis and presentation of results.

The first planning consideration is to establish your hypotheses, based on the information provided in the RI Brief for the selected topic. The RI Brief will also include important information about the research design to be used – this will be an 'independent measures', 'repeated measures' or 'matched pairs' design for an experiment, or a non-experimental design such as a 'correlation'. You should think about who the participants will be and how these will be obtained (see 'obtaining a sample', below). All such details will go into the 'research plan'.

At this stage the materials and apparatus should be planned in all possible detail. If you are using a worksheet with words or numbers, these can be drafted out. Something as apparently simple as forming two lists of words for a memory experiment can pose unexpected problems and should not be left until the last minute.

You may have the choice of running your RI as either a field or a laboratory study. Although you might not have a proper psychology laboratory available to you, a classroom or room in someone's home or workplace can make a reasonable substitute, as long as you have some control over the environment (e.g. eliminate noise, remove distractions and have control over the door to avoid interruptions).

Finally, the way the study will be conducted should be planned out in every detail. This means drafting out standard instructions for participants, a step-by-step standard procedure for researchers and a debriefing sheet. If more than one person is collecting data, each should be totally clear about what they will be doing at any given time and ensure that each goes through the process in exactly the same way.

Box 2/2.1

Activity 1

Imagine you were running the following study:

In a repeated measures study on memory, participants' memories are to be tested twice - first in silence and the second time with music playing. It has been decided that the form of the test will involve the participants reading a list of random words each time.

- What materials would you use?
- What difficulties might arise?
- Discuss this in pairs.

(See the end of this Chapter for answers/discussion.)

The RI Brief includes information on the procedure for your study and this should be referred to as these plans and instructions are drawn up.

It is advisable to test out the procedure before you actually collect data. How this is done can range from running a full 'pilot study', which is similar to the actual experiment but with fewer participants, to researchers simply trying the tasks themselves. As well as highlighting any flaws in the procedure or materials, a pilot study also provides practice in running the investigation, to help researchers come across as well prepared and professional (Harris, 2002).

The planning and running of the research will be documented in a portfolio comprising a plan and log, which will be marked by teachers/lecturers internally.

It will help you to use the checklist in **Box 2/2.2** to help keep track of the research process and ensure that nothing is missing from the portfolio. Tick each step once it has been carried out.

Box 2/2.2

Planning Checklist

- Are you clear as to which of the possible RI studies you will run?
- Are you aware of which areas of psychology are relevant to the RI Brief?
- Have you chosen a partner or group (if you wish to collaborate in running the study)?
- Have you completed the research plan and begun filling in a progress log?
- Have you taken a note of which theories and research are related to the study and begun background reading?
- Do you know which design your study will use (i.e. 'independent measures'/'repeated measures', 'matched pairs', 'correlation')?
- What are your variables (IV and conditions, DV)?
- What materials are you going to use (worksheets, etc.)?
- Are the brief, standard instructions, procedure and debrief drafted?
- Do you know what kind of data will be obtained and how it will be recorded? Have data sheets been prepared?
- Which data analysis techniques will be employed?
- Have you gathered all apparatus you will need?
- Is the room arranged/booked (if needed)?
- Sampling method selected and participants obtained? (Remember to obtain full consent).
- For experiments, have you randomly allocated participants to each experimental condition (or with an independent measures design, randomly counterbalanced your participants in terms of which condition they will do first)?
- Have you collected your raw data and included it in the portfolio and as an appendix to the report?
- Have you (individually) analysed the data? (Include analysis in portfolio).
- Have you (individually) written up the draft(s) of the report?
- Have you (individually) written up the final version of the report?

Throughout this process, record every step in your log. Take a note of all important details (e.g. type of sampling to be used) for inclusion in the practical portfolio.

Tips:

- Do not copy notes from others in your group. You can share ideas, but the wording of the RI should be your own. Likewise, avoid copying sections of text from books or lecture notes. This is known as plagiarism and is a serious breach of academic practice.
- To avoid making a task such as a memory test too difficult or too easy, consider running a pilot-study.

Keeping a research log

Throughout the research process, you should fill in a research log. This comes in a standard form from the SQA and is available either on paper or as a computer file.

It is very helpful if elements of your planning and research process are logged as soon as possible, while they are fresh in your mind. It is a good idea to photocopy the log and then to write up a copy when you are ready to hand it in. Bear in mind also that the log will be essential when it comes to writing up the Research Report, so you will need more than one copy.

Obtaining a sample

You will recall that there are several different types of sampling and random sampling is superior, as it normally provides a representative sample of participants, thereby allowing results to be generalized to the population as a whole. Ideally, you would also like a random sample taken from a broad cross-section of society. In practice, however, you may only have access to friends, classmates and family. For the purposes of the investigation, it is perfectly acceptable to use 'opportunity sampling', i.e. selecting participants on the basis of convenience and this type of sampling is widely used in social science research (Rudner and Schafer, 1999). However, you should bear in mind the limitations of this technique when drawing conclusions. Also, remember that for ethical reasons, participants must be at least 16 years of age.

A common question asked by students at this stage of their project is 'How many participants do I require?' Unfortunately, the answer is likely to be 'it depends'. For statistical purposes, the greater the number, the stronger the conclusions can be, since the more participants that are used, the less chance there is that the results are particular to a small group only. However, as a general guideline for the RI, around twelve or more per condition should be enough, bearing in mind that in repeated measures designs, the same people participate in more than one condition. Access to a larger pool of participants is one advantage of carrying out your research in a group. One way of obtaining a very large sample would be to combine results with those of other pairs or groups. Of course, the studies would have to be run in exactly the same way.

Some studies can be done on students from your own class – this can be a reciprocal arrangement. However, it may be that your research requires 'naïve participants' – people who do not know about the nature of the study – in order to avoid 'demand characteristics', or because there is an element of surprise (see Part 1 of this Chapter).

Box 2/2.3

Activity 2

A popular RI topic in recent years has been a comparison of estimates of IQ between males and females. Some previous research has found that males estimate higher IQ scores for themselves than women do (Hogan, 1978) suggesting that they have higher self-esteem.

Why might it not be a good idea to run this experiment on psychology classmates?

(The answer can be found at end of this Chapter.)

Remember, that to students of other subjects a 'psychological experiment' might sound quite intimidating. If asked nicely and reassured about the nature of the study – that they are only required to do a short memory test, for example – most people will be willing to help. It might be an advantage if you can tell them how long it will last and offer them some refreshments.

If the research is experimental, the next stage is to allocate participants to the experimental conditions (in the case of independent measures and matched pairs designs) or to the order in which they do the conditions (in the case of repeated measures designs). This should not be the researcher's choice, as there is a strong likelihood of experimenter bias, for example, putting brighter participants into a certain condition, having predicted that people from this condition will do better on a test or task. Instead, a list of random numbers can be used. These might appear as illustrated in **Table 2.2/1**.

Table 2/2.1

Using Random Numbers as a Means of Avoiding Researcher Bias

21	56	12	09	83
47	73	75	14	98
03	66	29	49	46
27	85	10	35	18
64	67	59	44	91

A full table is usually about twenty-five numbers wide. The experimenter should allocate each participant a number between 00 and 99. They then start at any point in the table and move in any direction, up down or diagonally. The first time they come to a number that corresponds to one of the participants, that participant is allocated to the first condition. The next participant is allocated to the second condition (and so on, if there are three or more conditions in the experiment). This continues, allocating participants alternately until all have been assigned.

Such tables can be found in any statistics book, for example, Coolican (1996). If this seems too complicated and if the study has only two conditions, you might choose to allocate participants to 'condition 1' or 'condition 2' by a simpler method, such as tossing a coin. This is acceptable, but should be mentioned in the log and report.

Once you have a list of participants for each condition, you are ready to gather your data.

Tips:

- Do not state in your report that you have used random sampling if you have not, simply to make your investigation sound better. An assessment/exam marker will give you more credit if you are truthful.
- Explain how you obtained your sample in as much detail as possible.
- Make sure to record 'demographic' details of the participants (i.e. age, sex, occupation) at the time of the experiment, provided they are relevant to the hypothesis. They will be harder to obtain later.
- Keep your participants' details in a coded format in your practical portfolio and in your RI; do not identify any participants' names.

Gathering the data

The next stage of the Research Investigation is to actually collect the data from the participants. In many ways, this is the fun bit, but it is important to follow the plan and to use a standardised procedure, for any random variation could invalidate the results. It is also essential to treat people ethically (see 'Ethical considerations', below).

Give participants as much information as possible about the study, without risking 'demand characteristics'. This will allow them to make an informed decision about whether to take part. Distribute the consent forms on the following page to the participants, or draft your own, making sure you cover all ethical aspects. These inform them of their rights and also provide the opportunity to obtain their written consent to take part in the study.

Box 2/2.4

Consent Form for Research Participants

I hereby consent to take part as a participant in this psychology research study. I have received information about the nature of the research and I understand that I have the right to withdraw at any time. I also understand that the researcher(s) are working under a code of ethics, which prohibits them from putting me in harmful situations and that the data obtained from my participation will be treated confidentially.

Name ______________________________ Date ___________________

I hereby consent to take part as a participant in this psychology research study. I have received information about the nature of the research and I understand that I have the right to withdraw at any time. I also understand that the researcher(s) are working under a code of ethics, which prohibits them from putting me in harmful situations and that the data obtained from my participation will be treated confidentially.

Name ______________________________ Date ___________________

I hereby consent to take part as a participant in this psychology research study. I have received information about the nature of the research and I understand that I have the right to withdraw at any time. I also understand that the researcher(s) are working under a code of ethics, which prohibits them from putting me in harmful situations and that the data obtained from my participation will be treated confidentially.

Name ______________________________ Date ___________________

I hereby consent to take part as a participant in this psychology research study. I have received information about the nature of the research and I understand that I have the right to withdraw at any time. I also understand that the researcher(s) are working under a code of ethics, which prohibits them from putting me in harmful situations and that the data obtained from my participation will be treated confidentially.

Name ______________________________ Date ___________________

You should also write up a suitable debrief, which comprises information given to participants after the study is complete, to give more details about the research, thank them and ask them if they have any questions or concerns (and if so, what they can do or who they can contact).

Another essential research skill is to ensure that there is no 'random error' in your procedure – the procedure is standardised for all participants. Consider the task in **Box 2/2.5**.

Box 2/2.5

Activity 3

To give you more practice in issues concerning research skills, consider the following study and information and identify what the researchers could do differently, to ensure more robust methodology.

> Two higher psychology students are running a memory experiment as part of their classwork. They decide to run a laboratory experiment, with an independent measures design. One of the groups is going to see a list of words, e.g. the words 'pig, chair' (condition1) and the other group will see the same items as a group of pictures, e.g. a picture of a pig, a picture of a chair (condition 2). Then they will be asked to recall the items and scores for the two groups will be compared, to discover whether it is easier to remember words or pictures.

1. All of the participants of the study are friends of the researchers.
3. Having selected their participants, they allocate the females to condition 1 and the males to condition 2. (Females are group 1, males are group 2).
2. The researchers invite all the participants to the canteen and discuss their expectations of the study before they start.
4. The researchers then take all the participants to a classroom. Group 2 (the males) are asked to sit quietly at the back, while group 1 (the females) start the task.
5. Group 1 are halfway through the task when the researchers realise that they have forgotten to read the instruction sheet. They decide to start again - they read the instructions out loud and then re-issue the task to group 1, who complete it in five minutes.
6. After they have finished, group 1 are asked to leave and group 2 are told to come to the front of the room. The experimenters read the instructions out loud and then group 2 begin the task.
7) It is now nearly lunchtime, so group 2 are told that they have only two minutes to complete the task.
8) When the two minutes are up, it is clear that nobody in group 2 is finished, so the experimenters wait another minute before they gather in the sheets and thank group 2 for their participation.
9) One of the experimenters takes group 1's answer sheets home to analyse and the other experimenter takes group 2's sheets.
10) When the analysis is complete, the experimenters draw up a sheet with each participant's name and score on the task. They post this up on a notice board in the corridor.

(See the end of this Chapter for the key to this task.)

Tips:

- Be organised, plan carefully and allow enough time.
- Try to see things from the participants' point of view.
- Ensure that participants in different conditions experience the same experimental treatment in all ways, apart from the IV.
- For any research, it is vital to choose a workable design and stick to it. Do not, for example, aim to run a laboratory experiment, but then at the last minute ask participants some questions (an interview) to get further information, or try to analyse variables that are not in the experimental hypothesis.

Ethical considerations

The British Psychological Society (BPS) provides guidelines for all researchers in psychology, as all research must be conducted ethically (BPS, 2000). There are also guidelines specifically for student research from the Association for the Teaching of Psychology (ATP, 2003). It is essential that you, too, conduct your research ethically and these guidelines can be a great help. The most important elements are as follows:

- Participants should give informed consent to take part in the study – and for student research, no participants under the age of 16 can be used.
- Participants should be informed of their right to withdraw from the study at any time (if the experiment has been completed, they can still withdraw their data).
- Participants have a right *not* to be endangered or harmed (including psychologically) in the experiment and should be informed of their rights to non-harmful treatment.
- Participants should not be deceived and any information that is kept from them (e.g. not telling them the aim of the study to avoid demand characteristics) should be given them at the earliest opportunity.
- Colleagues and research partners should likewise *not* be endangered, harmed, or deceived.
- Laws should *not* be broken.

Informed consent means that the participants agree to take part in the study having been given information on what is going to happen.

The notion of 'harm' to a participant or colleague is broad and difficult to define – it could include a variety of things from minor physical dangers to psychological trauma. In the real world, it is impossible to be absolutely certain that participants will not come to any harm during the research, but it is important to avoid procedures where participants could sustain injuries and not to put them into embarrassing situations. The guidelines in the SQAs RI Brief will not intend harmful treatment of participants, so it is important to stick closely to these. If you are in any doubt at all about research ethics, check with a teacher or lecturer before proceeding.

Tips:

- Read the *ATP Guide to Ethics for Teachers and Students of Psychology at pre-degree level* (ATP, 2003), which is contained in the SQAs (2004) *RI guidance for Higher Psychology*; your teacher or lecturer may also have a copy.
- Consult with your teacher or lecturer before you start your research.

Analysing the data

For the purpose of the Higher, we will use *descriptive statistics* – these are techniques that summarise or describe a set of data. They include:

- Measures of central tendency (averages).
- Measures of dispersion.
- Graphs and charts.

In more advanced psychology courses, such as at Advanced Higher and university level, psychology students learn 'inferential statistics'. These are more difficult to calculate, but they allow the researcher to draw inferences and conclusions about what a set of data shows.

For example, with two sets of data, descriptive statistics tell us useful information about each set, such as the average score and patterns such as a difference, a trend or a relationship. Inferential statistics would allow a comparison between the two sets of data and say whether there is a true difference between them, rather than just a chance variation.

Measures of central tendency – the *mean*

The mean is the arithmetic average of a set of data. It is calculated by adding together all of the values and dividing by **n** (where **n** = the number of scores).

It is very *powerful* as it includes all of the scores in the calculation. However, it falls down where there are extreme scores at one end of the distribution. For example, the following scores show how long nine participants took to do a task:

Data set A: number of seconds taken by students to complete a lateral thinking problem:

34 38 41 42 42 45 53 67 2961

The mean of data set A is 369.2. This is not a very useful summary of the data, as it is so different from all of the scores. It may be the average, but it is not a typical or representative central point. It is also important to remember the mean requires arithmetic division and often contains decimal places. This is fine when the measurement is of something like time, but cannot be used to find an average of, for example, people's favourite colour.

The *median*
This is the 'middle' of the data, the midpoint in the set of scores. You find it by placing the scores in increasing order of size and choosing the one in the middle. For example, if you have three scores, the second one is the median. In set A, above, the median is 42, as it is the fifth score in order of size out of nine scores. For such distributions, this is a much more useful average than the mean in that it can never be an extreme value since it is always to be found 'in the middle'. In this case, it happens to be the same as the mode for set A, but this need not be the case.

If there is an even number of scores, select the middle two and find the *mean* from these as described above. The middle two scores in data set B, below, are underlined:

Data set B scores out of 50 for the Psychology Research Investigation:

24 28 31 33 $\underline{36 \quad 39}$ 40 42 45 47

In the above set, the median would be:

$$\frac{36 + 39}{2}$$

So, it would be 75/2, or 37.5.

The *mode*
You might have come across the term *mode* as meaning something fashionable or popular. Similarly in statistics, the mode is the most common or popular score. In data set A, the mode is 42, as there are more cases of the score 42 than any other score. The modal (mode) age of a group of people is the most common age. What is the modal age in your class?

This is a useful summary where data consist of frequency counts, rather than a measure such as time. However, it relies on there being at least one score which is shown more than once in the data. Also, data can have more than one mode, making for a less clear summary. Consider the following distributions:

Data set C, numbers of pets each member of a psychology class (of ten students) have:

1 2 3 4 5 6 7 8 9 10

Data set D, numbers of paid days off members of staff in a small company had last year:

14 15 16 <u>16</u> 17 18 19 20 22 23 25 <u>25</u>

Data set D is *bi-modal*, meaning there are two modes (16 and 25). Data set C is *multi-modal* (several modes), but in fact there is no true mode as each score occurs only once.

What should be clear from the above examples is that the most suitable measure of central tendency depends on the type of data. Usually, the mean is the most informative, but there are cases where the median will be as useful or even more so. The mode can be helpful, but is not frequently used in psychological research.

Measures of dispersion

Measures of central tendency give us a single value which represents the central point of the data and provides a typical value in some way. They do not, however, give a complete description of the data, as can be seen from the following example:

Data set E:	10	15	20	25	**30**	35	40	45	50
Data set F:	26	27	28	29	**30**	31	32	33	34

In both sets of data above, the value for both the mean and the median is 30. However, it is clear that the data are not particularly similar. What is needed is a statistic to show how much the values are spread around the average. This is the purpose of 'measures of dispersion'.

The range

The range is simply the difference between the lowest and highest scores. It is calculated by subtracting the lowest score from the highest score. In the last two sets of data, the range can be shown as:

$$50 - 10 = 40$$
&
$$34 - 26 = 8$$

So, if we say that a set of data has a mean of 30 and a range of 40, it tells us more than the mean alone.

However, the range is very open to distortion by a single very low or very high number. It does not tell us anything about the distribution of the other scores, except that they fall within these limits.

The standard deviation

A more powerful and commonly used measure of dispersion is the standard deviation (or 'SD'). It shows the typical amount by which the scores in the distribution differ from the mean. Unlike the range, all of the data is included in the calculation and it is, therefore, more powerful and more representative.

It works best with normally distributed data and in these cases the standard deviation has certain mathematical properties that allow us to determine the position of a value in the set of scores. For example, 68.26 per cent of values lie within one standard deviation on either side of the mean, while 95.44 per cent lie within two times the standard deviation (or 'two standard deviations') each side of the mean and 99.74 within three standard deviations each side of the mean, as shown below. If the mean of a set of data was 40 and the SD was 6, for example, then we would know that 99.74 per cent of scores would fall between 22 and 58. A score of 21 would, therefore, be very unusual indeed, as less than 0.3 per cent of scores would fall this far from the mean. (See **Box 2/2.6** for how standard deviation is calculated.)

Box 2/2.6

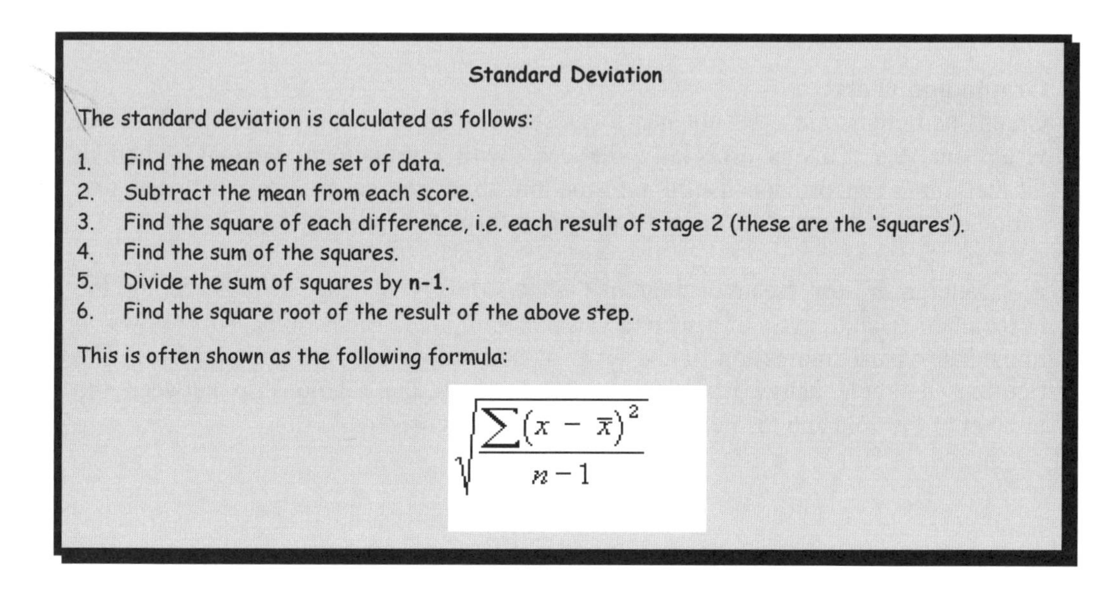
Standard Deviation

The standard deviation is calculated as follows:

1. Find the mean of the set of data.
2. Subtract the mean from each score.
3. Find the square of each difference, i.e. each result of stage 2 (these are the 'squares').
4. Find the sum of the squares.
5. Divide the sum of squares by **n-1**.
6. Find the square root of the result of the above step.

This is often shown as the following formula:

$$\sqrt{\frac{\sum(x-\bar{x})^2}{n-1}}$$

Box 2/2.7

Activity 4

Try to find mean, median, mode, range and standard deviation for the following sets of data:

Sample data:

Scores on condition 1:

3 7 10 8 14 2 9 8 7 13 7 5 11

Scores on condition 2:

19 10 11 8 9 9 11 14 3 6 3 10 17

(Answers to this Activity can be found at the end of this Chapter.)

Tips:

- Calculate means more than once, to check that you get the same result.
- Include the working of any complicated calculations as an appendix at the end of your report.

Graphs and charts

Graphs and charts are used not just to present results, but also to perform a useful visual analysis. This is especially the case with correlational designs, where a 'scattergram' can provide useful information about the relationship between two variables. (See Chapter 2, Section 1 for more information on scattergrams.)

A 'scattergram' (or 'scatter diagram') shows levels of one variable along the horizontal axis and levels of a second variable along the vertical axis. This allows an immediate visual impression of the level of correlation between the variables. The fictitious example below in **Diagram 2/2.2** shows the relationship between the number of lies told and the number of compliments received.

Diagram 2/2.2

Number of Lies Told and Number of Compliments Received

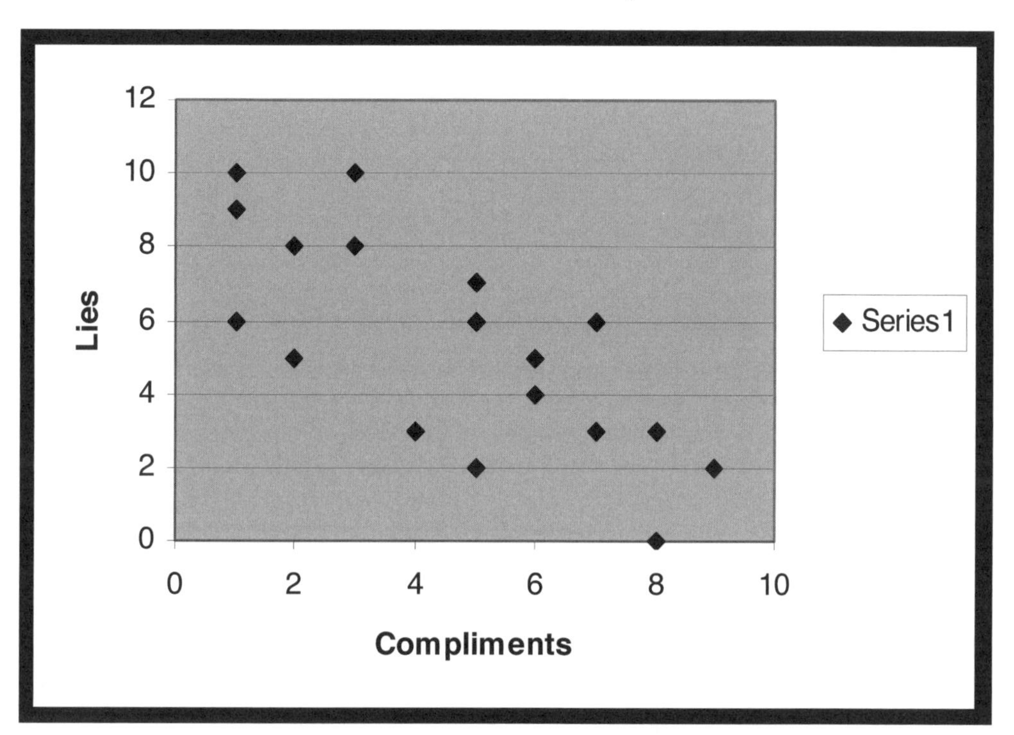

A general downward pattern can be observed, clearly indicating that the more somebody lies, the fewer compliments they get (a 'negative correlation'). Of course, the graph cannot tell us anything about *why* this might be the case.

A 'bar graph' shows scores as heights on two or more vertical 'bars'. These should be separate 'categories', e.g. scores from different groups or on different tasks and as they are distinct categories, the bars should have a gap between them (Coolican, 2004). The bar graph can allow for a useful visual comparison of mean scores of the DV between different conditions. The example below in **Diagram 2/2.3** shows the scores on two conditions of a verbal recall memory experiment – one with normal meaningful words and the other with 'nonsense syllables'.

Diagram 2/2.3

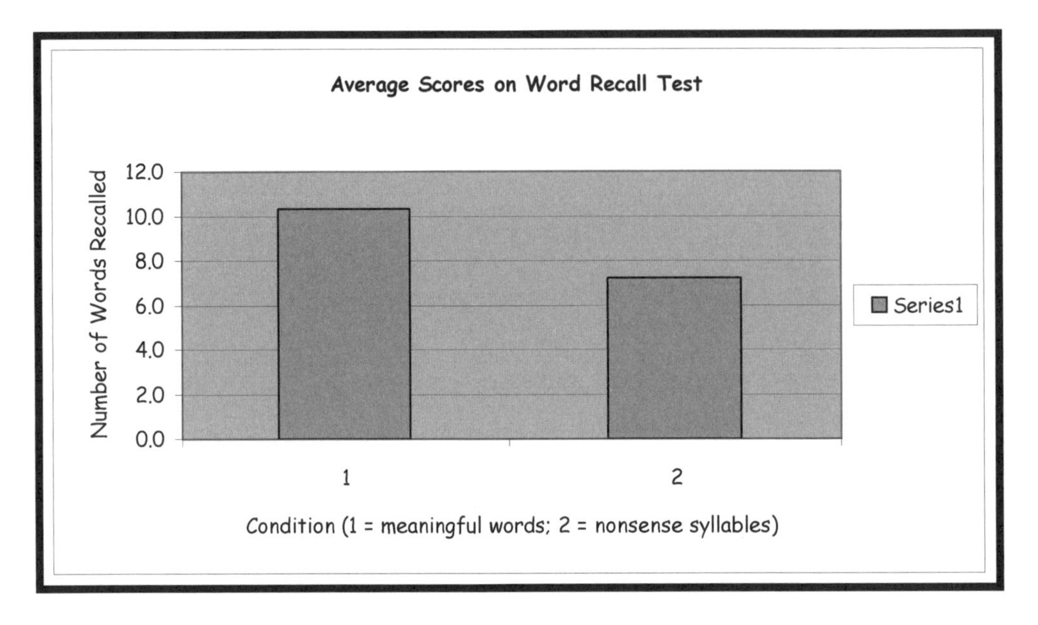

A histogram looks superficially similar to a bar graph, except for the lack of gaps between the bars. In fact, a histogram shows a range of values from the same category and, therefore, shows the pattern of a set of data, rather than a comparison between two or more categories. Columns in a histogram can *only* represent frequencies.

Section summary

The above Section is a guide to the process of planning and carrying out research. Throughout this process, the research investigation project plan and log should be filled out and this process will comprise 50 per cent of the internal assessment of the *Investigating Behaviour* Unit.

All students undertaking Higher Psychology are also expected to produce a full research report of their Research Investigation, which will be marked externally by SQA markers and will contribute to their overall mark/grade for Higher Psychology. The next part of this Chapter explains how to write this report.

Writing up the Research Investigation

Section summary

This Section aims to help you to write up and present the Research Investigation as a report and will cover the following:

- Writing up the Research Investigation.
- Overview.
- Title and Abstract.
- Introduction.
- Method.
- Results.
- Discussion and Conclusion.
- References and Appendices.
- Presentation.

General comments

A published research report is intended to provide readers, usually professional psychologists, with information. Although you are probably not going to publish your work, you should write a report in the same format and with the same aim in mind. For this reason, the report should be clear and to the point. It is not an essay, so avoid 'showing what you know' by including bulky but irrelevant background material. It should inform the reader, but not attempt to convince or persuade them (Rudner and Schafer, 1999).

Finding the correct writting style can by tricky. It is worth remembering that the use of 'I' and 'we' is generally avoided to make the report sound more formal and scientific (saying, for example, 'an instruction sheet was handed out' rather than 'we/I handed out an instruction sheet'). A report is an account of something that has been completed. Therefore, write in the past tense throughout (this is important to remember if you start drafting your report before collecting the data). A simple general rule is the 'ABC' of writing – be **a**ccurate, **b**rief and **c**lear. Ensure the accuracy of comments by checking sources and be truthful. Reports should be fairly brief – include enough information, but never include things just to fill space.

Be clear by defining all terms used, explaining things and writing in a way that is not over-complicated. A good assumption to work with is that the reader will possess a broad knowledge of the field, but will not be familiar with the particular studies and models that you describe (Rudner and Schafer, 1999).

Box 2/2.8 gives some general suggestions on writing style.

Box 2/2.8

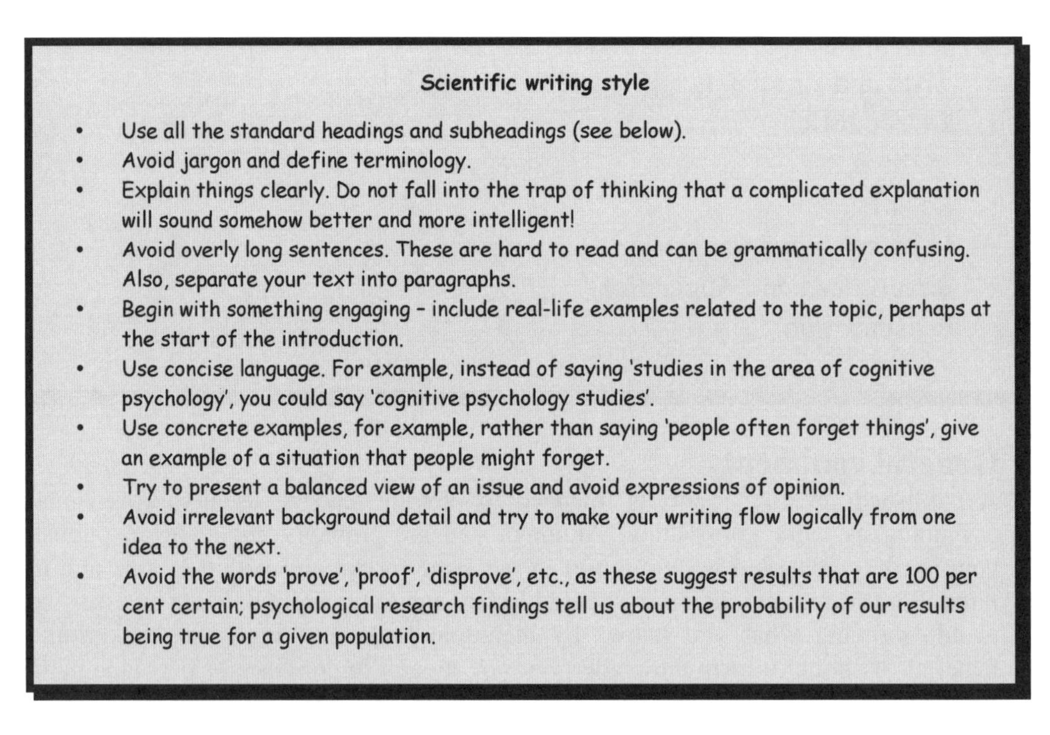

Scientific writing style

- Use all the standard headings and subheadings (see below).
- Avoid jargon and define terminology.
- Explain things clearly. Do not fall into the trap of thinking that a complicated explanation will sound somehow better and more intelligent!
- Avoid overly long sentences. These are hard to read and can be grammatically confusing. Also, separate your text into paragraphs.
- Begin with something engaging - include real-life examples related to the topic, perhaps at the start of the introduction.
- Use concise language. For example, instead of saying 'studies in the area of cognitive psychology', you could say 'cognitive psychology studies'.
- Use concrete examples, for example, rather than saying 'people often forget things', give an example of a situation that people might forget.
- Try to present a balanced view of an issue and avoid expressions of opinion.
- Avoid irrelevant background detail and try to make your writing flow logically from one idea to the next.
- Avoid the words 'prove', 'proof', 'disprove', etc., as these suggest results that are 100 per cent certain; psychological research findings tell us about the probability of our results being true for a given population.

Of course, all of the issues of good grammar, spelling and punctuation are as relevant to scientific report writing as to any other form of writing in school or college. Poor use of commas, for example, can make a sentence very unclear.

Note that in terms of length, the SQA sets a guideline of 1500-2000 words. You will *not* be penalised if you go slightly over 2000 words. The same is true if your report is less than 1500 words, but in this case, you should be careful that you have not missed anything out. The length of your sections will vary, but it is important to keep the *abstract* (see below) short – less than two hundred words.

Tips:

- Read classic research studies, which are available in shortened versions (see 'Further reading' at the end of this text), for examples of good written style.
- Write at least two drafts. The first draft can be checked against the above length guidelines.
- Make sure you know your final word count, as you have to declare it on the SQA flyleaf.

Overview

There is an internationally acknowledged format for psychology reports and anyone who submits an article to a scientific journal has to write in this style. This is what writers of Research Investigations should be working towards and the required sections are shown below in **Box 2/2.9**, together with their value in marks (out of 50) according to the Higher Psychology marking guidelines.

Box 2/2.9

Acknowledged Format for Psychology Reports (and Marks Weighting for Higher Psychology)

Title:	States the aim of the study in terms of the variables under investigation.
Abstract (5 marks):	Gives a very brief overview of the entire study.
Introduction (10):	Presents the background and links to the aim and hypotheses.
Method (8):	Explains how the study was performed.
Results (8):	Shows the results in terms of data and statistical analysis.
Discussion (12):	Interprets the results, comment, suggests further research, concludes.
References (3):	Directs reader to the sources/books you have mentioned.

(A further 4 marks will be available for presentation and style for the purposes of your RI.)

Please note that although the title is not awarded marks, it must be present and in the standard format (see below). The report must also include appendices, where information/materials, e.g. instructions, questionnaires, raw data and calculations are included. A further *four marks* are available for presentation and style, bringing the total up to fifty. Therefore, with the exam out of 100 marks, the RI report is worth the equivalent of 25 exam marks, i.e. a fifth (20 per cent) of the overall grade. While this might not sound like much, it could make the difference between an A and a B, or a pass and a fail.

There now follows a section-by-section description of what goes in each of these parts of the report (and what does not!).

Title and abstract

The title of your report is quite different from the title of an essay. It should express the nature of the study in terms of the variables being investigated as accurately as possible. This is more important than the title sounding good, being snappy or humourous! It should read something like: 'An investigation into the effect of (insert IV) on (insert DV)'. For example, a title for a study which measured the effect of sleep deprivation on driving performance could read:

> 'An investigation into the effects of different levels of sleep deprivation on number of mistakes made in a driving simulator.'

You may vary the style, but the information should be the same. This example puts the DV first:

> 'The emergence of the word length effect in young children: the effects of overt and covert rehearsal.'

For a correlational study, the title will be phrased slightly differently, as you are looking for a relationship between the variables, rather than the effect of one on the other. For example:

> 'A study of the relationship between the number of hours of driving lessons taken and the number of errors made in the driving test.'

The title should first appear centred on a separate title page. It should then be repeated at the top of the first page of the report proper, where it will be followed by the abstract (Burton, 2002).

An abstract is a summary that allows a reader to see at a glance what the experiment involved. Unlike other summaries, which usually come at the end, the report abstract is at the start, allowing busy researchers to get a quick overview of a new study and decide whether it is sufficiently relevant for them to read. As well as the main ('take-home') message from your study, the abstract should include:

- A short statement of the issue being investigated, including the aim of the study and mentioning background theories and/or research.
- The method and design being used.
- Who the participants were, how many there were and how they were selected.
- The variables being studied and the research hypothesis.

- Summary of the main results (a sentence should be enough; include figures).
- Brief conclusions in relation to the hypothesis (again, a sentence should do it).

If a previous piece of research is central to your study, it should be mentioned in the abstract. It is important to remember that an abstract does not just set the scene of the research, but does summarise all parts of the report, including results and conclusions. This example shows how an abstract might end:

> '[T]he study found a higher mean estimated IQ from males (124.8) than from females (112.1) and it was concluded that males are likely to estimate their own IQ higher than females' estimates of their own IQ. This suggests that males may have higher self-esteem than females and/or are less likely to play down their abilities in public situations.'

There are five marks available in the external assessment of the RI for the abstract.

Tips:

- The title page could also include your name and SQA candidate number, the school/college's name and the date or session.
- Many writers choose to leave writing the abstract to the end and this is a sensible strategy – it is difficult to make a summary before writing the conclusions!

Introduction

It is vitally important to be clear that an introduction in a scientific report is *not* just a short lead-in to the topic, but will be one of the longest sections, putting the study in its theoretical context. It is nothing like the introductory paragraph of an essay, but instead has to do three things: (1) outline the previous research, (2) give the aim and rationale for the study and (3) state the experimental/alternative and null hypotheses (Coolican, 1996).

Outlining previous research, also called a 'literature review', is essential in introducing the concepts and debates in the topic. For example, if you wanted to do a new experiment which was closely related to the 'working memory model' of memory, you would try to mention some of the most famous studies that relate to this area:

> 'Baddeley and colleagues have done several experiments into short term memory and have tried to show that this is better viewed as 'working memory' used for everyday tasks such as reading and performing calculations. It comprises both visual and verbal components, suggesting that we can perform both visual and verbal task simultaneously' (Baddeley and Hitch, 1974). This is supported by neurological evidence of patients who have lost one or the other area of short term memory, but not both (Shallice and Warrington, 1970). Their model suggests that the 'multi-store model' of memory (Atkinson and Shiffrin, 1968) is too simplistic.

As shown in the example above, previous research studies mentioned should be followed by a citation in brackets, which links to a 'reference' at the end (see 'References and appendices', below). This allows the reader to find the books and articles which you are talking about. If the author of the study is mentioned by name, only the year goes in brackets. Do *not* include full titles and publication details at this stage – these go in your references section at the end.

For the investigation, the research you outline does not have to be an exhaustive review, but should show that you understand the background. It is best to describe the work of several psychologists, as there are many areas of disagreement where it is useful to view an issue from more than one side and these should usually be presented in chronological order of research and theory development. At least some of the research you mention should be recent. Note also that the previous research cited must be relevant to your study – there is no point in mentioning irrelevant studies just because you have read them.

A good plan is to *briefly* outline the main ideas on the general topic (e.g. memory or stress, etc.) and then mention in more detail the specific study/studies that are closely related to your own study. You could also include a real-life example of the issue, perhaps at the start.

Ideally, the research background will move from a clear statement of previous ideas and findings on the topic through to information that supports your hypothesis. This means presenting a coherent argument of why the study is useful and necessary, in the light of previous research and background theory and why a certain outcome is being predicted. This may involve highlighting a weakness in a previous study, or a conflict between two theories that needs to be resolved. You may remember how Ainsworth and Bell's (1970) 'Strange Situation' experiment has been done in many different countries around the world to help clarify the role of culture in the process of attachment.

This theoretical justification of the study – the rationale – should lead into the aim of the study, which is (usually) to discover whether the research hypothesis is supported, or, more generally, to provide evidence for or against a certain view or theory. You should, therefore, now state the aim of your study.

The experimental or (if a 'non-experimental design' is being used) 'alternative' hypothesis is the most important part of your study, in that it says what you expect to find, as a scientific prediction. Without this, your results will be meaningless – what matters, is whether your results support your hypothesis or not.

An experimental hypothesis must:

- Include the 'independent variable' (IV), stated as specifically as possible.
- Include the 'dependent variable' (DV), stated as specifically as possible.
- State that the IV will have an effect on the DV, or that there will be a difference between the sets of DV values found.

Instead of an experimental hypothesis, the hypothesis in any non-experimental study is commonly called the 'alternative hypothesis'. In the case of a correlation study, this hypothesis has a special format, which predicts that there will be a relationship between the two co-variables and can predict whether the relationship will be positive or negative. For example:

> 'The alternative hypothesis is that the number of lies people tell will be negatively correlated with the number of compliments they receive'.

It is important to state variables in such a way that it is clear what you are doing. For example, you could predict that 'music affects memory', but it would be much more precise to say that 'the presence or absence of classical music will affect the number of words remembered on a verbal memory test'. Such wording narrows down the scope of your variables so that they can become the basis of an experiment.

Published research often uses the term 'significant difference' – this means a *real* difference, after taking chance factors into account. No two groups of measurements will be the same, but the difference between them may or may not be statistically significant. However, statistical testing is not required at Higher level and, therefore, as a general rule avoid the word 'significant' in your hypotheses. (See 'Results', below, for more details.)

Another example of an experimental hypothesis might be:

> 'The experimental hypothesis is that the level of stress (high or low) will have an effect on the number of errors made on a spelling test.'

Note that the above example does not say the *direction* of the difference – that is, it does not say whether stress will increase or reduce errors, just that it will have some effect. If you have a theoretical reason from your background research, you will be able to predict a direction, so it could be better to say, for example:

> 'The experimental hypothesis is that people will make more mistakes on a spelling test when they are in a high stress rather than in a low stress situation.'

Your null hypothesis has to cover all possible outcomes other than the prediction made in the experimental or alternative hypothesis, so that the results will support one hypothesis or the other. Usually, this means saying that there will be *no difference* found between conditions, or no effect of the IV on the DV and any difference that is shown will be due to chance factors. It is not correct to say that the null hypothesis is the opposite of the experimental hypothesis. So, as a typical example:

> 'The null hypothesis is that stress will have no effect on the number of errors made on a spelling test and any difference found will be due to chance factors.'

Again, the null hypothesis will have a slightly different form with a correlational design that will state that no relationship between the two co-variables will be found, or that a relationship in the predicted direction (positive or negative) will not be found. The following null hypothesis could go with the above example of an alternative hypothesis:

> 'The null hypothesis is that the number of lies people tell will not be negatively correlated with the number of compliments they receive'.

It should be clear that saying there will be no negative correlation found is different from saying that a positive correlation will be found.

When your RI is externally assessed, it is important to note that there are 10 marks available for the Introduction – five for the research background, two for the aim and three for the hypothesis.

Method

Use a new major heading to begin this section. The method, as mentioned above, should clearly describe the design, the variables and the ways in which the experiment was controlled. It should state what was done in the experiment and how. Your RI plan and log will be very helpful in writing up this section. The aim of a good method section is that another psychologist could easily replicate your work to test your results (Robson, 1983). It may even be possible to write most of this section before you run the study, but remember to use the past tense.

The Method section usually has four sub-sections: design, participants, materials/apparatus and procedure. (Note: sub-headings should be used – *do not* use continuous prose!). For external assessment purposes, there are four marks available for design and four marks available for the other three sub-sections put together.

Design

This section should start by saying whether your study was an experimental or non-experimental design. If it is non-experimental, the method (e.g. correlation) should be specified. With experiments, design has a specific technical meaning – it refers to whether a 'repeated measures', 'independent measures' or 'matched-pairs study' is used, which should be stated along with a rationale for the choice of design. This is central to the research and it is important to bear in mind the design and reason for selecting it as you write up the results and conclusions of your study.

This section should also clarify what the variables were and, in the case of experiments, the *conditions* (i.e. the two or more values of the IV – 'condition A: 5 hours of sleep and condition B: 8 hours of sleep). Remember that variables can be described in varying levels of precision and in this section they should be given as precisely as possible. You should also precisely describe how the DV (or each co-variable, in the case of a correlation design) was measured. This might be quite simple – in a memory test, the DV might just be 'the number of words recalled'. Many other measures will require more detail, for example, in a survey, the kind of scales used must be described (e.g. Likert scale), along with how the scores were obtained and what they mean.

The design section should say how participants were allocated to groups (which should normally be randomly) and describe the controls used (such as 'counterbalancing' and testing different groups at the same time of day).

Participants

This simply says who your participants are in terms of their age, sex and background. Age or age band (e.g. 16-19) and sex of members of each group used should be stated, including an average age (usually the mean). If relevant, participants' occupations and nationality could be mentioned. The section must also say how they were selected and whether they were 'naive' to the aims of the experiment. It should be quite easy to write. See **Box 2/2.10** for an example.

Box 2/2.10

Participants

The participants in the experiment were twenty college students, eight male and twelve female. These were divided randomly into two groups of four males and six females. The mean age of group 1 was 19 years 3 months and the mean age of group 2 was 20 years and 1 month. All were Scottish except for one member of group 1 who was English and one member of group 2 who was Swedish. The participants were selected using opportunity sampling, which involved asking passers by in the college refectory to help with the study. None had any prior knowledge of psychology or of the experiment.

Materials and apparatus

In this section, list or describe your briefing materials: brief and de-brief, standard instructions, consent form. Also, any worksheets, pictures, videos, etc., that you used to conduct the research should be clearly described. If they are very short you could include them here – otherwise put copies of the sheets in an *appendix* (see below) and refer to it in the text, for example, 'this questionnaire is shown in Appendix 1'.

It is helpful to give details of the materials that are in an appendix. For example, if you use a list of words or objects for a memory test, you could give three or four examples here and include the full list as an appendix.

If you use a questionnaire, this will go in an appendix, but again it is useful to give details here such as an example question and explanation of where the materials came from. If it is taken from another source, you should state where; if you designed it yourself, you should state the guiding principles used.

Perhaps you used certain apparatus, like TVs, videos, timers, etc. These should be included with technical specifications, e.g. 'A Canon MV630I camcorder was used'. If apparatus used was substantial, it can be included under a separate subheading.

Procedure

The procedure details exactly how the study was run. In it you describe exactly what was done with the participants. As you know, it is very important to treat participants ethically and in your procedure section you should refer to every ethical principle you followed, including giving information and obtaining consent.

Remember to keep the procedure in the passive voice, e.g. 'participants *were* asked to...', *not* '*I* asked the participants to...'. Although it is tempting to use bullet points, the standard format is to use continuous prose within this sub-section. Mention timings, instructions given and other relevant details. Do *not* give the word-by-word instructions here, but include a written/typed copy of these in an appendix (again, referred to in the text).

Remember that the main thing about a Method section is that it should give enough detail that another researcher could run a study in exactly the same way. This means the procedure should include even apparently trivial details, such as where participants were seated and whether participants were tested all together or individually.

If you have two conditions that are quite similar, it is perfectly acceptable to describe the procedure for one and then say, 'The procedure for condition 2 was exactly the same as for condition 1, except that....'

Your procedure should end on an ethical note, too, such as 'participants were thanked and informed that they could obtain further information from...' Of course, there is no limit to how much detail you could use and some – such as the brand of carpet in the room or whether the windows were clean – will almost certainly be unnecessary. Like all other sections it should be as clear and concise as possible.

Tips:

- Use a main heading for 'Method' and subheadings for 'design', 'participants', 'materials and apparatus' and 'procedure'.
- Do not describe materials or apparatus in the procedure sub-section. For example, any questionnaire used should be described under 'materials', so in 'procedure' it is sufficient to say 'the questionnaire'.

Results

A new major section starts here, showing the results of your research. This material can vary widely, but as a minimum it will include a statement of how the data were collected, such as counting correct answers on a test, an explanation of descriptive statistics used (e.g. averages/standard deviations/percentages), table(s) and graph(s) showing percentages/averages, etc., and comments stating all the main findings clearly in terms of the experimental or alternative hypothesis.

Descriptive statistics summarise what the results are. This usually involves showing means and/or medians, ranges and/or standard deviations and drawing graphs of results. Raw data, i.e. every result from every participant, are usually not included here; a raw data table should instead be presented in an appendix (see below). For correlational research, it may be sensible to include a full data table in this section and, of course, a 'scattergram'.

It may be useful to include all of the descriptive statistics mentioned in Part 1 of this Chapter, although there are cases where certain measures of central tendency need not be used, for example, if no 'mode' exists. Often, two graphical representations of the results will be sufficient (e.g. a table and a bar graph or scattergram), but in some cases, more will be necessary to fully illustrate all results. Do *not* include full calculations here – these should go in an appendix. Remember to state clearly *why* you analysed the data the way you did.

Graphs and tables should be clear and accurate and *must be referred to in the text* – they should never stand alone. All rows, columns and axes must be labelled. Furthermore, the tables must be numbered and each should have a 'legend', i.e. a short text underneath it, explaining what it is. This is all in order to make things clear for your reader and you will lose marks for not doing it. A graph can show exactly the same results as a table – it is justified in that it makes any pattern or difference clearer and more obvious. The following example in **Table 2/2.2** shows how a simple table can clearly show all major descriptive statistics.

Table 2/2.2

Total and average scores on Word Recall Test, n=13

	Meaningful Words	Nonsense Words
Total number of words recalled	134	94
Mean number of words recalled	10.3	7.2
Standard deviation	3.2	2.8

Each participant's answer sheet was collected and their score was calculated on the basis of one mark for each word correctly recalled. These results were collated and mean scores and standard deviations were calculated.

There are various types of graph that can be used. With typical data, scores on two or more conditions, a bar graph like the example in **Diagram 2/2.4** (which we saw in **Section 1**) is usually appropriate.

Diagram 2/2.4

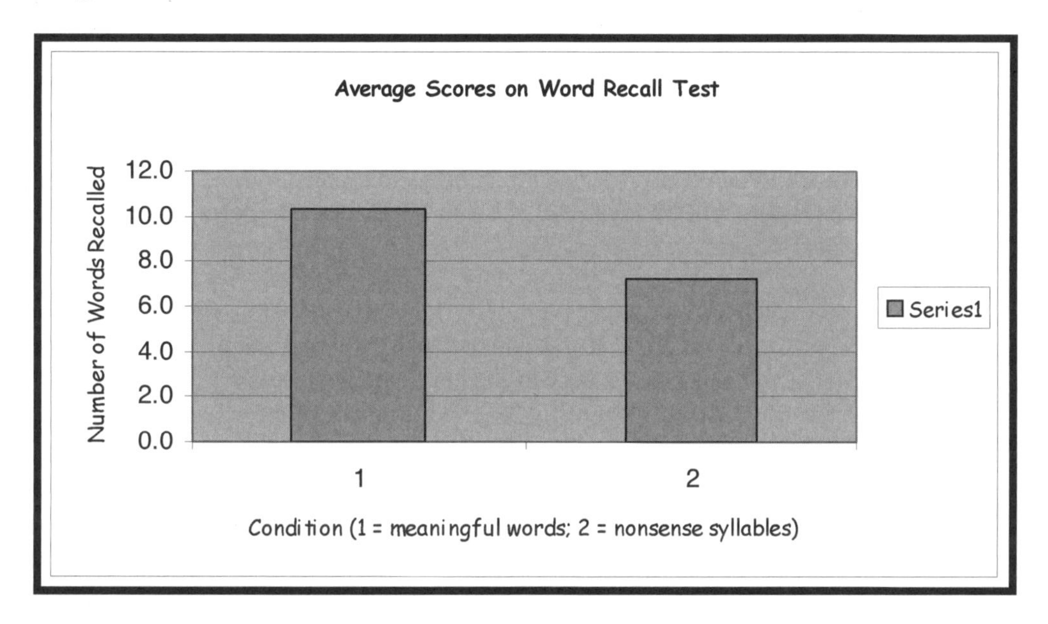

Pie charts are popular, but are not suitable for data like the example above (**Diagram 2/2.4**) and, therefore, not suitable for the majority of RIs. They should only be used when the results form portions of a whole, such as percentages of respondents to a questionnaire survey. This would look as indicated in **Diagram 2/2.5**.

Diagram 2/2.5

Example of a Pie Chart

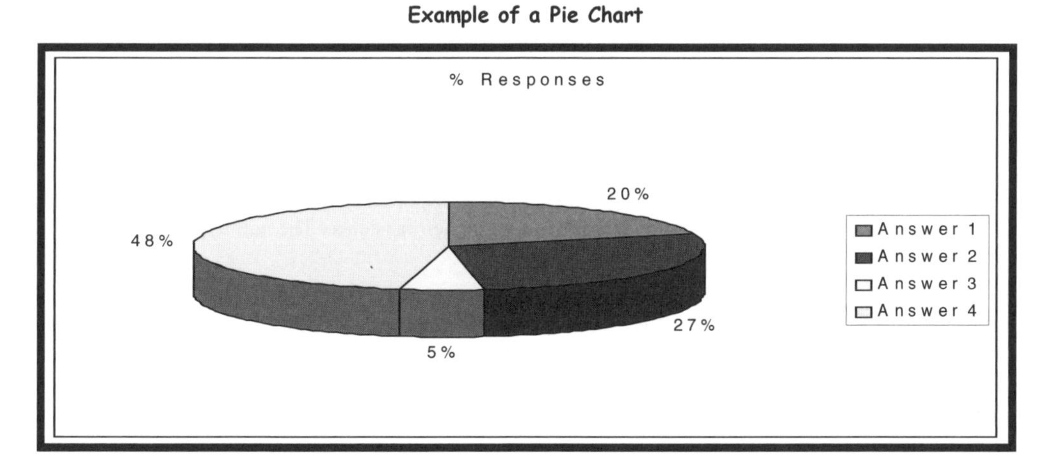

Finally, the results section will state whether the results support the hypothesis or not. Statistically, if there is a 5 per cent or less chance that it could be due to random factors, then they support the experimental hypothesis and if there is a greater than 5 per cent possibility, then the null hypothesis is supported. We describe results that meet this threshold as being 'statistically significant'. However, the statistical techniques needed to discover these probabilities are *not* included in the Higher Psychology course. Therefore, you could simply state that there *is* a difference between the conditions – what meaning this difference has can be explained in the under the heading, 'Discussion', below.

Correlational hypotheses will be accepted or rejected according to whether the correlation found is of the strength predicted and of the direction (positive or negative) predicted. As you know, this will be apparent from the direction and spread of the points on your scattergram (refer to Part 1 of this Chapter for further examples of scattergrams).

This will bring the results section to a close. Generally, it should not include much comment. Also, do not discuss your results, do not mention theories and do not mention aspects of your procedure in this section.

Discussion and conclusion

Discussion

Now the findings should be discussed and analysed. The discussion is the last major section and you should begin by re-stating the main results – although it may seem repetitive, it makes the discussion much clearer to read.

Next, the results should be interpreted in terms of the hypotheses. The following example relates to a study on stereotyping. Notice that the difference (a fact of the results) is followed by what it means in real terms – x has an effect on y (these examples are based in part on MacRae et al, 1994):

> 'The results show a significant difference between the experimental group and the controls. This shows that when people attempt to suppress unwanted thoughts, they are likely to subsequently reappear with even greater insistence. The null hypothesis can, therefore, be rejected.'

The section will then analyse the results in more detail and attempt to explain them. In explaining the results, it is useful to relate them to the background theory. For example:

> 'Devine (1989) and Fiske (1989) both argue that people can consciously control stereotyped thinking. Our results, however, suggest that there may be a range of behavioural side-effects in doing so.'

With a replicated experiment, the discussion will include a careful comparison of the current results with the original findings and will state whether they provide further support of the researchers' theories or not. It may be, for example, that your results did not support your experimental hypothesis and you feel that this is because of a flaw in the procedure used.

You must also point out any potential criticisms of your study. This is totally normal and although it may seem harmful to your conclusions, doing so might actually serve to justify methods and stave off criticisms. For example:

> 'Although the sample was non-random, it was felt that the number of participants used was large enough to remove the chance of systematic bias.'

As well as the problems of sampling, which are common to student research, be sure to identify any flaws that are specific to the design and procedure of your study, for example, any uncontrolled variables, order effects or demand characteristics. Ethical issues should certainly be discussed, (see Chapter 2, Part 1 for ethical principles in research). For every problem identified, you should suggest how it could be remedied.

You should also suggest further research – this usually derives from the analysis of your findings. For example, perhaps something has come up that you cannot explain, or maybe it would be helpful to test a similar hypothesis using a different methodology.

> 'As the participants used in this study were all in their late teens, it would be helpful to replicate the existing study with other age groups, to check whether the findings can be generalised to older people in society. The experiment is also limited by using only verbal material in the test of memory. As it is well known that verbal and visual material can be independently processed in STM (Baddeley and Hitch, 1974), it is recommended that future research make use of visual cues such as pictures and colours.'

Conclusion

The next stage is the 'conclusion'. The discussion has gone into a lot of detail, so it is useful to present the 'big picture', the take home message. This section will form a brief summary of what was found and concluded. In this respect, the conclusion will be quite similar to the second half of the abstract. Generally, conclusion sections are much shorter than discussions – only a sentence or two – stating what you found (statistically) and what you concluded from this, in terms of the hypotheses and/or previous researchers' findings. The conclusion can be formatted as a separate section or as a subsection under the 'discussion'.

References and appendices

The references section provides the reader with the information they need to find all sources referred to during the text (the year, publisher, journal volume, etc.). It is *not* a bibliography – it should only contain the details of books or research papers that you have directly cited in your text such as '(Miller, 1956)', not your more general background reading (e.g. this book). In this respect, the references section functions rather like a list of footnotes.

There is a very specific format for references. In addition to sticking as closely as possible to the examples below, bear in mind the golden rule for references – formatting should be consistent.

The list of references should be ordered alphabetically by the first named author. There is a standard format for references that is preferable and ideally you should include publication details, but at least include the name, title and year of a publication.

The format for a journal reference is as follows:

Author, initials (Year) 'Title of journal article', Name of journal (in italics), Volume (issue number), first page-last page. For example:

> Craik, F. I. M. and Lockhart, R. S. (1972) 'Levels of processing: A framework for memory research', *Journal of Verbal Learning and Verbal Behaviour*, 11, 671-684

Note that after the first line, subsequent lines can be indented to make the first author's name stand out.

The format for a book reference is as follows:

Author, initials (Year) Title with Capitals (in italics), Town/city of publication, Publishing company. For example:

> Baddeley, A.D. (1999) *Essentials of Human Memory*, East Sussex, Psychology Press

For a website, the author's name, the year of publication (if no year is available on the website, give the date you accessed it) and the title of article should be given, followed by the full internet (http) address. For example:

> Hall, T.M. (1998) 'Culture-bound syndromes', *http://weber.ucsd.edu~thall/cbs_glos.html*

If you refer to an article that is discussed in another book (e.g. this textbook), you could, of course, simply 'lift' the reference from the back of the textbook! However, you should, technically, cite it like this in the body of your text:

Lynch (1999, cited in Staddon *et al*, 2005)

In this case it is acceptable to include the reference just to Staddon et al (or to both) in the main text of your RI and in the references section. You could do this several times; it looks bad, though, if you only have one reference, so if you are taking many references from the textbook, you should probably include all of the original references, as well as the source. They can then be cited as normal and the entry in the reference section would look like this:

Lynch, T. (1999) *Communication in the Language Classroom*, Oxford: Oxford University Press, cited in Staddon, Duffy, Cherrie, Firth and McDermott (2005) *Psychology for Higher*, Paisley, Unity Publications Ltd

An appendix is for including relevant additional material referred to in the text. Any worksheets or questionnaires used should come in this section. A table of raw data (i.e. all of the participants' actual responses without any analysis or averaging) and calculations can also go in an appendix and must be included if details from these are referred to in the discussion. Some other things commonly found in appendices include observation schedules, briefings and instructions (written down in order to ensure consistency), pictures and other easily reproducible materials/responses and full details (perhaps with pictures) of apparatus used if these seem too lengthy for the apparatus section in 'Method'.

As with references, an appendix cannot stand alone – it must be referred to in the text as follows: 'A memory worksheet was given out to each participant; this is shown in Appendix 1' or 'A memory worksheet was given out to each participant (see Appendix 1)'.

Different appendices should be numbered and titled and these numbers and titles should appear on your contents page. If there are two parts to a worksheet, or if an appendix is quite long, consider subdividing it using decimal fractions, e.g. Appendix 1.1, Appendix 1.2, etc., or simply 'Appendix 1 part 1, part 2', etc.

Tips:

- Take a note of all sources as you do your reading from resource books and websites. This will save going to check them later.
- Be consistent! For example, refer to all books in the same way. This is important to remember if you are taking references from the back of other books that may not all use the same format.

- Ensure that appendices are neat and well presented and note that they should be page numbered.

Presentation

The investigation should be word-processed and printed double-spaced on white paper, one sided only. Pages should be numbered and a contents page provided. Start each section on a new page. Hand-written RIs are acceptable, but word-processing will save you time and effort when it comes to revising drafts. A hand-written RI should also use one side of a page only and writing should be as neat as possible (and must be readable!). Use black or blue ink. Remember that there are four marks available for presentation and style.

Graphs used in the 'Results' section can be drawn up using computer software, but if you are unsure how to do this then write them by hand on a separate piece of graph paper and include it in your submission. Remember to give this a page number!

The research investigation plan and log will go on a standard template provided by your centre. It is acceptable to write this by hand – try to be neat and avoid cramming in too much information. If you are concerned about the presentation of this form, photocopy it so that you can write a draft. Alternatively, the form may be provided as a Word document, which you can then type your work into and print off.

Your centre will have flyleafs supplied by the SQA that you must sign and date. These go over the front cover of your investigation and contain information about you and your school or college. They will also have plastic pockets for the RI to go in. For this reason, you need not put the document in any special binding – it is quite sufficient to simply staple the sheets together at the top corner. Make sure that you retain a copy of your RI, for security reasons and for exam revision.

Checklist

Use this checklist (Table 2/2.3) as you prepare the final version of your RI to ensure that all of your sections are in and that you have done what you should have to make your report as good as possible.

Table 2/2.3

Checklist

TASK	TICK ✓
Includes separate title page with your name, title of study and college/school.	
Includes a contents page with page numbers; pages are numbered throughout.	
Abstract includes summary of results and conclusions.	
References in introduction cited in the form: (Miller, 1956).	
Correctly expressed experimental/alternative hypothesis and null hypothesis.	
Introduction clarifies why you are doing the study (aim, rationale).	
Method section divided into four subsections.	
'Participants' includes age, sampling method and how allocated to conditions.	
'Procedure' includes briefing/instructions and debriefing to participants.	
Results section states how data were obtained.	
Includes at least two graphs or tables.	
Measures of central tendency & standard deviations have been calculated.	
Tables/graphs have name/legend (e.g. Table 1: Average scores).	
Tables/graphs referred to in text (e.g. see Table 1, above).	
Main results made clear and null hypothesis rejected or accepted.	
Discussion summarises main results only.	
Discussion states if experimental or null hypotheses supported/accepted.	
Any unusual or unexpected data are discussed.	
Results discussed in terms of theories.	
Method criticised where necessary; remedies and further research ideas suggested.	
Conclusion states main findings and principle conclusions drawn.	
References section written, in alphabetical order.	
Appendices included, one per item (e.g. Appendix 1: Consent form and brief).	
Double spaced text.	
Printed one sided, clipped in top left corner.	
Filled out, signed and dated pink flyleaf sheet.	

Answers to Activities

Activity 1 - Box 2/2.1

With a repeated measures study, each participant does both conditions. This means that the test cannot be exactly the same, otherwise there will be practice effects. However, it cannot be completely different, as the two conditions must be comparable. The experimenters might choose to make two lists of words that are similar in terms of the frequency and length of the words. The following issues arise:

- Are the lists of words equally difficult to remember? If not, this will influence the results.
- Are some of the words likely to be particularly memorable to some people?
- What kind of words do you use? Words which easily spring to mind are usually concrete nouns (things, objects) - but if you wish to use a mixture of words you should probably also include verbs and adjectives.
- How do you select words which are truly random? Due to the way our memories work, thinking of a string of words will tend to result in words which are related to each other. One possibility is to use ready-made lists prepared by another researcher. Another is to look through the dictionary, choosing the first word off every 10th page. These would then be randomised, so that they were not in alphabetical order.
- Another problem is to determine what music to play - not everyone will agree on what is normal music and even in a particular genre, such as classical, there are a huge number of possibilities.

Activity 2 - Box 2/2.3

This is a typical case of research which requires naïve participants. If people who take part know that the experimenter expects males to give relatively high IQ estimates and females to give relatively low estimates, people may 'play up' to the experiment and give the estimates which they feel are wanted. Alternatively, they may try to 'disprove' the hypothesis by giving estimates of the opposite size. Either way, these results would be hard to compare to results of a similar study done on non-psychology students.

Factors which put participants under pressure to behave in ways expected of them are known as demand characteristics (Orne, 1962). It also might place them under stress to conform, which is ethically unacceptable.

Activity 3 - Box 2/2.5

1. Experimenters could have sampled randomly, or at least avoided using people who know them because of possibility of bias.
2. Should have allocated participants randomly to conditions. Having males in one group and females in another group introduces another variable (sex of participant) - a 'confounding variable' that will lead to systematic error.
3. It is not a good idea to discuss expectations and hypotheses with participants and they may 'play up' to the study - resulting in demand characteristics.
4. Group 2 should have sat somewhere else while they waited - they may distract group 1 and could also get an insight into the study which could lead to error in the results. Alternatively, they could have done their condition simultaneously, as there are two experimenters, but ideally each participant should be treated individually.
5. Obviously, instructions should have been given in advance. Starting again will affect the results, as group 1 will already have had a chance to learn some of the items. It would be better to continue without the instructions, as the task is not particularly complex, or to ask participants to stop for a moment while the experimenters read them out.
6. Group 2 are not being treated the same as group 1 and this leads to systematic error in results. For example, they have had a second chance to hear the instructions.
7. Group 2 are being given a constraint that was not given to group one. Again, both groups should be treated the same except for the IV.
8. Having given instructions it is best to stick to them - the experimenters needn't wait until people have finished the task. They are attempting to compensate for giving group two a time constraint that group 1 did not have, but it will not make up for the fact that the two groups have not received the same treatment. Note, also, that group 2 were thanked and group 1 simply asked to leave - both groups should have had a proper debriefing.
9. In the RI, each person should take a separate copy of the data and do their own analysis.
10. There is a serious breach of confidentiality in posting names and results up publicly. This might be humiliating for the people who scored low on the memory test and is an unethical practice. Results can be posted up, but names should be excluded.

Activity 4 - Box 2/2.7

Condition 1: Mean is 8, mode is 7, median is 8. Range is 14-2, =12. Standard deviation - sum of squares is 148, SD=3.51.
Condition 2: Mean is 10, modes are 3, 9, 10 and 11, median is 10. Range is 19-3, =16. Standard deviation - sum of squares is 268, SD=4.73.

Chapter 3
Social Psychology

Introduction

Social psychology is one of the key domains in the 'Psychology: The Individual in the Social Context' Unit of Higher Psychology. The aim of this Chapter, therefore, is to develop knowledge and understanding of social psychological theories and research studies. As such, you are encouraged to analyse, interpret and evaluate psychological explanations of the following topics:

1. Prejudice.
2. Conformity and Obedience.
3. Anti-social behaviour.
4. Social relationships.

One of the main debates in social psychology is whether an individual's social behaviour is the result of his/her:

1. Social context ('behaviourist approach').
2. Personality ('psychodynamic approach').
3. Attachment style ('developmental approach').
4. Interpretation of social information ('cognitive approach').

Psychological explanations of human behaviour are drawn from a range of theoretical perspectives that are supported or challenged by classical and contemporary research studies. The findings of the research studies are critically interpreted and methodological concerns are evaluated in terms of their validity and reliability. This promotes the importance of logical argument as opposed to common sense explanation.

The contribution made by social-psychological research to our understanding of social behaviour and its application in the following areas, is examined:

1. Sexism and racism.
2. Strategies for the reduction of prejudice.
3. The effects of media violence on aggression.
4. Anger-management intervention.
5. Effects of divorce on children.

To assist you with exam revision a summary of the main points and self-test questions are presented at the end of each section within this Chapter.

The domain of social psychology examines inherently social motives for all aspects of human behaviour. According to Allport (1935), social psychology involves 'the scientific investigation of how the thoughts, feelings and behaviours of individuals are influenced by the actual, imagined or implied presence of others'. Election campaigns influence who we believe the best candidate to be, food advertisements affect what we buy in the supermarket, media images determine particular body shapes that we find attractive and the person sitting next to us in the class will have an impact on our learning experience.

Since romantic relationships are an important part of our social lives, social psychologists are interested in explaining things like why we fall in love with some people and not others and why some relationships last and others do not. Both individual and group behaviour are of importance in this area of study. Relations between groups are investigated and in particular why people tend to be prejudiced in favour of their own racial and ethnic groups and against 'outsiders'. Such prejudice may lead to discrimination, which can manifest itself in extreme forms of both hostility *and* altruism.

Explaining and understanding human interaction, in its many forms, is the main focus of social psychology. In an attempt to attach meaning to human interaction, social psychologists consider the wider contexts in which behaviour occurs, that is:

1. The *physical contexts*, e.g. aggression induced by overcrowding.
2. The *social contexts*, e.g. the expected relationship between pupil and teacher in school.
3. The *cultural contexts*, e.g. British people forming queues at the Post Office.

Social psychology is closely related to the discipline of sociology in that it attempts to understand the causes and consequences of major societal problems, such as sexism, racism, anti-social behaviour, and relationship breakdown. You are encouraged, therefore, to also read what sociologists say about topics such as the prejudice, since much of the subject matter overlaps.

Prejudice

Section summary

The objectives of this section are to investigate:

- The link between stereotyping, prejudice and discrimination.
- The components of prejudice.
- Sexism and racism.
- Theoretical perspectives of the formation of prejudice.
- Research studies on the formation of prejudice.
- Strategies for the reduction of prejudice.
- The reduction of institutional racism.

The social psychological phenomenon of 'prejudice' is one of humanity's pressing issues, as it is associated with human suffering ranging from verbal taunts to the extermination of an entire social group. Prejudice can produce profound hatred that may lead to the 'dehumanisation' of an 'out-group', as in the relationship between the Palestinians and the Israelis in the Middle East, pro-Unionists and Republicans in Northern Ireland and between the Hutu and Tutsi tribal groups in Central Africa. Almost any social group can become targets of prejudice, although enduring victims tend to occupy lower social positions in society in terms of status, wealth and prestige. In Western industrialised societies, prejudice is also based on sex, age, ethnicity, sexuality and physical and mental disability. Social psychologists examine the *causes* and *consequences* of prejudice and its relationship to 'discrimination'.

Link between stereotyping, prejudice and discrimination

To stereotype is to create an *over-generalised mental image* of a group of people. Such generalisations are based on very little information and do not allow for exceptions or individual differences between members of the group. Stereotypes can be positive, for example, 'Glaswegians are friendly, but tend to be mostly *negative* – Glaswegians get drunk and fight on the streets every weekend.' Inaccurate stereotyping often leads to prejudiced attitudes that involve 'pre-judgements' about a group or its members, for example, 'He is from Glasgow and has a scar on his face, therefore, he is a troublemaker.'

Stereotyping and prejudice become more harmful when they foster negative discrimination, which is 'unfavourable behaviour' towards a group or its members, for example, 'I do not employ the Glaswegian with the scar even though he is the best qualified applicant for the job.' Discrimination, therefore, is *prejudice in action.*

Possible links between stereotyping, prejudice and discrimination may be seen in the following speech by Saudi dissident, Osama Bin Laden, who has, by many, been accorded responsibility for orchestrating the terrorist attacks on the Pentagon and World Trade Centre, which killed over 3000 people, on 11 September 2001:

> 'The killing of Americans and their civilian and military allies is a religious duty for each and every Muslim. [...] We [...] – with God's help – call on every Muslim who believes in God and wishes to be rewarded to comply with God's order to kill Americans and plunder their money whenever and wherever they find it. [The September 11 attack] gave a harsh lesson to those arrogant peoples, for whom freedom is but for the white race. [...] God willing, America's end is near'. (Composite of two Osama Bin Laden statements made in a February 1998 appeal to Muslims and a videotaped statement in November 2001.)

1. A 'stereotypical belief' present in the excerpt is that Americans are arrogant. This may have led to a prejudiced attitude towards Americans.
2. A 'prejudiced attitude', which incited anger, was the assertion that Americans think freedom is only for the white race. This may have led to negative discrimination towards Americans.
3. An extreme form of 'discrimination' was displayed in the 11 September 2001 attack on the World Trade Centre in New York city, which ended in a large number of deaths of people from various countries and ethnic backgrounds.

Although stereotyping, prejudice and discrimination frequently occur together, they can also exist distinctly. Prejudiced attitudes do not always lead to discrimination. For example, we may feel a strong dislike towards people who skip the queue to get on the bus, but we may not display this feeling in our behaviour. In other words, we do not necessarily *act* in accordance with our attitudes.

La Piere (1934) claimed that the results of his study demonstrated the relationship between attitudes and behaviour. He was interested in investigating whether there was consistency between prejudiced attitudes towards Chinese people in general and specific discrimination towards two of his Chinese friends. La Piere concluded that attitudes and behaviour could be inconsistent. (See details of the study in **Box 3.1**.)

Box 3.1

Research: La Piere's Attitudes Versus Actions (1934)

Participants: People working in 66 hotels, caravan parks and tourist homes in the United States. People who were working in 184 restaurants in the United States took part.

Method: Field experiment.

Procedure: The researcher travelled across the United States with a young Chinese couple at a time when there was widespread prejudice against Asians and there were no laws against racial discrimination. They stayed in over 200 hotels, motels and restaurants. They were refused service only once. Six months later a letter was sent to all of the establishments asking: 'Will you accept members of the Chinese race in your establishment?'

Results: Of the 128 who replied 92 per cent said they would refuse to serve Chinese people, 7 per cent said they were uncertain and that it would depend on the circumstances, 1 per cent said they would not refuse to serve Chinese people.

Conclusion: Attitudes can be contradicted by behaviour. The attitudes people say they have may be different from the attitudes implied by their behaviour.

Evaluation: Staff members who served the Asian couple may not have been the same people who answered the letters. Questionnaires do not have high predictive validity. Ajzen and Fishbein (1980) argued that La Piere was attempting to predict *specific behaviour,* i.e. towards these two specific Chinese people on these particular occasions, from *general attitudes* - towards Chinese people in general, and that more valid findings could be derived from an investigation into the relationship between general attitudes and general behaviour.

(See 'Research methods' Chapter for methodological evaluation of field experiments and questionnaires.)

The components of prejudice

Baron and Byrne (1999) define prejudice a (typically negative) attitude 'towards the members of some group, based solely on their membership of that group.' Hence, the unique characteristics of any particular group member are subsumed by attitudes toward the group in general.

Prejudice has *three* components, which are common to all attitudes (Allport, 1954, Harding *et al*, 1969):

1. The 'cognitive' component encompasses the 'beliefs' – stereotypes – about a

particular group and its members. This is a learned belief, e.g. all overweight people are greedy.
2. The 'affective' component is the 'feelings' that are stimulated by a particular group, e.g. one may feel contempt towards overweight people.
3. The 'behavioural' component encompasses how a person 'acts' – discrimination – towards the group, e.g. one may avoid associating with overweight people.

Brown (1995) views this traditional model as over-simplistic and proposes a definition of prejudice that includes the concept of discrimination:

> 'The holding of derogatory social attitudes or cognitive beliefs, the expression of negative affect, or the display of hostile or discriminatory behaviour towards members of a group on account of their membership of that group.'

Sexism and racism

Sexism

'Sexism' could be defined as prejudice and discrimination against people based on whether they are male or female. In the UK, women are disadvantaged relative to men in business, government and employment and, therefore, most research focuses on women as victims of sexism. Although women outperform men academically and over half of all undergraduates are female, gender inequalities remain in the workplace (Equal Opportunities Commission, 2004). Forty four per cent of women and only 10 per cent of men who are in employment work part-time. Women face discrimination in achieving equal pay and having the same promotion prospects as men. In the UK, there is a 19 per cent pay gap between male and female earnings (Social Trends, 2004). Regardless of whether they have the same degree, the same qualifications and do the same job, women are paid less than men.

It was reported on the BBC News on 10 April 2001 that a woman who claimed she was forced to resign from her high-flying City job over a pay dispute won a sex discrimination case against her former London employer. Julie Bower, 35, was earning £120,000 per annum as a senior analyst with Schroder Securities Limited, but resigned because her complaints about unequal pay went unanswered. An employment tribunal has ruled that the company discriminated against Mrs Bower by paying her far less than her male colleagues. She was given a £25,000 bonus in 1998, while some male co-workers received up to £1.5m.

Gender segregation

There is 'gender segregation' in the workplace; that is, there is a tendency for men and women to be employed in different types of occupations. Modern apprentices in hairdressing and in early years care and education are mainly women, while those in construction, engineering and plumbing are mainly men (Equal Opportunities

Commission, 2004). Women hold 80 per cent of administrative and secretarial jobs, while men hold 92 per cent of skilled trades. Only 18 per cent of Westminster MPs are women. Eighty-six per cent of primary and nursery teachers are women while 84 per cent of ICT managers are men.

Gender stereotypes of occupations are manifested in the belief that certain occupations (e.g. nurse, teacher, secretary, etc.) are 'women's' occupations and others (e.g. automotive mechanic, engineer, medical doctor, etc.) are 'men's'. Such gender-stereotyping of occupations may discourage individuals from pursuing careers in occupations typed as gender-inappropriate for them, even though they may actually be well-suited for such careers. This stereotyping may also discourage managers from hiring qualified individuals for non-traditional occupations, though such actions are not lawful. In addition, occupational gender stereotyping may affect pay, promotion, and other rewards based on perceptions that 'women's work' is not as important or as difficult as 'men's work'. Finally, such stereotyping and the resulting outcomes contribute to the pervasive gender segregation of occupations.

Racism

'Racism' can be defined as prejudice and discrimination against people based on their ethnic origin. This has led to many different kinds of negative treatment of black and Asian people, including violent attacks and discrimination in employment. According to the Labour Force Survey (Spring 1997), people from ethnic minority groups are more likely than white people to experience unemployment, regardless of qualifications. Eleven per cent of black people with degrees and 6 per cent of Asians with degrees were unemployed in 1997, compared with only 3 per cent of white degree holders. Among those with no qualifications, 34 per cent of black people were unemployed, compared with 13 per cent of white people.

In a study carried out by Devine and Elliot (1995), they found that 45 per cent of respondents considered African-Americans to be lazy, and over 25 per cent characterised African-Americans as athletic, rhythmetic, low in intelligence, criminal, hostile and loud. Such stereotyping may explain why black American youths are more likely to be stopped and searched, and why black Americans are two and a half times more likely to go to jail. Black people get longer prison sentences and make up 12 per cent of the male and 18 per cent of the female prison population in the United States.

Theoretical perspectives of prejudice

There are many psychological explanations for the formation of prejudiced attitudes in society. Included among the causes suggested by more established psychological theories are *stereotyping*, *scape-goating*, *authoritarian personalities*, *inter-group conflict* and *conformity*.

More recently, Hoyle and Wickramasinghe (1999) proposed an *evolutionary* explanation of prejudice, which highlights that historical and sociological factors also need to be considered when attempting to understand prejudice.

Psychodynamic perspective: 'frustration-aggression hypothesis'

The Freudian concept that people's hidden unconscious thoughts and feelings influence their behaviour was applied by Dollard *et al* (1939), when they proposed the 'frustration-aggression hypothesis'. This theory suggests that when we are prevented from reaching our goal we feel frustrated, which is an excitable state that leads to aggression. If we cannot display aggression towards the source of our frustration, e.g. our boss, we *displace* it onto a *scapegoat*, such as the cat. Both prejudice and discrimination can be perceived as forms of aggression.

For example, it has been argued that, in Britain, when asylum seekers are placed in under-privileged areas, the number of racial attacks may increase in times of recession, because the British residents feel disempowered and displace the anger they have for the government and other decision-makers onto the asylum seekers, thus making them scapegoats. In the article in **Box 3.2**, the British National Party (BNP) attempt to explain racism by arguing that white people did not have the power to demonstrate aggression towards the source of their frustration – the council and the police – and so displaced it onto asylum seekers in the form of prejudice and discrimination.

Box 3.2

Far Right Political Groups

The Far Right groups, Lijst Pim Fortuyn and the British National Party (BNP), have been marginalised for years, but have recently been united in their common use of asylum seekers and economic migrants as scapegoats. Fortuyn, the late leader of the Lijst Pim Fortuyn Party, was determined to reduce the number of asylum seekers and immigrants in The Netherlands. Nearly half of the 18-30 year olds polled wanted a ban on Muslim immigration. In April 2002, Fortuyn was shot and killed by an animal rights activist and 10 days later his party became the 2nd largest in The Netherlands. At the same time there was a rise in support for the BNP, who won 3 seats in the local government elections in Burnley on 3 May 2002. The BNP put forward the argument that white people had been discriminated against by the council through funding and by the police ignoring them when they complained of being victims of racist attacks.

(Source: Adapted from 'Pay the right' Burhan Wazir, 'The Observer', Sunday December 22, 2002.)

Frustration, however, does not always lead to aggression. Some individuals may simply shrug their shoulders while others may burst into tears when frustrated.

Likewise, not all aggressive acts arise from frustration. (See also the 'frustration-aggression hypothesis' in the 'Anti-social behaviour' Section of this Chapter.)

Psychodynamic perspective: personality theory – the authoritarian personality
'Personality theories' emphasise the importance of personality traits when investigating the source of prejudice. Adorno *et al* (1950) argued that individuals, with what they term as an 'authoritarian personality', are particularly predisposed to prejudiced attitudes. The characteristics of an authoritarian personality include excessive conformity, submissiveness to authority, intolerance, insecurity and rigid, stereotyped, thought patterns. Adorno *et al* designed what they classed as the 'F scale' to measure fascist personality tendencies. Respondents were given a questionnaire and asked to state how strongly they agreed with each statement. A high score on the 'F scale' indicated an authoritarian personality and, therefore, a propensity to prejudiced attitudes. Some of the statements were:

1. Obedience and respect for authority are the most important virtues children should learn.
2. Young people sometimes get rebellious ideas, but as they grow up they ought to get over them and settle down.
3. People can be divided into two distinct classes: the weak and the strong.
4. No sane, normal, decent people could ever think of hurting a close friend or relative.
5. Homosexuals are hardly better than criminals and ought to be severely punished.

(Source: Adapted from Adorno, Frenkel-Brunswick, Levinson, and Stanford, 1950: 255-57.)

Adorno *et al* found that those who scored high on the 'F scale' had had a very strict upbringing and rigid discipline. The researchers adopted a 'psychodynamic perspective', by suggesting that these authoritarian personalities *repressed* – i.e. did not allow their feelings to be expressed – the hostility they felt for their parents, allowing it expression through the *displacement* of hostile feelings onto more vulnerable groups in society.

Adorno *et al*'s authoritarian personality theory may be evaluated thus:

1. Adorno *et al*'s sample was biased, comprising over 2,000, mostly middle-class, non-Jewish, white Americans from California.
2. Agreement to the statements always indicated authoritarianism. Those who agreed with most of the statements may have been the type of people who are inclined to agree with what is put before them and were not necessarily

authoritarian types. A high 'F' score may suggest a *conforming* personality rather than an authoritarian one.

3. Adorno *et al*'s authoritarian personality theory cannot explain why whole societies, or whole groups within societies, become prejudiced. A society often adopts a consistently racist approach towards one particular group, e.g. over half a million Rwandan Tutsis – 90 per cent of the Rwandan Tutsi population – were killed in 1994, yet there will be huge individual differences among the people involved in the killings in terms of authoritarianism.
4. Many social groups are uniform in their prejudices, so perhaps conformity to group norms is more responsible for prejudice than authoritarian personality type.

Adorno *et al*'s Freudian type of explanation was rejected by Altemeyer (1988), who prefers a simpler conceptualisation based on 'social learning theory'. Altemeyer (1988) sees authoritarianism as a social attitude, or cluster of attitudes, that is learned through interactions with peers, parents, schools, the media and through experiences with people who hold conventional and unconventional beliefs and lifestyles. His measure of right-wing authoritarianism (RWA) is considered to be more reliable and unidimensional than Adorno *et al*'s 'F-scale' and its components were balanced for agreement response set. However, Feldman (2003) suggests that it is almost impossible to distinguish between authoritarianism and social conservatism on Altemeyer's scale. Social conservatism is the distrust or dislike of social change and is, arguably at least, much less socially damaging than authoritarianism. Some of the items on a recent version of Altemeyer's (1998) measure are that:

1. Gays and lesbians are just as healthy and moral as anybody else.
2. There is absolutely nothing wrong with nudist camps.
3. Homosexuals and feminists should be praised for being brave enough to defy 'traditional family values'.
4. A 'woman's place' should be wherever she wants to be. The days when women are submissive to their husbands and social conventions belong strictly to our past.
5. There is nothing wrong with pre-marital sexual intercourse.

Altemeyer (2003) conducted a study in which Canadian students, who had been identified as being high in right-wing authoritarianism, were asked to pretend that they ruled the world. According to Altemeyer, authoritarians created a *simulated* world that was cruel and dangerous. Knafo (2003), however, was more interested in examining the *actual* social world that authoritarians create by how they raised their children according to their own standards, practices and values. He was particularly interested in violent tendencies and in values that influence inter-group attitudes and behaviours. Eighty-two authoritarian and 252 non-authoritarian Israeli fathers and their adolescent children participated in the study. The authoritarian fathers predicted that their children would give higher than average importance to power, tradition and conformity values but lower than average importance to the values of benevolence (kindness and generosity), universalism (consideration for others, unselfishness) and self-direction. The findings showed that in comparison with the children of non-authoritarian fathers, children of authoritarian fathers placed more importance on *power* and less importance on *universalism.* Altemeyer (1998) points out that power correlates negatively with interpersonal cooperation as is evident in levels of Israeli Jews' readiness for social contact with Arabs. Power, he argues, correlates positively with all sorts of prejudice, whereas universalism is negatively correlated with prejudice and positively correlated with interpersonal cooperation. Knafo (2003) found that when universalism is highly valued there are low levels of bullying, whereas in cases where power is valued, high levels of bullying are demonstrated. The children of authoritarian fathers also tend to make friends with bullies.

Knafo (2003) suggests that children of authoritarian fathers have become used to a coercive, sometimes even abusive, relationship and are inclined to associate with friends who have similar qualities to their fathers. In the same way that a right-wing authoritarian may seek to reduce perceived threats to the self by following a strong leader who will maintain the status quo, so might the offspring of authoritarian fathers feel safer in the company of strong, aggressive friends.

Knafo (2003) concluded that authoritarian fathers raise children who are non-accepting of out-groups and who tend to associate with bullies. The combination of both high adolescent power values and having been raised by an authoritarian father is associated with the highest degrees of bullying by adolescents. Although authoritarian fathers do not influence all of the child's values, they transmit values that emphasise social dominance and rejection of the out-group. (See 'the authoritarian personality' in the 'Anti-social behaviour' Section of this Chapter.)

Social psychological perspective: 'realistic conflict theory'

According to 'realistic conflict theory' (Sherif, 1966) the main cause of prejudice is conflict of interest. Competing groups develop negative stereotypes of each other that are used to legitimise discrimination. For example, the stereotypical view of women being caring, sensitive and nurturing can be used to explain the lack of women in powerful positions, especially when such jobs are scarce. Prejudice and discrimination evolve from competition for scarce resources, such as jobs, houses, income and power. Evidence for this explanation comes from 'The Robbers' Cave field experiment' conducted by Sherif *et al* (1961), who set out to investigate the relationship between *competition* and prejudice and discrimination. (See **Box 3.3** for details of the study.)

Box 3.3

Research: Sherif *et al's* 'The Robbers' Cave Field Experiment' (1961)

Participants: 22 white, middle-class well-adjusted 11-12 year old boys at a three- week summer camp in Robbers' Cave State Park, Oklahoma.

Method: Field experiment.

Procedure: Participants were randomly assigned to two groups. The groups were kept separate for most of the first week. They were unaware of each other's existence. Teamwork activities were specifically designed to produce group cohesiveness and identity. The camp counsellors were as non-directive as possible. The groups adopted the names of 'Eagles' and 'Rattlers'. At the end of the first week the two groups were introduced. Researchers arranged a tournament, which comprised of ten team games with prizes (scarce resources) for each member of the winning team. Researchers later set up activities that encouraged the boys to cooperate with each other to reach a common goal. Sherif *et al* ensured that a truck (that was to carry their food to a cookout) had gotten stuck in the mud.

Results: At the end of the first week the boys described members of their own group as 'tough' and 'brave', but members of the other group as 'cheats' and 'bums'. Fights between members of the two teams had to be broken up throughout the tournament. The 'Eagles' won the tournament and the 'Rattlers' stole the prizes. When faced with the truck being stuck in the mud, the Rattlers and Eagles worked together to free the truck. This had a dramatic effect in creating a friendlier atmosphere.

Conclusions: At the end of the first week teamwork activities had established group coherence and identity. Stereotypical views of in-group and out-group members were displayed. Conflict for material resources (prizes) led to in-group cohesiveness and out-group hostility. Prejudice and discrimination was the product of competition for scarce resources. Having a superordinate goal *reduced* prejudice and discrimination between the two groups

Evaluation: The experiment was as natural as possible. However, the experiment used American boys only, so findings cannot be generalised. The conflict began very early on. The groups became hostile as soon as they discovered each other and before there was any competition for material goods. Competition between groups does not always produce prejudice and discrimination ('social identity theory', Tajfel (1971)). Tyerman and Spencer (1983) carried out a very similar study with English boy scouts who knew each other before the camp. Competition was very friendly and notions of in-group and out-group did not emerge.

(See the 'Research methods' Chapter for a methodological evaluation of field experiments.)

'Realistic conflict theory' can also be used to explain prejudice attitudes and discriminatory behaviour towards asylum seekers in Britain. Tabloid newspapers frequently portray migrants and refugees as 'scroungers' trying to take advantage of the health, education, housing and benefits system, thus inflaming prejudices by creating a sense of hostility and fear between groups.

In *The Sun*, 18 August 2003, it was reported that asylum seekers were the 'country's biggest crisis,' with Britain being the 'Number 1 destination'. In fact, the UK has less than 0.5 per cent of the world's refugees and is ranked 9th among West European countries in the number of asylum applications received (Scottish Asylum Seekers Consortium, September 2003). *The Sun* article also claimed that Britain was being hit by a record number of new cases of HIV with lots of immigrants carrying the virus. This report has not been supported by any research. The editorial went further by complaining, without any evidence, that foreigners coming to Britain were defrauding the National Health Service (NHS) of £2 billion a year and had to be stopped. However, in February 2003 the Royal College of Nursing stated that the NHS is *dependent* upon the 42,000 immigrant nurses currently working in this country.

Likewise, an article in *The Daily Mail* on 28 May 2003, entitled 'Asylum seekers have brought NHS to its knees,' blamed asylum seekers for the waiting time in hospital casualty departments rising from a few minutes to over two and a half hours. The same article also claimed that pharmacists were overstretched as a result of giving out methadone to asylum seekers. No supporting evidence for such actions was offered.

Cognitive perspective: social identity theory

Inter-group discrimination can occur even where there is no competition present (Tajfel, 1971). This notion challenges the realistic conflict theory proposed by Sherif *et al* (1961). Humans are motivated to organise and make sense of all the information they receive about the world around them. They do this by putting people, objects and events into *categories*, highlighting the differences between each distinct group and overestimating the similarities among items in the same group. Therefore, they are likely to perceive people in groups other than their own as very different to themselves, while almost ignoring the individual differences among members of other groups. Such categorisation forms the basis for stereotyping.

Tajfel (1981) further developed his ideas culminating in 'social identity theory', that states that membership of a social group contributes to the development of one's personal identity. In the pursuit of a positive self-image, therefore, we tend to see groups to which we belong in a favourable light, thus 'in-group favouritism' and 'negative out-group bias' occurs. Tajfel *et al*'s (1971) research aimed to show that simply putting people into groups is enough for people to discriminate in favour of their own group and against members of the other group. The research findings can be linked not only with the social identity theory, but *also* with the realistic conflict theory, if status is perceived as a scarce resource. (See details of Tajfel's study in **Box 3.4**.)

Box 3.4

Research: Experiments in Inter-group Discrimination (Tajfel, 1971)

Method: 2 laboratory experiments. The independent variable was the type of allocation they were asked to make and the dependent variable was the choices they made, i.e. being fair or showing discrimination.

Participants: Sixty-four 14 and 15 year old boys from a comprehensive school in a Bristol suburb.

Procedure: Participants were instructed to complete a number of tasks independently. There was no face-to-face interaction within or across groups. Participants were randomly split into two groups - they were 'minimal' groups, i.e. there was nothing to distinguish them. Participants were asked to distribute money to the people in both groups. They were presented with the choice of either giving £2 to their own group and £1 to the other group or £3 to their own group and £4 to the other group.

Results: Participants chose the first option and gave £2 to their own group and £1 to the other group.

Conclusion: In-group profit was sacrificed for in-group superiority. In-group members were favoured over out-group members. The participants favoured their own group and discriminated against the other so displaying in-group preference in order to boost their self-esteem and self-image. Sustained competition for resources may not be necessary for in-group preference.

Evaluation: According to Hodson and Sorrentino (2001), only certain types of people are insecure enough to allow group identification to lead to prejudice and discrimination. Social identity theory cannot explain the slaughter of millions of Jews in Nazi camps (Brown and Lint, 2002). The relationship between groups is based on more complex issues than the need for people to obtain in-group status. Wider social forces, such as conflict over scarce resources like power, wealth and income, generate prejudice and discrimination. However, within many Western societies, status may enhance power, wealth and income. Therefore, it becomes a scarce resource and can lead to prejudice and discrimination.

(See the 'Research methods' Chapter for a methodological evaluation of laboratory experiments.)

Social identity theory can be applied to the issue of *racism* against immigrants in Britain. Daily newspapers in Britain frequently portray immigrants as a threat to the British way of life, a threat reinforced by the then Home Secretary, David Blunkett, in August 2003, when he proposed that asylum seekers should undergo a language and citizenship test when applying for asylum. Interestingly, however, many so-called 'British' things like fish and chips were first introduced into the UK by Russian immigrants in the nineteenth century. Such things are overlooked when developing common sense notions of 'Britishness'.

Despite this, on 26 February 2004, the first citizenship ceremony in the UK in Brent Town Hall took place. Prince Charles and David Blunkett were in attendance to give medals and certificates to 19 immigrants, each of whom had to swear allegiance to the Queen and sing The National Anthem. It could be argued that shopping in Marks and Spencers, reading *Heat* magazine and watching *Eastenders*, may provide immigrants with more insight into British culture than appreciating the Prince of Wales' double-breasted suit and the Mayor of Brent's fake furs. It was contrary to the concept of an inclusive multi-cultural society to hear Prince Charles implying 'out-group bias' when he stressed 'in-group favouritism' in his speech, by pronouncing that 'to be British is to win the first prize in the lottery of life.' This particular phrase was quoted from a speech made by Cecile John Rhodes (1853-1902), a British imperialist who conquered Rhodesia (known as Zimbabwe since 1980) and aimed to bring all of Africa under British rule.

Ethnic stereotypes are further reinforced by some sections of the printed press. Tabloid stories that focus on perceived differences between immigrants and the indigenous population, without considering that all humans display a similar range of behaviours and emotions. This has the effect of fuelling the notion that immigrants are somewhat less human than other citizens.

The popular British tabloid newspaper, *The Sun* (4 July 2003), ran the headline 'Asylum seekers steal the Queen's birds for barbecues,' thereby accusing asylum seekers of stealing the Queen's swans for barbecues. According to the paper, an official Metropolitan police report had stated that East European poachers had killed hundreds of royal swans after luring them into baited traps and that police had swooped on the thieves as they were about to cook the birds. *The Sun* commented that it was tragic that people from abroad did not respect British traditions. Within 24 hours the report was exposed as a lie. There had been no police swoop and no metropolitan police report.

On 21 August 2003, *The Daily Star's* front page bore the headline 'Asylum seekers eat our donkeys.' This article reported that nine donkeys had been stolen from Greenwich Park in south-east London and, according to a 'police insider', may have been taken by immigrants who liked donkey meat. *The Daily Star* went on to speculate that the donkeys had been spotted with Albanian immigrants who were offering rides on beaches in Kent. Such stories create 'moral panics' by exaggerating the perceived threat of immigrants and focusing on the similarities among members of the indigenous population, whilst magnifying the differences between immigrants and the indigenous population.

Psychologists are interested in explaining such behaviours. For instance, social psychological research has focused on the effect of what is known as 'perceived in-group similarity' on stereotyping and prejudice. Zarate *et al* (2004) investigated how the *quality* or *type* of similarity influences inter-group relations. In a study based in the United States, they presented participants with either *interpersonal* or *task-related traits* and asked one group to rate how similar they perceived their in-group to be in relation to Mexican immigrants. A second group was asked to evaluate how the groups differed on interpersonal and work-related tasks. Control groups evaluated themselves on the given traits. Negative attitudes towards immigrants were demonstrated when participants were asked to assess the differences between groups in terms of interpersonal traits, thus supporting the notion proposed by 'social identity theory' that perceived 'cultural threats' and the 'categorisation' of people can lead to prejudice. In addition, when work-related traits were salient, similarity comparisons led to more negative attitudes towards immigrants, supporting the 'realistic conflict hypothesis' that claims perceived 'economic threats' can produce prejudiced attitudes. It was concluded that a perceived threat to either cultural norms or economic well-being leads to prejudice.

Biological perspective: evolutionary theory

Hoyle and Wickramasinghe (1999) proposed that the evolutionary development of prejudicial attitudes contributed to basic human survival in prehistoric times. Although they no longer have this function in contemporary 'progressive' societies, they still exist today. (See the 'Anti-social behaviour' Section of this Chapter.)

This evolutionary theory states that because humans originated in tropical climates, probably West Africa, darker skinned people would have been healthier, since the pigment melanin that colours the skin helps protect the skin from cancers developed from excessive exposure to the sun. In line with the Darwinian notion of 'natural selection', the healthier darker genes would be successfully transmitted to offspring. Paler people would have diminished survival rates and would, therefore, produce fewer children, resulting in a lower contribution to the community. Consequently, a prejudiced attitude towards white skinned people may have emerged. As humans moved northwards from Africa, the sunlight would not have been strong enough to stimulate the production of vitamin D in dark-skinned people, which is vital for strong, healthy bones and teeth. Therefore, paler people would be healthier and so prejudiced attitudes towards black people may have developed.

Evolutionary theory suggests that the link between skin colour and health would have become so deeply ingrained in the human mind that prejudiced attitudes would become, via social learning and conditioning, a natural part of our thinking. Unfortunately, it is impossible to conduct empirical research to find out if adaptation to the environment was a major factor in the evolution of behaviour.

However, Bentley (2000) has pointed out that socio-biologists have argued that units of cultural learning, 'memes', can be inherited by being passed from mind to mind as a result of experience. The notion of a 'prejudice meme' would support Hoyle and Wickramasinghe's theory.

Reduction of prejudice

Inspired by the brutal murder of Martin Luther King in 1968, a third-grade teacher in Iowa, Jane Elliot, conducted an exercise (Zimbardo, 1979) in an attempt to show white children what it was like to be a victim of prejudice. She began the exercise by announcing to the children that it was well known in society that blue-eyed children were more intelligent and generally superior to brown-eyed children. Eye colour was chosen because the children had no control over it, but the method of choice has historical roots of a sinister nature. During World War II, the Nazis frequently used eye colour to determine if someone was to be sent to the gas chamber or not. In the exercise conducted by Elliot, she instructed the brown-eyed children to treat the blue-eyed children with respect. They were told that they were inferior to the blue-eyed children and had to sit at the back of the class, stand at the end of the line and use paper cups instead of drinking directly from the water fountain. The blue-eyed children were afforded preferential treatment, allowed extra time at breaks and given second helpings at lunch. After just one hour of the experiment the brown-eyed children's work deteriorated. They demonstrated signs of depression and described themselves as stupid. The brown-eyed children became mean.

On the second day, Jane Elliot told the children that she had made a mistake. Actually, it was the brown-eyed children who were more intelligent and superior to the blue-eyed children. A switch in attitude occurred at once. The confidence of the blue-eyed children deteriorated and the work of the brown-eyed children improved. The children were debriefed at the end of the study. At school reunions years later the participants all agreed that they had learned about the effects of prejudice from the exercise and were glad that they had taken part. Since 1984, Jane Elliot has been conducting an adult version of the brown eyes and blue eyes exercise in corporate and government institutions.

The contact hypothesis

The 'contact hypothesis' (Allport, 1954) states that the more positive contact we have with different groups in terms of ages, sexuality, physical/mental abilities, mental health and race, the lower the level of prejudice and discrimination will be.

Allport recognised, however, that contact alone would not determine lower levels of prejudice. Extensive contact between the Tutsi and the Hutu in Rwanda, for example, did not prevent 800,000 people being slaughtered in 100 days (Prunier, 1995). Hewstone (2003) points out that for contact to promote positive out-group attitudes and increase the perceived variability of the out-group it has to be promoted in conditions that have the effect of lowering anxiety, increasing perspective-taking, providing normative support and maintaining awareness of each individual's membership of the group. He argues that successful inter-group contact requires that group members have the opportunity to become personally acquainted with each other under conditions of *equal status*. The importance of equal status in reducing prejudice was demonstrated by Clore (1976), who set up a summer camp experiment in which black and white participants shared all responsibilities, duties and roles equally. Power and status were evenly distributed between blacks and whites. It was concluded from her findings that the conditions of equal status had significantly reduced prejudice.

Hewstone (2003) also proposes that the presence of 'super-ordinate goal's – common goals that can only be reached through cooperation among all groups – contribute towards the reduction in prejudice. Sherif *et al*'s (1961) summer camp study (details of the study can be seen in **Box 3.3**) supported this idea when it was found that when a group of boys had to work together to pull a truck that had broken down back to the camp, friendships developed between the two groups and hostility was greatly reduced.

The article in **Box 3.5** discusses how the contact theory could enable schoolchildren to cross the racial divide.

There are ongoing contact schemes in the educational and community relations sectors in Northern Ireland and ongoing debates over single faith schools in Scotland. A journalist and TV presenter who studied in Belfast stated that 'many of my Protestant friends had not met a Catholic, and Catholics had scarcely met a Protestant, until they got to university' (Ross, 1999). Perhaps, then, attempts to increase social contact in such contexts may have the effect of lowering prejudiced attitudes.

In *The Sunday Times* Scotland (1 February 2004), Bishop Joseph Divine – Roman Catholic Bishop of Motherwell, Scotland, and advocator of denominational schools –

postulated that the claim that children who are not schooled together cannot live harmoniously with each other in adult life is absurd, pointing out that half of Scotland's Catholics are married to 'non-Catholics'. He proposed that sectarianism, like racial discrimination, is not taught in schools but in homes and throughout wider society. Bishop Divine stressed that parents should maintain the right to educate their children within the moral framework as prescribed by their chosen faith.

Box 3.5

Contact Theory and School Children

Bruce Berry is head-teacher at Bradford's Belle-Vue boys' school. He was invited to Oxford University to discuss his previously written article, 'Parallel Lives', in which he reported that there was increasing segregation between Asians and white people in Bradford.

The social psychologist, Hewstone, had used the article to discuss the contact theory that begins with the premise that if we get to know people from different groups prejudice will be reduced. However, the theory does recognise that it can be difficult to encourage people to generalise these positive attitudes from individual acquaintances to the whole social group. Another social psychologist, Pettigrew, found that the contact theory was most significantly supported when adolescents were involved, regardless of the type of group. In his 516 studies, he found contact to have the most pronounced effect between gay and straight communities and secondly between ethnic groups.

Berry responded to the psychologists' comments by describing how Bell Vue had started as an all-white grammar school, gradually becoming a truly integrated place of learning with 50 per cent Asian pupils and 50 per cent white pupils. In 1984, Honeyford, the head of Bradford primary school publicly claimed that, because of the increase in the number of Asian pupils at the school, the education of the white children was suffering. Two years later 80 per cent of the pupils were Asian and now 98 per cent of the 500 pupils have Asian backgrounds.

According to Berry, Asian and white families are not mixing with each others' cultures in school or at home, as Asian families live mostly in the city centre and white families live on the periphery. Hence, segregation is increasing in the city. None of the theories are able to suggest how we can improve the situation and in the meantime all that we can do is encourage children to value different cultures equally and not simply accommodate them.

(Adapted from: David Ward (14 January 2003) 'Culture Class', 'The Guardian'.)

Hewstone (2003) is quick to point out that contact is not the only 'cure' for prejudice. Other interventions that do more than just require a degree of contact, such as the promotion of empathy, multicultural educational programmes and the maintenance of group identities, are also necessary.

Society is becoming more diverse not only in relation to culture, but also in terms of age. An increase in the ageing population has led to concern about the associated economic and healthcare issues, but the social and relational implications have largely been ignored. Intergenerational contact has been tainted by age-based prejudice that can lead to inter-group conflict, which could be of concern to society as intergenerational relationships within and outside the family are on the increase. Soliz and Harwood (2003) investigated the effect of perceived contact between grandparents and grandchildren on stereotypes of older adults. They found support for the contact hypothesis. (See **Box 3.6** for details of the study.)

Box 3.6

Research: 'Perceptions of Communication in a Family Relationship and the Reduction of Intergroup Prejudice,' Jordan Soliz and Jake Harwood (2003)

Aims:
(a) To examine the links between variation in young adults' perceptions of communication with their grandparents and attitudes towards older adults.
(b) To investigate the association between the perception of grandparent-grandchild relationships and the formation of stereotypes of older adults.

Hypotheses:
(a) More positive perceptions of communication experiences with grandparents will be related to more positive attitudes towards older adults.
(b) More perceived variation in grandparent-grandchild communication will be associated with increased perceptions of heterogeneity among older adults.

Participants: 102 young adults with ages ranging from 18-25 with a mean age of 20.25. They were all in an introductory speech class at a large American Midwestern university and received a course credit in exchange for volunteering. Sixty-one per cent were female and 39 per cent were male. Seventy-nine per cent were white/European-American, 9 per cent were African-American, 6 per cent were Hispanic/Latino and 6 per cent indicated that they were of other ethnic groups.

Procedure: Each participant completed 3 different questionnaires:
1. A 'grandparent relationship questionnaire' (GRQ) to elicit the number and type (lineage, gender) of grandparent relationships the participant had.
2. A 'grandparent relationship questionnaire' (GQ) to measure specific perceptions of aspects of communication in each of these relationships.
3. An 'older adult questionnaire' (OAQ) to measure more general attitudes towards older adults and intergenerational communication.

The GRQ measures the extent to which grandchildren perceive both themselves and their grandparents to adjust conversations in response to the other's perceived needs, capabilities and expectations.

It was assessed if grandparents go too far or not far enough in accommodating their grandchildren. The degree to which the grandchild feels the grandparent engages in interesting and relevant conversation was investigated.

Design: 56 of the participants completed the GRQ and the GQ before completing the OAQ. The remaining 46 participants completed the OAG before the surveys on grandparents. A correlational design was used.

Results: Both hypotheses were supported. In support of the 'contact hypothesis', perceived communication satisfaction between grandparents and grandchildren was positively associated with attitudes towards intergenerational communication. However, grandchildren who perceive their grandparents to go too far or not far enough in accommodating them are more negative towards their perceptions of older adults. The number of grandparents was not a significant predictor of attitudes towards older adults. Variability in grandparent-grandchild communication satisfaction was significantly positively related to variability in perceptions of older adults' traits. Variability in communication satisfaction is positively related to heterogeneity of perceptions of intergenerational communication.

Conclusions: More negative perceptions of communication behaviours with grandparents are related to more negative attitudes towards older adults. Positive perception of the grandparent-grandchild communication behaviours is associated with positive intergenerational attitudes. There is an association between qualitative variability in grandchildren's communication with their grandparents and perceptions of out-group homogeneity. Findings suggest that more diverse communication experiences with out-group members might be a recommended strategy for improving attitudes. In most cases it appears, however, that more variation in perceptions of communication with grandparents is associated with more negative perceptions of older adults and negative attitudes towards intergenerational communication.

Evaluation: 'Perceptions' of communication rather than *actual* communication in the grandparent-grandchild relationship were examined. The research assumes age group membership to be a salient dimension of the interaction, but family members may be both in-group in terms of religion, ethnicity, gender, social class, and out-group in terms of age, gender.

Findings only suggest that there is an association between diversity in the grandparent-grandchild relationships and greater variance in perceptions of older adults; they *do not* determine causality. The age and educational level of the sample *does not* represent the wider population. Health-related issues may affect whether the nature of the grandchild-grandparent relationship influences perceptions of older adults generally.

(See 'Research methods' Chapter for an evaluation of the correlational design.)

The 'jigsaw technique'

In an attempt to reduce prejudice and discrimination, the school system in Texas was *desegregated* in 1971. However, this had the effect of producing conflict and a decrease in self-esteem among minority group students as their previous schooling had not equipped them to compete with the white students on equal terms. Allport (1954) proposed that desegregation would only produce positive effects if:

1. All groups were in pursuit of 'common goals', as supported by Sherif *et al*'s (1961) findings.
2. Group members were under conditions of 'equal status contact', as supported by Clore's (1976) findings.
3. The groups were 'sanctioned by authority'.

Aronson (1971) set up what he called a 'jigsaw classroom' to encourage the attainment of common goals and so reduce prejudice and discrimination. He placed the students in groups of six, with membership directly proportionate to the ethnic composition of the school. Each member of the group was given a piece of information that was essential to the successful completion of a group project. In total, therefore, there were six pieces of the jigsaw that had to be put together.

Consequently, each student experienced some time as the 'expert'. After several days, the students shared their information with other group members and cooperated effectively as they shared a common goal and each had equal status. The jigsaw technique was successful in decreasing prejudice and discrimination and raising self-esteem. By the mid-80s over 25,000 teachers in the United States had set up jigsaw classrooms (Aronson *et al*, 1999).

Categorisation

According to 'social identity theory' (Tajfel *et al*, 1971), prejudice is the result of the 'categorisation' of people into 'in-groups' and 'out-groups'. Therefore, in an attempt to tackle prejudice, it is necessary to modify the categorisation process in order to alleviate social conflict.

'Recategorisation' is about changing the category by which people are grouped together. It is concerned with the creation of a larger, more inclusive group. According to research conducted by Gaertner *et al* (1989, 1993), the more students see themselves as a single student body, the more positive their feelings towards the ethnic population.

In an increasingly multicultural world people can classify themselves, and others, along multiple dimensions of category membership, e.g. female or male, young or old, black or white, Scottish or English and working class or middle class. Thus, a 17 year old working-class girl can perceive herself to share group membership with other 17 year old girls, but simultaneously perceive herself as being different to 17 year old middle-class girls. Would, then, a 17-year-old working-class girl identify more with 17-year-old working-class boys or with 17-year-old middle-class girls?

Multiple social categorisations *can* effect social judgments and reduce prejudice (Crisp, 2002) by taking into account the additional shared bases for categorisation and not focusing on one criterion for group membership. For example, sex discrimination in the workplace may be reduced when people are encouraged to consider shared group memberships – level of education, motivation, ambition, talents, as well as non-shared, such as sex.

Crisp, Hewstone and Rubin (2001) conducted a study with Cardiff and Bristol students who were categorised as 'psychologists', 'females', 'living in university accommodation', '18 to 20 year olds' and 'born in the U.K'. Hence, they were categorised as group members on a number of dimensions. The researchers hypothesised that using more than just two categorisation criteria would improve attitudes towards the out-group as a whole and that the categorisation strategy would be abandoned as a useful way of making social judgements. The researchers reasoned that people would assess others as individuals rather than on the basis of their membership of a particular group. As predicted, participants did think less categorically and judged each other individually, thus improving inter-group relations. This study demonstrated that 'decategorisation', which involves the removal of *all* categories, has the effect of reducing prejudice. Gaertner *et al* (1989, 1993) encouraged two groups of three students to re-categorise themselves as six *unique* individuals. This produced a reduction in former positive in-group bias and negative out-group bias.

Reduction of institutional racism

The concept of racism is central to most social psychological research studies of prejudice. Although racism traditionally has its roots in biologically-based assumptions, 'new racism' views some groups as being inferior to others in terms of cultural or ethnic differences. If their cultures are perceived as a threat to the British way of life, black people and Asians in Britain may suffer from racism in the following forms:

1. Racial violence and harassment.
2. Inequalities in housing, employment, education and social welfare provision.
3. Derogatory humour and stereotypical representations in the media.
4. Unfair treatment in the criminal justice system.
5. A greater likelihood of being detained in a psychiatric hospital.

Prince Philip, the Queen's husband, appears to believe his ethnic origin and nationality to be superior to others. This attitude is reflected in apparently racist comments he has made in public.

In 1986, he met a group of British students in Beijing and is reported to have said, 'If you stay here much longer you'll all be slitty eyed.' Similarly, in 1994, he is alleged to have asked a wealthy Cayman Islander, 'Aren't most of you descended from pirates?' Shortly after, in 1995, he is said to have asked a Scottish driving instructor, 'How do you keep the natives off the booze long enough to get them through the test?' and, in 1998, when touring a high-tech electronics company in Edinburgh he noticed a fuse box that looked less sophisticated than the other state-of-the-art equipment and said, 'It looks as if it was put in by an Indian.' On 27 May 2004, another Royal, Princess Michael of Kent, allegedly told a group of black people in a restaurant in New York, 'You need to go back to the colonies.'

Despite the fact that the British Royal Family has long been publicly lauded as all that is 'Great' about the Establishment in Britain, the media do not vilify such examples of compulsive racism. Unfortunately, they laughingly refer to the offensive comments as 'gaffes' and present Royals as quaintly eccentric when acting in a racist manner. Such an approach does little to support attempts to tackle racism at the level of public attitudes.

The Macpherson Report, 1999

Racism needs to be understood not only as prejudiced attitudes and behaviour at an individual level, but also as an important aspect of the social structure. 'Institutional racism' occurs where racism is built into the policies and practices of the social system, becoming a taken-for-granted feature of society. It has been argued that the British police force is institutionally racist, since racism forms a part of the constructed policies and practices. In the *Macpherson Report* (1999), 'institutional racism' is defined as:

> '[T]he collective failure of an organisation to provide an appropriate and professional service to people because of their colour, culture or ethnic origin. It can be seen or detected in processes, attitudes and behaviour which amount to discrimination through unwitting prejudice, ignorance, thoughtlessness and racist stereotyping which disadvantage minority ethnic groups.'

The *Macpherson Report* began as an inquiry into the failure of the Metropolitan Police to successfully apprehend the killers of Stephen Lawrence, a young black man murdered by a gang of white racists in 1993. On 26 July 2001, the director of public prosecutions, David Calvert-Smith, accepted that the Crown Prosecution Service (CPS) had been shown to be 'institutionally racist.'

The National Assembly Against Racism's (NAAR) submission to the Lawrence Inquiry stated that only if the existence of institutional racism in the police force and the criminal system is acknowledged, could it be eradicated. Comprehensive and on-going race training in challenging racial stereotypes should be a basic part of staff development in all police areas. Recognition of how institutional, cultural, personal and historical factors maintain institutional racism leads to the development of strategies to combat them. However, in order for prejudice reduction exercises, conflict resolution programmes and cooperative learning to be effective, the underlying issues of power and privilege must be addressed.

NAAR suggests that the ethnic composition of the police force at every level must reflect that of the community it polices, even if this means the setting of short-term targets for fast-track appointment and recruitment of black judges. The mere presence of culturally diverse groups is not sufficient to ensure that members will be treated fairly by those holding power in the institution or society in general. The barriers to understanding cultural differences are still existent in institutional cultures. All too often the presence of diverse cultures is taken as evidence of the non-existence of institutional racism, but this may not be indicative of the situation beneath the surface level.

Application of theoretical concepts to the Macpherson Report
As a useful application of the theoretical concepts introduced above, we might argue that if institutional racism is to be eradicated in the police force:

1. All members of the force, black or white, need to be given *equal status* for an *increase in contact* to be effective.
2. There needs to be more members of minority groups in high status positions for personal contact to be increased at that level.
3. *Common objectives* need to be set and *sanctioned by authority*, as demonstrated in the jigsaw technique.
4. Staff training should highlight the importance of viewing people as individuals, not as group members, thus discouraging *stereotyping* and *labelling*.
5. In order to tackle prejudice and discrimination in the police force, the *categorisation* of people needs to be avoided. Jane Elliot demonstrated that in order to reduce prejudice and discrimination it is essential for people to know how it feels to be a victim of such attitudes.

Section summary

1. *Stereotyping* can lead to *prejudice,* which can lead to *discrimination.*
2. Prejudice (attitude) does not always lead to discrimination (behaviour) – La Piere (1934).
3. The three aspects of prejudice are *affective, behavioural* and *cognitive.*
4. The 'frustration-aggression hypothesis' (Dollard *et al*, 1939) is used to explain prejudice and inter-group aggression as it proposes that all frustration leads to aggression and all aggression comes from frustration.
5. Adorno *et al*'s (1950) 'authoritarian personality' proposes that children whose

parents adopt excessively disciplinarian practices develop a predisposition to be prejudice.

6. According to 'realistic conflict theory', groups become prejudiced towards one another because they are in conflict over material resources. Evidence comes from 'The Robbers Cave field experiment' (Sherif, 1961). The theory is used to explain prejudice towards asylum seekers in the UK.
7. The 'social identity theory' challenges the 'realistic conflict theory' and proposes that prejudice occurs even where there is no competition between groups. The premise of this theory is that social categories provide members with a social identity. Evidence comes from Tajfel's study in 1971. The theory is used to explain racism towards immigrants in the UK.
8. According to 'evolutionary theory' (Hoyle and Wickeramasinghe, 1999), prejudice comes from the relationship between skin colour and health.
9. To reduce prejudice the 'contact hypothesis' suggests that positive contact between groups is important. It is recognised that the contact should be between groups of *equal status* and there should be a *superordinate goal.*
10. The 'jigsaw technique' involves giving small multi-ethnic groups a joint task to perform and giving each member of the group one bit of information that is vital to complete the task. The group are compelled to work together in the pursuit of a superordinate goal, so prejudice is reduced.
11. 'Re-categorisation' and 'de-categorisation' contribute to the reduction of prejudice.
12. Institutional racism is the formalisation of personal attitudes and behaviours.

Practice exam questions

1 Explain the ***cognitive***, ***affective*** and ***behavioural*** aspects of prejudice. **(9)**

2 Describe and evaluate the ***authoritarian personality*** as an explanation of prejudice. **(11)**

3 Describe the ***jigsaw technique*** as a way of reducing prejudice. **(5)**

4 Using research evidence, evaluate the ***social identity theory*** to explain the cause of prejudice. **(15)**

Anti-social behaviour

Section summary

This Section on anti-social behaviour will investigate:

- Definitions of anti-social behaviour.
- Theoretical perspectives of aggression.
- Aggression and the media.
- Gender differences in aggression.
- Approaches to the control and reduction of aggression.

Introduction

Most people in the UK are bombarded by reports of child abuse, assaults, muggings, rapes and wars in the media everyday. The number of non-sexual violent crimes reported to police in Scotland increased by 9 per cent to 16,500 between 2001 and 2002. Recorded cases of 'serious assaults, etc.' increased by 5 per cent to 7,600. Such increases may partly reflection the success of zero tolerance campaigns, but it is estimated that only 2 per cent of violent attacks on women are reported to the police, and that two women are killed by their male partner or ex-partner in the UK every week (Zero Tolerance Charitable Trust, Edinburgh, 2000).

Regardless of whether or not individuals have actually been the victims of anti-social behaviour, individual *perception* of levels of public aggression often places constraints on daily behaviour. Many people have become wary of leaving their children with strangers, avoid walking in unlit areas at night, lock their doors before going to bed and avoid groups of people standing on street corners.

Social psychologists focus on *actual* incidences of aggression and examine the reasons *why* people aggress against others and *how* to reduce/control the levels of aggression in society.

Definitions of anti-social behaviour

Baron and Richardson (1994) define anti-social behaviours as those 'which show a lack of feeling and concern for the welfare of others.' One form of anti-social behaviour is aggressive action that Aronson *et al* (1997) define as 'behaviour aimed at causing either physical or psychological pain.' Whilst this is a useful definition in that it is fairly specific, it is not clear whether it would cover self-mutilation or suicide. In addition, there is growing controversy over whether or not the smacking of a child is an aggressive act.

This definition is also limited in that it would imply that actions such as kicking and pushing a chair or smashing a window are not aggressive acts, since inanimate objects cannot feel pain. A similar definition is provided by Baron and Byrne (2000), who categorise aggression as 'the intentional infliction of some form of harm on others.' It is unclear if this definition includes harming animals. Overall, there is little consensus about the components of aggression. Some definitions incorporate physical parameters, while others include features such as facial expressions and threatening language. In addition, what is considered aggressive varies cross-culturally and between social groups. It is generally agreed, however, that there is an element of *intention* to cause harm present in aggressive behaviour. *Impulsive* or *emotional* aggression includes actions in which the aim of the act *is* to cause harm, whereas *instrumental* aggression includes intentional actions that indirectly cause harm, despite the fact that they are aimed at something other than causing harm.

Theoretical perspectives of aggression

'Biological' explanations argue that aggression is innate while 'behaviourist' explanations claim that it is learned. The debate over which of the two factors contribute more to the production of aggressive behaviour is an example of the nature-nurture controversy (see Chapter 1). Most scientists accept that it is neither exclusively biological inheritance nor the social environment that determines human behaviour, but, rather, an interaction of both.

The biological explanation(s) is an umbrella term that includes the 'psychodynamic theory', the 'ethological theory' and the 'evolutionary social theory'. These theories view aggression as an instinct and propose that human beings are genetically programmed for aggression. Learning theories and social learning theories are derived from 'behaviourist' explanations. 'Biosocial' standpoints, on the other hand, come from the 'frustration-aggression hypothesis' and the 'excitation-transfer model'. Social explanations emphasise learning processes and environmental factors that appear to be linked with aggression, whereas biosocial explanations regard aggression as a general drive – innate or learned – that is elicited by social events or circumstances.

Psychodynamic approach

The psychoanalyst, Sigmund Freud (1930), argued that the *libido*, the 'life instinct', and the *thanatos,* the 'death instinct', are two conflicting sources of energy. The libido governs pleasure-seeking tendencies while the thanatos is initially directed at self-destruction, but is later *displaced* as aggression towards others, or is *sublimated* into other physical activities, such as going to the gym, which release these aggressive urges. Although this theory suggests that aggression is 'natural', it also implies that non-destructive behaviours can be used to control destructive behaviours.

Ethological approach

According to Lorenz (1950), antagonistic behaviour towards others is the result of *innate* aggressive energies that continuously build up within the individual and spill over if the level becomes too high, or if specific environmental stimuli ('releasers') are present. Lorenz, therefore, considered it important for society to provide opportunities for aggressive energies to be discharged safely.

Aggressive energies accumulate in a 'reservoir' until they are released by a stimulus (represented by weights on a scale) or until the pressure on the valve causes an action to occur spontaneously (see Chapter 1 on 'Stress'). The fixed action patterns released vary depending on how much action specific energy is released from the valve.

This 'hydraulic model of aggression' proposes that aggression can be used up through *catharsis*, i.e. acting aggressively by pounding a punch-bag or simply viewing aggressive acts, and reduces pent-up feelings of anger or aggression. Loew (1967), however, found that when people were allowed to 'attack' someone to express anger they became even angrier.

Bushman et al (1999) tested the 'cathartic hypothesis' by asking students to read one of three fake articles. The first article was 'pro-catharsis', claiming that cathartic behaviour reduced the tendency towards aggression. The second article was 'anti-catharsis' and claimed that there no link between catharsis and the reduction of aggression. The third article was unrelated to the link between aggression and catharsis. The students were then requested to write an essay that was to be critiqued by another student – the experimenter was the critic. The experimenter produced extremely negative comments in an attempt to induce anger. The results showed that those students who had read the 'pro-catharsis' essay were more likely to choose a punch-bag exercise as an optional task, thus indicating that popular belief can influence people to select catharsis stress relief.

In the second part of the study, the students were asked to read one of the three articles and were informed that they could meet the critics of their essay later. Some of the students were asked to spend two minutes pounding a punch-bag. They were then instructed to take part in a competitive task in which they had to deliver varying levels of punishment, i.e. varying noise levels to a competitor on each occasion that his/her reaction time was slower. The students were told that the competitor was the negative critic of their first essay. The students who had been told that they would meet their critics were keener to punch a punch-bag before the meeting. Those who had read the *pro-catharsis* article delivered louder noises – were more aggressive – even after having punched the bag. It was concluded that punching the punch bag did not act as a catharsis and that catharsis does not relieve stress and could actually lead to *increased* aggression.

Evolutionary social theory

'Evolutionary social psychology' assumes an innate basis for all social behaviour, including aggression (Buss, 1990, 1999). Aggressive behaviour has evolved because it promotes the *survival of the genes* onto the next generation. Evolutionary psychologists argue that women prefer dominant males; hence, males compete for mates by displaying dominance in the form of aggression. Aggression will allow males to gain greater access to resources, which is attractive to females, as these resources will enable them to successfully raise their children. Females make a higher parental investment than do males, therefore, lower rates of aggression by women reflect the importance of her survival for her own reproductive success (Campbell, 1999).

This can explain why males are more likely to participate in crime, dangerous sports, and risk-taking behaviour, such as volunteering for drug experiments. Campbell notes that, in patriarchal societies, female aggression is perceived as being a 'gender-incongruent aberration' or is dismissed as evidence of irrationality. She suggests that these cultural interpretations have 'enhanced' evolutionary based sex differences by stigmatising aggressive expression by females and causing women to provide excuses for their aggression, whereas males are more likely to offer justificatory accounts.

The evolutionary model has also been employed to explain prejudiced attitudes (Hoyle and Wickramasinghe 1999). (See the 'Prejudice' Section of this Chapter.)

However, Green (1998) argues that evolutionary social psychologists' contribution to an understanding of aggression is limited, as it is of little use to the prevention or control of aggression and depends on immeasurable and unknown levels of energy.

Biological theories may contribute to our understanding of male/male aggression, but it is difficult to apply them to male/female aggression or parent/child aggression. In addition, they fail to explain the huge cultural differences in aggression.

The frustration-aggression hypothesis

The 'frustration-aggression hypothesis' (Dollard *et al*, 1939) has been used to explain both aggression and prejudice. (See the 'Prejudice' Section of this Chapter.) According to this theory, a 'drive' – state of arousal – is a precondition for aggression.

Aggression is caused by a frustrating event or situation, so in order to reduce aggression the source of the frustration must be controlled. This can be very difficult if the frustrated state derives from social inequalities produced by no easily identifiable source. For example, lack of job opportunities, shortage of decent housing and limited number of beds in NHS hospitals.

The frustration-aggression hypothesis does not specify what kinds of frustration can lead to aggression and, as Seligman (1972) argues, frustration does not always lead to aggression but could lead to *depression* or *learned helplessness.*

Likewise, Bentley (2002) claims that the frustration-aggression theory – or 'relative deprivation theory', as it is also known – is too simplistic and that frustration can either lead to helplessness or apathy or, alternatively, to the pursuit of positive, problem-solving strategies.

The social learning theorist, Bandura (1977), also points out that people do not always respond to frustration with aggression – *learned responses* may range from drug-taking to rationalisation to aggression.

Cue-arousal theory

'The cue-arousal theory' (Berkowitz, 1964, 1974) builds on from the frustration-aggression hypothesis. This theory proposes that frustration produces anger that may provoke aggression if there is a *stimulus* present that acts as a *cue* to aggression. Therefore, external stimuli can play a part in increasing the chances of an aggressive act occurring. The stimulus will only act as a cue if the angry person associates it with aggression. Donnerstein and Wilson (1979) found that people were more likely to become aggressive in noisy than in quiet situations, although participants in their study were less aggressive when they believed they had control over noise levels.

Excitation-transfer effect

According to Zillmann (1979), *arousal* caused by one source can be *transferred* to a new situation. Evidence for this theory of aggression is derived from an experiment (Zillmann, 1971) in which participants were provoked by verbal abuse and later offered the opportunity to give electric shocks to people who provoked them. In between the provocation and the opportunity to give electric shocks, participants either exercised on a cycling machine or quietly sat down and watched slides.

Participants in the 'cycling condition' gave higher levels of electric shocks than those in the 'watching slides condition'. It was concluded from this that the participants had *transferred* physical arousal from one situation, exercising, to another – giving electric shocks. Kerr (1994) also provides support for the excitation-transfer effect by investigating how the excitement at football matches can overspill into violence between the fans of opposing teams. The excitation-transfer effect cannot, however, explain planned aggressive acts.

The threatened-egotism theory

According to Bentley (2002), it has been suggested that aggression can be produced as compensation for low self-esteem. Aggression in this instance is a cry for help. The aggressor has the intention of harming others in order to displace their own feelings of inadequacy or to feel empowered. The 'threatened-egotism theory' does not seek to claim that attempting to boost self-esteem is an effective way to reduce aggression, as there has been no research that supports a direct link between low self-esteem and aggression. On the contrary, Bentley (2002) suggests that psychopaths show more violence, but have inflated self regard, whereas people with low self-esteem problems, such as those suffering from depression, are *less* violent than the norm.

Further research evidence (Baumeister, 2001) indicates that the majority of war-makers are very proud people who believe that they are not receiving the respect they deserve. In addition, bullies display higher levels of self-esteem than do their victims. Baumeister pronounces that '[C]onceited, self-important individuals turn nasty towards those who puncture their bubbles of self-love.' Kernis *et al* (1989) point out that all individuals with high self-esteem cannot be grouped together, as some are quietly self-confident and non-hostile, while others are arrogant, conceited and overly assertive. The latter type feels superior to others and can be described as *narcissistic* in their self-esteem (Rhodewalt *et al*, 1998). Bushman and Baumeister (1998) conducted a laboratory experiment to test the relationship between self-esteem and aggression. Participants were asked to write an essay and in order to provoke the experimental group a negative evaluation was presented to them. The control group were not given this negative evaluation. The participants were then provided with the opportunity to be aggressive towards the critic. Findings indicated that the narcissistic individuals displayed the most aggression towards the critics who had offended them. It was concluded that self-esteem did *not* predict aggression, but, rather, it was narcissism that did.

Learning theory and social learning theory

The 'social learning theory' is derived from 'behaviourism', which makes the assumption that all behaviour is learned through *direct experience*. Skinner's 'operant conditioning theory' – a behaviourist perspective – focuses on how behaviour is maintained through reinforcement. However, the social learning theorist, Bandura (1977), sees people as active manipulators of their own environments, rather than being passive recipients of experiences. He proposes that aggressive acts can also be learned by *vicarious experience* via the process of *observation* and *imitation*. Social learning theory suggests that we learn to aggress by being directly rewarded for aggressive acts or by watching others being rewarded in some way. The influence of cognitive factors on learning needs to be considered in explaining observational learning. For example, we are likely to pay more attention to models who are reinforced – models who are admired, respected and liked – and models who are similar to ourselves in terms of gender and age. In addition, past and present experiences will determine our expectation about the consequences of an observed behaviour. Social learning theorists investigate the importance of *positive role models* in the reduction and control of aggression. Bandura *et al* conducted an experiment to demonstrate how readily children mimic others. (See **Box 3.7** for details.)

Box 3.7

Research: 'Transmission of aggression through imitation of aggressive models,' Bandura, Ross and Ross (1961)

Research method: Laboratory experiment.

Experimental design: 8 experimental groups with 6 participants in each group.
1. Two groups of boys and 2 groups of girls were exposed to the aggressive model.
2. Two groups were exposed to the same-sex model and 2 were exposed to the opposite-sex model.
3. Two groups of boys and 2 groups of girls were exposed to the non-aggressive model.
4. Two groups were exposed to the same-sex model and 2 were exposed to the opposite-sex model.

There was 1 control group of 24 participants. The control group never encountered the model.

Participants: 72 nursery school children (36 boys and 36 girls), aged between 37 months and 69 months (with a mean age of 52 months). All children were enrolled in the Stanford University Nursery School. One male and one female adult role model were used.

Procedure: Children were brought into a room in the nursery school. They were directed towards one corner to play with toys of high interest. The model was seated in the opposite corner with a 5-foot 'Bobo doll' - an inflatable toy that does not fall over when pushed - and tinker toys.

In the non-aggressive condition the model ignored the Bobo doll and played quietly with the tinker toys. In the aggressive condition the model repeatedly punched the doll, sat on it, kicked it around the room, hit it with a mallet and shouted out exclamations such as 'Pow' and 'Kick him'.

The whole session lasted 10 minutes and participants could only play with the toys they had been given.

Participants were then taken to another room where there was a selection of aggressive and non-aggressive toys. Participants were observed for 20 minutes through a one-way mirror.

Results: Children in the aggressive condition reproduced much more physical and verbal aggression than those in the non-aggressive or control condition who showed virtually no imitative aggression. Boys reproduced more imitative physical aggression than girls. There was no difference between the sexes in the imitation of verbal aggression. Boys demonstrated more aggressive and more non-aggressive imitation after being exposed to the aggressive male model than did the girls. Girls exposed to the female model performed more imitative verbal aggression and more non-imitative aggression than did the boys.

Conclusion: Observation of the behaviour of others, especially if the role model is similar to us in some way, is an effective way of eliciting responses that are extremely unlikely to have been produced otherwise. Children can learn to imitate aggressive behaviour purely by seeing someone else act in that way.

Evaluation: The experiment only involved harm to a doll that was designed to be hit. Baron and Richardson (1994) criticised Bandura for suggesting that children passively absorb the events they see around them. Bandura (1973) did, however, make an important distinction between learning aggression and actually performing it.

(See 'Research Methods' Chapter for an evaluation of laboratory experiments.)

Bandura's findings on observational learning provided fuel for critics who argued that graphic presentations of violence in films and on TV could have serious consequences for children's future behaviour. Likewise, non-aggressive modelling in the media and in the home can contribute to the control of aggression levels in young people. With the growing social costs of violence, changes are taking place at a societal level to prevent observation learning. In Scotland, it is illegal not only for teachers to physically punish pupils, but also for parents/guardians to hit children under two years of age.

Aggression and the media

According to Bandura *et al* (1961), children observe and then imitate behaviour during the 'socialisation process' (see Chapter 1). The media is an important source of information for modelling, but the extensive research into the likely effect of TV violence has been inconclusive.

Eron *et al* (1972) conducted a 'longitudinal study' and collected data on the amount of TV watched by 9-year-old American boys. They measured the levels of aggression demonstrated by the boys 10 years later and found a high positive correlation, i.e. boys who had watched a lot of television at nine years old displayed high levels of aggression 10 years later. However, a causal relationship between television viewing and aggression was *not* established. It is difficult to ascertain whether aggressive children are attracted to watching violence on TV, or if it is the violence on TV that produces the aggression.

Thomas *et al* (1977) proposed that TV violence has a 'desensitising effect'. The findings of their research indicated that those who habitually watched violent TV programmes were less distressed by violent images than those who did not watch violent TV. The researchers suggested that watching violence of high realism encourages people to become callous and indifferent to real-life violence.

On 20 April 1999, Eric Harris and Dylan Klebold, who were 18 and 17 years old respectively, went to their high school – Colombine High in Denver in the United States – and killed 12 pupils, one teacher and, finally, themselves, with sawn-off shotguns and home-made bombs. Widespread coverage of the shootings was followed by 'copycat crimes' in the United States. In May 1999, 15-year old T.J. Solomon was charged with the shooting of six classmates at his Georgia High School. A letter expressing his admiration for Harris and Klebold was found under his bed. FBI agents also found instructions on bomb building that had been taken from the Internet. Classmates testified at the hearing that Solomon had boasted that he could do a better job than the Colombine High School shooters.

Harrower (1999), however, claims that the results of research frequently show that those who are involved in violent crime have an unhealthy interest in violent horror videos. Although *Natural Born Killers* was said to be Harris and Klebold's favourite film, the link is not clear-cut. According to Browne and Pennell (1998), violent family background is a more reliable predictor of violent criminal behaviour. It was, however, reported that both of the young men were intelligent and had stable, affluent, family backgrounds.

Harris and Klebold are said to have replaced sports with computer games (Harrower, 1999). The game, *Doom*, in which players use a variety of weapons, including a chainsaw, to kill the enemy, was one of their favourites.

The two killers admired the 'shock rock' artist, Marilyn Manson, who is renowned for his supposed Satanist and nihilistic ideas. Fans of the so-called 'Antichrist Superstar' at Colombine High school, formed a group that cultivated a Nazi mystique with members using Nazi salutes to greet each other. Members of the group wore a uniform of long black coats, berets and sunglasses. Harris and Klebold performed the killings on the anniversary of Hitler's birthday while wearing the 'uniform'. This feeds into Tajfel *et al*'s (1971) argument that individuals define themselves in terms of their social group, which can lead to in-group favouritism and negative out-group bias. Athletes and black students were not members of Harris and Klebold's group.

One of their victims was Isaiah Shoels, who was a successful athlete and one of the few black students at the school (see the 'Prejudice' Section in this Chapter.).

Explanations of why Harris and Klebold carried out the shootings varied from blame being placed on the school, the parents, US gun laws, violent movies, the Internet and the fact that Harris was taking the psychiatric drug, Luvox, at the time of the shootings.

Terrorism

Since the events of 11 September 2001 when two hijacked passenger jets flew into New York's World Trade Centre, a third crashed into the Pentagon and a fourth went down outside Pittsburgh, there have been many myths surrounding terrorism and terrorists. According to 'attribution theory', we tend to view the behaviour of others as stemming from internal forces, such as their personality (Quanttrone, 1982). Hence, it is common to assume that terrorists have extreme and violent personalities as they are involved in extreme and violent acts. However, in his working role as a psychiatrist, Rasch (1970) was in close contact with captured German terrorists, and found there to be *no* evidence of psychological abnormality.

The understanding of social processes such as 'inter-group behaviours' provide us with valuable insights into explanations of terrorism (see the 'Prejudice' and 'Conformity and obedience' Sections of this Chapter). Minority groups in any society may, rightly or wrongly, perceive that they are being treated harshly by the world and experience a sense of injustice, persecution, intimidation and discrimination that could lead to *frustration.* Such deep-rooted feelings can compel members of the disaffected group to shift to a violent extremist group in the pursuit of revenge, especially if a *catalyst* event, which heightens the anger, occurs. Kushner (1996) pronounced that most suicide bombers have had at least one relative or friend who has suffered at the hands of terrorists. According to Silke (2002), however, many terrorists claim that it was violence committed by the police or soldiers that finally forced them to join a terrorist group.

In order to build a psychological profile of the terrorist, it is important to have detailed knowledge of all relevant theories and to consider the historic, social, economic and political context in which acts of terrorism occur, as, to paraphrase an old adage 'One person's terrorist is another person's freedom fighter'.

Gender differences

According to Gladue (1991), higher levels of overt aggression are found in both heterosexual and homosexual males as compared to females, implying that biological sex is more important than gender in determining the difference between male and female aggression levels. His findings showed there to be a correlation between testosterone levels and levels of aggression as displayed by male participants when instructed to administer electric shocks to a contrived opponent. However, Gladue's (1989) earlier findings suggest that this does not necessarily indicate that high testosterone levels directly cause aggression, since activities such as playing and winning a game of chess can cause an increase in testosterone levels that is only temporary.

More conclusive evidence was provided when sex hormones given to transsexuals in the Netherlands as part of their sex reassignment led to an *increased* tendency towards aggression when the change was from female to male and a *decreased* tendency when the change was from male to female (von Goozen *et al*, Cohen-Kettanu and van Goozen, 1997). It is uncertain, however, whether such increases in aggression might have been elicited from factors such as negative social reactions to the practice, stress of the experience of reassignment on the individual, or even the individual adopting stereotypical gender roles after reassignment.

Nurturists, on the other hand, claim that males are encouraged to be more aggressive than females throughout the whole socialisation process. Campbell (1999) suggests that patriarchal culture has imposed a 'meme' – a unit of cultural learning – that exaggerates sex differences by equating female aggression with social or individual pathology. According to Burns (1992), a woman appearing before a British court is twice as likely as a man to be dealt with by psychiatric rather than penal means. Allen's (1987) investigation of 129 London court cases concludes, '[R]eports on males frequently cite histories of criminal delinquency and sexual promiscuity, but hardly ever suggest that these indicate any medical abnormality. A woman who manifests these traits, however, may be labelled as a psychopath.'

Harris (1992) found that men are more likely to be physically violent and possess more aggressive attitudes than women. Women, however, were almost as likely as men to use verbal attacks in similar situations, although the extent of the aggression displayed by women was lesser.

Reduction and control of aggression

Early learning theories

'Early learning theories' gave rise to a range of strategies, termed 'behaviour modification', which were aimed at changing behaviour. Behaviour change can be attempted by modifying the consequences that follow a given behaviour. A specific behavioural goal is set and any behaviour that is vaguely related to the required behaviour is systematically reinforced. The behavioural principle of rewards in the form of sweets, computer games, praise, smiles and television viewing time can be applied to reinforce non-aggressive behaviour in children. Punishments, such as timeout, chores, disappointment and homework, can be applied to stop aggressive behaviour or can be removed to reinforce non-aggressive behaviour. Applying a reward and/or removing a punishment can have the effect of reinforcing non-aggressive behaviour, whilst removing a reward and/or applying a punishment can reduce the likelihood of aggressive behaviour being repeated. The child learns that changing behaviour will elicit different outcomes from the environment. In turn, these new outcomes reinforce and strengthen the new behaviour, thereby successfully bringing about behavioural change.

Cognitive-behavioural therapy

'Cognitive-behavioural therapy' in the form of 'problem-solving training', 'self-instructional training', 'emotional control training', 'social skills training' and 'thought stopping' has now largely taken over from behaviour modification as the recognised method of encouraging behavioural change. This method is based on the belief that effective changes in behaviour occur only if psychological and/or physiological processes are altered. It gives individuals more control and responsibility over their behavioural changes.

One of the central features of stress is loss of control. Stress may result in feelings of anger and aggressive behaviour due to this lack of control. Increasing a sense of being in control of one's own life is fundamental to effective stress management; one can only change what one feels in control of. The 'biofeedback technique' requires the individual to monitor his/her particular stress-related physiological symptom, e.g. blood pressure or muscle tension. The individual is trained in cognitive-behavioural techniques to control it. These may be progressive muscle relaxation, mediation, or just a change in posture. Although it has been suggested that biofeedback is no more effective than training in relaxation alone, children do benefit, as they tend to like the technology used and see the practice as similar to a game.

'Cognitive-behavioural therapies' are used widely with young offenders (Hollin, 1990b), although Coie and Koepple (1990) point out that the highly aggressive child is least responsive to social skills training. Research conducted by Patterson (1989) on parenting skills found that mutual provocation was the typical interactional style of families with highly aggressive children; hence, whole families would need to be examined in order to develop appropriate intervention strategies. Only when the nature of the family's coercive cycle is established might parental training in the use of techniques such as 'time out' procedures be undertaken.

Rosenkoetter *et al* (2003) conducted a year long classroom-based intervention programme with young children in an effort to minimise the harmful effects of violent television. (See **Box 3.8** for details.) This intervention is focussed on encouraging children to actively evaluate the behaviour of aggressive role models on television. The objective was to change the children's attitudes and behaviour towards violence on television.

Box 3.8

Research: 'Mitigating the Harmful Effects of Violent Television,' Lawrence I. Rosenkoetter, Sharon E. Rosenkoetter, Rachel A. Ozretich, and Alan C. Acock, (2003)

Participants: 177 first, second and third grade children.

Aims: There were four aims:

1. To reduce the amount of violent TV viewed by participating children.
2. To encourage children not to identify with TV heroes who solve problems with force and violence.
3. To reduce the frequency of aggression for those children participating in the intervention.
4. To alter participants' attitude regarding the attractiveness of violence on TV.

Hypothesis: A year long intervention with a sustained focus opposing TV violence will result in participating children watching fewer violent TV programmes, identifying less with violent TV heroes, behaving in less aggressive ways with their peers and reporting less positive attitudes regarding violence on TV programmes.

Design: 130 participants were placed in the experimental condition and received the intervention. There were 9 experimental classrooms. Forty-seven participants were in the control condition and received no intervention. There were 3 control classrooms. There was no significant difference between the experimental and control groups on any of the major dependent variables.

The intervention consisted of the delivery of 31 lessons, lasting 20-30 minutes each. The intervention emphasised that:

1. TV is a powerful teacher.
2. All TV programmes teach something.
3. Different programmes teach different lessons.
4. Some programmes teach that the best way to solve problems is to use violence.
6. Violence is not the real world's great problem-solver.
7. Violence often produces more problems.
9. TV violence is contrived to attract viewers so that the television industry can make money.
10. Some TV programmes teach us that thinking and talking can solve problems.
11. We can actively choose which programmes to watch.
12. TV programmes that teach good lessons are the best choice.
13. We should not imitate or wish to be like TV characters that use violence to solve problems.
14. TV is staged by special effects to look real.

'Lesson mastery' was measured by asking true/false questions that were designed to assess the participants' learning of key themes in the curriculum.

To assess the level of 'TV violence viewing' the participants selected the most frequently watched programme during the last 4 or 5 weeks from 8 groupings of 10 programmes each.

In an attempt to measure 'identification with violent TV characters', participants were asked if they got upset when popular TV characters got hurt, if they acted like the TV characters and if they wanted to be like the character.

'Aggression' was assessed by asking the children to 'guess who in the classroom shares things', 'guess who says mean things about other children' and similar questions.

'Attitude' towards TV violence was assessed with true/false questions.

Results: Mean score for 'lesson mastery' for those in the intervention classes was significantly higher than those in the control condition. There was a negative correlation between viewing violent TV and performance on the lesson mastery exam, i.e. participants who viewed violent TV were less likely to learn the key themes in the curriculum.

1. 'TV violence viewing' was significantly higher in the control condition than in the experimental condition. Girls in the control group were watching TV violence more than girls in the intervention group, but also more than boys in either the control or experimental group. At the outset, the boys were watching substantially more violent TV than the girls. The boys in the intervention and the control groups were equivalent as were the girls in the intervention and the control groups.
2. Boys reported higher levels of 'identification with violent superheroes' than girls did. Identification with violent characters was higher for the control group than for the intervention group. There was a correlation between levels of viewing violent TV and levels of identification with TV heroes that use violence to solve problems.
3. Mean scores for 'aggression' were higher for the control group than for the intervention group. Boys scored higher than girls in aggression levels. Girls in both the intervention and control groups had lower aggression scores than boys in the control group. The effect of the intervention on aggression was substantial only for boys. There was a significant decrease in aggression for boys who were initially high viewers of violent TV, while boys who were initially low viewers showed little change.
4. Girls in the intervention group had a more negative 'attitude' towards violent TV than girls in the control group. Although more negative views were displayed in the intervention groups than in the control groups, the difference for boys was not significant. Children watching high levels of violent TV had more positive attitudes towards violent TV and were rated by their classmates as displaying more behavioural aggression.

Conclusion: An intensive and systematic intervention can mitigate some of the harmful effects of violent TV. Girls in the intervention group, but not in the control group, reduced their viewing of violent TV, their identification with violent TV heroes, and their attitudes towards TV violence became less positive. The behavioural aggression of girls was not affected by the intervention. For boys, the intervention resulted in a reduction of behavioural aggression but not in viewing, identification or attitudes.

Evaluation: When measuring the extent to which participants identify with violent TV characters, 15 per cent of the children had to be eliminated because they were unfamiliar with the stimulus characters selected by the researchers. Children who watched very little TV had a higher chance of being eliminated. Pre-existing classrooms were used. Therefore, the researcher could not randomly assign participants to conditions.

There was a degree of self-selection since 35 per cent of the children could not be interviewed, as their parents' did not return the consent forms, which implies that the sample was not representative. All the participants lived in, or near, a community of approximately 50,000 inhabitants, hence the diversity of large urban areas was limited. Most of the children in the intervention classrooms realised that they were being persuaded to watch less violent TV, identify less with violent TV heroes and decrease their positive appraisal of violent TV. This, therefore, raises the possibility that the children could have been telling the researchers what they wanted to hear.

Section summary

1. It is difficult for social psychologists to agree on a non-ambiguous definition of aggression. However, most argue that aggression involves an element of intention.
2. Instinct theories (*psychodynamic*, *ethological*, *evolutionary social theory*) are developed from the premise that aggression is an innate drive that is genetically transmitted.
3. Biosocial theories (*frustration-aggression hypothesis*, *excitation-transfer model*, *cue-arousal theory*) emphasise an innate component, although not the existence of a full-blown instinct. Such theories view aggression as a general drive that is elicited by social circumstances.
4. Learning theory proposes that aggressive behaviour is maintained when it is reinforced.
5. According to social learning theory, aggressive behaviour is learned from appropriate role models. Social learning theory can be applied to a discussion on the relationship between aggression and the media.
6. The theories can be applied to acts of aggression such as the Columbine killings (1999) and worldwide terrorism.
7. Gender differences in aggression can be explained in relation to the interaction between the socialisation process and genetic factors.
8. *Behaviour modification techniques*, *cognitive-behavioural therapies* and *intervention strategies* are used to reduce and control aggression.

Practice exam questions

1. Describe and evaluate how the ***frustration-aggression hypothesis*** explains the development of anti-social behaviour. **(10)**
2. Explain one way of ***reducing aggression***. **(5)**
3. Describe and evaluate research findings of **one** study into the effects of media violence. **(10)**
4. Explain **gender differences** in aggression. **(5)**

Conformity and obedience

Section summary

The objectives of this section are to investigate:

- The nature of conformity and obedience.
- Theoretical explanations of conformity.
- Research studies on conformity.
- Minority social influence.
- Theoretical explanations of obedience.
- Research studies on obedience.
- Strategies for the resistance of social pressure.

Introduction

In most Western societies people are socialised from a young age to value the attributes of *individuality* and *independence*. Parents fear that their children may be easily led and succumb to 'peer pressure' that might result in danger. Although parents can be heard boasting about their children 'having a mind of their own' and 'knowing what they like and dislike', it is still generally considered desirable for a schoolchild to adhere to school rules and follow the orders of the teacher. Some degree of consensus appears to exist that in order to avoid social chaos and have the security of a degree of predictability it is preferable that people follow the core norms of society. In our everyday interactions we are influenced in how we think, feel and behave by means of persuasion, argument, example, demand, propaganda and sometimes even force.

Nature of conformity

'Social influence' refers to the effect the presence of others has on our behaviour, thoughts and feelings. Conformity is one aspect of social influence that can be used to explain, for example, the emergence of cultural fads, from flat-pole sitting in the 1920s, stamp collecting in the 1930s, to break-dancing in the 1980s and tattoos in the 1990s.

The term, *conformity*, refers to generally following the accepted and expected pattern of behaviour within particular social groups or societies. It is also about the influence of the majority over the minority in relation to behaviour.

Informational and normative influence

According to Deutsch and Gerard (1955) there are *two* types of influence that direct individuals towards conformity:

1. **Informational influence** that is 'internalised' by the individual and leads to genuine attitude change. If members of the reference group are perceived to be competent, individuals might rely on them to determine what is correct in uncertain situations. Informational influence is assumed to cause change in public and private behaviours. This type of conformity is referred to as 'internalisation'.
2. **Normative influence** that does not imply genuine attitude change, but rather a strategic effort on behalf of an individual to be accepted and to avoid social censure. According to Abrams *et al* (1990), normative influence is stronger when individuals feel they belong to the group as the costs of non-conformity would be higher than in groups of strangers where there is no identification. The assumption is that normative influence will cause changes in public, but not private behaviours. This type of conformity is referred to as 'compliance'. Hogg and Vaughan (1995) associated compliance with low self-esteem, a high need for social approval, low IQ and feelings of inferiority, insecurity and anxiety.

Research studies on conformity

The earliest study on conformity was conducted by Sherif in 1936. He demonstrated by using the 'autokinetic effect' – a perceptual illusion in which a point of light seen in darkness appears to move about – participants would take the judgements of others in 'unambiguous' situations. Sherif asked participants to estimate how far the light moved. The responses varied greatly when participants were tested individually, but the estimates converged and a group norm was established when participants were tested together. The participants adhered to the group norm even when they were alone.

Asch (1951) suggested that Sherif's study was not a valid test of compliance as the autokinetic effect is an illusion that has no 'right' answer. Asch, therefore, aimed to find out if participants would even give answers that they know to be wrong, rather than ones that deviated from the views being expressed by others. (See **Box 3.9** for details of Asch's study.)

Box 3.9

Research: 'Effects of Group Pressure on the Modification and Distortion of Dudgements,' Asch, S.E. (1951)

Participants: 123 American males.

Aims: To test compliance under unambiguous situations. To show that if one is certain about what is correct, then others' behaviour will not be influential.

Hypothesis: If the object of judgement is entirely unambiguous, then disagreement will have no effect on behaviour: individuals will remain independent of group influence.

Design: Participants were informed that they were taking part in a visual discrimination task. They were seated round a table in groups of 7-9 people. They were given the simple task of publicly matching the length of a standard line to one of three other comparison lines.

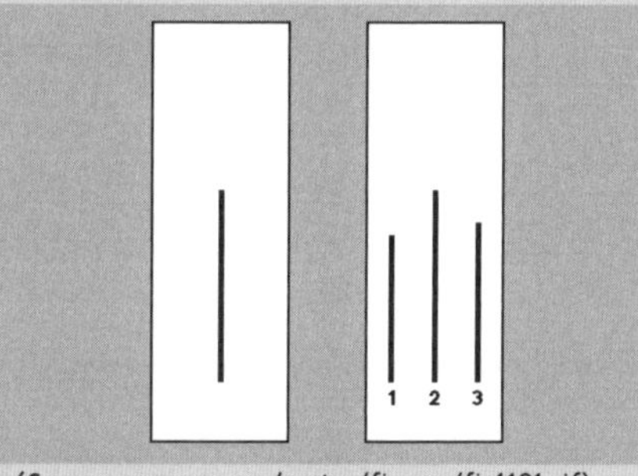

(Source: www.awa.com/norton/figures/fig1101.gif)

In the experimental condition, only one person was a true naïve participant, and he answered second to last. The others were confederates of the experimenter who had been told beforehand to give all the same wrong answers on 12 out of 18 of the trials. In the control condition, the participants performed the task privately with no group influence.

Results: Less than 1 per cent of the control participants' responses were errors. Out of the 123 naïve participants, the average rate of conformity was 32 per cent, 75 per cent conformed at least once, 25 per cent did not conform at all and 5 per cent conformed on every trial.

Conclusion: People will give the wrong answer even if they know it to be untrue, rather than giving the right answer, if it means deviating from the norm. Accounts by the participants suggested that people conform, even when the stimulus is unambiguous, to avoid censure, ridicule and social disapproval.

Evaluation: The high level of conformity may only reflect the norms prevalent in the United States in the 1950s. Conformity was tested under artificial conditions with meaningless stimulus.

(See 'Research Methods' Chapter for an evaluation of laboratory experiments.)

Bond and Smith (1996) collected data from cross-cultural studies that used Asch's (1951) paradigm to measure conformity. They calculated the conformity rate for 15 nations. The results indicated that *individualistic* nations such as the United States, the UK, Belgium, France, The Netherlands, Germany and Portugal, displayed significantly lower levels of conformity in comparison to *collectivist* nations like Japan, Brazil, Fiji, Hong Kong, Arab states and African countries. Individualistic countries define identity by personal choice and achievement, whereas collectivist countries define identity in terms of the collective group a person belongs to, e.g. religion or family.

Most experiments on compliance have used fairly trivial and morally neutral tasks, such as judging the length of lines, to measure the influence of group norms. Very few researchers have experimentally examined the influence of group norms on social issues with a moral component. Hornsey *et al* (2004) pronounce that in situations where people have a strong moral basis for their attitudes they will not conform to the opposing group norm and will publicly move away from it in order to defend their deeply held convictions. (See **Box 3.10** for details of Hornsey *et al*'s study.)

Box 3.10

Research: 'On Being Loud and Proud: Non-conformity and Counter-conformity to Group Norms,' Hornsey *et al* (2003)

Aim: To examine, experimentally, how the moral basis of an individual's attitude can moderate his or her responses to group norms.

Participants: 280 introductory psychology students. One hundred and fifty-two females and 53 males who held a position contrary to the status quo (pro-gay reform). Seventy-five anti-gay law reform students. The average age was 19.88 years.

Hypotheses:

1. On issues with a moral component (e.g. gay law reform), people will choose to use the public domain to reassert their original position in the face of majority opposition.
2. People do not conform more in *public* than in private. The motivation to present one's position *publicly* will outweigh fears of social isolation, resulting in non-conformity or even counter-conformity.
3. People will be more likely to act in line with their attitude in *private* when they have group support.
4. People with a weak moral basis to their attitude will assimilate to the group norms, and those with a strong moral basis for their attitude will show non-conformity or even counter-conformity.

Procedure: Pro-gay law reform participants were asked to rate to what extent they had a moral basis for their attitude. Participants were informed that, generally, students at their university (University of Queensland) either agreed or disagreed with their attitude towards the recognition of gay couples in law. They were then asked to complete a questionnaire assessing their willingness to act out their attitudes in the private (signing a petition, voting in a referendum, and voting for a political party that had pro-gay reform policies) and public (signing a letter to the editor, distributing information leaflets, and attending a rally in favour of gay law reforms) domain.

Results:

1. Overall, participants intended to act in line with their attitudes when they had a moral basis for their attitude.
2. Participants who had a weak moral basis for their attitude were more intent on *privately* acting in line with their attitudes when they had group support than when they had group opposition. For participants who had a strong moral basis for their attitude, group norm had no significant impact on *private* intentions.
3. Participants' intentions to *publicly* act in line with their attitudes were greater the stronger the moral basis for their attitude. Those who had a weak moral basis for their attitude were not significantly affected by the group norm.
4. There was a marginal trend for participants who had a strong moral basis for their attitude to be more willing to act *publicly* in line with their attitudes when they had group opposition than when they had group support.

Conclusion: Moral basis for attitude moderates responses to group norms. Participants who had a weak moral basis for their attitudes shifted towards the group norm in relation to their private behavioural intentions (conformity), whereas those who had a strong moral basis were not affected by the group norm. There was a trend among those who had a strong moral basis towards counter-conformity (stronger intentions when they perceived group opposition than when they perceived group support). Group norms can influence behaviour in different ways: just as sometimes people may be motivated to move towards the group norm, in some situations people will be motivated to resist the group norm or even move away from it.

Evaluation: It is unclear if the effects of moral basis are operating independently of attitude strength. Evidence for counter-conformity is weak. The study does not address why people who have a strong moral basis for an attitude should move away from the group norm. The public behaviours used in the study did not imply that University of Queensland students - the group providing the group norm - would be the audience.

Minority social influence

Minority influence occurs when a minority rejects the established norm of the majority of group members and induces the majority to move to the position of the minority. Moscovici (1969) concluded from the findings of his study that the minority were most likely to influence the majority if the minority showed consistency in their views, both among themselves and over time.

First, participants were given an eye test to ensure that they were not colour blind. Four participants were allocated to a group with two confederates of the researcher. There was a control group with no 'stooges'. They were shown 36 slides with distinctly different shades of blue and were instructed to identify aloud the colour of each slide.

In the first part of the experiment, the two confederates answered 'green' for each of the 36 slides, thus displaying *consistency*. In the second part of the experiment the confederates showed *inconsistency* by answering 'green' for 24 of the slides and 'blue' for the remaining 12. Among the control group's answers, 0.25 per cent were 'green' and the rest were 'blue'. When the confederates in the experimental group answered inconsistently, 1.25 per cent of the participants identified the colour of the slides to be 'green', but 8.42 per cent of participants answered 'green' when the confederates were consistent. The findings support the notion that the minority can influence the majority, especially if the minority is consistent in their views. It is pointed out by Mugny and Papastamou (1980) that for the minority to have influence over the majority their views should not only be consistent but also flexible, compromising, moderate and reasonable, rather than dogmatic, rigid and extreme. In addition, minorities exert more influence if the majority perceives them as an in-group.

Unlike 'majority influence', which is usually caused by 'normative influence', i.e. based on public compliance and the power of the majority to punish through group rejection and to reward through group acceptance, minority influence is more likely to be the result of 'informational influence'. According to Clark (1990), minorities that can refute the arguments of a majority are *more* likely to persuade a change to occur and the more members of the majority who deflect, the more likely the remaining members are to deflect too. In the process of changing thoughts, feelings and behaviours to match the minority group, the majority are provided with new ideas that lead to the active re-examination of existing views.

Nature of obedience

Compliance becomes obedience when requests are put in the form of an *order*. The requests come from someone in a perceived position of *power*.

At the end of World War II it was estimated that over 6 million Jews, Slavs, homosexuals, Jehovah Witnesses, communists and others had been targeted by the Nazis and killed in the Holocaust. An infamous SS officer, Eichmann (1906-1962), was charged with the destruction of millions of Jews. He was convicted for crimes against humanity and hanged on 31 May 1962. Eichmann had appeared to be an average bureaucrat with no particular criminal tendencies and claimed he was not a 'monster', but was merely carrying out Hitler's orders to transport Jews to their death.

During the Vietnam War inhabitants of the village, My Lai, were rounded up by a platoon of American soldiers and shot to death. The leader of the platoon, Lieutenant William Calley, claimed he was not to blame as he was simply fulfilling his duty by following orders. A military court found him guilty, but he was released after a short sentence. Before the My Lai massacre, Calley had not demonstrated any pronounced criminal tendencies. He had been a fairly average college student and became an ordinary officer. He is now living a respectable life as a civilian.

Social psychologists investigate whether individuals like Eichmann and Calley were 'monsters', or if the average person would inflict harm on others if ordered to do so by someone in a perceived position of power.

Theoretical explanations of obedience

Obedience theories can be put into two main categories: those that focus on 'personal characteristics' – the 'psychodynamic perspective' – and those that examine the 'social situation' – the 'behaviourist perspective'.

The authoritarian personality and situational factors

Adorno *et al*'s (1950) 'authoritarian personality theory' suggests that some people have a greater propensity towards obedience than others (see the 'Prejudice' Section of this Chapter). Individuals with authoritarian personalities have been brought up by strict and punitive parents who instil fear of authority figures in their children from a very young age. Such children learn absolute obedience to people in positions of authority.

Miale and Selzer's (1975) 'psychopathology thesis' claims that Nazi war criminals who underwent psychological tests demonstrated high levels of depression, violence, and a lack of guilt or concern for others.

Aronson *et al* (1997) consider the 'social situation' to be more important than personality in determining obedience levels. One is more likely to follow orders if the person giving the commands is perceived to have 'legitimate authority'. In Milgram's (1963) study (see **Box 3.11**, below), the experiment took place in the prestigious Yale University, suggesting to participants that such an establishment could not be involved in anything untoward. Therefore, orders were followed. Removal of personal responsibility for the consequences of obeying an order encourages obedience. The participants in Milgram's study saw the experimenter and not themselves, as responsible for the torture. Milgram referred to this as 'being another person's agent,' a situation known as the 'agentic state'. When in an agentic state, people stop acting according to their consciences. Milgram proposed that the other state of consciousness is the 'autonomous state'. This occurs when we voluntarily direct our actions because we are aware of the consequences. UK citizens live in an hierarchical society and from a young age are socialised in obeying a wide range of authority figures, such as parents, older siblings, childminders, park attendants and teachers. Consequently, subordinates learn to exonerate themselves by passing the responsibility up the ranks of a hierarchy.

Research studies on obedience

More hideous crimes have been committed in the name of obedience than in the name of rebellion. From 1939-1945, the Nazis systematically slaughtered 6 million people on command during Hitler's regime. Many historians have attempted to explain such horrors by arguing that Germans have some sort of character defect, which makes them more obedient.

Milgram's (1963) experiment on obedience was an attempt to test the 'Germans are different' hypothesis, which suggests that the cause of the behaviour comes from the individual's own personality or characteristics – 'dispositional attribution'. Milgram believed that the situation had led to the inhumane behaviour of the Nazis – 'situational attribution'. Details of Milgram's study can be found in **Box 3.11**.

Box 3.11

Research: Milgram, Stanley (1963) 'Behavioural Study of Obedience'

Aim: To investigate what level of obedience would be shown when participants were told by an authority figure to administer electric shocks to another person.

Method: Laboratory experiment (the independent variable was the verbal prods provided by the experimenter for the participant to continue and the dependent variable was the level of obedience, as measured by how far up the shock scale the participant went).

Participants: Forty males between 20 and 50 years of age were recruited from the New Haven, Connecticut area. They responded to an advertisement looking for volunteers to take part in a study of learning and memory at Yale University. They were each paid $4.50 just for turning up.

Procedure: The participants turned up at the laboratory and were introduced to the researcher, Jack Williams, a 31-year-old biology teacher in a grey technician's coat, who informed the volunteers that they were taking part in a study on the effects of punishment on learning. Unbeknown to the participants, a draw was fixed so that they always played the role of 'teacher' while a confederate of the experimenter played the role of 'learner'. The 'teacher' is shown the 'learner' who is strapped into a chair with electrodes attached to his wrists. The 'teacher' is taken into an adjacent room with a shock generator, which he is told can deliver shocks from 15 to 450 Volts, with 15 Volt increments.

Each switch is labelled to indicate the severity of the shock. The 'teacher' is instructed to read a list of word pairs to the learner, then test his memory by giving him only one word and asking to select the paired word. The 'teacher' was ordered to give increasingly higher shocks with each incorrect answer. (No real shocks were administered apart from one sample shock of 75 Volts that was given to the 'teacher'.)

The 'learner' was instructed to give loud protests with each increased shock. At 180 Volts the 'learner' yelled that he could not stand the pain. At 300 Volts he complained of pains in his heart. At 320 Volts there was silence. At this point if the 'teacher' turned to the experimenter, unsure what to do, he was instructed to continue with prods such as: 'Please continue'; 'The experiment requires that you continue'; 'It is absolutely essential that you continue'; 'You have no other choice; you must go on'. The experimenter assured the 'teacher' that although the shocks might have been painful, there would be no permanent tissue damage. Participants in a control group were not given orders to continue.

Results: Twenty-six out of 40 (65 per cent) participants continued up to 450 Volts (labelled 'Danger: Severe Shock'). Only 5 dropped out at 300 Volts when pounding on the wall was heard. Most participants showed signs of distress during the experiment. Participants in the control group delivered very mild shocks only. Yale psychology undergraduates had predicted, before the experiment, that 1.2 per cent of participants would continue administering shocks up to 450 Volts.

Conclusion: The situation - the prestigious location, the professional researcher in a laboratory coat - and not the disposition of the participants, produces high levels of obedience to instructions. Ordinary Americans will obey an authority figure and inflict harm on others.

Ethical considerations: Participants did not give their informed consent; participants were deceived; participants were psychologically distressed; verbal prods could have prevented participants from withdrawing.

Methodological considerations: Unrepresentative sample; deliberately ethnocentric. Participants were paid to take part in study. Orne and Holland (1968) criticised Milgram's experiment on the grounds of ecological validity.

(See 'Research Methods' Chapter for an evaluation of laboratory experiments and ethical guidelines in psychological research.)

Meeus and Raaijmakers (1986) followed a similar procedure to Milgram, but conducted the study in Holland with job applicants. Participants were ordered to make 15 stress remarks to try and put off interviewees. Twenty-two out of 24 delivered all 15 remarks in spite of the high unemployment rates in Holland at the time.

Hofling *et al*'s (1966) 'Astroten study' was conducted to investigate obedience levels in a real-life situation. It was carried out to investigate if a female nurse would intentionally do serious harm to a patient if a male doctor ordered her to do so. The researchers set it up so that a nurse would receive a phone call from a 'doctor' whom she had not met before. He ordered the nurse to administer 20 mg of the drug 'Astroten' to a patient. This order was against the rules in two ways: first, it was against hospital policy to accept prescriptions by phone and, second, the nurse was aware that the maximum daily dosage for this drug was 10mg. The nurse, therefore, knew that she was being ordered to give the patient an overdose. Twenty-one of the 22 nurses started to give the medication before being stopped by a psychiatrist. After the study, the nurses claimed that doctors had given such orders in the past and became extremely annoyed if questioned by nurses. In their role as nurses, it was the norm to accept orders from doctors who held a higher position in the hierarchy. The doctor took the responsibility since he was signing the authorisation forms.

The study was described to a similar group of nurses and 10 out of 12 said that they would refuse to follow the doctors' orders. These findings suggest that what people report in interviews may be very different to how they actually behave. Rank and Jacabson (1977) carried out a follow-up study, but gave the nurses the opportunity to get advice. Only two out of 18 obeyed the order to give the drug to a patient.

Strategies for resisting social pressure

In individualistic societies, such as the US, the UK and other West European countries, one's identity is defined by freedom of choice and personal achievements. Therefore, conformity is usually perceived as a *negative* attribute to possess, although it is generally accepted that to avoid social chaos a certain degree of conformity is desirable. Most individuals attempt to create a balance between asserting their own individuality and conforming to societal norms.

Conscientious objectors

Conscientious objectors have resisted authority through refusal to join the armed forces when conscripted to do so – either through opposition to the war or for self-preservation. German citizens, during the Nazi regime, put their lives at risk to shelter and protect Jews. In Tiananmen Square, Beijing, thousands of students gathered in April 1989, to protest against the authoritarian leadership of the People's Republic of China. Government orders to disperse were ignored by the protesters who occupied the Square. People from all walks of life supported the students. Tragically, hundreds, perhaps thousands, of the students were killed on 20 May 1989 when the army was ordered by the government to clear the Square. This extremely costly resistance in terms of the number of lives lost, ultimately led to the collapse of communism in Eastern Europe and in the former Soviet Union. The fight for freedom and democracy became unstoppable.

Dangers of conformity

According to Krebs and Blackman (1988), 'There are obvious dangers to conformity. Failure to speak our minds against dangerous trends or attitudes (for example, racism) can easily be interpreted as support.'

Individuals are more likely to resist authority and to disobey directives from above when provided with social support and/or role models. In another version of his teaching experiment, Milgram had three 'teachers', two of whom were confederates. The first confederate refused to continue to administer shocks beyond 150 volts, despite the experimenter's insistence that he should continue. The second confederate also stopped after 210 Volts. In that situation only 10 per cent of the participants continued despite being ordered to do so.

However, it may be difficult to ascertain if conformity to the group norm or resistance to authority is the motive for disobedience. At a demonstration in Glasgow on 20 March 2004, to mark an International Day of Action against the continued occupation of Iraq by US, UK and 'coalition' forces, three of the protesters were arrested. Tommy Sheridan, then leader of the Scottish Socialist Party, encouraged demonstrators to block one of the main roads through the city centre until the protestors were released. Despite orders from the police officers on duty, authority was resisted and the three protesters were released. In this situation, the individuals had the opportunity to show disobedience with the support of like-minded others and in the presence of a role model. Variations of the Asch study on compliance have shown that even a minimal amount of dissenting support is enough to give people confidence in their opinion against the majority. As suggested by Hornsey *et al* (2004), people with a strong moral basis for their attitudes are more likely to resist social pressure to act against their beliefs.

Gamson *et al* (1982) demonstrated the importance of social support in an experiment designed to encourage resistance to authority. A fictitious company, Manufacturers' Human Relations Consultants (MHRC), contacted participants and asked them to take part in discussions about how the views of the local community influence legal cases. MHRC asked for permission to videotape the discussions that were to take place in groups of nine. **Box 3.12** describes how these fictitious discussions were presented to each of 33 discussion groups.

Box 3.12

Manufacturers' Human Relations Consultants (MHRC), Gamson *et al* (1982)

The manager of a petrol station was Mr C. A private detective, who was hired by the oil company that owned the station, investigated his lifestyle. Subsequently, Mr C's franchise on the station was cancelled as the company claimed that, because he was co-habiting with a woman, his behaviour offended the moral standards of the local community, which would lead to a loss of business. Mr C sued the oil company for invasion of privacy and beach of contract.

Participants were first of all asked to complete a questionnaire on Mr C's behaviour and their attitudes towards authority. After a general discussion of the case, three members of each group were asked by the experimenter to present the argument that Mr C's domestic arrangements had caused them offence. Then another three participants from each group were asked to do the same. Lastly, each group member was asked to speak individually. Each individual was ordered to report that they found Mr C's behaviour offensive and that they agreed with the loss of his franchise. They were also told to say that they intended to boycott the petrol station. The experimenter then asked the group members to sign affidavits that would allow MHRC to edit the videotapes and to use them as evidence in court. Realising that their 'evidence' was being distorted, most of the participants objected to the procedure and insisted that the court be told their real views were not being presented. According to the results of the questionnaires, which were distributed before the discussions, most participants saw nothing wrong with Mr C's behaviour.

In 16 of the 33 groups, every member refused to sign the affidavit, a majority refused in nine of the groups and a minority refused in the remaining eight. Individuals with previous experience of dissent - classed as such due to their participation in strikes, protests and demonstrations against authority - were included as members in most of the groups who disobeyed. Such 'dissenters' provided role models for other group members. The questionnaire results indicated a positive correlation between anti-authority attitudes and disobedience on the one hand, and pro-authority attitudes and obedience on the other. Those group members who scored high on pro-authority attitudes were most likely to obey and sign the affidavit. Attitudes and beliefs alone do not always lead to resistance to authority as situational forces and constraints also contribute to the decision-making process.

Resistance to authority was encouraged in the design of the experiment as, to most fair-minded people, the oil company's treatment of Mr C was clearly unacceptable. By asking participants to argue against their own views and to sign affidavits giving MHRC permission to use their statements as court evidence, normal standards of behaviour were clearly violated. In addition, the participants had the support of other group members to resist authority. Throughout the discussions they were given plenty of chances to share their views with each other and question the morality of the experimenter's directives. People were able to define and clarify the situation for one another. *Defining the situation* is an important factor in the development of rebellion. The decision to disobey was formulated at these times and often became a group norm. Therefore, the group members could have succumbed to social pressure to comply with the group norm of disobedience.

The researchers observed that participants had to decide between the urge to obey and the urge to conform to the group norm.

'Granfalloons'
There are many techniques used by advertisers and propagandists to increase the likelihood of persuasion. A 'granfalloon' – a loosely connected group that forms solely because its members believe they have something special in common – is created to give people a sense of belonging. For example, appeals for donations may be addressed to 'Dear Friend...', salespeople give their product a 'personality' by using celebrities in advertisements and politicians in election campaigns refer to what 'we' as parents, patients, homeowners, taxpayers, etc., want. This technique is also used by religious cults.

The new member is persuaded to cut off from others, give up their possessions and adopt a particular diet and style. It then becomes difficult to integrate with people outside the group and a feeling of identity with in-group members is created. Granfalloons originate from Tajfel's (1982) notion of 'minimal groups', which are usually based on tenuous links, but provide individuals with a sense of 'group identity'. To resist granfalloon techniques, individuals need to accept not being part of the 'special' group and consider other ways of raising their self-esteem. It is also important to acknowledge the vast differences among members of the in-group, while accepting the similarities between the out-group members and yourself. (See the 'Prejudice' Section of this Chapter.)

The elaboration likelihood model
The 'elaboration likelihood model' (Petty and Cacioppo, 1981) states that there are *two* routes to persuasion:

1. The 'central route' involves allowing the audience to draw their own conclusions by encouraging them to actively process a message and carefully consider its content. Cult leaders may use this self-persuasion technique by sending potential converts to give the message to non-converts. In order to resist persuasion, individuals need to play 'devil's advocate' and try to present a counter-argument. Audiences may be gently encouraged to conduct mental role-plays in 'slice of life' adverts that show people in situations not too unlike the viewers own. If the viewers fail to realise they are being sold a dream, it is easy for them to imagine themselves enjoying the benefits of the product. Advertisers often create a sense of scarcity by advising the public to 'Buy now while stocks last!', so that we are discouraged from looking at alternatives if we have the promise of possessing something rare and desirable. It is important, here, for the potential buyer to recognise that frustration is a response to being thwarted and should be prepared to walk away and cool off. Another technique is to create 'factoids', i.e. facts that did not exist before the media created them. For example, Hitler created factoids about the Germans being the 'master race'. Cult leaders may create myths about a 'promised land'. To decrease the probability

of accepting the new information the audience has to *question the motives* of the persuader and *consider the consequences*.

2. The 'peripheral route' involves shallow processing of the message with very little attention to the content. Attention is distracted from the message with humour, action or music. This may lead the resistant audience to ask why it is necessary for the persuader to distract them. Phrases such as 'best ever' are used to deceive the audience. To resist this persuasive technique the individual could try rephrasing the message for him or herself.

'Psychological reactance' is the tendency to behave in the opposite way to others in order to reassert one's personal freedom. This is especially likely to occur where we feel ourselves to be coerced by others. Heilman (1976) stated that telling people someone else has declared, 'Petitions should not be allowed to be distributed concerning this topic,' will increase petition signing rates. We are more likely to resist persuasive tactics if we are *inoculated* by receiving a prior warning that a particular message is being used to persuade us in some way. This will allow the recipients to formulate counter-arguments and make them more resistant to persuasion.

Section summary

1. Collectivist societies value conformity and obedience more than individualistic societies.
2. Informational social influence (in uncertain conditions one is more likely to refer to others to know how to react) leads to internalisation (one's behaviour and opinions coincide with that of the group). The motive for internalisation is the need for certainty.
3. Normative social influence (in potentially embarrassing situations one is more likely to adhere to the group norm) leads to compliance (publicly agreeing with the group, but privately maintaining one's own opinion). The motive for compliance is the need for social approval or acceptance.
4. Sherif (1936) found that individuals conform to the group norm in ambiguous situations. Asch (1951) found that individuals conform to the group norm in non-ambiguous situations.
5. According to Hornsey *et al* (2004), if one has a moral basis for one's attitude, conformity rates decrease.
6. The minority can influence the majority, especially if the minority is consistent in their views (Moscovici, 1969).
7. Obedience is complying with the demands of an authority figure.
8. The authoritarian personality theory (Adorno *et al*, 1950) argues that some individuals have a greater propensity towards obedience, whereas Aronson *et al* (1993) claim that the social situation determines obedience levels.
9. The findings of Milgram's (1963) study show that it is the situation and *not* the

disposition of the individuals that produces high levels of obedience.

10. Social support and/or role models encourage resistance to authority (Gamson *et al*, 1982).
11. The motives of advertisers, politicians and cults need to be questioned in order to resist social persuasion.

Practice exam questions

1. What is meant by **informational social influence**? **(2)**
2. Briefly explain **one** strategy that may be used to resist social pressure. **(3)**
3. Using research evidence, explain **conformity** and **obedience**. **(15)**
4. Describe and evaluate research findings in **one** study of minority influence. **(12)**
5. Explain **situational** and **individual** factors that contribute to obedience. **(6)**
6. What is meant by **normative social influence**? **(2)**

Social relationships

Section summary

The objectives of this section are to investigate:

- Stages of relationships.
- Gender differences in the benefits of relationships.
- Theoretical explanations for the formation, maintenance and dissolution of relationships.
- Dissolution of relationships.
- The effects of divorce on children.
- Attachment styles.
- Cultural and sub-cultural variations in relationships.

Introduction

For Reis (1996), a relationship is 'any ongoing association between two or more individuals.' Social psychologists suggest that humans are motivated towards forming connections and making contact with others. Humans have a basic need for the company of others, i.e. 'affiliation'. Cutrona (1986) found that stress levels were highest among people who had the least social interaction.

Stages of relationships

Most relationships go through predictable stages as they develop. This is especially true for romantic relationships. Kelley *et al* (1983) identified *four* stages of love.

Stage 1: Acquaintanceship

Two people meet and begin to interact with each other. With some contacts the relationship never goes any further than this. Sometimes we are introduced to people, get on well with them but the contact is not continued.

Stage 2: Discovery

This stage starts between three and six months and can last for years, depending on how willing the couple is to reveal personal information. Both partners begin to discover each other's quirks and vulnerabilities. They find evidence that they have selected the right person and the attractiveness of each partner is accentuated in the eyes of the other. The two people share their activities and interactions with each other.

Stage 3: Build-up

There can be stumbling blocks at this stage as one partner might discover things about the other that they find irritating. The couple may realise that they have completely different interests and have opposing plans for the future. This is often a time of choice regarding whether or not to continue with the relationship. Each partner has to decide if they are willing to make the necessary sacrifices to meet the other's needs. In order to protect the relationship deception might be used, e.g. you do not tell your partner if someone else has asked you out. As the level of commitment grows jealousy arises. Jealousy in men is related to self-esteem and status. A man's virility is dependent on his ability to maintain the relationship. According to Shettel-Neuber *et al* (1978), male jealousy manifests itself in feelings of anger and behaviour that could jeopardise the relationship. Women, however, experience jealousy because they want to protect the relationship, which they perceive as being more rewarding than any alternatives. Shettel-Neuber *et al* (1978) found that women are likely to express the jealousy in depressive symptoms and attempts to improve the relationship.

Stage 4: Commitment develops

The couple makes a deep commitment to each other at this stage. They know they are together and they can finally relax. The danger is that many people begin to take each other for granted during this stage and pay less attention to the relationship. Blais *et al* (1990) believe the most important thing at this stage to be the motivation behind the commitment. People remain happy with the relationship and activities that contribute to its maintenance if motivations to remain committed are intrinsic and self-determined. Although one partner's perceptions of the relationship will affect the other partner's view, Blais *et al* found this to be more applicable to women than to men. It appears, therefore, that women play a more active role in the development of a relationship than men.

Gender differences in the benefits of relationships

The majority of people in the UK are still expected to marry and remain in the relationship throughout their natural lives. Church leaders and politicians have extolled the virtues of marriage in terms of the economic and psychological benefits for the individual and society at large. In the past several decades, however, this view of marriage as the preferred way of life has been undermined by the rise of non-traditional family living patterns, such as cohabitation, same-sex couples, reconstituted families and single parenthood. In spite of the increasing rejection of the importance of marriage within modern life the health benefits of marriage have been consistently confirmed in national and international research.

Cochrane (1983, 1996) found that there was a high positive correlation between *marital status* and the risk of admission to a mental health hospital, with divorced individuals being five and a half times more likely than married people to be admitted to a mental hospital within any one year. Cramer (1995) reported that married people have not only lower rates of mental and physical disorders than single, widowed or divorced people, but also live longer. This is not to suggest that all unmarried people are equally at risk of health difficulties. Research findings in the US, UK and elsewhere confirm that among the unmarried population those who have never married are healthier than those who were married previously (Wyke and Ford, 1992).

Duck (1992) reported that people in disrupted relationships are more likely to suffer from coronary heart disease, alcoholism, drug dependency and sleep disturbance. Fincham (1997) concluded that, for men, depression predicted marital stress, whereas for women marital stress predicted depressive symptoms. According to Brehm and Kassin (1996), women tend to report more relationship problems than men and the extent of female dissatisfaction is a more reliable predictor of whether the relationship will end.

Bee (1994) suggested that men benefit more from marriage, partly because they are less likely than women to have intimate relationships outside marriage and partly because they receive more emotional support than they give. However, from a sample of 55-year-old men and women in the west of Scotland, Wyke and Ford (1992) found that good health among married men and women alike could be linked to higher levels of material resources and lower levels of stress. (Refer to **Box 3.13** for a study that investigates the relationship between marital status, gender and physical health.)

Box 3.13

Research: 'The relationship between marital status and health: An Empirical Investigation of Differences in Bed Occupancy within Health and Social Care Facilities in Britain, 1921-1991,' Prior and Hayes (2003)

Aim: To study the association between marital status, gender and physical health in health and social care institutions in England and Wales.

Participants: The total population of individuals (excluding staff and visitors) who, on the night of the census in 1921, 1951, 1961, 1971, 1981 or 1991, occupied beds in communal establishments designated as general health or social care facilities.

Design: A detailed investigation of census returns from 1921 to 1991, excluding 1931 and 1941, was undertaken. Individuals, excluding visitors and staff, who occupied beds in hospitals, nursing homes, homes for the elderly and homes for people with physical disabilities (all sectors - public, private and voluntary) were included. Hospitals and other facilities designated for people with mental illnesses or learning disabilities were excluded from this study. Bed occupancy in health and social care institutions were used as an indicator of health status.

Results:

1. Married individuals showed the lowest level of bed occupancy within residential health and social care facilities across all six census periods.
2. In contrast to the earlier half of the century, it is the previously married, specifically widowed individuals and not single people, who have occupied the highest proportion of beds in residential health and social care facilities.
3. Throughout the 20th century, married men have constituted a much larger proportion of the male sub-population in residential health and social care facilities than have married women in their equivalent female sub-population. In 1991, married women in these facilities formed only 7 per cent of the female subpopulation, whereas the equivalent figure for men was 17 per cent.
4. By 1991, within the male sub-population, the proportion of beds occupied by single (never married) men was 7 per cent higher than that of previously married men - 45 per cent as compared to 38 per cent.
5. Since 1981, the most vulnerable women are the previously married, but the most vulnerable men are those who have never married.
6. In 1991, exactly 45 per cent of all beds occupied by men in residential health and social care facilities were filled by men who had never married. This contrasted with the situation for single women, who made up just 26 per cent of the female subpopulation in these facilities.
7. Widowed women have much worse health than widowed men, but the reverse is true for the divorced.
8. In contrast to young single women, young single men are showing signs of an increasing vulnerability to ill health.

Conclusions: Across all census years, married individuals demonstrated much higher levels of physical health than the non-married (widowed, divorced and single). Married people are healthier than the non-married and this positive association between marriage and health has increased dramatically over time.

The benefits of marriage, particularly among women, have increased dramatically over time. Married men had poorer health than married women. There has been increasing vulnerability among the older female widowed sub-population and the young never-married male sub-population.

Discussion: Unhealthy people are thought to be less likely to marry or stay married as ill health can interfere with the establishment and maintenance of relationships. According to Wyke and Ford (1992), the more advantaged tend to marry and obtain the protective effects of marriage. For the most vulnerable groups (female widows and young never-married males), it may not be their current lack of a marital partner *per se* that explains their greater ill health, but rather the absence of an adequate support system.

Theoretical explanations for relationships

McDougall (1908) claims that individuals have an innate tendency to gather together. 'Evolutionary social psychology' emerged more recently, stating that social behaviour has a biological base. 'Behaviourist' approaches view human behaviour as being motivated by the gaining of pleasure and the avoidance of pain, whereas 'cognitive' approaches focus on the need to maintain cognitive consistency or balance.

Evolutionary explanations

Darwin's theory of evolution (1859) proposes that people choose partners who will maximise their *reproductive success*. This notion was supported by Buss (1988), who found that males show a preference for young and attractive females, whilst females desire partners who can provide wealth and support and can participate in a long-term relationship. Buss *et al* (1990) conducted a cross-cultural study comparing females' descriptions of desirable qualities in a partner and males' descriptions of desirable qualities in a partner. They found that females ranked things like 'good financial prospects', 'ambition' and 'industriousness' higher than males, whilst males rated 'physical attractiveness' higher than females. It could be argued, however, that women's attraction to men with earning potential and men's attraction to young, beautiful, women could be explained from a socialisation perspective as well as from an evolutionary perspective.

Within the UK, men are still earning more than women in the workplace and women are still the main carers in the home, so to an extent the social structure compels women to continue to be economically dependent upon men and to seek a partner who can provide support.

The British media constantly comment on the appearance of all women from supermodels to pop idols to politicians, thus reinforcing the importance of physical attractiveness in females. From a socialisation perspective, we could predict that as women and men become valued more equally they will no longer be attracted by such different attributes in a mate.

Research conducted by Buunk *et al* (2002) investigated mate preference for five different levels of heterosexual relationships – marriage; serious relationships; falling in love; casual sex; and sexual fantasies among individuals aged 21, 30, 40, 50 and 60. They found, in support of the 'evolutionary perspective', that men preferred mates who had higher levels of physical attractiveness than themselves, whereas women showed preference for those who had higher levels of income, education, intelligence, self-confidence, dominance and social position than themselves. For both men and women, higher levels of physical attractiveness were more important in sexual fantasies than in real relationships. There were few age differences in mate preferences, although older people did consider levels of education to be a prime factor.

Smith *et al* (2002) examined the content of personal advertisements to determine what people want in partners and what people believe others desire. They analysed the physical descriptions given in 357 advertisements written by lesbians, 135 written by bisexual women looking for female partners and 334 advertisements by heterosexual women. The findings showed that bisexual women offered the most physical descriptions of themselves, including weight and requested the most physical attributes in potential partners. Lesbians gave the least physical descriptions of themselves. It was concluded that what women want and what they perceive others to want, differs according to sexual orientation.

Critics of the evolutionary perspective have complained that it is unable to explain mate selection between same-sex individuals. Bassett *et al* (2001) investigated the differences in partner preference and jealousy among lesbians who identified themselves as either *butch* or *femme*. The researchers hypothesised that the *butches* would be more attracted to a partner's physical attributes and more jealous of a partner's sexual behaviour, thus reflecting the attitudes of a man in a heterosexual relationship. The *femmes*, it was hypothesised, would be more attracted to a partner's financial resources and more jealous of her emotional behaviour, thus mimicking the attitudes of women in heterosexual relationships.

Eighty-four lesbians at a Gay Pride event were asked to rank attributes that would provoke jealousy towards potential competitors in whom their partners might be interested. Participants were also instructed to rate their willingness to go out with hypothetical others who differed in levels of physical attractiveness, income and 'masculine' or 'feminine' personality. There was no difference between the butches and the femmes in terms of sexual versus emotional jealousy. However, the femmes were more jealous of physically attractive competitors, whereas the butches were more jealous of wealthy competitors. In addition, femmes were more influenced by the financial resources of potential partners and butches by physical attractiveness. The researchers recognised that the labels of *butch* and *femme* were social constructions, modelled after heterosexual sex roles, but concluded that a complex interaction of socialisation and prenatal development underlie lesbian sex role identification.

Reinforcement-affect theory

This theory is based on *conditioning* – humans are attracted by what they like, i.e. what produces a positive affect or emotion. They are also repulsed by what they dislike, i.e. what produces a negative affect or emotion. It is postulated that we like people who are around when we experience positive feelings, just as the Pavlovian dog learns to associate the sound of a bell with the positive reinforcement of food, humans can associate another person with other positive features of the environment. Consequently, people can be liked or disliked, depending on whether they are associated with positive or negative feelings. Griffit and Veitch (1971) placed participants in either physically comfortable or physically uncomfortable (i.e. too hot or too cold) conditions and presented them with neutral statements by strangers. Participants in the more uncomfortable conditions liked the stranger less. It was concluded that the stranger's statement (i.e. the neutral stimulus) had become associated with negative feelings about physical comfort in the uncomfortable condition. Baron and Byrne (1999) claim:

> 'It is simple but true, that we tend to like others when our emotions are positive and to dislike them when we are experiencing negative feeling, no matter what caused the emotions.'

The 'reinforcement-affect theory', however, does not consider the role of cognition in our decision to form or maintain relationships, suggesting that behaviour is deterministic.

Economic theories

Economic theories were first produced in the United States in the 1950s. They provide an explanation of *all* relationships, from romantic to business, focusing on interactions between two people. As the name suggests, economic theories make a *cost-benefit analysis* in explaining the formation, maintenance and dissolution of relationships.

Social exchange theory

Thibaut and Kelley (1959) proposed one of the earliest economic theories, the 'social exchange theory', which states that in relationships we take the costs – e.g. effort, embarrassment, time wasted and money spent – away from the rewards to measure the *profit.* According to this theory, the greater the profit, the more likely we are to stay in the relationship. Like other theories that stress the importance of behavioural principles, exchange theory suggests that socially significant behaviour – i.e. the relationship – is maintained only if it has been suitably reinforced. Each person has a 'comparison level', a standard that is the product of past experiences and general expectations of social exchanges, that allows one to judge whether a new relationship is profitable or not. If a person's *profit* exceeds his or her *comparison* level, then the relationship will be perceived as satisfying and the other party will appear attractive.

Like the reinforcement-affect theory and the evolutionary theory, the social exchange theory supports the notion that we are motivated by self-interest. The latter differs, however, in that it suggests people rationally calculate whether or not to maintain a relationship rather than being driven by learned or innate emotion.

Equity theory

Equity theory stems from exchange theory, but is more specific as it investigates how people decide when an exchange is fair and what they do if they decide it is not. Unlike social exchange theory, it recognises that sometimes we happily accept less than we give as the two people involved may be looking for different things from the relationship. The relationship is more likely to last if both parties are content with the exchange. According to Walster *et al* (1978) everyone strives for *balance.* Relationships are equitable when the ratio of profit to contribution is *perceived* to be the same by each partner. It is based on the principle that within Western societies fairness and justice are valued in social exchanges. Equity in a relationship is defined as a situation where all individuals' outcomes, i.e. rewards minus costs are proportional to their contributions to the relationship. (See **Box 3.14** for details of a study that provides support for the equity theory.)

Box 3.14

Research: Oswald and Clark (2004) 'Best Friends Forever? High School Best-friendships and the Transition to College'

Aim: To investigate if best friend relationships formed at school can be maintained when one or both parties head off to university.

Method: Survey.

Participants: 249 first year American undergraduates. Virtually all were white/Caucasian with an average age of 18. Fifty-three per cent of the participants lived far from their school best friend - median of 350 miles - and 47 per cent still lived in the same town.

Procedure:

1. All participants were surveyed during their first week at university, and 137 of them again one week before the end of the spring semester.
2. They were asked to indicate the 'rewards' and 'costs' of their best school friendships, rating it in terms of level of satisfaction and personal commitment towards it.
3. Participants were also asked to describe any alternative friendships.
4. A friendship maintenance scale was completed where the participants indicated the amount of mutual support they and their best friend gave each other; how upbeat they were when they were together; how much they confided in each other; and how often they socialised together.
5. Loneliness felt by the participants was also measured in both surveys.

Results:

1. 54.7 per cent of the participants considered their best friend from school still to be their best friend by the spring. These participants socialised frequently with the friend, confided in the friend and the friend confided in him/her, the friends were positive together and provided each other with support.
2. Overall, however, it was reported that by the spring school friendships had become 'more costly', 'less rewarding' and there were more 'alternatives' now available. Participants who spoke to their best friend from school on the phone more often were more likely to remain friends and less likely to complain about the increasing 'costs' of the relationship.
3. The people who had maintained their best friends from school were less likely to feel lonely in the spring. Those who still lived in the same town as their school friends were not any more likely to maintain the friendship.

Conclusion: Findings support the equity theory. When benefits such as mutual support and positive feelings are perceived to outweigh costs, e.g. time and effort, a relationship is more likely to be maintained. Regular contact is more important than physical proximity in the maintenance of relationships.

Evaluation: Unrepresentative sample. There has been no follow-up study to find out if the friendships were still strong in the 2nd or 3rd year of university.

(See 'Research Methods' Chapter for an evaluation of the survey method.)

Matching hypothesis

This explanation stems from equity theory, but is concerned only with romantic relationships and marriage. According to the matching hypothesis, the more *equitable* the relationship the more likely it is to lead to marriage. The main assumption of the matching hypothesis is that people aspire to be in a relationship with a partner who is socially desirable, i.e. has sought-after qualities, such as a nice personality, attractive appearance, good social skills, wealth, status and intelligence, but this aspiration is balanced against the perceived probability of attaining it. Subsequently, people tend to be attracted to others of approximately the same level of attractiveness – this is the notion of *homogamy*. The matching hypothesis claims that romantically involved couples tend to be matched in levels of physical attractiveness. The 'Computer dance' study was carried out by Walster *et al* (1966) to test the matching hypothesis – details of the study can be seen in **Box 3.15**.

Box 3.15

Research: 'Computer Dance Study', Walster *et al* (1966)

Aim: To test the matching hypothesis.

Procedure: A 'computer dance' was advertised during 'Freshers' Week' at college. Four independent judges assessed each student's physical attractiveness as a measure of social desirability. The participants completed a questionnaire to use in the pairing of couples. The questionnaires were actually used to provide data about similarity and participants were paired randomly (although males were never coupled with taller women). Participants attended the dance two days later. They were given a questionnaire about their date to complete during the dance. Six months later they were asked if they had been on a date with their dance partner.

Participants: 376 male students and 376 female students.

Results: When they were asked about their date during the dance the more physically attractive participants were liked more by their partners than were the less attractive participants. However, when the participants were contacted six months later they were more likely to have been on a further date if they were similar in levels of physical attractiveness.

Conclusions: Physical attractiveness was the most important factor in liking the partner, above intelligence and personality. The matching hypothesis was not supported in the initial stages of the study. However, the matching hypothesis was supported by the later findings that those who were similar in levels of physical attractiveness had highest rates of having been on a further date six months later. People use different criteria for a long-term relationship than for a short-term one.

Evaluation: A 'real-life' event was used to test the matching hypothesis. The computer dance is not a realistic test of the matching hypothesis as the dates were assigned for the students and assessments were made before any rejections could have occurred. As the interaction was brief, interpersonal assessment had to be based on superficial characteristics. The measurement of physical attractiveness was unreliable. The participants were not representative (students) so findings may apply only to young people who are not making long-term choices.

Dissolution of relationships

Most of the social psychological theories and studies on relationships focus on the formation and maintenance of relationships. However, it also important to look at the complex nature of relationship dissolution as this can affect an individual's social, emotional, family and financial life. Hill *et al* (1976) conducted a longitudinal study with 231 couples in Boston, Massachusetts, a high proportion of whom were college students. Over the two-year period of the study, 103 of the couples had split up, 65 were still going out together, nine were engaged, 43 were married and 11 could not be contacted. The maintenance of the relationships depended more on women, whose feelings were also a more accurate measurement of the state of the relationship. It was most likely to be the woman who made the decision to end the relationship. The couple often remained 'good friends' when it was the man who had initiated the break-up, but this was much less likely to happen when it was the woman. The findings showed that those couples who were similar in terms of age, education, verbal test score, numerical test score, attractiveness and views on gender roles were more likely to stay together.

Duck (1988) investigated marriage break-ups and identified factors that make it more likely a marriage will end either in divorce or in unhappiness:

1. Marriages between younger couples are more unstable, especially if they have children early. The individuals are not ready to make a commitment to one person since they have yet to fully establish their sense of identity. If a new baby arrives, the couple has very little time to adjust to the responsibility of marriage, financial and housing concerns.
2. Couples from lower socio-economic groups and lower educational levels tend to have more unstable marriages. These couples are also more inclined to have children early in the marriage.
3. Couples from different demographic backgrounds tend to have more unstable marriages.
4. Individuals who experienced parental divorce in childhood and who have had an above average number of sexual partners are more likely to have unstable marriages.

Duck (1988) recognised that not all break-ups fit neatly into these categories. Some marriages between young, working class, individuals from different cultures are secure, whilst many divorces occur between couples that meet none of the above criteria. Duck (1988) investigated reasons for relationship break-ups that affect all types of couples regardless of age, class, educational level, religion and culture. According to Duck, communication skills (both verbal and non-verbal) play a major role in the breakdown of relationships. A common problem in marriages is that one of the partners, usually the husband, is over-confident about how precisely they give and receive non-verbal messages. This can produce a 'negativity cycle' where each partner perceives faults in the other that leads to arguments and scoring points off each other. The relationship is more likely to end when one partner is perceived to have broken the 'relationship rules'. These rules include the expectations that the individuals have of each other, such as support, loyalty, fidelity, honesty, spending time together, balance in terms of effort and resources and the existence of a 'magical quality'. Duck (1988) proposes that if one partner deceives another then the most important relationship rule has been violated. Lack of stimulation, boredom and the feeling that the relationship is not going anywhere are commonly given reasons for ending a relationship.

For Duck (1988) the break-up of a relationship should be regarded as a process that occurs over a period of time. Although it is recognised that each break-up is unique, Duck proposed that there were *four* phases in the dissolution process:

1. The 'intrapsychic phase' begins when one partner feels unable to tolerate the relationship any longer. The individual focuses on the negative aspects of remaining in the relationship and positively evaluates aspects of alternative relationships. At his stage there is little outward show since the processes are happening only in the individual's mind. This phase comes to an end when the discontented partner starts to share his/her complaints with others, but not their partner and feels justified in leaving the relationship.
2. In the 'dyadic phase' the unhappy partner reaches the decision that something has to be done and he/she confronts their partner. Negotiations over whether the relationship can be repaired and the costs of withdrawal occur. If it is decided that the relationship cannot be saved the dissatisfied partner shows he/she is serious about splitting up.
3. The 'social phase' involves declaring the break-up to family and friends, which will bring about a change in both partners' social networks.
4. Finally, the 'grave-dressing phase' is when the individuals attempt to get over the relationship. This involves giving a socially acceptable account of the relationship to save face, preserve memories and justify the original commitment to the ex-partner.

Duck's model provides the typical story of a break-up, but does not apply to those who leave a relationship very quickly with very little or no discussion, nor can it explain the break-ups that occur in a cloud of passion because of infidelity or jealousy. Some dissatisfied individuals may take a more passive role and simply neglect things until the relationship naturally declines.

Effects of divorce on children

(See the 'Attachment and separation' Section in Chapter 1 of this book for further discussion on the effects of divorce on children.)

Changes in family structure, especially when this involves the removal of a parent, will cause a certain amount of stress. Divorce and separation can sometimes be perceived as liberating for the adults, particularly women, but disastrous for the children. Amato (1991) suggested that being labelled the child of divorced parents may be hard for children to cope with and other children at school may make life difficult for them. Furthermore, immediately after a divorce, children become more defiant, more negative and more aggressive or they become depressed or angry (Hetherington, 1989, 1991a, 1991b). The researchers found these effects to be more severe in boys than in girls, although girls show more disruption in adolescence. Hetherington (1982) conducted a study of 2,500 people in 1,400 families over a 25-year period and concluded that the negative effects of divorce have been exaggerated, while the positive effects have been ignored.

The findings of the study indicated that approximately 80 per cent of children with divorced parents function well, with little long-term damage and that within two years the vast majority were starting to 'function reasonably well'. It is also worth noting that 70 per cent of parents reported to be happier after the divorce than before.

It is prudent, however, to address the difficulties faced, as Hetherington (1982) did acknowledge that about 20 per cent of children with divorced parents had serious or emotional problems compared with 10 per cent from intact families.

It is fashionable for politicians to blame single parents for unruly behaviour in children and to view non-nuclear families as main contributors to social problems. Divorce and separation have been seen as liberating for the adults, especially women, but disastrous for children in terms of the psychological, social and financial effects. Rodgers and Prior (1998) pronounce that the complex factors affecting families before, during and after separation need to be examined, thus recognising divorce as a *process*, rather than an *event*. According to Dowling and Gorell Barnes (2000), children need an *explanation* throughout the whole process.

It is essential that children understand that even though their parents cannot live together they are still interested in them and responsible for them. On the one hand, researchers claim that the effects of divorce are mitigated when children maintain good relationships with both parents. Continuing parental conflict after divorce, on the other hand, has a negative effect on children. Thus, it can be concluded that it is the quality of care, *not* parental separation that is an important contributory factor in children's future happiness.

See **Box 3.16** for details of a study that investigates the long-term consequences of parental conflict and divorce for offspring. The findings suggest that mitigating factors such as low parental conflict during divorce, positive child-parent relationships and social support will protect children from the negative effects of parental divorce.

Box 3.16

Research: 'Parental Marital Conflict and Divorce, Parent-child Relationships, Social Support, and Relationship Anxiety in Young Adulthood,' Heidi R. Riggio (2004)

Aims:

1. To explore the consequences of parental conflict on the psychological and social adjustment of young adults by comparing individuals from divorced and intact families.
2. To investigate the links between parental conflict and divorce and the young adults' relationship with their parents.

Hypotheses:

1. Compared to individuals reporting lower levels of parental conflict, individuals reporting high levels of parental conflict will report significantly lower quality relationships with fathers and mothers, fewer numbers of and lower satisfaction with available social supports and significantly stronger feelings of anxiety in personal relationships with others.
2. Compared to individuals from intact families, individuals from divorced families are expected to report significantly more negative relationships with fathers, and fewer numbers of and lower satisfaction with available social supports.
3. Individuals from divorced families are expected to report significantly more positive relationships with mothers than are individuals from intact families.
4. Individuals from divorced families are expected to report significantly less anxiety about personal relationships, given their less negative view of relationship failure, than are individual from intact families.
5. For individuals from intact and divorced families, high quality relationships with parents are expected to be positively related to number of and satisfaction with available social supports and negatively related to feelings of anxiety in personal relationships.

Participants: 208 men, 358 women with ages ranging from 18 to 32 (mean age of 21.4 years). Four hundred and one participants were from intact families (biological parents married) and 165 were from divorced families (biological parents divorced). Mean age at parental divorce was 9.4 years. Ninety per cent were undergraduate students and 10 per cent were graduate students. Sixty-two per cent lived with one or both parents. Of those from divorced families, 9 per cent had been brought up by fathers, 64 per cent by mothers, 26 per cent by both parents, 3 per cent by neither parent. Forty-nine per cent reported that their mothers had remarried, 52 per cent reported that fathers had remarried (both parents/neither parent remarried = 32 per cent each). The students participated for extra or research participation credit.

Design:

1. 'The Social Support Questionnaire' (SSQ) - a 27-item measure of the perceived number of social supports and satisfaction with available social support.
2. 'The Anxiety Subscale of the Relationship Awareness Scale' (RAS-A) - a 9-item measure of relational anxiety, defined as the tendency to experience anxiety and discomfort in close relationships.
3. 'The Personal Attachment Questionnaire' (PAQ) - a 48-item measure used to assess affective quality of relationships with each parent, parents as sources of emotional support and degree to which parents facilitated independence.
4. 'The Parental Conflict Scale' (PCS) - a 9-item measure of the nature, duration and severity of parental marital conflict.
5. Demographic information was collated (sex, age, parental marital status and, if relevant, age at divorce, annual household income and parental educational attainment.

Procedure: All participants completed the SSQ, the RAS-A, the PAQ, gave demographic information and lastly completed the PCS. Sessions lasted 45-60 minutes.

Results:
1. 'Hypothesis 1' was partly supported. Young adults from high-conflict families reported significantly lower affective quality, independence and emotional support in relationships with fathers and with mothers compared to those from lower-conflict families; significantly lower numbers of available social supports and significantly greater anxiety in personal relationships.
2. Consistent with 'Hypothesis 2', individuals from divorced families reported significantly lower affective quality and emotional support in relationships with fathers compared to individuals from intact families. Contrary to Hypothesis 2, individuals from divorced families reported significantly greater numbers of available social supports and marginally significantly greater independence facilitated by fathers.
3. 'Hypotheses 3 and 4 'were supported. Individuals from divorced families reported significantly greater affective quality, greater independence and marginally significantly greater emotional support in relationships with mothers. Individuals from divorced families reported significantly lower anxiety in personal relationships.
4. 'Hypothesis 5' was partially supported. For young adults from intact families, results indicated significant positive correlations between quality of both parent-child relationships and satisfaction with and number of perceived available social supports. For young adults from divorced families, results indicated significant and marginally significant positive correlations between quality of both parent-child relationship and numbers of available social supports and significant positive correlations between satisfaction with social support and qualities of mother-child relationships and emotional support from fathers.

Conclusion: Divorce and conflict have significant independent effects on outcomes in young adulthood. Effects of conflict are uniformly negative for quality of parent-child relationships, perceived social support from others and anxiety in personal relationships. Parental divorce is associated with lower quality father-child relationships, social support, independence facilitated by both parents and reduced anxiety in relationships. These effects occur regardless of sex, parental remarriage and parental socio-economic status.

Evaluation: Custody arrangements and frequency of contact with fathers were not specifically assessed for individuals from divorced families. Retrospective accounts of parental conflict may have been affected by memory relapses and current attitudes. The sample was taken from the student population.

(See 'Research Methods' Chapter for an evaluation of the correlation design.)

Attachment styles

(See Chapter 1 of this book regarding 'Attachment' and 'Separation'.)

Attachment refers to the strong, emotional and lasting bond that is developed between a young child and his/her carers. When a child, or indeed an adult, has formed an attachment with someone they feel a sense of comfort and security when they are with that individual. For a young child, being securely attached to another person is essential for healthy emotional development as it provides him/her with a safe base from which to explore the world.

Bowlby (1953) insisted that babies have a biological need for a warm and continuous attachment with a mother or mother substitute and that the attachment bond was 'monotropic', which means that it is between the infant and one other person (usually the mother). He suggested that infants develop a bond with their mother that is qualitatively different from any other, claiming that a baby needs to maintain virtually constant contact with his/her mother or permanent mother substitute until the age of five. If, according to Bowlby, the child experiences 'maternal deprivation', i.e. the bond has never been formed or is broken by fairly long periods of separation, the child is at risk of suffering from emotionally disturbed behaviour in the long-term.

Bowlby's monotropy theory of attachment suggested that the father is not emotionally important to the young child, but is only indirectly valuable in providing emotional and economic support for the mother (Gross *et al*, 2000). Contrary to Bowlby's theory, children often form 'multiple attachments' with caregivers (including the father) and the formation of a secure attachment does not depend on the caregiver's continued presence, but rather on the sensitivity of the caregiver to the child's needs (Schaffer and Emerson 1964). Shaffer and Emerson (1964) pronounced:

> '[B]eing attached to several people does not imply a shallower feeling towards each one, for an infant's capacity for attachment is not like a cake that has to be shared out. Love, even in babies, has no limits.'

Secure and insecure attachments

In order to investigate the formation of childhood attachments, Ainsworth *et al* (1978) devised the 'strange situation' in which 26 mother-infant pairs were brought into an unfamiliar room with toys. The 12 month-old child's reaction was observed as a stranger entered, as the mother left and, finally, on the mother's return. The findings showed that babies explored the room more enthusiastically when the mother was present and appeared less confident when the mother was absent and when the stranger was in the room. Ainsworth *et al* were interested in the children's behaviours when reunited with their mothers as such behaviours form an important part of the mother-child attachment.

Seventy per cent of the children were classified as 'securely attached'. They used their mothers as a 'home base' for exploring the world and felt secure in their attachment to her even when they were not in contact. These children played happily when the mother was there, irrespective of the presence of a stranger. They were clearly distressed when the mother left and went to her immediately for comfort when she returned. Fifteen per cent of the children were classified as 'anxious-avoidant' and appeared to be unconcerned about who was in the room with them. In new situations, these children explored the environment less and cried more. These children showed no signs of distress when their mother left the room and either ignored or avoided her when she returned. They showed the most distress when left on their own. Fifteen per cent of the participants were classified as 'anxious-resistant' and showed reluctance in exploring the new surroundings even when their mother was present. They became very distressed when the mother left. On the mother's return they were very clingy, but at the same time also demonstrated anger by hitting her and crying.

Ainsworth *et al* concluded that the mother's sensitivity to the child determines the quality of the child-mother attachment. Sensitive mothers tend to have babies who are securely attached as they can view events from the baby's perspective, interpret his/her signals appropriately, respond to the baby's needs and be accepting and cooperative. Insensitive mothers, on the other hand, are more likely to have babies who are insecurely attached, i.e. either 'anxious-avoidant' or 'anxious-resistant'.

Research indicates that children with secure attachments in infancy are more likely to be popular with their peers, independent and confident with strangers, eager to learn and have a positive and emotionally mature outlook (Carlson and Stroufe, 1995). According to Bretherton (1985) insecurely attached children are more likely to demonstrate hostility in their relationships.

Feeney and Noller (1990) pronounce that different *attachment styles*, i.e. anxious, secure or avoidant that develop in childhood, will influence the formation of our adult romantic relationships. Feeney (1994) concluded that securely attached individuals were likely to be paired with similarly secure partners. They are likely to have a close and trusting relationship with their partner. People who had established insecure-avoidant attachments are more likely to be uncomfortable about forming a close relationship with their partner and are fearful of commitment. If an insecure-resistant attachment had been formed in infancy, adults may worry that their partner might leave them and that they were not receiving enough love from them. It is worth noting that Levitt (1991) argues that early attachment styles could be a contributory factor in the quality of adult relationships, but experiences in the intervening years should not be ignored.

Hazan and Shaver (1987) argued that love was a form of attachment and a person's adult romantic attachments should, therefore, have some association with other attachment experiences. The researchers gathered extensive information on the romantic experiences and reactions of over 1,200 people. Hazan and Shaver found that the participants' reported histories of their relationships with their parents were related to their different adult attachment styles. Adults who had experienced secure attachments in childhood found it relatively easy to get close to people and were comfortable depending on others and being depended on. Their romantic relationships were happy. People with a secure attachment style recognised that their relationships would have 'ups and downs'. They believed that the extremely intense feelings often experienced at the start of a relationship could reappear and that romantic love need not fade at all. 'Avoidant' lovers on the other hand, thought that heart-fluttering happy-ever-after romantic love was merely fictional and that real love was very rarely found. They found it difficult to get close to others and their romantic relationships often involved high levels of jealousy. Adults who had developed an anxious/ambivalent attachment style reported that others were often reluctant to satisfy their desired level of closeness. Although they felt that real love was rare, they fell in love often.

Gross (2003) points out that attachment type need not be a fixed characteristic of the child as it could change according to family circumstances, such as the mother's stress levels. It is also important to consider the individual differences in babies, e.g. some infants like cuddling while others do not. Similarly, a child could form a secure attachment to its mother, but an insecure attachment to its father.

The classification of attachment types was based on studies of American infants, as Ainsworth's (1978) 'strange situation' was based in the United States. The influence of culture should not be ignored when investigating attachment, as norms and values vary about childrearing and the interaction between parents and children. Cross-cultural studies (van Ijzendoorn and Kroonenberg, 1988) based on the 'strange situation' found that although secure attachment was the most common type of attachment, Germany had a relatively high proportion of insecure-avoidant attachments and Japanese infants showed a relatively high proportion of insecure-resistant attachments.

Grossman *et al* (1985) explained the high incidence of insecure-avoidant relationships in Germany by examining childrearing norms and values. The researchers concluded that German mothers were responsive and sensitive to their children's needs and were keen to instil the values of *independence* and *self-reliance* in their children. The German parents considered some of the behaviour in the 'strange situation' that was supposed to indicate secure attachment as displays of 'spoilt' and 'clinging' children. Likewise, Takahashi (1990) concluded that the high proportion of attachments in Japanese infants classified as insecure-resistant was due to the norms and values that determined childrearing practices. In Japanese culture, children are very infrequently left alone at 12 months and their mothers rarely leave them in the care of anyone else. Therefore, in the 'strange situation' experiment they are more likely to experience distress when left alone or left in the company of a stranger.

Cultural and sub-cultural variations

The psychological research into social relationships focuses on Western heterosexual, romantic interactions, even though arranged marriages are the most common method of 'mate selection' worldwide. Moghaddam *et al* (1993) argued that this concentration among social psychologists on romantic couples and first time acquaintances is the result of a 'Western cultural perspective'.

As Goodwin (1995) argued, love 'at least in its passionate stomach churning Hollywood manifestation,' is mostly a Western, individualistic phenomenon. For most Westerners, love is considered to be a necessary prelude to marriage, but, as Bellur (1995) points out, in arranged marriages the marriage is a prelude to a loving relationship.

As well as being 'ethnocentric', social psychological research largely ignores gay and lesbian partnerships, concentrating on heterosexual relationships. Bee (1994) proposes that there are far more similarities than differences between homosexual and heterosexual relationships. Kitzinger and Coyle (1995), however, point out that homosexual couples are less likely to *cohabitate* – perhaps 'closet' homosexuals are reluctant to openly live with someone of the same sex. They are less likely to be *sexually exclusive* – having sex outside the main relationship may be in agreement with the negotiated sexual activity guidelines and are less likely to adopt conventional *sex-roles*. The researchers also suggested that the maintenance of gay or lesbian relationships might be more difficult if the couple do not have family support or are discriminated against in financial matters.

Douglas *et al* (1999) conducted research into homophobic bullying in 307 secondary schools in England and Wales. Most of the survey respondents were aware of homophobic verbal bullying, and over one in four knew of homophobic physical bullying. According to the research findings, existing school policies on bullying rarely referred to gay or lesbian issues. Recommendations included the modernisation of national bullying policies, new initiatives in citizenship training and supporting teachers and policy-making in schools through training.

Such recommendations do not sit comfortably with Clause 28, Section 2 of the Local Government Act 1988, which states that local authorities shall not intentionally promote homosexuality or publish material with the intention of promoting homosexuality. The repeal process of this Act became very public in Scotland when Stagecoach tycoon, Brian Souter, funded the 'Keep the Clause campaign', which involved a private referendum. Only 34 per cent responded to the poll, with 86.8 per cent voting in favour of keeping the Act and 13.2 per cent voting for repeal. Incidentally, Brian Souter was embarrassed two months later when *The Sun* newspaper revealed that the chair of his UK buses division, William Hinkley, had been charged with soliciting for a male prostitute while on business in Houston. Throughout the debate over Clause 28, the National Union of Teachers argued that the repeal was essential to protect pupils from intimidation and bullying.

On 31 December 2003, *The Scottish Daily Mail's* headline read, 'Fury at Gay propaganda in schools' (see **Box 3.17** below). This suggests that the promotion of homosexuality is still a controversial topic in Scottish schools, which may have implications for prejudiced attitudes and homophobic bullying.

Box 3.17

News Article: 'Fury at Gay propaganda in schools'

A scheme, funded by taxpayers' money, will advise teachers on how best to promote homosexuality in Scottish schools. Teachers will be encouraged to integrate homosexual issues into the secondary school curriculum and to replace the term 'husband and wife' with more inclusive language such as 'partner'.

The Executive's Healthy Respect sex education project initiated the scheme in Lothian schools and has been met with outrage from family groups and the Catholic Church. Healthy Respect was launched in 2001 at a cost of £3 million, which has already angered parents since nearly half of all Scottish 13 and 14-year-old pupils have been assessed as falling below national literacy and numeracy standards.

(Adapted from Kate Foster, 'The Scottish Daily Mail,' 31 December 2003.)

Section summary

1. Humans have a need to form connections and make contact with other people.
2. There is a positive correlation between marriage and mental health. According to Prior and Hayes (2003), the most vulnerable groups in terms of physical health are older widows and young males who have never married.
3. The evolutionary perspective claims that individuals choose mates who will ensure species survival and reproduction.
4. The reinforcement-affect explanation emphasises socialisation and learning rather than evolution.
5. The social exchange theory considers relationships in terms of the cost-reward ratio.
6. The equity theory defines a relationship as equitable when the ratio of profit to contribution is perceived to be the same by each partner.
7. The matching hypothesis predicts that individuals will become romantically involved with others who are fairly closely matched in terms of desirability.
8. Duck (1988) investigates some of the complex reasons for the dissolution of relationships.
9. The findings of Riggio (2004) show that children of divorced parents experience most distress when there is a high level of conflict between the divorcing couple.
10. Attachment is an enduring bond to a particular individual.
11. There are cultural and sub-cultural variations in relationships.

Practice exam questions

1. Explain the **economic theory of relationships** and evaluate relevant research evidence. **(15)**
2. Explain the possible **effects of divorce** on children. **(2)**
3. Describe **the role of mitigating factors** that may protect children from the negative effects of divorce. **(3)**
4. Explain the **matching hypothesis** and evaluate relevant research evidence. **(15)**
5. Explain a stage theory of relationships. **(5)**

Chapter 4
Individual Differences

Introduction to individual differences

Since psychology had been variously defined as the scientific study of behaviour and experience, psychologists have attempted to use systematic and objective research to explore the ways in which human beings behave and experience the world in which they live. Most visibly, psychologists will do this through assessing and testing the ways in which people are 'different'. The study of 'individual differences' is the subject matter for this Chapter and includes the topic areas: 'Intelligence', 'Atypical behaviour – definitions and approaches' and 'Atypical behaviour - therapies'.

As is the case with other social scientists, individual differences psychologists tend to subscribe to particular viewpoints. There is no single perspective, or domain, that all psychologists use to inform research or theoretical framework. To some onlookers, this may give the impression that psychology is divided in how it explains human behaviour, but to others it shows the richness and variety of perspectives used in explaining the complex issues pertaining to *how* and *why* humans behave. A key focus for psychologists, regardless of perspective taken, is on why humans differ in the way that they do. Various perspectives influence how psychologists conduct research and how they view individual differences, but *all* are interested in the subject matter. Perspective also affects how psychologists assess and test for individual differences. Therefore, consideration of *philosophical issues*, such as those given in this Chapter, is crucial to any understanding of individual differences.

Key issues in Individual Differences

In this introduction three key issues will be addressed – free-will and determinism, nature and nurture, and idiographic and nomothetic approaches. These will be useful to widen your understanding of individual differences and will show how these issues apply in all areas of psychology but particularly in the areas of *intelligence* and *atypical behaviour*.

Free will and determinism debate

The issue of 'free will' and 'determinism' is probably one of the oldest philosophical issues influencing psychology and the social sciences at large. The debate focuses on whether, or to what extent, human behaviour results from an act of free will, or volition on the part of the individual, or whether, or to what extent, that behaviour has been caused, or at least influenced, by determining factors. This key debate also provides a backdrop to the other areas to be discussed in this Chapter – the 'nature-nurture' and 'idiographic' and 'nomothetic' debates.

The free will approach regards human beings as having the capacity and freedom to choose our experiences and how we behave. In essence, human behaviour is seen as self-determining. This does *not* mean our behaviour is totally random but, rather, that external environmental influences or innate instinctual behaviours can to some extent be overridden as determinants of how we behave, if we so desire.

The determinist approach, on the other hand, claims that all physical events can be seen as 'effects' that are 'caused'. Since much of human experience and behaviour manifests physically – as opposed to *metaphysically*, or *spiritually* – it follows that anything we do and feel must in some way be caused by factors other than individual choice. As a result of this, it could be assumed that future experiences and behaviour could be predicted. In other words, if we know the causes of certain behaviours, then we could predict that in any future situation if the cause occurred, it would determine a particular effect.

It is important to understand how this debate applies to psychology and how the positions taken by the different domains impact on how individual differences are interpreted and explained.

'Humanistic' and 'cognitive' psychologists are, to varying extents, 'free-will' psychologists. Carl Rogers (1963) is the strongest proponent of free will, claiming that we, as individuals, positively direct our lives towards our own chosen goals and beliefs. This will become more apparent when we discuss 'therapies' dealing with 'atypical behaviour' – where the humanistic based therapies expand the idea that the individual has the power to solve their own mental problems. Cognitive psychologists favour a more moderate version of the free will approach, which is referred to as 'soft determinism'. This states that the individual's capacity for freedom of choice ultimately has the potential to override the impact of the constraints of the environment on choice. They point to the fact that humans can think out how to override restraints on their behaviour through 'problem solving' and can choose to pay 'attention', or not, to identified influences on behaviour.

The 'behaviourists' take a more extreme deterministic approach, asserting that learning is conditioned by environmental stimuli. Skinner (1938) takes this deterministic view of behaviour and regards the human perception that individuals' have free will as merely an illusion that in itself is a product of learning.

The 'psychoanalysts' also view behaviour as determined. They claim that the unconscious mind controls behaviour and, by definition, the conscious mind is unaware of this. They refer to this by the use of the concept 'unconscious determinism'.

The 'biological' approach is also determinist. Their position is informed by the assumption that biological and physiological forces, such as genetics, biochemistry and the nervous system, directly cause predictable behavioural effects.

It will be shown later in the chapter the ways in which the free will and determinism debate informs both theory and research into individual differences. For now, however, we should think of free will and determinism as polar opposites on a continuum, with various positions taken by psychologists featuring somewhere along the line, rather than at either end. We should also note that the debate is more accurately referred to as the free will *and* determinism debate, rather than free will *or* determinism.

Nature-nurture debate

The concepts, free will and determinism, influence another key issue in psychology – the 'nature-nurture' debate. The 'nature' side of the debate focuses on the extent to which biological and genetic heredity influences behaviour. The 'nurture' side focuses on the extent to which behaviour is learned and taught by social and environmental factors. Essentially, *both* sides of the debate are determinist.

Nature

The 'naturist' (or 'nativist') side of the debate shows 'genetic determinism'. It places the roots of behaviour in heredity factors such as 'bio-physiological instinct'. Behaviours develop throughout the lifespan as innate, inborn, evolutionary forces provide for us a maturational blueprint. Nature has provided us each with a unique and complex behavioural code forged with the need for survival at its core. Environmental factors *do* elicit particular behavioural responses, but *only* insofar as they provide the stimuli for pre-programmed responses. Since the roots of behaviour are seen as bio-physiological from this approach, any attempt at behavioural change should be targeted at this level. Thus, behavioural therapies should take the form of genetic manipulation, drug administration and, in its most extreme and racist form, selective breeding of human beings.

Nurture

Whilst those on the nature side of the debate are known as 'genetic determinists', those on the nurture side are known as 'environmental determinists'. 'Nurturists' take a position similar to the English philosopher, John Locke (1632-1704), who first claimed that the human mind is born as a 'blank slate'. All knowledge and behaviour is learned from experience in the world and no innate determinants of behaviour exist. It is the environment that determines behaviour for 'nurturists'. The environment referred to here encompasses everyone and everything in the social world that may influence an individual's knowledge and behaviour. Behaviour is, therefore, learned and, as such, any attempts to change behaviour should be focused on changing environmental conditions in order to *unlearn* certain behaviours.

What follows are examples of positions taken by psychologists with regard to this debate in various topic areas in psychology.

Aggression
Biological psychologists take a naturist approach and would argue that hormones, neurotransmitters and specific areas of the brain cause aggression in human beings. Nurturists, such as 'social learning' theorists, argue that aggression is learned from the environment through observing and imitating (Bandura, Ross and Ross, 1961).

Abnormality (commonly known as 'atypicality')
Naturists following the medical approach have stated that mental disorders have a clear and direct link to both genetic and neurochemical imbalances within the brain. Nurturists would strongly advocate that the environment plays a critical role in any aspect of abnormal behaviour and would cite illnesses such as stress, anorexia and phobic disorders as being clearly rooted in the person's environment and, in particular, with learning through imitation.

It is important to note that although the position taken in this debate has significant implications for how a topic area is explored, modern psychologists tend to take a position somewhere along the nature-nurture continuum rather than a hard and fast position at either extreme. In other words, nature and nurture interact in a complex relationship. Behaviour is both genetically and environmentally determined.

Earlier, we looked at the examples of aggression and abnormality from opposing sides of the debate. Below are examples of psychologists taking account of *both* sides of the nature-nurture interaction.

Certain mental disorders such as schizophrenia may have a genetic predisposition. Those people who have an inherited susceptibility from their parents and families *may* be more likely to develop the illness if they are exposed to certain environmental stressors, such as those that may have experience of living in socially deprived areas.

Cognitive development
Piaget introduced us to the idea that we all have an innate 'schema', or framework, for individual development. However, he clearly argues that in order for this to develop adequately, individuals need to interact with the environment in order to adapt to our individual environment and lifestyle. Piaget believed that both the nature and nurture elements are major influences in the maturation of the individual.

Thus, different approaches in psychology tend to view the nature-nurture interaction differently. The behaviourists clearly identify with nurture as the root cause of behaviour. Psychoanalysts emphasise the role of nature, but are willing to accept that the external environment will influence a child during maturation and the psychosexual stages of development. Biological psychologists are clearly on the nature side when they focus on the effects of physiology and genetics and imply that behaviour can only be modified through physical means. Both cognitive and humanistic psychologists assume that both nature and nurture interact as they impact on human development and experience.

The implications of this particular debate are fairly profound and these will be explored later in this Section when we look at 'Intelligence' and both Sections on 'Atypical behaviour'.

The idiographic and nomothetic debate

One very simple way to remember the distinction between these two terms is to think of the 'I' in idiographic as standing for 'individual' and the 'N' in 'nomothetic' as standing for 'numerous' (individuals). Both terms refer to research methodologies; that is, the theoretical approaches informing choice of research methods. The idiographic approach focuses on discrete individuals in a personal and in-depth way in order to produce a complete and unique understanding of them as an individual. A typical research method used by psychologists taking this approach would be the 'case study', since it provides deep and comprehensive understanding at the individual level. This focus on the level of the individual has led some to assert that this approach is *non-scientific*. The nomothetic approach, on the other hand, is considered to be scientific in that it takes large groups of people and attempts to advance principles or laws of behaviour that can then be generalised to wider populations. Typical research methods used by psychologists taking this approach would be those that produce quantitative, statistical data (see Chapter 2, Part 1). By doing so, general patterns and trends of human behaviour may be detected.

There are many examples in psychology where both approaches are used simultaneously:

Nomothetic

- In social psychology, Stanley Milgram's (1974) famous work, *Obedience to Authority*, established general conclusions on people's attitude to authority.
- In the study of individual differences, personality and IQ tests place subjects' scores on a scale for the purposes of statistical measurement and analysis. The classification manuals used in atypical behaviour classify individuals in populations by category of mental illness.

Idiographic

- Freud (1909) based his theory of personality development on several clinical case studies, including the famous study of 'Little Hans'. He kept detailed notes on behaviour and, using the technique of 'free association', he was able to build up a pattern of patients' experiences and behaviour.
- Piaget (1953) kept a highly focused and extensive diary of the cognitive development of his own children, into which he gained tremendous insight. This led to the theoretical construction of many of his ideas.

As is the case with the two other debates considered above, many psychologists use an approach that recognises *both* stances. Perhaps this is necessary for a balanced and complete study of psychology. It is important to recognise the importance of philosophical issues in psychology as they provide the setting against which theoretical and conceptual frameworks are constructed.

Self-assessment questions

1. Distinguish between the concepts of **free will**, **determinism** and **soft determinism**.
2. How do **environment** and **heredity** interact when influencing behaviour?
3. Define the terms **idiographic** and **nomothetic**. Search for examples from what you have already studied to illustrate how and where they were used in psychology.

Intelligence

Section summary

The learning objectives for intelligence are to:

- Explain what psychologists mean by the term intelligence.
- Describe the different models and theories of intelligence.
- Explain the techniques we use to measure intelligence.
- Identify where and why intelligence testing is used.
- Critique intelligence testing.
- Understand the debate on the *determinants* of intelligence: the nature-nurture issue.
- Describe research evidence relating to nature and nurture in intelligence.

The meaning of intelligence

The study of intelligence is one of the most challenging areas in psychology. It may surprise you that there is no single universally accepted definition of intelligence. Nor, in fact, is there common agreement over whether intelligence is a singular concept or whether many different forms exist. Modern psychologists tend to develop explanations of aspects of intelligence rather than define it in its entirety.

At the core of any study of intelligence are the terms *ability* and *capacity*. Humans have varying levels of ability to learn new ideas and skills. They also have varying capacities to take these new learned ideas and skills and apply them to new processes, such as learning to construct sentences and then paragraphs and then essays. The development of an ability leads to increased capacity, which in turn leads to further and higher levels of ability. Many humans develop such complex abilities and capacities that they are able to perform difficult mathematical equations, learn to drive, operate a computer *and even score an 'A' grade at Psychology Higher!* It is intelligence that is the wonderful underlying ability that enables all these different processes to come together. It gives us the capacity to gather and use all our thoughts and abilities and apply them to the world in which we live and work.

Models and theories of intelligence

There are *two* broad theoretical categories that look at the topic of intelligence:

1. The 'factor theory' approach.
2. 'Cognitive' or 'information processing' theory.

Factor theory approach

The factor theory approach uses statistical techniques, such as analysing a person's scores by different categories of intelligence in an IQ test, to measure correlation. Various tests using different categories of abilities such as spatial, problem solving, language, numeracy, etc., are given to a large group of people. Individual scores are then 'inter-correlated' or inter-related, and these relationships are entered into a grid. When the grid is analysed it will show a high relationship between two tests, e.g. language and spatial ability, or numeracy and problem solving. It is often found that scores by category of ability are related. For example, scores tend to be similar between related abilities such as numeracy and problem solving. The factor approach interprets this as indicating that an underlying *ability* or factor is present.

Charles Spearman (1904) was the 'inventor' of what we call 'factor analysis'; his model or theory is called 'Spearman's two factor theory – g and s factors'. According to the theory, there is what Spearman called a 'general factor' of intelligence – which he called the 'g factor', which all intelligence tests should measure for. Levels of ability specific to the person can explain varying scores between individuals, or, what he called 'the s factor'. Louis Thurstone (1938) challenged Spearman's two-factor theory as being too narrow and simplistic. He claimed that intelligence should be viewed as comprising 'primary mental abilities'; seven separate but unrelated factors that would clearly identify the individual's own strengths and weaknesses in particular areas (see **Table 4.1** below). He considered Spearman's 'g factor' to be too vague and not specific enough for the purpose intended.

Table 4.1

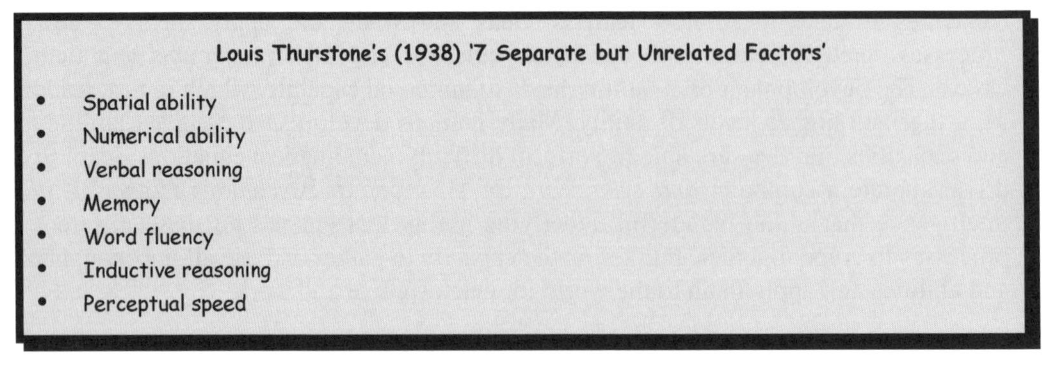
Louis Thurstone's (1938) '7 Separate but Unrelated Factors'

- Spatial ability
- Numerical ability
- Verbal reasoning
- Memory
- Word fluency
- Inductive reasoning
- Perceptual speed

Other theoretical models using the factor approach include Guildford's 'structure of intelligence model' (1967) and Vernon's 'hierarchical model' (1950). Guildford states that there are over 150 factors based on various combinations, whereas Vernon placed intelligence within an hierarchical model with general intelligence at the highest point of the triangle, less general factors next and numerous specific factors at the bottom. Cattell (1963) claims general intelligence is made up of two quite *distinct* but *related* forms of intelligence – 'crystallised intelligence' and 'fluid intelligence'.

Crystallised intelligence is formed from an accumulation of knowledge and skills over time (common in older people) and can be called on to solve problems and deal with new concepts and ideas. On the other hand, fluid intelligence is the ability to take on new ways of thinking and is fuelled by a willingness to do so (common in young people). Cattell maintains that fluid intelligence peaks before the age of forty, whereas crystallised intelligence increases towards senescence. When tested on vocabulary skills, 85 year olds obtained the same test scores as young adults (Blum *et al*, 1970).

Factor theories can be evaluated on a number of points. There is a great deal of variation between theories, suggesting that factor analysis has no objective roots in a singular approach. Data derived can vary by how it is produced and by whom. An apparently objective scientific approach, therefore, would appear to be very subjective. The various theoretical models are more concerned with *measuring* intelligence than *defining* it. Finally, they assume that intelligence is inherited, which as we will see, is debatable.

Cognitive or information processing theory

The cognitive or information processing models were developed in the early sixties and represented a dramatic move away from the 'factor theories' that had dominated the study of intelligence to that point. Two of the most prominent theorists are Howard Gardiner and Bob Sternberg. Gardiner (1983) proposed the theory of 'multiple intelligences' and saw intelligence as a complex and multi-dimensional process. He viewed intelligence as the capacity to do, and be, something of value to others in society. Humans have 'multiple abilities' that are not necessarily directly related – a genius with numbers may lack linguistic skills. For Gardiner, intelligence is:

> '[A]n ability or set of abilities that permits an individual to solve problems or fashion products that are of consequence in a particular cultural setting.' (Walters and Gardiner, 1986: 165)

He set out *seven* different concepts in which he saw each of us being able to excel in our own way – note he is *not* using the factor analysis method; he sees each of us as processing all of these 'intelligences' to a greater or lesser extent (see **Table 4.2** below). These are:

- **Bodily intelligence**: The use of body movement and the control of that movement to a great degree of excellence. We can see this in sports persons and dance and theatre artists. Think for yourself where you can identify people who have taken body movement to the highest level.
- **Interpersonal intelligence**: How people are sensitive and empathetic in how they communicate with others.
- **Intrapersonal intelligence**: The sensitivity of one's own abilities and feelings and expression of that in society.
- **Language**: The use of the spoken and written word in all aspects of society. For example, some people have created lasting pieces of worthwhile text in literature and in the dramatic arts.
- **Abstract intelligence**: The ability to solve logical and mathematical problems in astrophysics, maths, philosophy, as well as everyday problem solving.
- **Music**: The ability to play, write and perform music and sing.
- **Spatial intelligence**: How to effortlessly move around the environment and even be able to encapsulate the dynamic aspects of designing buildings and see how that detail will transform itself.

Table 4.2

Gardner's 'Multiple Intelligences' (1983)	
Bodily Kinaesthetic	Dexterity and dance.
Intrapersonal Intelligence	Recognise your own feelings and actions.
Interpersonal	Recognise correctly how you deal with your feelings and intentions towards others.
Linguistics	The ability to communicate and learn other languages.
Mathematical	Manipulate and be able to use numbers and abstract thought.
Music	Create and use pitch and sounds.
Natural Intelligence	Ability to classify the world around us.
Spatial	Be able to perceive and manipulate shapes and objects.

Interestingly, Gardiner claimed that whilst some may excel in more than one area, all humans have high-level skills in at least one area (we are all good at something!) and that all kinds of intelligence have importance as determined by any particular culture.

It could be said that Gardiner offers us a richer and more humane view of the concept of intelligence than anything offered by factor theorists. However, some would argue that all of the 'intelligences' identified by Gardiner are of equal importance, regardless of cultural values. His theory is more descriptive than explanatory and offers no indications of how and why some excel over others in particular areas.

Triarchic theory of intelligence

Bob Sternberg (1985) prefers to view the different areas of intelligence as coming together in unity in what is known as the 'triarchic theory of intelligence'. Sternberg claims that to understand intelligence we have to relate the concept of intelligence to various factors in the world around us. These include the *internal*, the *external* and the *experiences* we have as individuals. From this, he maintains there are *three* types of intelligence:

1. **Contextual intelligence**: This considers the person's external world and how that person uses their practical abilities to get through the demands of everyday living, in work, in travelling and communicating and interacting with other people within their environment.
2. **Componential intelligence**: This deals with the person's internal world and all the cognitive systems that we use such as memory, thinking and language. This, Sternberg would say, is the only one of the triarchic system aspects that we can test successfully in IQ tests.
3. **Experiential intelligence**: This deals with the effect of our experiences on intelligence and the relationship between both the internal and external world. How do we cope with new and novel situations as we go through life? How are we creative with new ideas and situations?

There is no doubt that Sternberg provides a very rich and comprehensive theory of intelligence. He gives us the first clear indication of how information processes that are internally represented interact with the world we live in as individuals and help us to produce the strategies that may be referred to collectively as 'intelligence'. There are limitations of the triarchic model, in that (like Gardiner) he provides us with a structure rather than a comprehensive account of what processes are actually involved in intelligence. There is also little indication of how the three sub-theories relate to each other and how they come together in unity as he claimed.

Measuring intelligence

The Frenchman, Alfred Binet, presented the first intelligence tests assessing children's intelligence in 1905. He produced an intelligence test that included memory, comprehension and a variety of cognitive processes. The aim of the test was to discover if children with no special training could answer intellectual tasks, rather than specific knowledge acquired in school. This was followed by what has become known as the 'Simon-Binet test' (1916). The purpose of the test was to provide an objective test measurement and was based on the previous testing of children of different ages whose average scores were taken as benchmarks. Each individual child's performance could thus be compared to the average for other children of the same age. This produced a measurement known as 'mental age'.

Before the mental age can have any bearing on the concept of intelligence testing it has to be compared with the 'actual' or 'chronological' age of the child. The following formula has been developed to calculate the Intelligence Quotient (IQ) of the child:

$$\frac{\textbf{Mental Age}}{\textbf{Chronological Age}} \ \mathbf{x\ 100 = IQ}$$

So, for example, a child who has a mental age of 5 but an actual age of 4 would have an IQ of 5 divided by 4 times 100, which would equal an IQ of 25. In the form of an illustrative equation, it would look like this:

$$\frac{\mathbf{5}}{\mathbf{4}} \ \mathbf{x\ 100 = 25}$$

The Simon-Binet test is still used. However, since 1986 there have been *four* specific categories used to measure the relative strengths and weaknesses of the particular individual. These are:

- Visual reasoning.
- Verbal reasoning.
- Quantitative reasoning.
- Memory (short-term).

This test of 'general mental ability' was perceived as being useful in identifying children who were performing below the average score.

Measuring intelligence in adults

A set of questions consisting of the specific categories were developed that would produce a 'normal distribution' in a large sample of people representative of the wider population. In an IQ test the mean or average score is 100 and the standard deviation is 15. See **Diagram 4.1** for an illustration of how this works.

Diagram 4.1

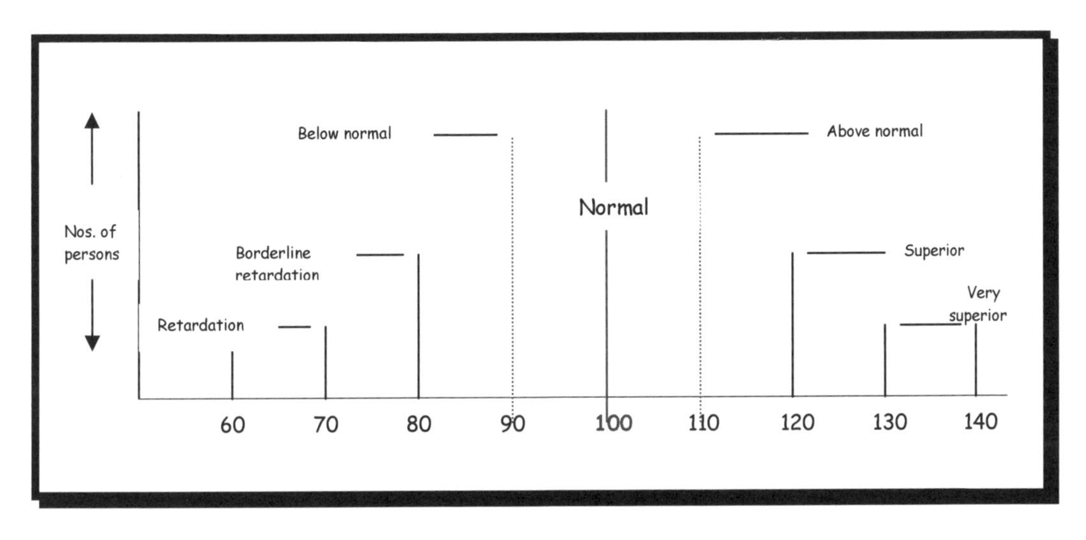

Box 4.1

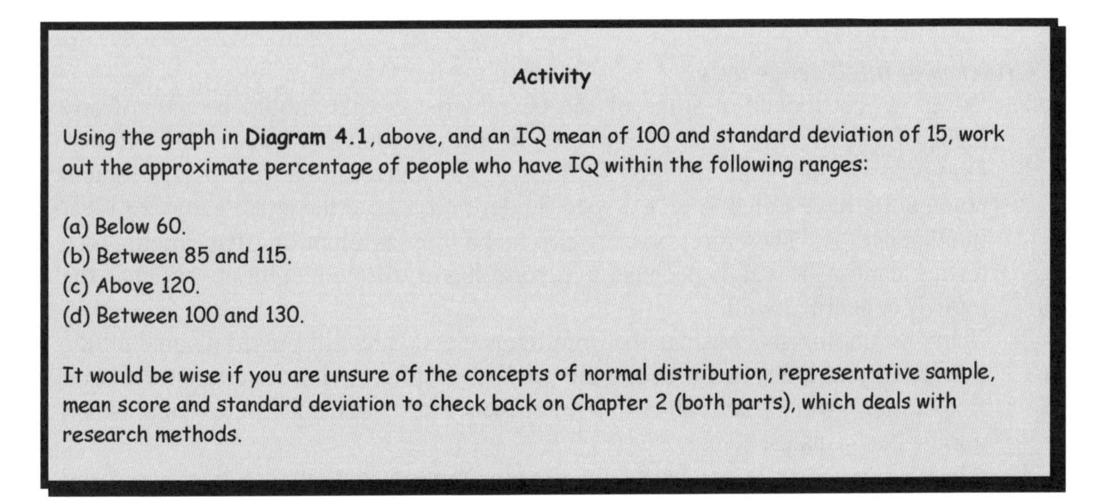

Activity

Using the graph in **Diagram 4.1**, above, and an IQ mean of 100 and standard deviation of 15, work out the approximate percentage of people who have IQ within the following ranges:

(a) Below 60.
(b) Between 85 and 115.
(c) Above 120.
(d) Between 100 and 130.

It would be wise if you are unsure of the concepts of normal distribution, representative sample, mean score and standard deviation to check back on Chapter 2 (both parts), which deals with research methods.

In many intelligence tests, the score is given as an IQ. The concept of IQ is purely statistical and it must be remembered that any individual's IQ will always vary depending on the particular test and on the specific sample on which the test was standardised. The IQ score enables one individual's performance to be compared with the IQ score of others. Since Binet's (1905) original work, there have been other tests dealing not only with children but also adult performance, one being the 'Wechsler tests – 'Wechsler adult intelligence scale'. This takes a series of scales – both verbal and performance – of various tasks in order that a clear picture of an individual's strengths and weaknesses can be identified. Many tests are based on verbal and literary skills. However, some are non-verbal, such as those asking participants to arrange pictures in order that will present a story or a logical progression. The best known of these is Raven's 'progressive matrices test'. The test has been developed to test abstract reasoning and does *not* require the individual to have any verbal abilities or any formal education. It is free of cultural bias and requires no level of understanding beyond appreciation of two-dimensional figures.

All forms of effective intelligence tests should have basic common characteristics:

- They must be *reliable*. In other words, they must be consistently *replicable*, no matter when they are taken or by whom. They have to measure similarly on a consistent basis.
- They must be *valid*. They have to measure exactly what they say they measure; in this case it has to be intelligence (containing all the correct elements that are required, e.g. verbal, mathematical, etc.).
- All tests must be *standardised*. They have to be given to a large and representative sample so that you can comfortably compare an individual's score with others with a high degree of certainty.

Criticism of intelligence tests

1. We have just looked at some of the characteristics that should be part of any form of intelligence testing and one of the factors discussed was validity. However, at the start of this section it was agreed that the psychological community have failed to give a specific definition as to the exact nature of what intelligence is. Therefore, you could make the assumption that intelligence testing cannot be valid, because everyone has a different opinion of what the topic is concerned with.
2. Many psychologists consider that intelligence tests are still biased against ethnic minorities and lower socio-economic groups, despite the introduction of 'culture free' tests. Critics also claim that intelligence tests are biased towards white, middle class, males.
3. All intelligence tests are based on the assumption that intelligence is a fixed characteristic, which is not necessarily the case. Doubt remains over when, or whether, students, for example, should stop studying as they have reached the limits of their intellect.
4. Intelligence testing is based on comparative data and is, therefore, relative.

These criticisms are only some that are levelled against IQ testing and what it attempts to achieve. Before we discuss the uses of intelligence tests, it is worth now getting to grips with untangling one of the more fiercely contested debates within the psychological community – the nature-nurture issue in relation to intelligence.

Nature or nurture?

The nature side of the debate looks at the 'genotype' of the individual, which includes all the areas connected with biological composition, innateness, genetic composition, heredity factors and what is commonly known as 'grey matter'. The nurture side focuses on everything around us; that is, the 'environment'. This will include where we live, what we experience, where we work, what we learn, with whom we associate and so on.

There have been many extensive studies and designs used in an attempt to unravel the contribution of the 'heredity' or nature side of the debate. 'Kinship studies' attempt to analyse the relationship between pairs of individuals who are related genetically – the most obvious being twins. If we accept the nature side of the debate, then those individuals sharing the same genes would have more or less the same level of intelligence, unlike those who have no genetic link whatsoever. Much of the early research looked closely at the similarities or differences between identical twins and non-identical twins and compared twins who had been raised together with those who had been raised apart.

Monozygotic and dizygotic twins

Identical twins share exactly the same genetic material and are called 'monozygotic' (MZ) as they come from the same single egg (zygote). Non-identical twins ('fraternal') come from two separate eggs and are referred to as 'dizygotic' (DZ).

Many studies of intelligence compare test results for identical twins (MZ) and fraternal twins (DZ). They seek to measure and compare 'correlational' relationships between twins of different types. Such correlations may also be compared with those in non-twin groups.

Shields (1962) advertised on the BBC for twins reared together or apart and found that the 34 pairs of twins reared together showed a correlation of 0.76, whilst the 40 pairs reared apart showed a correlation of 0.77. Same sex DZ twins showed a correlation of only 0.51. This would suggest that genetic inheritance plays a greater role than the environment. (See Chapter 2, Part 1 for more information on 'correlation'.)

Bouchard and McGue (1981) provided similar correlations, which further supported the argument that genetic factors play a very strong influence:

MZ reared together	0.86
MZ reared apart	0.72
DZ reared together	0.60
DZ reared apart	0.47

Ongoing studies by the 'Swedish Adoption'/'Twin Study of Ageing' (Pederson, 1992) found their correlations to be very similar those found by Shields in 1962 with correlations of 0.80 for MZ twins reared together and 0.32 for DZ twins reared apart. Other studies by Newman *et al* (1928) and Herman and Hogben (1932), display similar correlational results, but notably *do not* exclude environmental factors.

Before any conclusions can be drawn from the research, we should evaluate the evidence presented:

1. Almost all of the evidence from the various studies is correlational; therefore, other factors such as the environment may have a larger part to play than has been accorded. For example, Benton and Cook (1991) found a positive correlation between sugar intake and IQ ratings.
2. The data used for correlational analyses derives from IQ tests and are, therefore, subject to such limitations as noted above.
3. Many of the subjects used in the studies of MZ twins reared apart, had shared very similar home environments and had open access to each other throughout their childhood.

It might be fitting to conclude this consideration of twin studies with Gould's slightly sceptical comment (1981: 234):

> 'If I had any desire to live a life of indolent ease, I would wish to be an identical twin, separated at birth from my brother and raised in a different social class. We could hire ourselves out to social scientists and practically name our fee.'

Adoption studies

Another area of research used in the study of genetic factors is 'adoption studies', which allows researchers to compare IQ correlations of children with both their biological parents *and* their adoptive parents. Two of the most interesting studies have come from the United States – Scarr and Weinberg (1983) and Horn's 'Texas adoption project' of the same year.

In a unique study, Scarr and Weinberg examined black American children who were adopted by white parents. In all cases, the families who adopted the black children had a higher social, economic and educational status than the children's biological parents. It was discovered that the average IQ of the adopted children was 106, whereas the average score of similar black children with similar genetic, environmental and socio-economic backgrounds was only 90. From this, they concluded that environmental aspects have a direct and positive correlation to environmental conditions.

Horn (1983) used a sample of 469 children from various ethnic backgrounds who were adopted after birth by 310 families and concluded that IQ level of the adoptive mother more closely associates with the child's level than the biological mother. Schiff *et al* (1978) examined children who had been born into poverty but had been adopted by high socio-economic families. The children in the adoptive/fostered environment scored an average IQ of 111 compared with an average score of 95 for their siblings left in poverty.

Evaluation of twin and adoption studies

As we have seen, there are problems with both twin studies and adoption studies. Samples are small, there are issues regarding reliability and validity and a significant lack of clarity as to the extent that effects are biological or social in origin. It must be very clear that both genetics and the environment contribute in a critical way to individual differences in intelligence and it is now worth more fully considering the environment – the nurture side of the debate.

Nurture

Harrell *et al* (1955) showed that the 'pre-natal environment' had an effect on intelligence. He compared diets of two groups of pregnant women from very low socio-economic backgrounds: one group were given supplementary diets of vitamins, whereas the second group were given placebos. When the children were tested between the ages of three and four, those whose mothers had been given the vitamin supplement scored higher on IQ than those whose mothers were given placebos. Benton and Cook (1991) supported these findings. In their study, it was the children themselves who were given vitamin supplements, but again their scores overtook the children who had been given placebos.

Birth order has also been found to have a high correlation with children's' IQ scores. Zajonc and Markus (1975) examined the relationship between IQ, family size and birth order and concluded that intelligence scores decreased with birth order. As families grew in size, IQ scores of the next sibling fell. The results were composed from a study in Holland involving 40,000 nineteen year olds in an attempt to create a large and representative sample and to negate any possible influence of genetic factors. They noted that, for various reasons, first-born children were treated differently from the other siblings in many aspects including the amount of parental time and interactive communication, which was associated with higher IQ scores.

Home background would, therefore, appear to play a significant part in a child's intellectual development. Sameroff *et al* (1993) conducted an important longitudinal study, known as the 'Rochester longitudinal study', which traced the development of hundreds of children from birth in the early 1970s through to adolescence. From the study, Sameroff and his colleagues identified *ten* major environmental factors in the home that were shown to have a significant effect on children's intelligence level. **Box 4.2** indicates the environmental factors affecting IQ scores, according to Sameroff and Seifer *et al* (1993).

Box 4.2

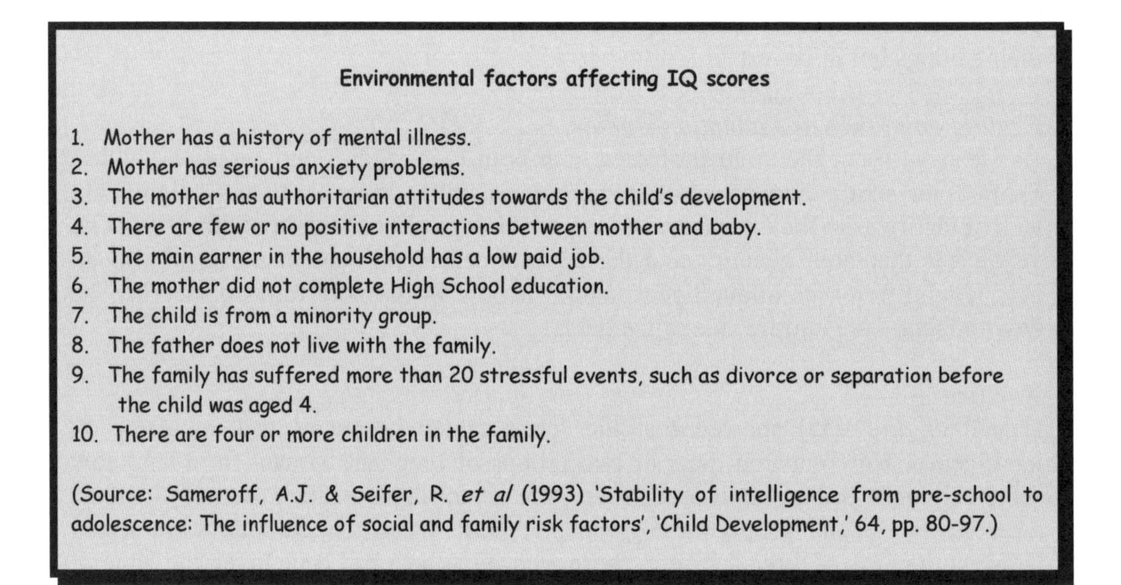

Environmental factors affecting IQ scores

1. Mother has a history of mental illness.
2. Mother has serious anxiety problems.
3. The mother has authoritarian attitudes towards the child's development.
4. There are few or no positive interactions between mother and baby.
5. The main earner in the household has a low paid job.
6. The mother did not complete High School education.
7. The child is from a minority group.
8. The father does not live with the family.
9. The family has suffered more than 20 stressful events, such as divorce or separation before the child was aged 4.
10. There are four or more children in the family.

(Source: Sameroff, A.J. & Seifer, R. *et al* (1993) 'Stability of intelligence from pre-school to adolescence: The influence of social and family risk factors', 'Child Development,' 64, pp. 80-97.)

In Sameroff and Seifer's study, IQ scores decreased proportionately to the amount of the above factors impacting on the child. The more factors from the list that applied to the child, the lower their tested IQ by four whole points for each factor.

Deprivation and privation studies, such as those by Koluchova (1972, 1976, 1991), show very clearly that IQ is lowered by lack of both mental and physical stimulation in the early stages of infancy. Other studies by Goldfarb (1944) and Skeels (1966) show that children reared in institutions show marked intellectual deficits and make remarkable progress when transferred to more stimulating and loving environments.

In the field of formal education, Rosenthal and Jacobsen's (1968) classic study clearly demonstrated how a teacher's *expectations* of success can have a profound effect on a child's IQ score (see **Box 4.3**).

Box 4.3

Case study: Rosenthal and Jacobsen (1968) 'Teacher's Expectancies: Determinants of Pupils' IQ Gains'

The authors used IQ testing to investigate the concept of the 'self-fulfilling prophecy'. The aim of the study was to look at the *expectancy* of teachers of future pupil performance in the primary school sector in the United States and to ascertain if this had any influence on the IQ gains made by the children in the school. They used an IQ test called TOGA (Test of General Ability). It was considered to be a pretty fair measurement of intelligence and not the *primacy* of school-learned subjects. The participants were 18 classes of primary children where 20 per cent of each class were assigned to the experimental condition with the remainder being the control group.

(Remember the experimental group consists of those participants who receive the 'independent variable' in the study – the control group do not receive the independent variable.)

The TOGA Test was 'sold' to the teachers as a test that would 'predict' intellectual potential and was given to all children within the school. Then 20 per cent of the children were selected to be the experimental group. The children's names were handed to their own individual teachers who were told as a consequence of their scores in the TOGA test that these children would be expected to excel intellectually during the course of the term. After the end of the academic year, all the children were re-tested using TOGA.

The results clearly demonstrated that within the whole school the children in the experimental group obtained a higher gain in IQ scores than those in the control group. Those children in whom the teachers expected to see an improvement produced the better results.

Uses of IQ testing

One of the main consequences of IQ testing is that the results produce an expectation effect regardless of ability to predict what is claimed of them. To many modern psychologists, they offer little or no indication of intelligence level. To others, however, they are still seen as contributing to the assessment of intellectual abilities. It can be argued that trying to make sure that people who are appointed to do certain tasks have the intellectual ability to execute the task properly can save a lot of time and money. Yet it is debatable whether IQ tests are fit for purpose here either.

The effectiveness of any form of IQ testing largely depends on what is being tested. Research by James Flynn (1992) demonstrated that IQ scores do not always show a person's level of ability and achievement. His study looked at Chinese immigrants in the United States after the Second World War. He discovered their IQ scores were lower than indigenous white Americans. In practice, however, their work-related achievements exceeded those of the indigenous white Americans. Despite findings such as these, IQ and aptitude tests are still commonly used to provide data about an individual's capacity to succeed in certain types of education and employment.

The practical application of intelligence tests

Intelligence tests are perhaps best known for their practical application within education. In some countries, such as the United States, intelligence tests are often used to place children in classes according to their level of ability. This is known as *tracking*. Here it is argued that all students benefit from their use, as they are allocated to classes geared to teaching to an appropriate level of intellectual capacity. Those against the process argue that once a child is identified and 'labelled' as having low ability, they will perform accordingly. Other factors, such as creativity, special talents, perseverance and motivation, are considered by many to be just as important as the result gained in a test. Critics have argued that by administering an intelligence test in this way, an individual may have their opportunities restricted rather than maximised.

In the United States, intelligence tests are also used to determine entry to colleges and the likelihood of obtaining a scholarship. Intelligence tests can also be employed in education to diagnose potential problems and predict future performance. However, the tests do provide some measure of success and relying purely on subjective observations and judgement would inject a wide variety of biases and inaccuracies that the tests are designed to avoid.

The IQ test, which formed part of the '11 Plus' exams, was removed from Scottish schools in the early 1970s, but their legacy remains in the form of National Testing. This focuses on a variety of subjects, such as numeracy and all its various components of mathematical skills, including mental and spatial ability and reading and writing skills, including comprehension and literacy. In actual fact, a child is being tested on a wide variety of subject matter that previously would constitute the original IQ testing. The tests are used as predictors of a child's progress at primary school and also the level in which they will be 'streamed' at secondary school just like their '11 Plus' predecessors.

One major factor shaping the development of a child's abilities is their own unique experiences and interpretation of them. An example cited in Michael Howe's (1997) book, *IQ in Question*, describes how two people can be in the same place at the same time, seeing exactly the same event and yet they will experience it in different ways. The keen reader in a library of books will be excited and stimulated, whereas the non-reader may find the experience boring and totally uninteresting.

Tests that examine both general and specific mental abilities have been developed for use in employee selection, such as the Otis 'self-administering test of mental ability' and the 'Wonderlic personnel test', which are both general mental ability tests. More specialised tests include the 'Bennett mechanical comprehension test, which is used in jobs that need a good comprehension of physical relationships and mechanical principles.

Intelligence tests can be utilised to address issues regarding atypical behaviour. For example, an individual who has perhaps suffered some form of head injury may return to their place of work and discover that they cannot carry out their tasks as well as before. Using an intelligence test in this situation may help to deduce whether the problems with the person's performance are due to the injury. Intelligence tests are often used as part of a series of 'neuropsychological performance tasks' of cognitive functioning. Neuropsychological assessment is an approach to cognitive assessment that tests a range of cognitive functions with the goal of identifying the nature and extent of possible brain impairment.

The role of IQ in the workplace produces an even wider spectrum of opinions, because in many areas of the military, commerce and industry, psychometric testing is used as a measure (or predictor) for job fit and achievement. (Psychometric means the 'measuring of the mind', though some psychologists would argue that the term 'mind' should not be used in this context.) Basically, a psychological test is given from a standard format and this will produce a numerical score. Usually, it will be a questionnaire or a series of different questionnaires. The idea is to measure certain cognitive abilities as in IQ tests or factors of 'personality' using personality tests or an aptitude test that will test the individual in the skills required. They are widely used in all sectors of business and the Armed Forces, especially for senior ranks within the Royal Air Force and Royal Navy.

However, the notion of psychometric tests throws up a number of critical issues and one of the main considerations is the difference between *performance* and *ability*. Performance is linked to what you actually do as an individual, e.g. how fast an athlete runs a particular race. Ability, on the other hand, is what the individual is capable of – how many times has your tutor stated to someone in your class, 'you have the ability, but you are not performing!' So, psychometric testing may test performance on that specific test on that particular day rather than ability or future capabilities. Those companies who consistently use such tests assume that performance *implies* ability. For the role of a fighter pilot, for example, intellectual and spatial ability have to be extremely high because of the speed and movement of the aircraft. They must have the ability to perform at every level and in every situation and, therefore, undergoing a series of tests may best determine whether their performances measure up to predicted ability.

The effects of cultural, political and environmental factors on the validity and use of IQ testing

One of the major problems of IQ testing is *ethnocentrism*. This describes a situation where we take a particular perspective based on how people think, behave and believe in our culture or part of the world. This usually means that we exclude, or fail to account for, alternative perspectives and cultural norms and values that may enrich an understanding of the phenomenon or issue. IQ tests that are constructed ethnocentrically directly favour respondents who share the ethnic background of the tester. To deliberately do so, or fail to amend the test when bias becomes evident, could be construed as institutionalised racism.

Racism in psychology

One major source of this kind of bias is *racism* in psychology. Racism – that is, the feeling of physical and intellectual antipathy towards another human being whom you perceive to be different from yourself – is still alive and well and did not die with the Nazis or the vivid pictures of genocide in Bosnia and Rwanda. They are all too real and close to home. Unfortunately, psychology has entertained racist ideas in its history as a discipline. In fact, just as was the case with other disciplines of the time, racist notions were common among pioneers of the study of intelligence in the early 1900s. Indeed, similar views are still advocated by eminent psychologists such as J.P. Rushton (1995), author of *Race, Evolution and Behaviour*. One of the most disturbing cases was Christopher Brand (1996) of the University of Edinburgh, whose book, *The g Factor*, was withdrawn by the publishers because they found ideas in the book both repugnant and repellent. Like Rushton and Brand, there are some who favour the practice of 'eugenics' – the successive and selective breeding of particular genetic groups.

A key study that had a ripple effect on the development of eugenicist ideas was that carried out by Yerkes (1971). His main concern may have been to improve the status of psychology as a science in the real sense, but, equally, Yerkes believed that intelligence was inherited and could not be changed. In order to demonstrate this, he used mental testing on a sample of nearly two million US Army recruits at the start of World War I. The data were analysed by one of Yerkes' colleagues who manipulated the data in order to find racial and national averages. When the 'facts' were presented it showed some startling statistics on average US citizens:

- The average mental age of white American adults stood at 13. This was seized on by proponents of eugenics as evidence that racial inbreeding had lowered the IQ of the average white American.

- The data also showed that immigrants from Europe could be graded by their area and country of origin. The dark skinned Southerners and Slavs appeared far less intelligent than the fair skinned people of Northern Europe.
- Blacks had a mental age of 10.

Yerkes and his fellow 'scientists' appeared to do little to defuse the resultant public controversy and the study impacted directly on the military, who subsequently introduced IQ screening for the officer corps and mental testing for any form of promotion. The most sinister impact of the results was on minority ethnic groups. A plethora of 'scientific research' on the topic of race and intelligence followed the study and fuelled propaganda for racist ideologies. Jews in particular were subject to claims that they had low levels of intelligence. Despite Yerkes' spurious methodology, his results may have provided the perfect pretext for the passing of the 1924 Immigration Restriction Act. This was to have the most profound consequences in a number of ways; immigration from Southern and Eastern (Slavic) Europe dwindled to nothing, but worse was to come when Jews, fleeing the Nazi genocide were not admitted into the United States. Figures suggest that six million were denied entry into the United States from 1924 to 1939. Many of these would have perished in the Nazi concentration and death camps.

A closer inspection of Yerkes' (1917) study reveals many of the problems of such testing procedures. The tests were designed for literate recruits and required a solid understanding of the English language, which could only be acquired through some form of formalised education. The test was extremely biased *towards* those with a firm grounding in American history as the following question from the test shows:

'Washington is to Adams as first is to ....'

Pictorial depictions of cultural artefacts in American society were also used in the test for those who could not read or had failed the main one, thereby further disadvantaging immigrant groups. Instructions were given in English and answers had to be written. All this for people who probably had no formal education and may never even have used a pen or pencil.

The focus of this Section was to introduce the topic of intelligence and the problems of defining, measuring and operationalising it. A good deal of debate exists over whether intelligence has usefulness as a concept and whether it can be adequately measured using IQ tests. The nature-nurture debate regarding intelligence tends to take the form of an *integrative* approach rather than viewing one side of the debate in isolation. To ask how much is due to nature and how much is due to nurture is, as Hebb (1949) states:

'[L]ike asking how much of the area of the rectangle is due to width and how much to length.'

Self-assessment questions

1. Distinguish between **factor theories** and **cognitive theories** of intelligence.
2. Briefly describe **four** types of intelligence that Howard Gardiner explored.
3. Give **four** criticisms of IQ tests.
4. What do we mean by **cultural bias**?

Content of exam questions

1) Discussion of theories of intelligence.
2) Consideration of the nature versus nurture debate.
3) Appreciation of the use of IQ testing.

Exam question

Discuss the functions of intelligence tests and the controversies that relate to their usage.

Atypical behaviour – definitions and approaches

Section summary

Learning objectives for definitions and approaches to atypical behaviour will include:

- Definitions and origins of atypical behaviour.
- Explanations of approaches to atypical behaviour.
- Explanations of aetiology of specific disorders/causes of abnormal behaviour.
- Explanations of the classification system.
- Explanations of culture, gender and ethnic problems in diagnosis.

Definitions and origins of atypical behaviour

In this part of the Chapter on Individual Differences we will look at the various ways in which we can define human behaviour and experiences that are considered 'atypical' or 'abnormal' and look at a range of approaches that attempt to explain disorder, including the medical model, cognitive model, behaviourist, psychoanalytic and humanist approaches. We will also spend time looking at what we know to be the cause of some specific common disorders – depression, schizophrenia and phobic disorders. We will also examine in detail the systems for classification and diagnosis of mental disorder. Finally, as with intelligence, we will examine a range of cultural issues in the classification and diagnosis of mental disorder and the existence of culture-bound syndromes.

Definitions and origins

What is abnormality? This is the most fundamental of questions and one of the most difficult challenges facing psychology and related subjects. What precisely makes us believe that a specific pattern of behaviour or experience is abnormal? Again, like intelligence, there is no universal or, for that matter, fully adequate definition of what abnormality is. There are no precise boundaries that separate those who are considered normal and those who are considered abnormal. They can only be viewed in terms of time and place and the prevalent social system of a particular culture. Rosenhan and Seligman (1989) present certain characteristics and suggest behaviour based on these criteria may indicate the nature and presence of some degree of a psychological disorder. Although no single definition is adequate, a combination of characteristics may lead us to criteria for an informal definition and at least offer the clinician a feasible framework of definition.

The criteria are as follows:

1. Statistical Infrequency.
2. Personal Distress.
3. Maladaptiveness.
4. Unpredictability.
5. Observer Discomfort.

Statistical infrequency

The easiest way of describing something as abnormal is simply to consider how often it occurs. Therefore, anything that is considered a rare occurrence could be described as atypical or infrequent. Researchers who study the statistical degree of abnormal behaviour will use human characteristics that can be measured in a certain way, e.g. personality, intelligence and so on. Most people would score around the average and, in turn, as we move away from the average score there will be fewer and fewer people. One type of population distribution is the 'normal curve' or 'normal distribution'. A feature of this is that very few people fall at either end of the curve. The assumption that a person is normal implies that they do not deviate too much from what is seen as average for a particular behavioural pattern. Statistical infrequency, then, is used as an indicator of abnormal behaviour.

This is the case in diagnosing mental retardation. The normal curve is used to show the normal distribution of intelligence in the population. People with low tested IQ below the level of 70 would be considered as having mental retardation defined as seriously reduced cognitive ability. However, that is not to say that everything that is infrequent would be regarded as abnormal behaviour. The perceived genius of Steven Hawkins or the athletic ability of certain individuals occur very infrequently but are not considered abnormal behaviour. We cannot, therefore, accept statistical infrequency alone as a sufficient criterion for the definition of abnormal behaviour.

Personal distress

Personal suffering in the form of great distress and personal torment with no apparent cause may indicate that a person is experiencing some form of atypical behaviour, such as acute depression or anxiety. Most mental disorders involve varying degrees of personal distress, but it is essentially highly subjective and only the person suffering can communicate how they are feeling.

Maladaptiveness
This is behaviour that interferes with the person's ability to meet everyday responsibilities and cope with the demands of everyday living such as family, personal care and work. A cruder way of looking at maladaptive behaviour is to attempt to ascertain whether the individual could survive alone without assistance.

Unpredictability
This is behaviour that appears to have no rational basis and, more importantly, is disconnected from social reality. We have all acted irrationally from time to time. For example, some people smoke despite the very clear health warnings and sometimes we eat or drink substances that are unhealthy. Many of us have acted unpredictably, too. However, most of us could provide a rational explanation for that behaviour if only in retrospect. Unpredictability is associated with abnormal behaviour when behaviour does not conform to social conventions and norms, cannot be rationally justified and, more especially perhaps, when it disrupts the social and emotional lives of other people.

Approaches explaining atypical behaviour
Having gone some way toward defining abnormality, we will now examine ways of *explaining* abnormality. As we will see, there are similarities and differences between models of explanation.

The biomedical model
In this Section we will consider an approach that views mental instability similarly to physical instability, in that it explains it as being caused by problems within the physiological or biological makeup of the individual. Treatment of the mentally ill shifted away from degrading and inhuman practices with the emergence of modern psychiatry. Rather than assuming that the individual was to blame in some way for mental illness, enlightened medics began to view mental illness as pathological and sought means to 'cure' the individual. The assumption was that mental disorders like any physical illness, is be caused by biological dysfunction of the brain or body. Thus, the 'biomedical model' is alternatively known as the 'disease model'.

As is the case with physical illness, mental illness is investigated, classified, diagnosed and treated scientifically. Treatment tends to be physiologically based and may include the use of drugs, surgery or the application of electric shocks. Whilst the biomedical model has a long pedigree, many modern psychologists and psychiatrists influenced by the approach would tend to combine medical treatments with psychological therapeutic models.

There are several different ways in which the origins of mental disorders have been studied using the biomedical model. One such model focuses on 'behaviour genetics'. This is the study of how behaviour is influenced by genetic structure.

Behaviour genetics

The unique genetic composition of every human being is known as the 'genotype'. Genes carry the instructions for producing the physical features in the human body, which inevitably affects psychological characteristics. The combination of physical and behavioural patterns is caused by both genetic and environmental influences and is known as the 'phenotype'. An example may help to illustrate this. Two different children may be born with the same predisposition to suffering depression. If one is faced with a very depressing environmental situation they may grow into a very depressed adult and prone to bouts of depression. By contrast, the other might have a very stimulating and uplifting upbringing and become a mature and balanced individual capable of dealing with the everyday ups and downs of life. Their genotypes are very similar but their phenotypes differ dramatically.

The most critical factor to note in this discussion is that psychopathological conditions are disorders of the phenotype *not* the genotype. Individuals do not inherit genes for depression or anxiety – what they may inherit are genes that may make them vulnerable to that particular disorder. They inherit a genotype for that particular vulnerability but *not* the condition of depression or anxiety. This is what is called the 'diathesis model', which describes how vulnerable genetic structures can combine with the stress of the environment to produce mental disorders. In order to examine the effect of genes on mental disorders, psychologists focus on twin studies and adoption studies (see the Section on 'Intelligence', above).

The biomedical model can be evaluated thus:

- Much of the work into the causes of abnormality has been conducted on animals, which, of itself, may be ethically problematic.
- It is often unclear whether results from animal experiments can be replicated with humans.
- The biomedical model is 'reductionist' as it explains mental disorders through simple bio-physiological causes.
- Although certain biological functions do affect behaviour, the relationship is reciprocal rather than one-way.

The cognitive approach

Since the late 1960s and early 1970s, the cognitive approach has dominated psychology in terms of dominant ideas and pioneering research. Cognitive psychology broadly focuses on internal mental processes. It is the study of how the human mind works and analyses processes in the brain, such as perception, memory, attention and problem solving. When approaching the study of mental disorders, the cognitive approach prefers to focus on explaining specific symptoms that may be linked to cognitive elements, rather than explaining mental illness as a whole.

Perhaps the most important theory to emerge from the cognitive approach is Beck's cognitive theory of emotional disorders (1976). Beck attempts to explain mental disorders with a high degree of cognition, such as depression and anxiety at the level of the individual. He focuses on how individual thought processes, or cognition, lead to depressive or anxious reactions to unpleasant situations, or stimuli, in some individuals, but not in others. Negative early life experiences can create a series of dysfunctional beliefs in the individual, which can, in turn, create negative attitudes to self, attitude to one's life situation and future. Examples might include bad experiences with teachers at school, peer group or parents. Beck goes on to claim that if such beliefs are not resolved, they may become determinants of future depression and anxiety. He labelled this three-factored series the 'cognitive triad' of negative schemas.

The cognitive triad of negative schemas

Anxiety, for Beck, developed from what he termed as 'vulnerability schemas'. These describe a distorted way of thinking that leads to a person perceiving people or situations to be a physical or psychological threat. As the roots of such negative thinking lay in some critical life event in the person's past, combined with the individual's current negative state of mind, the basis of cognitive therapy is to change the thinking process at both the behavioural and cognitive levels. Attempts would be made to have the individual mentally revisit the critical life event and to reassess it in order to break the causal link between that and the individual's worldview. If that link can be disconnected, then the individual may be liberated from processing new information from a position of negativity. In such a way, Beck claims, the cognitive triad of negative schemas can be broken.

Beck's approach proved to be highly influential in the cognitive approach to mental health and in psychology at large. Subsequent research and practice has also vindicated the validity of his focus on negative thought processes and mental illness. His critics, however, argue that whilst the therapeutic method has proven to be effective, it does not necessarily demonstrate the validity of his theory. Another major criticism is the role that schemas play in Beck's theory – the schema (a store of information about previous experiences that is used to evaluate future experiences and make decisions about them) is inferred from patient testimony and is then used to explain the bias producing that particular response. This is called 'circular reasoning' and, to all intents and purposes, is unscientific.

Another major cognitive behavioural therapy that is based on the same principles that attitude and beliefs about self compound mental instability, is Albert Ellis's (1957) 'rational emotive therapy' (RET), but this will be examined in the next section when we deal with therapies that help those suffering from mental illness.

The psychoanalytic approach

The psychoanalytic approach is the oldest psychological model and stems from the work of Sigmund Freud (1896). Freud and the later proponents of 'psychoanalysis' ('psychodynamics') were primarily interested in the way that childhood relationships and experiences affect future mental health. The main features of the psychoanalytic approach are as follows:

- The critical importance of childhood relationships and experiences especially with parents. Psychoanalysts would suggest that this is a fundamental element of mental health both as a child and into adulthood.
- Any traumatic childhood experience in the relationships with parents, such as physical abuse, will cause a mental disruption that inevitably leads to episodes of mental illness in the future.
- The essence of these assumptions are embodied in the concept of the *unconscious mind*, which stores memories of negative early life experiences and affects later emotions, motives and behaviour.
- The *unconscious mind* can cause trauma experienced in childhood to resurface in adulthood when the individual was unaware that they still carried it as a burden.

Whereas the biomedical model treats mental illness as a physical phenomenon and the cognitive model sees it as an acquired pattern of behaviour, the 'psychoanalytic model' views mental instability as an *emotional* response to trauma resurfacing from the unconscious mind.

Freud used what has become known as the 'hydraulic model of the mind' in relation to the study of mental illness. This analogy compares the mind to a physical energy system in that the psychic energy of the mind can only be discharged or changed, but not destroyed. In other words, any failure to express adequate psychological accommodation of trauma will result in a build up of psychic energy that will inevitably lead to mental instability if left undischarged. A key therapeutic tool, here, is what is known as 'catharsis' – the *release* of this accumulated energy.

Freud and Bruer's (1896) famous case study on 'Anne O' illustrates these latter concepts. The subject of the study was treated, in terms of the 'hydraulic therapy model', as having excess psychic energy due to frustrated intellectual abilities. According to Freud, the use of catharsis released the pent up energy and her symptoms lessened. However, many psychologists view the hydraulic model in a metaphorical sense and note that there is no physical evidence of build up of psychic energy or of its discharge. The model does, in many ways, describe how people feel when they experience instability, but does not *explain* it. Although, the psychoanalyst would argue that it is critical to understand how a person experiences mental distress in order to explain it.

Without doubt the most controversial of Freud's work on mental illness is his focus on 'psychosexuality'. Freud identified the role of childhood sexual fantasy in determining future mental distress. He believed that as part of normal childhood development, children develop a sexual attachment to the opposite-sex parent and see the same sex parent as a rival. This he termed the 'Oedipus complex' and it formed the basis of his analytic approach in the classic case study of 'Little Hans' (Freud, 1909). Despite accusations of a sinister interest in sexuality in Freud's work, his refusal to shirk controversy has led to the development of a field of analysis that had been hitherto regarded as taboo. This has undoubtedly benefited many sufferers of sexual abuse in coming to terms with its traumatising effects. His psychoanalytic methods of free association and talking over past experiences and psychodynamic therapies such as 'group psychoanalysis' and 'brief dynamic', are still used in modern psychiatry. However, the concept of the Oedipus complex has been repudiated as a major element of mental instability and it is questionable whether every, or even any, child has this fantasy to any great extent.

The behaviourist or learning theory model

The 'learning theory model' or 'behaviourist approach' looks at mental disorders as behaviour, like all other behaviours, that have developed as a result of the learning process. Mental instability, therefore, is a learned behaviour but one that is maladaptive. It has been learned through classical conditioning; that is, through learning particular responses to specific stimuli, whether such responses are rational or indeed functional. For example, stimuli such as the very thought of appearing in public, or seeing a spider may elicit dysfunctional responses such as acute panic and phobia in the individual. Such responses can have the effect of greatly reducing the sufferer's quality of life and are not useful to the individual in the way that 'healthy' responses, such as running out of the way of an oncoming car, are. To compound the problem, 'operant conditioning', that is, the learning from the consequences of our responses, encourages and reinforces the maladaptive behaviour.

The behaviourist approach makes the following assumptions with regard to mental illness:

- Learning can be described as a change in behaviour as a result of some form of experience.

- The learning of maladaptive behaviour takes place through the processes of classical and operant conditioning and by means of association and reinforcement. Particular stimuli are associated with specific dysfunctional responses. The role of the therapist here would be to associate the stimuli with other, more functional, 'healthy' and rational responses.
- These new responses can be reinforced in the individual positively and negatively. Positive reinforcement strategies encourage particular responses by the presentation of pleasurable consequences for the individual. Negative reinforcement strategies may bring about the same desired behavioural response through the individual seeking to avoid unpleasant consequences. The difference between the two can be illustrated by considering the school pupil who faithfully completes homework tasks. This may have been positively reinforced by the pupil's sense of satisfaction with their completion of the task. Alternatively, it may have been negatively reinforced by the pupil's fear of what the teacher may say if the task was not completed.
- Both positive and negative reinforcement strategies have the effect of encouraging specific behavioural responses.
- The main characteristic of the model is the assumption that behavioural patterns can be observed and identified as distinct.
- It is further assumed that if the maladaptive behaviour is learned it can be unlearned and replaced by positive adaptive behaviour.

Behaviourists claim that another means by which we learn particular behaviours is through 'observational' or 'social learning'. In other words, we learn behaviour through imitating other people's behaviour. This is obviously highly significant with children since they tend to copy the behaviour of the people they see as most important to them, such as family members, teachers and influential people in sport, media, music and so on. The classic study by Bandura (1965), known as the 'Bobo doll study', is of interest here as he claims that it demonstrates that children will copy aggressive acts carried out by others, especially when the aggression is rewarded. In the field of abnormal behaviour, the suggestion by many theorists is that modelling can play a vital role in mental instability; for example, depressive parents can lead to depressive children. Equally, when we examine therapies we will see clearly how modelling has an important role to play in the healing of certain disorders.

Social learning theorists view people as being the *active* manipulators of their own behaviours and experiences rather than being merely *passive* bystanders. They recognise the role classical and operant conditioning play in the learning of maladaptive behaviour, but claim that observation and imitation are equally important determinants. Humans imitate the behaviour of those whom they respect and admire but also those perceived as similar. This approach is widely used in the study and treatment of abnormal behaviour especially in the fields of depression and anti-social behaviour.

We can evaluate the behaviourist model of learning by making the following points:

- It has been supported by a high degree of scientific studies and empirical data.
- It has built a reputation of successfully treating maladaptive behavioural patterns.
- One major shortcoming is that evidence for the claim that mental illness is caused by maladaptive learning is difficult to obtain.
- The behaviourist approach is 'determinist' and 'reductionist' and, as such, underestimates the complexity and flexibility of the human mind in directing behavioural responses.

The humanistic/existential model

Humanistic psychology emerged in the early 1950s and offers a completely different view of human experience than that presented by either the behaviourist or the psychoanalytic approach. Carl Rogers (1952), the 'founding father' of humanistic psychology, stressed what he regarded to be the basic goodness of people and that they have the innate ability to realise their own potential and freedom of choice as to how to behave. He assumes that the only valid reality is what the individual experiences at any given moment. These assumptions inform the therapeutic model used by humanistic therapists who tend to view the world from the client's frame of reference. They make minimal use of theoretical constructs. It claims to be the 'third force' in psychology after behaviourism and psychoanalysis respectively.

The main components of the humanistic approach can be summarised thus:

- People have the innate tendency to fulfil their own potential and psychological disorders result when environmental forces prevent the individual achieving their particular potential.
- Symptoms should always be understood as the person's response to the reason why their growth and potential are being stymied.
- The primary concern of the humanistic approach is the emotional aspect of the person and not the individual's cognitive or physical behaviour.
- Positive self-esteem, self-efficacy and self-image are all critical elements to the mental health of the individual. If any are adversely affected by external forces then this will have a bearing on individual mental health.
- The chief aim of both the theory and the therapy is to help the person move towards life choices that will allow for the recognition and achievement of their full potential.

Many people argue that this is *not* a psychological theory, but almost a quasi-religious belief system or philosophical stance that is at best naïve and at worst unworkable and misplaced. That claim, however, has not prevented it from greatly influencing the development of psychology since its rise to prominence

The actualising tendency

Rogers proposed that for full mental health two intrinsic elements have to come together – the 'actualising tendency' and the role of 'self-concept'. For Rogers (1959), humans are innately built with the ability to fully realise our potential – to 'actualise'. In order for this to come to fruition, environmental variables have to influence accordingly. Rogers also introduces us to the concept of individual values. These are unconscious motivations that guide the individual towards experiences and behaviours in accordance with realising the actualising tendency, but will collapse if self-image or self-esteem is restricted by environmental pressures and rules.

The self-concept

The second pillar of Rogers' theory is the role of 'self'. He placed an equal amount of concern on the development of the self as on the process of actualisation and he proposed that the most critical aspect of self is the notion of self-esteem. From childhood, we constantly evaluate our experiences and ourselves in an attempt to create personal identity. If the people we are close to and respect show us *unconditional* positive regard, that is, unqualified acceptance, we develop strong self-esteem. In other words, we translate the degree to which others value us into our own feelings of self worth. If, on the other hand, we are subject to *conditional* positive regard, or qualified acceptance, we are likely to behave as we think others would have us behave and develop a weak feeling of self worth. Rogers explains that high levels of self-esteem are present in individuals whose self-image is congruent with, or matches with, their image of what they would like to be. Only then can the individual fulfil potential and self-actualise. Coopersmith (1967) also stresses the importance of unconditional positive regard and self-esteem, stating the importance of liking the person that we are. He demonstrates this in a seminal and groundbreaking study that corresponded with Rogers' ideas and philosophy regarding self-esteem.

Another humanistic theorist, Abraham Maslow (1970) extended Rogers' original ideas and further emphasised the need in humans to strive towards self-actualisation (see **Diagram 4.2**). This, he illustrates in his now famous 'needs hierarchy', where he gauges the level of motivation and growth required for psychological well being. At the bottom of this hierarchy are the basic biological needs for survival, such as hunger and thirst, which must take precedence over all else. Unless these needs are met, other needs are not a major concern but, when they are, other needs will motivate behaviour, such as safety and security. In turn, once these needs are met we are motivated to move to the higher level needs of attachment, belonging and relationships, the need to accomplish and the need for prestige. Ultimately, we reach our full potential as a human being, self-actualisation, upon accepting ourselves and others. At this point we will enjoy full mental stability and health.

Diagram 4.2

A Representation of Maslow's Hierarchy of Needs (after Maslow 1959)

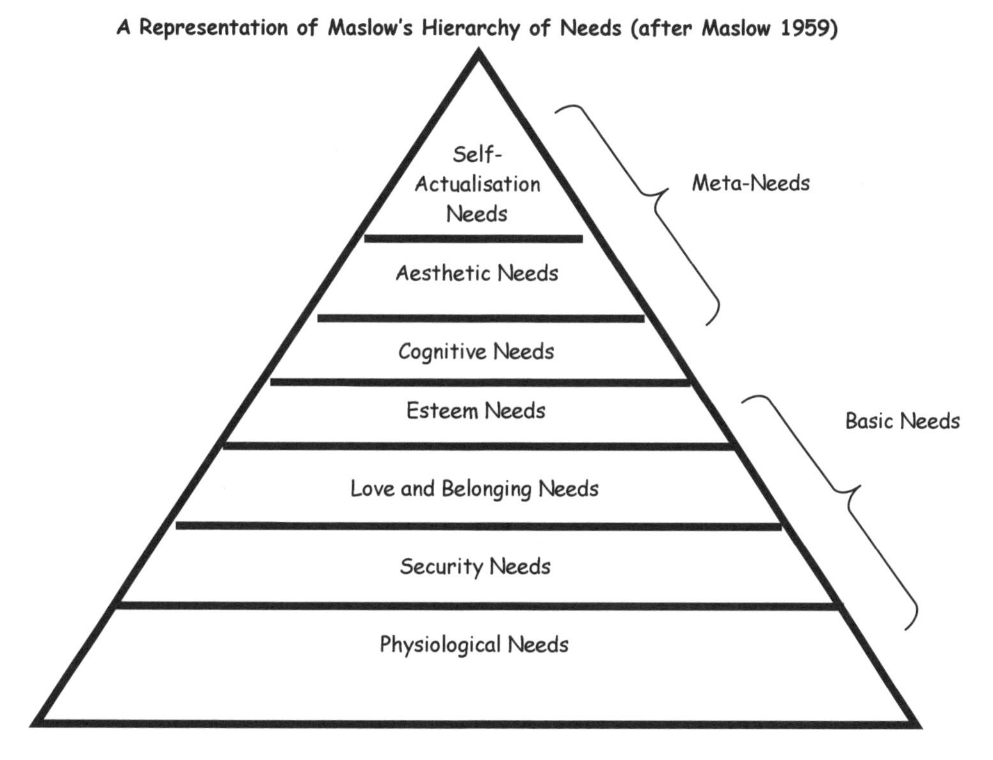

Thus, rather than explaining mental instability by identifying what is wrong with the individual, Maslow developed a more proactive system detailing what individuals need for mental health.

We can evaluate the humanistic model as follows:

- The theories of both Rogers and Maslow are optimistic about human ability to affect personal change.
- They offer an holistic insight into free will and motivation.
- The concepts are essentially philosophical and, therefore, open to debate – they can *neither* be proved *nor* disproved.

- The notion of self-actualisation is dubious. Its measurement depends on the subjective nature of self-report, which ultimately depends on the integrity of the person and whether they understand what the concept means.
- Humanistic therapeutic approaches tend to overlook the individual's past lives and experiences.
- Although they are *not* reductionist in the same manner as behaviourist models, they reduce personal development to the narrow process of self-actualisation and make no attempt to predict future behaviour.

Aetiology of specific disorders/causes of abnormal behaviour

This Section deals with the clinical characteristics of specific disorders: depression, schizophrenia and anxiety disorders, such as phobias. Before we explain the causes of these specific disorders, it is important to realise that there are usually multiple 'aetiological' – causal – factors for any specific abnormal behaviour and these can be categorised in *three* main factor areas:

1. **Predispositional**: These are mainly concerned with how vulnerable or susceptible a person is to certain disorders. This would involve consideration of genetic inheritance, personality, childhood experiences and socio-economic factors.
2. **Precipitating**: This is the immediate cause for the onset of an identified abnormal behaviour. Examples might include workplace stress, drug use or bereavement.
3. **Perpetuating**: Perpetuating factors prolong the suffering of the individual after the onset of the illness. This tends to encompass factors such as a loss of self worth, withdrawal, depression and problems associated with institutionalisation.

Depression

The term, 'depression', has been commonly used to describe the episodes of sadness or disappointment that all humans endure from time to time. Such episodes are usually relatively brief and contained to the specific issues or events at the root of the problem. The depression that psychologists view as mental illness is possibly the most common form of mental distress and is defined by a particular cluster of symptoms and termed 'clinical depression'.

By definition, the disorder broadly describes a state that the mood, expressiveness and functioning of the individual is sufficiently lowered as to detract from the quality of life of the individual and those close to them. Psychological symptoms include a feeling of worthlessness, meaninglessness, misery, helplessness, despair, poor self-image and low self-esteem. There is a high tendency to brood over real or imagined past failures and broken relationships and project such feelings in a way that makes the future appear bleak. A general cluster of associated problems encompass the following:

- Emotional factors such as sadness and melancholy.
- Motivational elements include being totally passive to what is going on around them.
- Cognitive areas include the lowering of self-worth and image with a high degree of pessimistic helplessness.
- 'Somatic factors' (that can be the first signs of the disorder) include loss of appetite followed by weight loss and the disturbance of a normal sleep pattern.

All the above characteristics are categorised under the heading of 'unipolar depression'. Within this category there are two quite distinct types of depression:

1. 'Endogenous depression'.
2. 'Reactive depression'.

Reactive depression

We will examine 'reactive depression' first as this tends to be the most common and within this sphere depressed patients tend to recover spontaneously after around six months. This tends to arise out of some disappointment or deprivation, for instance, the loss of someone close. The person tends to have difficulty in their sleep pattern particularly in the form of broken sleep and a higher degree of dreaming. Sufferers tend to be listless and find grave difficulty in motivating themselves. Moods tend to fluctuate between 'good days' and 'bad days' and can be lifted temporarily by people and events. This type of depression is clearly linked to external environmental stimuli. There is a tendency to comfort eat, especially sweet items such as chocolate and this can lead to very fast weight gain which, in turn, can have an influence on self esteem. Other sufferers may experience disinterest in pleasure seeking, usually including the loss of sex drive.

Endogenous depression

'Endogenous' or 'psychotic depression' tends to arise without warning and it is difficult to relate to external events. Symptoms include early morning waking and the inability to fall asleep easily and other physical signs such as complaints of general aching sometimes accompany this. Psychologically, it is much more damaging than reactive depression. There is a total lack of interest in the self and what is going on in the environment. Withdrawal from all aspects of social life is common and the disturbance of mood is apparent. From morning till evening the endogenous sufferer experiences little respite from the deep dark mood. Hallucinations, particularly those that are auditory in nature and feelings of delusion may present. Delusions tend to take the form of beliefs that the individual is suffering from some form of serious illness and resist despite results of any medical investigation proving the contrary. Other common delusions are guilt and feeling unworthy, persecution and feelings of nothingness in terms of the reality of their existence. The danger of death by suicide is extremely common and any talk or threat of this should be taken seriously.

There are, however, certain clinical features that tend to overlap both types of unipolar depression. Generally, any physical movement tends to be carried out in a slow and deliberate manner, there is a distinct lack of vitality and the person tends to brood for long periods of time usually in a sedentary position. There are usually periods of fatigue and this is often due to the sleep disturbance common to both types. Appetite is affected, but is polarised by type of depression. Weight loss is common with endogenous and weight gain through 'comfort eating' with reactive.

There are numerous possible *causes* for unipolar depression and consequently numerous explanations.

- **Genetics**: Several studies show higher rates of depression in close relatives, for example, McGuffin *et al* (1996) found MZ twins had a concordance rate of 46 per cent, compared with 20 per cent in DZ twins – thus suggesting a fairly strong genetic component.
- **Neurochemical**: There is inconclusive research evidence linking low levels of the neorotransmitter, noradrenaline, with a loss of movement and motivation and many antidepressants affect the production of noradrenaline, which may offer qualified support for this particular view.
- **Environmental**: It is unlikely that genuine clinical depression can be imitated or learned, but maladaptive behaviours *can* be learned. This may result in depression. Environmental stressors like work, exams and the weather can all trigger episodes of depression.
- **Triggers**: Certain types of depression such as post-natal or seasonal affective disorders have been clearly linked with hormonal changes in the body, as is the case with premenstrual syndrome.

The other major form of depression is 'bipolar' or 'manic depression'. The symptoms of this differ from those expressed in the unipolar category in that two distinct phases exist in extremity to the other – *high elation* at one end and *low depression* at the other. They may occur separately or fluctuate between each form over a period of time. In the manic state, the person may experience high states of arousal and excitement, be hyperactive, need significantly less sleep and have increased sexual appetite. They often act impulsively and make irrational and unrealistic judgements and plans. The syndrome seems to occasionally create highly creative situations for some comedians, writers and artists, but for most sufferers the horrendous mood swings are highly debilitating and greatly impact on quality of life and personal relationships. Sufferers can fluctuate between episodes of mania and depression for long periods of time.

Again, the explanations proffered are numerous:

- **Genetic**: Concordance studies with MZ and DZ twins have shown a higher degree of correlation with MZ twins and the same applies with adoptive studies. When allied to the 'neurochemical' argument, the case becomes stronger. A study by Egeland (1987) on the religious community known as the Amish, found that part of chromosome II was present in 65 per cent of those with the disorder. This chromosomatic defect could lead to a lack of certain 'neurotransmitters' throughout the body. More recent research has shown that noradrenaline is also on chromosome II.
- **Predisposition**: Evidence is inconclusive with regards to this as many sufferers of bipolar depression in particular do have family histories with previous sufferers. It is unclear, however, whether this has been brought about due to genetic or environmental factors as family members often share very similar environmental conditions.
- **Personality**: People suffering bipolarity tend to suffer a higher degree of neuroticism, which is an abnormal emotional reaction to disturbing situations, such as parental discord and child abuse, but does not deprive the person of a sense of reality. There is no disintegration of the personality, but it can be a crippling disability.

Given the high and growing incidence and public profile of depression, coupled with the fact that all humans are prone to at least mild bouts of the non-clinical variety, it is perhaps no surprise that a great deal of controversy surrounds the study and diagnosis of depression. One prominent concern is the gendered nature of diagnosing (see 'Classification systems', below).

Schizophrenia

Schizophrenia has a very confused public image and is often greatly misunderstood and misrepresented among the general public. Schizophrenia means 'split mind', but to most people it is understood to be split personality, which it is most definitely *not*. It is not a specific illness but a collection of debilitating circumstances that produce delusions, thought disintegration and hallucinations. It presents through specific symptoms that may vary dramatically from one individual to the other, but it does contain many common symptoms and specific clinical features:

1. **Thought disorientation**: The individual's powers of thought are gravely impaired and in most cases sufferers cannot think in abstract terms. In many

cases, they use a group of meaningless words called 'word salads' and, in some cases, will invent their own words, which only they understand – 'neologisms'. There is also usually 'thought blocking' where the individual thinks their thought processes are 'held up' in some ways.

2. **Delusions**: A delusion is a false belief that is out of keeping with the person's socio-cultural background, has no real basis in fact and is usually absurd. Delusions vary by type and may include persecution delusions where the individual believes himself to be the victim of a 'plot' to harm them; delusions of grandeur, where the individual believes that they occupy the level of status normally reserved for a god or legendary figure; guilt delusions, where the individual wrongly believes that they are guilty of some heinous crime or other misdeed in their past life; hypochondriacal delusions, where the person believes they suffer from various diseases and this is maintained in spite of medical evidence to the contrary; and somatic delusions, where the individual exhibits a high degree of passivity and professes not to believe in anybody or anything.
3. **Disturbances of perception**: We can broadly define perception as the mental awareness of people and objects in the external world through sensory perception. In the case of schizophrenia, the basic process of perception can be grossly disturbed and distorted. This usually happens through hallucinations. An hallucination can be understood as a false perception that arises without the presence of its usual external stimulus. Or, in simple terms, the sufferer perceives something that is *not* there in reality. Hallucinations may be pleasant or unpleasant and may affect any of the five senses despite the lay assumption that hallucinations are visual. Auditory hallucinations – 'hearing voices' – are common.
4. **Detachment**: Many sufferers become preoccupied with their own thoughts and beliefs to the almost total exclusion of everyone around them.
5. **Disrupted volition/psychomotor behaviour**: This is manifested in alternations between a complete lack of interest in anything and any form of activity and hyperactivity.

It should be noted, however, that whilst these groups of symptoms can be described as common, diagnosis remains very difficult since symptoms vary greatly by individual and *three* different sub-types of schizophrenia have been defined.

Sub-types of schizophrenia

1. **Catatonic**: This form or sub-type describes the polarity of extreme hyperactivity or extreme withdrawal to an almost 'mummified' state.
2. **Paranoid**: This is possibly the type most familiar to film goers and is most often misrepresented by film makers. It describes a condition of persistent and systematic delusions, commonly in the form of grandeur or persecution.

3. **Disorganised/hebephrenic**: This involves the disintegration of mental maturity and develops from an early age. It manifests in regressive behaviour such as childishness, behaviour perceived as 'silly', affective disorientation, thought disorder and highly disorganised use of language.

Both the sub-types and clinical features of schizophrenia span the major components of the human cognitive system – perception, thought, language and emotion. Therefore, sufferers displaying symptoms across the spectrum experience a general disintegration of identity and behaviour. The illness is prevalent in around 1 per cent of the world's population and is most common in young adults. Peak incidence has been detected in late teens and early twenties for men and in the thirties for women. Typically, it follows *one* of *three* distinct courses: one third of sufferers eventually recover and lead relatively normal stable lives, another third have relapses but otherwise maintain relatively stable lives. The remaining third, however, fall into a rapid state of total deterioration displaying chronic symptoms and often become psychiatric inpatients within mental institutions.

But what are the causes of such a devastating illness? As is the case with both types of depression, there are a number of causal factors and a number of explanations proffered.

Biological explanations of schizophrenia

Heredity

Evidence from genetic studies appears to indicate that heredity factors are of critical influence with many cases of schizophrenia. Twin studies by Kendler (1983) reported a concordance rate of 50 per cent for schizophrenia in monozygotic twins as against 15-16 per cent for dizygotic. Whilst common environment effects cannot be overlooked, neither can a high genetic component. Extensive studies of adopted children found that those children whose biological parents were schizophrenic were ten times more likely to suffer the disease than the average. Crow (1984) claimed that a virus that becomes embedded in the DNA and is thereby passed on to children causes the illness. Other researchers have found chromosomal evidence and claim that an abnormal gene or cluster of genes on chromosome 5 may increase susceptibility. As yet, however, these studies are unconfirmed despite major research in this particular area.

Chemical imbalance/biological

There is growing evidence that schizophrenia may arise from biochemical factors. One major influence here is the 'dopamine hypothesis', which suggests that excessive activity of the neurotransmitter dopamine is clearly related to schizophrenia. Despite a wealth of evidence apparently supporting this claim

(Comer, 2003), it remains unclear as to whether the incidence indicates cause or effect.

Other studies point to possible bio-chemical causes. When non-sufferers are given a large dose of drugs that increase dopamine levels in the body, such as amphetamines, they exhibit symptoms associated with paranoid schizophrenia. The same effects may be found with drugs like cocaine, LSD and L Dopa, the drug used to treat sufferers of Parkinson's disease, which is partly caused by too little dopamine. Conversely, if L Dopa is given to a schizophrenic patient it aggravates their symptoms. Phenothiazines, the generic drugs used in the treatment for some schizophrenics, act to reduce the action of the dopamine receptors in the brain. Neuroanatomy scans indicate that there is a higher density of dopamine receptors in the brain of untreated schizophrenics as compared to non-schizophrenics. There is also research evidence to suggest from anatomical scans that between 35 per cent and 50 per cent of schizophrenics have enlarged ventricles in the brain, particularly in the left hemisphere, suggesting some deterioration in brain functioning (Torrey, 2002).

However, the evidence is not conclusive and there is no clear explanation of how dopamine levels are related to the specific symptoms of schizophrenia. Also, no concrete evidence exists of large excesses of dopamine itself in the brains of schizophrenics, despite a clearly greater density of dopamine receptors on various cells in different parts of the brain.

Psychological and social-psychological explanations of schizophrenia

Social class

The 'social class hypothesis' argues that the lower social classes suffer more socio-economic deprivation, poor housing and high-density population, than higher socio-economic groups, which increases social stresses on the individual. In other words, stressful life events may precipitate a psychotic illness such as schizophrenia. Laing (1959) suggests that schizophrenia is in fact a sane response to a dysfunctional social environment and is the result of an individual's attempt to deal with the split between the internal and external world of the family and wider society.

Social studies have certainly indicated a higher incidence of schizophrenia among the lower socio-economic classes and especially those within highly densely populated inner cities and housing schemes. It may be that inherent stressors within such an environment could create conditions that lead to schizophrenia – an approach known as 'social causation'. It could also, however, be the case that the stresses associated with privation and poverty could aggravate a genetic vulnerability towards schizophrenia.

Alternatively, lower class position may be caused by the illness as is suggested by the 'downward drift hypothesis'. Sufferers are more likely to be unemployed, living in poor circumstances and ultimately end up living in areas with high urban and social deprivation. The individual may be ill-equipped to deal with employment and a stable relationship, so they drift downwards to low economic and social status. Lower social class position in this case is viewed as a *consequence* rather than *cause* of the illness.

Research evidence in this area is essentially skewed in that it focuses exclusively on deprived groups. However, numerous studies, including one carried out by Castle (1993), have shown that most individuals who suffer from the disorder were born into deprived urban areas characterised by innumerable negative social factors, such as higher rates of low-weight babies, birth complications, poor dietary habits, *in-utero* drug and substance abuse, poor housing and education.

The diathesis-stress theory

In order to establish a more comprehensive explanation of the causes of schizophrenia, then, it may be necessary to develop a multi-causal, integrative and holistic approach. The 'diathesis-stress theory' attempts to do so by focusing on both genetic vulnerability *and* environmental influences. The theory suggests that it is not the disorder itself that is inherited, but the *predisposition* to developing it. The interaction of vulnerability factors with environmental stressors may activate the predisposition, resulting in the manifestation of the disorder. The potential sufferer, that is genetically vulnerable individuals who experience little environmental stress, as may be the case in affluent middle or upper class areas, may *never* develop the illness.

Anxiety disorders – phobias

As with depression, anxiety and fear are common features of the human condition. Many of us become anxious of visiting the dentist or experience fear when flying. Such experiences are viewed as 'normal', since they are very common in varying degrees to the vast majority of people and they do not have lasting effects on our lives. Mild fears of flying can be overcome with accumulated experience of travelling by airplane or by simply avoiding flying altogether. Anxiety on visiting the dentist diminishes after our visit and does not typically spill over into other aspects of our lives. Some levels of fear and anxiety may also be of great use to humans in protecting our health and very survival. Imagine the possible consequences of holding no anxiety of driving at very high speed on a narrow road, or of fearlessly approaching a wild and hungry tiger! We probably have all experienced the state of anxiety in some part of our lives – going to the dentist, the day before or day of exams, going for an interview, etc. In other situations we may have genuine feelings of fear, for instance going on board an aircraft. Episodes or occurrences of anxiety and fear are typical to humans, then, in that although they may occur relatively frequently, we can adapt physically and mentally to accommodate them and as a means of alerting us to danger or threat, they are functional and rational.

Anxiety is viewed as a *disorder* when people develop irrational fears of certain everyday life situations that do not threaten the individual in the ways that they anticipate. In such cases, the irrational fear can greatly impact on the individual's quality of life. Patterns of behaviour are often developed in order to avoid situations or items that induce anxiety and often this leaves the sufferer unable to cope with everyday life. In most cases, the anxiety or fear will also induce unpleasant physiological arousal in the form of 'butterflies' in the stomach, sweating, laboured breathing and so on, which have the effect of exacerbating the initial sensation and further compounding the problem. Anxiety may be generalised and not focused on any particular fear. In such cases, feelings of anxiety may be severe, persistent and overwhelming. There are *four* main types of anxiety disorders: *generalised anxiety disorder*, *panic disorders*, *obsessive-compulsive disorders* and, the one that we will focus our attention on, *phobic disorders*.

There are some common clinical factors running through all of the anxiety disorders, namely:

- Insight into everyday life may be unbalanced, but the person retains ability to engage with reality in most situations.
- With most cases the difference between sufferers and non-sufferers tends to be *quantitative*; that is, sufferers experience considerably *more* episodes.
- The type of disorder may not be clearly evident as symptoms may overlap or confound simple diagnosis.

The American Psychiatric Association (1987) suggests that 'phobias' or 'phobic disorders' are characterised by an intense and disproportionate, or even inappropriate, fear of an object, activity or situation that elicits an overwhelming urge in sufferers to avoid the feared stimuli. The classification system, DSM IV (that will be discussed in the next Section), distinguishes *three* categories of phobic disorders:

1. **Agoraphobia**: This is an intense fear of being in places or situations from which some form of escape would be difficult. This would include the fear of going outside and being in either an open or public space. This type of phobia tends to be characterised by regular incidence of panic attacks – relatively short episodes of intense and distressing fear where the sufferer may feel loss of control and impending doom. The episode is often exacerbated due to the resulting acute physiological symptoms that develop very quickly, such as

sweating, chest pains, trembling and accelerated heartbeat. A spiralling effect is produced where physiological symptoms 'confirm' the perception that something is badly wrong, thereby increasing anxiety levels, which in turn further heightens physiological response and so forth.

2. **Social phobia**: Social phobias tend to relate to specific social situations such as using public toilets and eating and drinking in public. These tend to develop in late adolescence and early adulthood and are diagnosed as clinical conditions when they significantly interfere with daily life and persist beyond early adulthood.
3. **Simple/specific phobia**: This involves the persistent and overwhelmingly disruptive fear of specific items outwith the forms dealt with thus far, such as animals, insects, disease, dirt and heights. Such phobias have been associated with well-known individuals. Arsenal and Holland football player, Dennis Bergkamp, is reportedly so afraid of flying that when Arsenal were playing in European ties he would leave two days before the rest of the team to travel overland or avoid playing matches altogether if they were too far away. Famous Scottish player of the late sixties, Jimmy 'Jinky' Johnstone, shared the same fear of flying and in a famous quarter-final game of the European Cup run of 1967, scored three goals in the home game in an attempt to avoid travelling to the away leg. The movie actor, Kim Basinger, has an alleged fear of being seen in public that kept her housebound after the birth of her daughter.

See **Diagram 4.3**, below, which is a simple flow chart that illustrates the behavioural cycle associated with phobic disorders.

The crucial elements in this irrational and disproportionate fear of *specific* objects or situations are that the anxiety is experienced as a panic attack, which leads to *avoidance* of the object or situation. Both behavioural responses may greatly disrupt everyday life.

As with depression and schizophrenia, there is much debate over whether biological characteristics are the cause or consequence of the disorder. Eysenck's 'liability theory' suggests that it is the level of arousal in each individual's autonomic nervous system (ANS) that determines anxiety levels. Individual's with particularly sensitive ANS react much more to fear-provoking stimuli and thus suffer greater levels of anxiety. If the reactivity of the ANS is genetically inherited, then so, too, would be the predisposition to anxiety disorders. Concordance studies with MZ and DZ twins have shown that identical twins were significantly more likely to share phobic conditions than fraternal twins. Similar studies on other anxiety disorders, such as post-traumatic stress disorder and obsessive-compulsive disorder, have all shown that there may be an element of genetic susceptibility, but not enough to be definitively conclusive. Again, the role of the environment cannot be overlooked and using the 'diathesis model' may be most appropriate.

Diagram 4.3

Behavioural cycle associated with phobic disorders

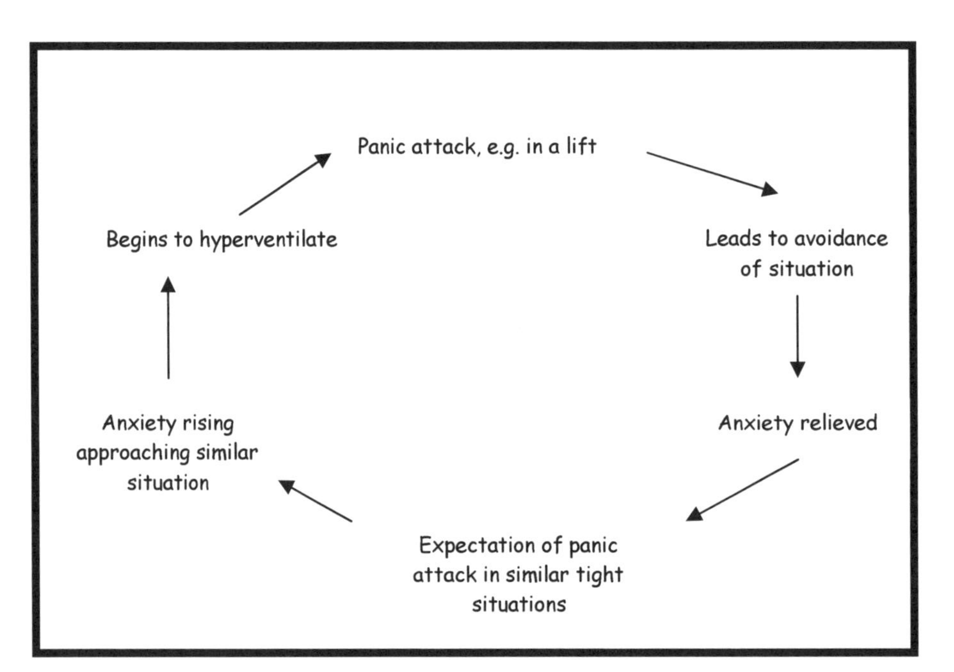

Theoretical explanations of anxiety disorders

Learning theory

Perhaps the most fruitful approach when seeking causal components of anxiety disorders is to be found in 'learning theory' – incorporating 'classical' and 'operant conditioning' and 'social learning theory'. At its simplest, the approach assumes that phobias are learned through association of trauma with a particular stimulus. This is known as the 'avoidance-conditioning model' and involves the cognitive pairing of the phobic stimulus with trauma, which provokes a degree of anxiety and fear from the mere anticipation of the stimuli's occurrence. The individual who has been caught up in a serious crush at a football ground or concert may become deeply afraid of going near another match or concert or even somewhere where there is a large crowd, such as a shopping centre. The victim has learned through conditioning to associate the fear with similar stimuli.

The famous classic research on 'Little Albert' conducted by Watson and Rayner (1920) illustrates this further. As part of the study, a baby was deliberately conditioned to develop a fear of furry objects. The baby learned to associate fear with any furry object resembling the one used in the study through the process of classical conditioning. This model has been used to explain phobias as a fear of fear itself. Behaviourists see phobias as developing from 'classical conditioning' and maintained through 'operant conditioning', which reinforces the avoidance behaviour that results from the phobic disorder. Avoidance of the situation that produces anxiety becomes a very strong negative reinforcement of this strategy.

'Social learning theorists', such as Bandura (1961), would suggest that phobic disorders could be learned through the principle of modelling. Specific people held in high esteem, such as parents, siblings or peers act as 'models' that others imitate. Studies have shown that the very act of observing certain emotions such as fear in the model can result in reproducing the same fear in the imitator through 'vicarious conditioning'.

There are, however, weaknesses in this approach. Many phobics cannot recall any unpleasant situation prior to the onset of the disorder, which means that the original situation may not have been learned in a maladaptive fashion. Again, the theory cannot explain why certain phobias are more common than others.

The psychoanalytic approach

The psychoanalytic approach commonly associated with Freud places great emphasis on the unconscious processes of early childhood development. This tradition would maintain that childhood trauma induced from abuse and the fear of parental disapproval could lead to what they describe as 'free floating anxiety'. Such anxiety could be focused on a specific stimuli, for example, spiders, which could, in turn, lead to phobic disorder. However, Freud suggests that some degree of anxiety can have *positive* consequences. It would promote the development of ego defence mechanisms such as denial, repression and suppression, which would protect the individual from mental instability. Many modern psychologists would, however, reject this notion as being overly simplistic, since the efficacy of defence mechanisms is dubious and the symptoms of anxiety and phobias persistent, even increasing.

Notwithstanding this, contemporary studies suggest that anxiety conditions in adulthood have a degree of association with early childhood and family experience. The research again raises the issues pertaining to the 'diathesis model', since family relationships and experiences can create a vulnerability to anxiety and phobias but, as the National Risk Survey in Canada (2001) concludes, a number of major issues such as parental discord, parental split and sexual abuse correlate highly with social phobias.

The classification system

With any physical or mental illness practitioners have to have a system for identification, categorisation and diagnosis in order to prescribe treatment of the condition. This is made all the more crucial with mental illness, since many of the concepts used are theoretical, contested and somewhat vague. Terms, such as 'abnormal behaviour' and the 'mind', are difficult to define and no universal agreement exists as to any one definition. Within each classification there will be a highly detailed description of the associated symptoms, characteristics and special features. Classification is essential for a number of other reasons, too:

1. The classification will provide the clinician with a set of parameters, within which symptoms may fall, thereby making the diagnostic process possible.
2. The classification system displays statistical frequency, which allows for quantitative data analysis across various groups and cultures.
3. It is an invaluable mechanism for communicating various symptoms between clinicians and creates a body of knowledge that can be shared in a formal and scientific manner.
4. It allows clinicians to map patterns of behaviour and relationships between variables in a representative way, which can aid with identifying causal factors.

There are two widely used classification systems for abnormal behaviour. One is the American Psychiatric Association's (APA) *Diagnostic and Statistical Manual of Mental Disorder*, commonly referred to as DSM IV, most recently revised in 1994. The other is the *International Classification of the Causes of Disease and Death*, commonly referred to as ICD 10 and is produced by the World Health Organisation (WHO). Both systems have undergone a series of revisions over time and as a result have become more similar, but both retain distinct differences, most notably in terms of coverage. DSM IV has many more discrete categories and also takes more consideration of environmental factors as part of the diagnostic regime. This is a critical element as can be seen by previous discussions on the social influences on mental disorders. New disorders have also been identified in DSM IV and others have been dropped, for instance, homosexuality!

DSM IV

This system consists of five separate dimensions or axes, which are used as diagnostic tools and in the formation of treatment. Each individual's symptoms are mapped on each of the five axes to give a broad spectrum of what the person may be suffering and in order to gauge possible biological and environmental influences.

DSM IV Axial classification

Axis I

This maps clinical syndromes, anxiety disorder, sexual disorders and mood disorders. Other relevant circumstances requiring intervention may also be included here, such as a history of physical or sexual abuse and marital or intimate relationship problems.

Axis II

This includes mental retardation, personality disorders and developmental disorders. Many of these disorders may accompany Axis I disorders and also include autism, specific learning disabilities and personality disorders, such as *schizoid* – severe thought disorder and sustained mood abnormality, and *narcissistic* – a pervasive pattern of grandiose fantasy and need for admiration and *obsessive-compulsive* disorder.

Axis III

This includes general physical disorders and conditions that may affect psychological functioning and treatment. These are *medical* problems that precipitate related psychological problems, such as may be the case with cancer and depression, for example.

Axis IV

This includes psychosocial and environmental problems, everyday life problems and experiences that influence the psychological health of the individual, such as the break up of relationships and bereavement.

Axis V

Assesses the individual's state of mind through the Global Assessment of Functioning (GAF) questionnaire.

The greatest advantage is gained from taking a multi-axial approach to diagnosing what are essentially complex problems. The model has facilitated a great deal of successful diagnosis and treatment, but has been criticised for not catering for ethnic and cultural variations.

Main categorisations ICD 10

Prior to 1993 there was a fair degree of disparity between the DSM and the ICD systems, but as successive versions have been produced, there has developed more similarity and the eleven categories within ICD 10 have a fairly close likeness to DSM IV. There are fewer categories within ICD but only because they cover a wider area and differences in language and presentation reflect the fact that the DSM was designed in the United States. Also, ICD 10 is more of a definitive *classification system* than diagnostic manual. (See **Box 4.3**.)

Box 4.3

Main categorisations ICD 10

F0	Organic, including symptomatic mental disorders.
F1	Mental and behaviour disorders due to psychoactive substance abuse.
F2	Schizophrenia, schizotypal and delusional disorders.
F3	Mood (affective) disorders.
F4	Neurotic, stress related and somatoform (biological) disorders.
F5	Behavioural syndromes associated with physiological disturbances and physical factors.
F6	Disorders of adult personality and behaviour.
F7	Mental retardation.
F8	Disorders of psychological development.
F9	Behavioural and emotional disorders with onset usually occurring in childhood or adolescence.
F10	Unspecified mental disorders.

In both systems, diagnosis is a long process, involving an initial history-taking interview, followed, in the UK, by what is called the 'Mental State Examination'**.** There are common difficulties at this stage of the diagnosis including language or cultural barriers, the mental state or cooperativeness of the individual and the presence of other non-visible disabilities. In these instances, it may only be possible to make observations of the person's behaviour or to have a relative or friend give information. The interview covers a wide area of components regarding symptoms and behaviour, appearance and behavioural patterns, speech and the form and sequence of thought, through content and perception of everyday factors, cognitive and intellectual functioning and insight. This process underpins the effectiveness of the classification system.

For either of the classification systems to operate effectively they have to be *reliable* and *valid.*

Reliability and validity

Numerous studies on the reliability of ICD 10 throughout Europe suggest that it is consistently high for most categories. In Rosenhan's (1973) study, *On being sane in insane places* (see **Box 4.4**, below and also see Chapter 2, Part 1 for further details of Rosenhan's study), it was found that there was a *high* degree of reliability but a very *low* degree of validity, since doctors were consistently and wrongly diagnosing 'pseudopatients' who were faking the symptoms of schizophrenia. However, after the study, major changes took place in the American psychiatric system.

Box 4.4

Case Study: D.L. Rosenhan (1973) 'On Being Sane in Insane Places'

The 'idea' behind this research was the question of whether the concept of an individual's 'abnormality' arises from the individual concerned or in the mind of the observer. Many, like Laing (1960), would argue that diagnosis is in the mind of the observer rather than from any scientifically based objective assessment. To test and challenge whether the sane could be distinguished from the insane in the 'insane' context of a mental institution, Rosenhan had eight pseudo-patients fake a symptom of a mental disorder.

The three women and five men pseudo-patients were all admitted to different hospitals after (falsely) complaining of hearing voices. From the point of admission, all acted 'normally', both within themselves and on report to the psychiatric staff. Whilst fellow patients declared them all to be fraudulent, none of the nursing or clinical practitioners did and all but one of the group was diagnosed with schizophrenia. Their average stay in hospital was 20 days, after which all were released on the basis that their schizophrenia was in remission.

The problem of labelling and stereotyping became apparent from the study. Once the 'abnormal' label was attached through diagnosis, future behaviour was interpreted accordingly. *All* the pseudo-patients reported feeling of depersonalisation; clothes were taken out of their possession and a number attached to their wrist. Any vestige of individual identity was removed and they felt totally powerless. This is still the case in many psychiatric institutions where many patients have limited legal rights and personal freedom is strictly monitored.

Social stigma

One of the major negative consequences that potentially accompany diagnosis and classification is the risk of 'labelling' and 'social stigma'. Unfortunately, many people do not treat physical and mental illness with the same degree of equanimity and there is a high degree of prejudice attached to the latter. The stigmatisation of the mentally ill has been caused by a number of contributory factors based almost entirely on misunderstanding, misplaced fear, ignorance and maliciousness. Such attitudes are perpetuated through the socialisation of children, education, common sense explanations and the use of negative stereotypes in the media. This public perception encourages sufferers to withdraw into isolation or remaining unemployed because of fear of disclosure, which has led some social commentators to suggest that mental illness should not be diagnosed at all!

Cultural, gender and ethnic problems in diagnosis

When diagnosing psychological abnormality clinicians necessarily make certain judgements that which might impact on moral, ethnic and cultural codes. This becomes problematic for psychologists, who, like other social scientists, have historically tended towards an ethnocentric approach.

Cultural problems in diagnosis

Notions of abnormality can be viewed as culturally relative since incidences of behaviour are, arguably at least, somewhat determined by what is considered normal and acceptable in that culture. Thus, the manifestation and treatments of certain disorders will vary by culture and Western models of diagnosis and treatment may not always be appropriate.

Interestingly, some mental and physical disorders are only found in certain cultures. These are known as 'culture bound syndromes' and an example is 'koro', an anxiety disorder found among Chinese males, where sufferers fear the withdrawal of the penis into the abdomen. Many tie string to the penis to prevent this from happening!

In the UK, black people are disproportionately represented among diagnosed schizophrenics and compulsory admissions to psychiatric hospitals. It is unclear here whether this is due to cultural bias in diagnostic processes, or a combination of genetic and environmental factors. It could also be that among black groups mental illness is viewed as less of a social stigma, thereby encouraging blacks to seek treatment, or, conversely, that other minority ethnic groups do not disclose it due to social pressures. Fernando (1991) suggests that the process of classification, including the medical interview, lacks objectivity and misunderstandings can occur to the detriment of the patient due to differences in language, religious beliefs and moral codes. Others point to the fact that most doctors are white, middle class and have been trained in institutions that are culturally bound by the Western model of medicine.

The most up to date version of DSM does now take account of cultural variations and, like ICD 10, includes a section on culture-bound syndromes. Both systems are, to all intents and purposes, highly sophisticated systems, but many still challenge their reliability and validity regarding certain cultural groups.

Gender problems in diagnosis

Gender also plays a significant part in the diagnosis of abnormality. There are often clear gender differences in terms of diagnoses, hospital admissions and type of mental illness suffered. If the act of suicide is taken as indicative of acute depressive illness, then it is notable that young males are five times more likely to commit suicide than females. Anorexia nervosa is ten times more common in women than men. Depression is more common in women and autism more common for men. This, then, raises some critical issues:

1. Are these differences due to biological or environmental and social variation between the sexes?

2. Are females more likely to disclose and seek treatment for 'mental problems'? This may be especially true in particularly macho 'cultures', such as that found in the West of Scotland, but also among men who view treatment for mental illness as 'faddy', or unnecessary. Clinicians can only report on those cases that are presented to them, which seriously skews incidence rates.
3. Are women diagnosed differently from men? This could be influenced by sex role stereotyping that panders to notions that women are neurotic and psychologically fragile. Some feminist psychologists argue that psychology, like other social sciences, fails to appreciate the particular social conditions experienced by women. Myths abound concerning the female body as *problematic*. Natural biological processes such as menstruation, pregnancy and menopause are misunderstood as pathologies. Gloria Steinhem (1983), in *If men could menstruate*, claims that:

> 'Menstruation would be an enviable masculine event and men would brag about how long and how much [...]. Young males would discuss it as the beginning of manhood. Gifts, religious ceremonies, family dinners and stag parties would mark the day [...]!'

Gender and depression

Whilst the figures for children are almost equal, almost twice as many adult females are diagnosed as suffering depression than men. It could quite simply be the case that the significant amount of hormonal imbalance experienced by women through puberty, menstruation, pregnancy (for many) and menopause explains the different incidence of depression. We should, however, be careful when interpreting this, as there are a number of possible causes for gendered diagnosing practices over and above any other considerations. For example, gender stereotyping may influence practitioners, intentionally or otherwise, into diagnosing females as depressive. It could be the case that cultural norms relating to gender dictate that women are more likely to report personal problems to a professional.

Conversely, many Scottish males tend to view psychological problems and the sharing of emotional distress as 'unmanly' or 'silly' and prefer not to admit to problems for fear of derision. Such sufferers may choose to attempt to bury their emotions through immersion in work, alcohol or drug abuse or simply withdraw into themselves. Due to the lack of professional medical guidance many cases of depression in males go unreported, but, interestingly, males show a far higher ratio of alcohol and drug abuse than females. In addition to these factors, it may well be the case that many modern women are particularly vulnerable to bouts of depression as they are often left with the overwhelming double burden of childcare and housework as well as paid employment. The types of jobs that working class women hold tend to be low paid, unskilled, repetitive and unrewarding and many are forced to become the main breadwinner in such jobs due to male unemployment.

Ethnicity problems in diagnosis

Ethnicity and racial stereotyping impact on the diagnosis of mental illness. The American psychologist, Cartwright (1851), developed *two* classifications that applied to black people only – 'dysaesthesia' and 'drapetomania'. The first portrayed blacks as having different personal traits to whites, such as being dirty, clumsy, idle and thieving and the second described the mental condition that induced black slaves to run away. These racist and contrived notions repel right-minded people today, but they do illustrate how overtly racially biased psychiatry was then. Recent studies in the UK show that Afro-Caribbeans were *twice* as likely to be diagnosed schizophrenic than other groups, including other minority ethnic groups. Fernando (1992) has vehemently argued that Western-based psychiatry and psychology is racist. He maintains that the medical and mental health systems are permeated with 'racist ideology' and he presents the following evidence to uphold his point:

- Afro-Caribbean and Asian people living in the UK are twice as likely to be diagnosed as schizophrenic.
- There is significantly greater use of locked wards in psychiatric hospitals for Afro-Caribbean, African and Asian patients.
- Black patients are more likely to receive sedatives and electro-convulsive therapy than their white counterparts.

Atypical behaviour – therapies

Section summary

Learning objectives for therapies for atypical behaviour will include:

- Explanations of medical and theoretical models of therapy.
- Explanations of therapeutic approaches to specific disorders.
- Explanations of care for people with mental health problems.

Introduction

Along with discussing the origins, definitions and approaches to atypical behaviour, it is also necessary to look at how we treat atypical behaviour. Using the models and approaches in the previous Section, we will examine the therapies used to treat disorders and then more specifically the common disorders of depression, schizophrenia and phobias. The importance of looking at mental health historically will also be addressed in conjunction with how the general public view mental health and, more importantly, the attitude formation that has taken place with the changes in how society deals with the problem.

Medical and behaviour models of therapy

Medical model: somatic therapies

The medical model of abnormality assumes that mental disorders result from biological disturbance. Accordingly, the treatments suggested focus on altering biological features or processes in the body rather than the mind. These are known as 'somatic' therapies and include the use of drugs, psychosurgery and electro-convulsive therapy (ECT).

The use of drugs in treating mental disorders has a highly controversial history. The use of psychotropic or 'behaviour altering' drugs that act on the brain was introduced in the 1950s. To many people at the time they were hailed as a panacea, until, that is, their side effects and addictive nature became apparent. Modern medicine uses newer drugs with less debilitating side effects.

The psychotropic range of drugs is divided into *four* main categories:

1. Anti-depressant.
2. Anti-anxiety.
3. Anti-psychotic.
4. Anti-bipolar.

Anti-depressant drugs

The anti-depressant drug helps to lift the person's mood and alleviate the depressive cycle and common examples tend to be known by their trade names such as Prozac and Seroxat. These are both classified under the general title of 'Selective Serotonin Reuptake Inhibitors' (SSRI). However, there is very serious concern both in the UK and the United States that there has been an ever-increasing spiral of prescriptions of such drugs by GPs who have not been trained in psychiatry. Also, usage of such drugs is significantly higher in Scotland per head of population than other parts of the UK and there is evidence of violence and/or suicide as possible side effects.

Anti-anxiety drugs

Anti-anxiety drugs tend to take the form of tranquillisers and produce calming effects on the brain. Well known examples include Valium and Librium, which have attracted media attention over their alleged high physical and psychological dependency rates. Prescription of such drugs tends now to be closely monitored and restricted to short time spans.

Anti-psychotic drugs

Anti-psychotic drugs are used only in the treatment of psychotic illness, such as schizophrenia and the latest in a long list of newer drugs include Clozapine and Olanzapine that have much fewer debilitating side effects than the previously used Phenothiazines such as Largactil, which have severe side effects.

Anti-bipolar drugs

Anti-bipolar drugs are used to treat manic mood swings. Lithium is by far the most common drug used, but it *must* be strictly controlled and monitored as too much may be lethal. However, Lithium is seen by many to be the success story of drug therapy and it has reportedly made dramatic improvements to the quality of many sufferers' lives.

Evaluation of the biomedical model

However, many psychologists and psychiatrists question the prominence of the 'biomedical framework' in modern research and practice, claiming that it overlooks social and environmental causes and treats symptoms rather than causes. Some question the efficacy of so-called wonder drugs like Prozac and question the extent of placebo effects.

The very thought of using ECT as a therapy tends to conjure up images of cruelty, pain and fear in many. This is compounded by images from early populist horror films as well as multi-Oscar winning films such as *One Flew Over the Cookoo's Nest*, but also by the fact that patients were often forced to undergo this treatment and without anaesthetic. Remarkably, though, despite this method's unpopular image and a distinct lack of medical knowledge as to what it actually does to the brain, clinicians and patients alike recognise that it has a degree of success in treating severe depression when drug therapies have failed. It is also still widely used in the UK in treating schizophrenia and epilepsy. A less controversial alternative to ECT is 'transcranial magnetic brain stimulation' (TMS), a non-invasive and painless method of brain stimulation. Whereas ECT uses electric current, TMS uses magnetic fields, which do not cause the convulsive seizures associated with ECT.

The practice of pre-frontal lobotomy was introduced by Moniz in 1935 and involves brain surgery in which the frontal or transorbital lobes are severed from the lower centre of the brain. It was hailed as a major breakthrough in mental health, but was in fact a very crude and often lethal procedure that left those patients that survived intellectually impaired, severely paralysed and with altered personalities. Modern psychosurgery may, as a last resort, use magnetic resonance imaging (MRI) and the use of tiny electrodes to create lesions in the brain as treatments for depression and chronic anxiety. As with ECT, there is no clear indication as to why such treatments work when they do.

The continued use of somatic therapies in modern medicine seems to imply that physical dysfunction is indeed related to mental illness, but this is not necessarily the case with all patients. Other strategies that accommodate social and environmental causes are available to sufferers and have been associated with relatively high degrees of success.

Behavioural therapies

'Behavioural therapies' focus on processes of 'operant conditioning' and assumes that abnormal behaviour is a *learned* process, which can be *unlearned* and replaced with a more appropriate behavioural pattern. The behavioural therapist has a wide range of therapies to choose from, depending on the individual patient's problems and needs and it is not unusual for a range of different therapies to be used. The range of treatments include:

1. Systematic desensitisation.
2. Flooding/implosion.
3. Aversion therapy.
4. Token economies.
5. Modelling.

Systematic desensitisation

This treatment was developed by Wolpe (1958) specifically to treat phobias and he devised a systematic procedure for the reduction of anxiety. This was based on earlier work, which advocated that the way to treat the phobia was to gently introduce the client to the actual object of their fear. Wolpe's procedure comprised *three* distinct strategies:

1. Deep relaxation training, even including hypnosis.
2. The provoked construction of a hierarchy of fear in order to create an increasing level of anxiety, e.g. moving the spider closer to the arachnophobic by stages.
3. The counteraction of past conditioning by pairing the phobic object with a deep relaxation response

The person will be systematically desensitised to the fear on a gradual basis. The method is considered most effective when the stimulus, the spider in the example above, is present and gradually introduced to the phobic. Alternatively, the process may be played out in the imagination using visualisation techniques.

Flooding/implosion

This strategy involves the phobic directly confronting the object or situation of fear for as long a period of time as is required for the fear to subside. Examples might include treating a fear of heights by exposing the phobic to an extended time on the top of a tall building or insisting that the agoraphobic occupy a seat in the middle of the crowd at a sell-out weekend rock festival. 'Implosion' works on the same principle, but the long exposure is imagined. Both techniques assume that given enough time, fear will subside since the body cannot maintain the associated state of anxiety for extended periods. It is hoped, then, that the individual will realise that they are not under threat in the presence of the object of fear, thereby diminishing it. As you can imagine, this form of therapy is controversial and has to be used with the utmost care by highly experienced therapists due to the severe stress the patient may suffer. However, it is a strategy commonly used by members of the public recovering from trauma. During World War II, many fighter pilots who were shot down were sent straight up into combat as soon as possible as a form of flooding and many victims of traumatic accidents, such as car crashes, drive as soon as possible in order to immediately confront the fear associated with the accident.

Aversion therapy

Here, the stimulus/response relationship fundamental to the 'classical conditioning' model is the subject of *intervention*. The intention is to discourage patients from engaging in the undesired behaviour by removing any pleasurable effects associated with it. This is done by manipulating the stimulus/response relationship by enforcing unpleasant responses from engagement with associated stimuli. For instance, the smoker is made to feel violently sick on lighting a cigarette, or the alcoholic suffers similar effects on consuming alcohol. Through this, it is hoped that the undesired behaviour is eventually eliminated altogether as patients avoid the stimulus. There are, however, problems with this method:

- Drop out rate is very high because of the obnoxious nature of the treatment.
- The existence of unpleasant responses may only last as long as the therapy and may, therefore, have *no* long-lasting effects.
- Patients can become hostile and aggressive.
- It is dubious whether the punitive aspects of the treatment are ethical and effective.

However, it tends to be used only as a last resort and is rarely used as the sole means of therapy. The success rate will depend largely upon the individual's determination and motivation.

Token economy

This method of behaviour modification uses the principle of 'operant conditioning' through reinforcement strategies. The system is predominantly used in institutions such as psychiatric hospitals, young offender institutions and specialist schools, where the subject is dependent on an authority figure for the provision of favours and concessions. The aim is to change undesired behaviour or, indeed, encourage desired behaviour by the use of 'secondary reinforcers', in the shape of tokens, for example, which can be exchanged for items such as tobacco, favourite foods, recreational visits and so on. Such systems of reward are reportedly highly effective in reducing undesired or abnormal behaviour, although their effectiveness may be limited to controlled environments. Some critics view it as derogatory and authoritarian while others emphasise that mainstream society itself takes the form of a token economy, where behaviour has to be modified in line with rules and incentives and rewards similarly arise from self-discipline and sacrifice.

Modelling

This method encourages the learning of 'correct' behavioural responses by observing and then imitating the behaviour of another person. It is based on the fact that as children, humans learn many aspects of their behaviour through imitating role models such as parents and teachers. It is extremely effective in teaching people with learning difficulties appropriate social and personal skills, such as feeding and clothing themselves. It can be integrated into everyday life and is practical and cheap to administer.

Evaluation of the behavioural model

Behavioural therapy at large has proven to be a relatively effective model for therapeutic intervention. It clearly defines the behavioural pattern it seeks to eradicate, although it is less effective in cases where stimulus/response relationships are difficult to detect. It is particularly of use in the treatment of phobic disorders, obsessive-compulsive states, social withdrawal and more minor conditions, such as bed-wetting. Some view the approach as superficial, since it focuses on removing symptoms without tackling the problem at source and the behaviour modification may not last beyond the duration of treatment.

Cognitive and cognitive-behavioural therapies

'Cognitive behavioural therapy' (CBT), as the name suggests, is a combination of cognitive and behavioural treatments. They are based on the principle that self-defeating perceptions, attitudes and personal beliefs first create and then maintain and even magnify the psychological disorder. One aim is, therefore, to turn these negative features into positive ones and this is done through 'cognitive restructuring'. Individuals are encouraged to monitor negative thoughts and emotions and any relationships between them. Another aim is for the individual to challenge irrational thought processes and create alternative, more rational interpretations of experiences. Focus is placed on thoughts, beliefs and attitudes that distort positive thinking. Examples of this approach in action may be inviting an individual suffering depression to change their lifestyle habits in an attempt to have them review how life can be lived or inviting the overeater to record what they eat and how they feel and think before and after eating.

Cognitive restructuring

A well-known therapy based on this model is Aaron Beck's (1979) 'cognitive restructuring'. The principal aim of Beck's restructuring therapy is to confront and challenge dysfunctional beliefs and attitudes before restructuring them. The individual is encouraged to seriously reflect on thinking patterns and then attempt to modify negative ones. The therapist will instruct and give guidance on how to focus, identify and monitor 'automatic' thoughts, such as feeling slightly depressed or anxious at given points in the day. Posing simple questions, such as the following, may help achieve this:

- 'What are you thinking about yourself?'
- 'What is going through your mind?'

Negative beliefs are then challenged using evidence of positive aspects from the person's life, such as personal or occupational achievements. Past 'failures' are reviewed in a positive way in order to have negative aspects approached differently.

Dysfunctional beliefs are always challenged and countered, which helps build an alternative, more positive and productive belief system.

Rational emotive therapy

Ellis's 'rational emotive therapy' (RET) was introduced much earlier than Beck's and is an example of a 'confrontational therapy', which seeks to identify and bluntly challenge negative self-image and its damaging effects of leaving sufferers with often overwhelming feelings of worthlessness, insecurity and self-loathing. He suggests that psychological disorders often result from internalising a series of beliefs that lead to the development of irrational thoughts. These often take the form of 'I must do this or I am a failure.' Examples might include, 'I must go to university, or my life will be over', 'I must get five Highers, or I will blame myself', 'I must own a big house in Newton Mearns (or Morningside), or I will have failed in life'. Ellis does *not* suggest, here, that individuals should not aim to do well in life and apply themselves accordingly. Rather, he emphasises the destructive and irrational aspects of the latter part of the statements; that is, 'or my life will be over' and so on. These beliefs place conditional self-acceptance in the mind of the individual and in many cases over overly ambitious goals. RET encourages clients to adopt unconditional acceptance of self through 'positive mental attitude'.

Evaluation of the cognitive and cognitive-behaviour models

Almost all cognitive and cognitive-behavioural therapists mix and match the techniques developed by Beck and Ellis and many studies have confirmed the efficacy of the ever-expanding CBT therapies and their multi-faceted use for treating depression and psychotic disorders such as schizophrenia. Some evidence exists to suggest that effects of CBT are only short term but given that the approach has only recently risen to prominence in clinical psychology, time will tell whether longer-term effects become evident.

Psychoanalytic treatment

The basic premise behind the 'psychoanalytic model' is that childhood experience impacts on psychological maturity into adulthood. Therefore, traumatic experiences or emotional disturbances in childhood may lead to mental disorders in adulthood.

Psychoanalysis

'Psychoanalysis' aims to unearth these unconscious conflicts in order to gain insight into the origins of the symptoms and thereby interpret the results of the individual's condition. The common goal of the therapy is to bring unconscious forces to the conscious level in order to discover the roots of the problem and encourage patients to develop an understanding of the problem, to recognise its effects and deal with it.

The basic starting point of the therapy is the 'talking cure' of free association, where the clinician listens to and interprets what is said and, equally important, what is omitted by the individual when asked to orally respond directly to the presentation of words or images. At this point, the analyst notes hesitations and the specific words used to describe what is presented to them. It is assumed that the information gleaned will betray what is stored in the unconscious mind. A specific characteristic of psychoanalysis is the use of insight into the origins of the problem. Freud suggested that a critical way that insight can be achieved is through *transference,* which is when the individual begins to see the therapist in the same light as a significant and important person from their past and feel confident enough to transfer inner thoughts and feelings such as anger, love, lust and hatred towards them. This may reveal insight into past events that may still impact on current relationships.

Freud, however, realised that people will not automatically open up their innermost secrets to just anyone and he was aware that the person will resist and deny certain aspects of their past lives. This is communicated to the individual on occurrence as their use of denial as a defence mechanism. All these elements of resistance and denial are open to interpretation by the therapist and would be used to build a profile of 'unconscious conflicts'.

Dream analysis

'Dream analysis' is also used. The content of the dreams is interpreted in an attempt to reveal hidden meaning and symbolism, since dreams are viewed as the free unravelling of the unconscious mind in circumstances where the conscious mind cannot interfere and distort. The assumption is that through this, true and unfiltered meanings of any past conflict are communicated.

Evaluation of psychoanalytical treatment

Psychoanalysis has been highly influential to the development of treatments of psychological disorder despite having been overtaken by its offshoot 'psychodynamic therapy' in terms of clinician preference in recent years. These methods range from modified classical psychoanalysis used by Freud and the early pioneers in the form of 'psychodynamic psychotherapy', 'group psychoanalytic therapy' – usually with groups of 6-12 patients – and 'brief dynamic therapy'. Conflicting evidence means that its efficacy is questionable and the long and protracted nature of diagnosis using these methods proves to be extremely expensive for clients. The assumptions behind the model are entirely theoretical and cannot be backed by empirical investigation and so even in cases where it has been shown to be effective, it may not be for the reasons claimed by the theory. For instance, patients may resolve issues through the practice of talking them through rather than for reasons outlined in the theory of the unconscious mind. Also, the model may be better at identifying the roots of problems than solving them.

Humanistic therapies

Humanistic psychology takes a holistic approach to psychological disorder. They assess all aspects of the individual and note the damaging effects of conditional acceptance on psychological well-being. According to the prominent humanist, Carl Rogers, if people feel that they have to act in particular ways in order to be accepted, loved and respected by others (i.e. these responses are conditional on meeting certain criteria), they develop poor self-esteem to the extent that can lead to psychological disorder. The placing of conditions on acceptance of others forces them to seek approval in ways that cause significant damage. Love, acceptance and emotional support need to be given unconditionally or freely to foster 'wholesomeness' in the individual.

Non-directive therapy

In terms of therapeutic intervention, Rogers viewed the individual as a 'client' who must be allowed to talk freely to a 'non-directive' therapist who merely guides the client to find their own solutions rather than offering 'professional' interpretations. The focus of discussion is confined to the *present* and the *future* rather than the *past*. The assumption behind this 'person-centred therapy', or 'counselling', is that humans can effect personal change through free expression and building towards personal fulfilment and growth. Rogers outlined *three* main elements of successful therapy with this regard:

1. **A degree of empathy**: The counsellor must understand how the person is feeling and be able to transmit that understanding to the client.
2. **Unconditional regard**: The client must value her/himself as an individual in order to grow and seek her/his potential through 'self-actualisation' and so a positive attitude must be retained at all times with the client.
3. **Genuine feeling**: The client must be able to relate to the counsellor as a 'real' person rather than a detached professional.

Evaluation of humanistic therapy

Humanistic therapy is open to significant criticism. It has been portrayed as more of a philosophical or spiritual approach than scientific and as overly optimistic over the individual's potential to bring about deep and lasting personal change. It has been shown to be effective with generalised anxiety and depression, although few would recommend it as appropriate for acute cases or psychotic disorders. It, too, is based on untestable concepts and, where it is effective, it is unclear as to why it is. It is certainly radically different from any of the other approaches and therapies in psychology and dominates the 'new social industry' of counselling with its simplicity and effectiveness. Interestingly, however, it has *not* been recognised by the British National Health Service (NHS).

Other humanistic therapies include the work of Perls (1966). Perls also assumes that people are essentially good, free and creative, but claims that they need to be pushed a little to achieve true potential and growth. 'Gestalt therapy', like RET, is very much a more confrontational and challenging therapy than the 'soft' approach taken in person-centred therapy. The techniques are highly controversial and anyone witnessing both therapeutic models in action would be surprised at the polarity of ideas used to achieve similar results.

Therapeutic approaches to specific disorders

Depression

This section will consider therapeutic approaches to the *three* specific disorders of 'depression', 'schizophrenia' and 'phobias'.

Treatment of depression using the cognitive-cognitive behaviourist model

Depression is the most commonly diagnosed mental disorder and is characterised by a varying degree of symptoms, such as overwhelming sadness, withdrawal, anxiety, negativity, gloom and doom, among others. Depressed individuals tend to perceive themselves and the world around them in a negative manner, which leads to a cycle of unrewarding behavioural patterns that serve to deepen the negative state of mind and further produce unrewarding behaviour. This cycle can be very difficult to break depending on the extent and duration of the illness. The cognitive/behavioural approach to dealing with the problem is based on the principle of the person taking control of themselves and their environment. They are encouraged to provide a more rational interpretation of their own behaviour and to develop new ways of thinking.

The major difference from other 'psychotherapeutic approaches' is the insistence on 'working together'. *Both* therapist *and* patient work together to identify and deal with the problem, to make specific strategies for change and then apply these changes and test their effectiveness. At all stages, both the therapist and patient can 'test' their strategy against the desired outcome of behavioural change. It is very much an 'evidence' gathering and testing approach. We can examine a specific theory on depression in order to illustrate its application here.

Cognitive restructuring model

Beck's 'cognitive restructuring model' encompasses the general points made above. Beck focuses on depression following loss where 'negative cognitive schemas' are formed. Simply put, these are negative assumptions made by the individual, such as, 'I am worthless, nobody likes me.' This automatically creates *negative* thought processes, which, in turn, create 'cognitive negative' actions. From this, the individual is left with negative schemas over the *self* and the *world* – 'I and everything around me is hopeless' – compounding feelings of failure and doom.

Even minor ambiguous situations are interpreted in negative ways. Beck called these errors of judgement 'cognitive distortions'.

CBT trains the individual to *monitor* occurrences of these negative assumptions and to immediately challenge and confront them. This method has reportedly proved to be just as effective as the use of drugs in alleviating the symptoms and evidence suggests that it has high relapse prevention.

Treatment of depression using the psychoanalytic model

Freud's (1917) theory is based on 'object loss', in the sense that the individual has *not* fulfilled various needs during the first phase of life-span development, the 'oral stage'. This experience of denial of need by others predisposes the child to states of depression in adulthood.

Incidences of depression will follow stressful events since the individual's psychological capacity to cope is used up continually seeking warmth from relationships with others. At the point of loss in adulthood, such as the loss of someone close through bereavement or the dissolution of a personal relationship, or loss of esteem or status, sufferers automatically regress to their 'object loss' state.

Psychoanalysis makes use of the following techniques over the longer term:

1. ***Free association***: Where the person is allowed to talk freely with the therapist, who interprets the material provided in order to 'unlock' the traumas within the unconscious and eventually is able to break down the defence mechanisms to release the person from the earlier depressive state.
2. ***Dream analysis***: Uncovering the meanings and symbols within dreams, therefore, like free association giving the patient insight into feelings that may be causing the depression.
3. ***Defence mechanisms***: Since the object of loss may be painful for the patient to recount, they may attempt to block the flow of information through resistance. Therapists use the concept of defence mechanism to illustrate denial of reality and to encourage the unravelling of the most intimate conflicts that may be masquerading behind the denial.
4. ***Transference***: The client is encouraged to transfer their anger and mistrust of their parents or carers on to the analyst. The purpose, here, is to *re-enact* the conflict and attempt to resolve it.

Treatment of depression using the behaviourist model

The behaviourists view depression, schizophrenia and phobias as a result of maladaptive learning through the principle of 'association' by 'classical conditioning', which is then *reinforced* through 'operant conditioning'. The basis of therapeutic intervention is 'behaviour modification', based on the assumption that what has been learned can be unlearned and replaced by a more *positive* and *effective* behavioural response.

This approach has proved more effective when treating phobic and anxiety disorders rather than depression and schizophrenia since it operates by specifically defining behaviour that needs to be changed. In the case of phobias and anxiety, this is appropriate, whereas depression and schizophrenia have less easily defined origins. Although behavioural therapy has little influence on the primary symptoms of schizophrenia and depression, it can aid development of improved communication through the use of operant conditioning based on the reward system.

Treatment of depression using the humanistic model

Regarding person-centred therapy, the principal emphasis is on personal growth and the essential 'goodness' of human nature. If the person is held back by groundless fear and restrictions, they will fail to develop normally, just as a flower only blooms in the right environment. Depression is indicative of the person being held back and prevented from flourishing.

In treating depression, as with other disorders, the therapist or counsellor would create an environment of trust and safety within which the client is encouraged to reveal the deepest inner workings of self. The client is encouraged to understand perceptions and feelings – the 'phenomenological world of reality'. The counsellor will try to understand *how* the person subjectively *experiences* the event(s) causing the instability. Since each person is unique, they are treated as such and encouraged to be aware of the particular roots of their symptoms. Unlike with psychoanalysis and behavioural therapy, the therapist does not attempt to manipulate proceedings, but rather creates conditions that encourage the individual to direct and effect their own change. This approach is most effective in treating mild conditions and Rogers himself warned that it was inappropriate for severe mental disorders.

Schizophrenia

Schizophrenia – cognitive-behavioural

The 'cognitive' and 'cognitive-behavioural' focus very clearly on the multiple cognitive defects or 'mental deficits' in the context of schizophrenia. It is these deficits, in fact, that define the disorder as the threads of interrelated cognitive factors break down, causing the impaired ability of the sufferer to process information required for normal activity. In 'healthy' individuals, the brain processes a great deal of information quickly and automatically and this is hampered for the schizophrenic, which can prevent the forming of systematic, logical and rational thought patterns. Psychotic experiences may inevitably result, but therapists challenge irrational beliefs.

Often these beliefs take the form of auditory hallucinations resulting from sensory overload, such as 'voices' relaying specific commands. Since the assumption here is that the commands are irrational, the therapist would invite the patient to systematically reject them until more rational thoughts arise. The same principle applies for depression – there are systematic and irrational cognitive deficits that need to be eradicated and replaced by more rational and positive thoughts.

It should be pointed out that psychological therapies may be most effective (or even feasible) when the person is already receiving drug therapy.

Evaluation of psychoanalytic, behavioural and humanistic approaches

1. Psychoanalytic approaches suggest the problem stems from childhood trauma resurfacing as conflict in later years and so the sufferer needs to deal with unresolved subconscious issues. Like the humanistic approach, the effectiveness of treatment is assessed by the therapist, which raises the issue of bias.
2. The learning and social learning (behavioural) theory would see learned maladaptive behaviour as being the primary cause and would recommend a process of unlearning before learning new behavioural patterns. The lack of a clear notion of causality, here, makes it very difficult to know *what* to change and *how* to change it.
3. Humanistic approaches would not be appropriate due to its non-directive nature, where the counsellor does *not* advise or interpret, but leaves the client to clarify the ideas that they are exploring. A person suffering from schizophrenia may not be able to contend with such a system or, for that matter, have the ability to understand how to achieve such a potential.

Phobias

Cognitive behavioural therapy

CBT would suggest that phobias are caused by 'cognitive distortions' and that these assumptions must be challenged and tested. This is done by instructing the individual to actively engage in situations that allow the validity of the individual's assumptions to be checked and re-checked, until such times as the person accepts that the problem stems from belief distortion.

The behaviourists are by far the most productive and effective group for dealing with what they consider to result from a 'learned irrational thought process'. The techniques of systematic desensitisation, flooding and modelling have all shown to be very successful in dealing with phobic disorders.

Psychoanalytic and humanistic therapies

There is little or no evidence to suggest that psychoanalysis and humanistic therapies would be useful for phobic disorders, because both theories and therapies tend to be centred on the finding of self or insight into self, rather than curing a specific and focused problem.

Evaluation of therapeutic approaches to depression, schizophrenia and phobias

The critical question for the three disorders we have examined and the different therapies that are used is quite simply whether or not they work. Each is effective for some disorders only and in some cases only. There can be no single prescribed 'cure', since success can only be assessed by the relatively unscientific methods of self-report and client observation. For instance, behavioural therapy has had tremendous impact on the treatment of anxiety disorders in terms of resultant behavioural change, but it is more difficult to assess whether belief-systems have changed.

In summary, the list below indicates which approaches are most effective for treating specific disorders:

- ***Behaviourism***: Anxiety and phobias.
- ***Drug treatment***: Most successful with psychotic disorders, such as schizophrenia.
- ***Cognitive/CBT***: Successful with depression. This, combined with anti-depressants, offers the best relief for sufferers.
- ***Humanistic***: Mild forms of depression and anxiety.

However, most modern therapists *do not* stick rigidly to any particular therapeutic model. Instead, they employ a mix and match approach to suit the individual and particular situation.

Care of people with mental health problems

Historical perspective

It is notable from considering the history of the study, perceptions and treatment of abnormality, that there has been a gradual change of emphasis on assumptions over the role of the sufferer, wider society and forms of treatment. Concepts of abnormality, then, must be viewed as having been shaped by social and historical context. For example, homosexuality was once universally seen as a psychological disorder and is still seen as such in some cultures and by some political and religious groups today.

In *The Human Experience of Psychological Disorders*, Halgin and Whitbourne (1993) suggest that there are *three* distinct and focused modes of explanation of abnormality that periodically rise to prominence throughout Western history. These are the:

1. Mystical.
2. Scientific.
3. Humanistic.

The 'mystical explanation' explains abnormality in the language of evil and demonic spiritual possession. Scientific explanations, on the other hand, probe the conventions of scientific disciplines, such as biology, to offer what could be described as the scientific basis of human behaviour – a claim that could perhaps be made of 'modern psychology', too. The humanistic/humanitarian approach takes the view that social inequality and living conditions underlie much of mental instability.

With regard to these approaches, Halgin and Whitbourne clearly favour the scientific over the humanist and mystical approaches and claim that had the development of historical explanations of abnormality been entirely linear and progressive, humanistic approaches would have been subsumed within the scientific and the mystical abandoned entirely.

The ancient Greeks, who believed that mental illness could be treated by purgation, forced excretions from the body, developed the first recorded 'scientific-medical' model of abnormality. This was not a universal view of the ancient Greeks, however. Plato suggested that the mentally ill should be *cured* instead of being *punished* by their families.

Perhaps the next era where the concept of abnormality became a public issue was in the period around the Dark and Middle Ages and stemmed from the widespread authority of the Catholic Church. By its authoritarian nature, the Church demanded allegiance to its teachings and dissenters were denounced as heretics and duly despatched in the most inhumane ways. The 'theology' of the sick was a direct descendant of Old Testament interpretations, which considered illness of any kind as divine retribution for sinfulness. The Church, in many cases, saw abnormality as being the work of the devil and many innocent sufferers were subject to horrific forms of exorcism or burned at the stake.

In England by the Middle Ages, 'asylums' began to spring up to house the insane. The first of these was Saint Mary of Bethlehem, which became commonly known as 'Bedlam'; a term that has entered modern parlance as an adjective for chaos. 'Abnormality' was still *not* seen as an illness, but as a form of spiritual or physical possession. The rise of science and humanist philosophy in the sixteenth to eighteenth centuries promoted more sympathetic views on abnormality, but failed to significantly impact on the inhuman or degrading treatment of sufferers. By the beginning of the 20th century, however, Emil Kraepelin (1896) had published the first recognisable textbook on what was to become known as psychiatry – thus returning abnormality to the medical level of analysis, which had diminished since the time of the ancient Greeks. Kraepelin's work was the first ever attempt to classify mental illness and it formed the foundations for the establishment of the classification systems DSM and ICD in the late forties.

Two major theoretical constructs emerged at the beginning of the 20th century, with the works of the psychoanalyst, Freud, and the behaviourist, Skinner. From here on, psychology and psychiatry extended their theoretical knowledge to the *problem* of abnormality. From then until now, there has been a shifting moral and ideological pattern, as witnessed by the rise of humanistic psychology in the sixties. The role of science and knowledge has transformed the subject in the past forty years with the advancement of somatic models of treatment and the rise of cognitive-behavioural therapies. As discussed earlier, advancement has brought with it many ethical and moral implications; the role of diagnosis and stigmatisation, the domination of white Anglo-American philosophy and gender and ethnic bias in the field of psychology.

Where are we now?

With the growth of psychiatry and psychology, there has been a dramatic shift away from the 'Bedlam' model of incarcerating people as the sole treatment for mental illness. From the 1980s onwards, more and more people were being treated 'in the community'. Regardless of the strengths and weaknesses of the UKs social policy initiative known as 'Care in the Community', it has at the very least refocused debates on how sufferers of mental illness should be treated and integrated into mainstream society. The problem of institutionalisation had been partly addressed, since many of those who had spent their lives under lock and key had never developed skills for independent living. This was made all the more possible with the advancement of drug therapies that dramatically controlled symptoms and allowed for individuals to be treated outwith a hospital situation. Formal policies of community care have been adopted and the individual is cared for at home, a task often left to the family, which in many cases has been extremely burdensome.

This process has been accelerated with the rapid expansion of 'commercial' residential care homes run by the private sector. This has been criticised as 'care on the cheap', especially with mental health patients whose lack of real funding has led to increased 'social drift', particularly for psychotic patients. This has led to an increase in homelessness among the mentally ill, which undoubtedly further exacerbates their problems.

Negative public perceptions of mental illness still abound at the turn of the 20th century, despite recent media campaigns sponsored by the Scottish Executive, such as the 'See Me' TV and billboard advertising campaign, to present all of us as susceptible to some form of mental illness at some time in our lives. Public information on mental illness needs to be more coordinated and structured if it is to adequately educate the public on the realty of mental illness for sufferers. The use of language is important in this respect, as many children in particular continue to use terms such as 'psycho', 'looney', 'nutter', 'schizo' as terms of abuse. This practice, whether conscious or unconscious, provides a platform for continued stereotyping and discrimination.

Self-test questions

1. What are **somatic therapies**?
2. Describe the **three** main somatic treatments.
3. With what type of **condition** is each of the main behavioural therapies particularly effective?
4. Describe the principle of **counselling**.
5. Briefly describe **rational emotive therapy** and **cognitive reconstruction**.

General areas for exam questions

1. Description of treatments.
2. Evaluation of treatments.
3. Problems with evaluating the effectiveness of treatments.

Some exam-type questions

1. Compare and contrast the **psychoanalytic** and **somatic** approaches used in the treatment of abnormal behaviour.
2. Describe and evaluate the learning approaches used in the **therapeutic treatment** of abnormal behaviour.
3. (a) Describe **ONE** type of therapy or treatment for a mental illness or disorder.
   (b) How difficult is it to **evaluate** this type of therapy or treatment?

Glossary

Abstract A brief summary of research aims, methods and conclusions that appears at the start of a report.
Acoustic coding The storage of information in memory by the way it sounds.
Adaptive Relating to behaviours that help us to adjust to the demands of our environment.
Advertising Promoting products, services, information or ideas via the mass media with a view to increasing sales.
Affective component Influenced by or resulting from emotions.
Agentic state A state of feeling controlled by an authority figure and, therefore, lacking a sense of personal responsibility.
Aggression Any form of behaviour that is intended to harm or injure some person, oneself, or an object.
Anticonformity Opposition to social influence on all occasions, often caused by psychological reactance.
Anxious/ambivalent attachment style An expectation about social relationships characterised by a concern that others will not return affection.
Appendix A section at the end of a report containing supporting materials or data.
Attachment A strong emotional tie that develops over time between an infant and its primary caregiver(s) and results in a desire to maintain proximity.
Attitude A relatively enduring organisation of beliefs, feelings and behavioural tendencies towards socially significant objects, groups, events or symbols.
Attribution The process of assigning a cause to one's own or others' behaviour.
Authoritarian personality Identified by Adorno *et al* as someone who is more likely to be obedient – they tend to hold rigid beliefs, be hostile towards other groups and submissive to authority.
Autokinetic effect A visual illusion where a small spot of light in a darkened room appears to be moving when in fact it is stationary.
Autonomic nervous system (ANS) A division of the body's peripheral nervous system that controls involuntary activities such as breathing.
Avoidant attachment style An expectation about social relationships characterised by a lack of trust and a suppression of attachment needs.
Behaviourism A school of psychological thought that advocates the study of observable behaviour rather than unobservable mental processes.
Biofeedback A stress management technique whereby an individual learns to recognise and control certain autonomic responses to stress, such as pulse rate and blood pressure.
Bi-modal Data where there are two modes (see '**mode**').
Capacity The amount of information that can be held in memory.
Categorisation The process of classifying people, objects and events into different categories.
Catharsis A dramatic release of pent-up feelings: the idea that aggressive motivation is 'drained' by acting against a frustrating object or a substitute, or else by a vicarious experience
Central executive The governing part of the working memory that co-ordinates how attention is allocated to tasks. Thought to be involved in demanding mental activities, such as decision-making and problem solving.
Chunking A method of grouping information together into meaningful units to allow greater amounts of information to be retained in short-term memory. STM capacity is approximately 7 items, or chunks.
Classical conditioning Learning that occurs when a reflex response becomes associated with a stimulus that would not normally be associated with it.
Cognition Any mental thinking process.
Cognitive component Influenced by or resulting from an individual's thoughts, knowledge, interpretation, understanding or ideas.
Cognitive development Changes in mental abilities and processes that occur throughout life.
Collectivist A culture where individuals share tasks, belongings and income. The people may live in large family groups and value interdependence.
Compliance The influence of a majority or minority, based on its power – the influence is more on public than private behaviour.
Confederate An accomplice of an experimenter whom research participants assume is a fellow participant or bystander.
Conformity Yielding publicly to group pressure and sometimes yielding privately as well.
Contact hypothesis The theory that under certain conditions direct contact between antagonistic groups will reduce prejudice.

Correlation A statistical measure of the relationship between two variables. They may have no relationship (zero correlation), a relationship where both variables increase, or decrease together (a positive correlation), or a relationship where as one variable increases, the other variable decreases (a negative correlation).
Correlation co-efficient The numerical value that indicates the strength of the relationship between two variables. Ranges from -1 (perfect negative correlation) through 0 (zero = no relationship) to +1 (perfect positive correlation).
Cross-cultural studies Studies in which similarities and differences between different cultures are examined.
Cue-dependent forgetting Where a memory is stored but is not retrievable unless a specific cue is available.
Culture The total lifestyle of a people from a particular social grouping, including all the ideas, symbols, preferences, and material objects that they share.
Demand characteristics Factors which result in participants feeling pressure to behave in ways that they believe are expected of them.
Dependent variable (DV) The variable which is measured in an experiment in order to determine whether the independent variable has affected it.
Deprivation Occurs when a child is separated from its primary caregiver. Attachments have been formed and are then disrupted. May also refer to the lack of emotional stimulation.
Descriptive statistics Mathematical techniques that summarise and show patterns in the data, such as measures of central tendency, measures of dispersion, and graphs.
Desegregate Abolish segregation.
Desensitisation A serious reduction in one's responsiveness to material that normally evokes a strong emotional reaction.
Design The shape of an experiment in terms of variables and conditions – the most typical designs are 'repeated measures' and 'independent measures'. Also the name of a subsection of the method section of a report detailing this information.
Despair Signs of hopelessness and unwillingness to participate socially, demonstrated by a child during separation from a primary caregiver.
Detachment Demonstrated by children who have been separated from their primary caregiver. An apparent state of normality is shown, but the child has become emotionally withdrawn.
Discrimination The behavioural expression of prejudice.
Displacement Psychodynamic concept referring to the transfer of negative feelings onto an individual or group other than that which originally caused the negative feelings.
Duration The length of time information can be retained in memory.
Ecological validity A situation where findings from research are meaningful in the real world.
Ego Part of the personality, according to Freud. The ego works on the reality principle and attempts to balance the demands of the id and the superego.
Encoding The process of coding information so it can be stored in memory.
Equal status contact Contact between individuals who share the same status or prestige.
Equity theory A special case of social exchange theory that defines a relationship as equitable when the ratio of profit to contribution is perceived to be the same by each partner.
Ethnocentrism Evaluative preference for all aspects of one's own group relative to other groups.
Ethology The study of animal behaviour in the natural environment, focusing on the importance of innate capacities and the functions of behaviours.
Evolutionary social theory A biological theory claiming that complex social behaviour is adaptive and helps the individual, kin and the species as a whole, to survive.
Excitation-transfer model This suggests that the expression of aggression is a function of learned behaviour, some excitation from another source and the person's interpretation of the arousal state.
Factoid A fact that did not exist until it was created by the media.
'Fight or flight' response The bodily response to a perceived threat. The body reacts by getting ready to repel or evade the threat.
Forgetting The loss of, or inability to access, information from memory stores.
Frustration-aggression hypothesis Theory that all frustration leads to aggression and all aggression comes from frustration.
General Adaptation Syndrome (GAS) A model devised by Selye that describes three stages of reaction to stress: alarm, resistance and exhaustion.
Gender stereotypes A society's expectations about the characteristics of females as a group and males as a group.
Granfalloon A technique used in persuasive communications to give a product a 'personality' so that buying it gives the consumer a sense of belonging to a special group.
Group norm Attitudinal and behavioural uniformities that define group membership and differentiate between groups.

Heterosexism A system of cultural beliefs, values and customs that exalts heterosexuality and denies, denigrates and stigmatises any non-heterosexual form of behaviour or identity.
Id Part of the personality, according to Freud. The id works on the pleasure principle seeking pleasure and avoiding pain. Present from birth.
Identification The process through which someone adopts the feelings, attitudes and behaviour of another person (or group) and becomes like them.
Independent measures The experimental deign which uses two (or more) separate groups of participants, one for each condition.
Independent variable (IV) The variable which is manipulated in an experiment resulting in two or more 'conditions' in order to measure its effects on another variable (the DV).
Individualistic Societies in which the ties between individuals are loose: people are expected to look after themselves and their immediate families.
Inferential statistics Mathematical techniques used for analysis of data, usually to determine the likelihood that a difference between two or more sets of sample data is representative of the target population.
Informational social influence The influence that results from the provision of information that reduces ambiguity.
In-group A group to which a person belongs and that forms a part of his or her social identity.
In-group bias The tendency to give more favourable evaluations and greater rewards to in-group members than to out-group members.
Innate Where a trait is inborn, rather than learned.
Inoculation The technique of presenting a weakened form of a message to allow people to form counter-arguments.
Insecure attachment A form of attachment between a child and its primary caregiver that occurs when the primary caregiver lacks sensitivity to the child's needs. Results in problems with social and emotional attachments in adult life.
Institutional racism A form of racism in which the policies and practices of society's institutions are racist.
Intergenerational contact Contact between people of different generations.
Internalisation The process through which standards, beliefs and values become part of one's own motive system.
Jigsaw classroom A situation in which superordinate goals produce cooperation rather than conflict between social groups.
Labelling Defining a person or group in a certain way – as a particular 'type' of person or group.
Laboratory An environment for experimentation in which it is possible to have complete control over external factors. Used to avoid distractions and unpredictability of 'everyday' environments.
Learned helplessness Seligman's term for a state of apathy or helplessness that may result when an animal or human is unable to escape from a traumatic situation.
Learning theory The explanation of behaviour using the principles of classical and operant conditioning. The view that all behaviour is learned.
Libido A form of psychic energy that Freud regarded as sexual in nature, compelling people to act in ways likely to reproduce the species.
Longitudinal study A research study that involves a single group of individuals being studies over a period of time.
Long-term memory (LTM) The memory store for past events and knowledge acquired. The capacity of LTM is thought to be unlimited and duration can last a lifetime.
Matched pairs design The experimental design that is similar to the independent measures design in that it uses two separate groups of participants, one for each condition, but each participant is matched up with a partner of similar characteristics (e.g. sex, age, education level) and one member of each pair is placed in each group.
Matching hypothesis States that people aspire to be in a relationship with a partner who is socially desirable, but that this aspiration is balanced against the perceived probability of attaining it.
Maternal deprivation Where a child is deprived of the care of its mother or primary caregiver. Some researchers believe that if a child suffers maternal deprivation before the age of 2½ years they will suffer problems in developing and maintaining relationships in adult life.
Mean The arithmetic average of a set of data, formed by dividing the total score by the number of scores.
Median The central point of a distribution of data, in that an equal number of observations or measurements will fall above and below the median.
Memory The storage of information and knowledge.
Method The means or techniques used to obtain data, for example, experiment, or survey. Also the name of the section in a report which details the design, participants, apparatus and procedure used in the research.
Minority influence Social influence processes whereby numerical or power minorities change the attitudes of the majority.
Mode The most common score in a distribution.

Monotropy The theory that the relationship between a child and their primary caregiver is of particular and special significance in the emotional development of the child.
Multi-modal Data where there are three or more modes ('see **mode**'). Normally distributed data that are normally distributed from the pattern of a bell curve, with a large number of measures towards the centre of the distribution, and few towards the extremes.
Multi-store model Memory is explained through the use of three separate stores: sensory, short-term and long-term.
Nature-nurture Nature is that which is inherited and genetic, as distinct from nurture, which refers to all influences after conception, i.e. experiences.
Nervous system The system in the body comprising the central nervous system and the peripheral nervous system. Information is transmitted through the nervous system via nerve impulses that travel through neurons.
Neuron A nerve cell in the nervous system that transmits information between the brain and the spinal cord and the rest of the body. There are three types of neuron: sensory neurons transmit information from the senses to the brain and spinal cord; motor neurons transmit information from the brain and spinal cord to the muscles and glands; interneurons are connectors mainly contained in the central nervous system – they relay information between sensory and motor neurons.
Normative social influence An influence to conform to the positive expectation of others to gain social approval or to avoid social disapproval.
Obedience Behaving as instructed, usually in response to an individual in a position of authority – unlikely to involve a change of private opinion.
Observational learning Learning through imitating or copying the behaviour of others.
Operant conditioning Learning that occurs through reward or reinforcement that increases the probability of a behaviour recurring. Punishment decreases the probability of a behaviour recurring.
Out-group Any group with which a person does not share membership.
Parasympathetic nervous system (PNS) Part of the autonomic nervous system that conserves energy and restores the body to a relaxed state following the 'fight or flight' response of the sympathetic nervous system.
Participants The people who take part in a study, the sample, also known as subjects. Also the name of a subsection of the method section of a report, detailing this information.
Pilot study A practice run, prior to an experiment or study, which allows techniques and procedures to be tried out and adjusted if necessary.
Population The group of people from whom a sample is taken from and to whom the conclusions of a piece of research will relate. A population in this sense need not refer to everyone in society.
Powerful A measure of how well a statistical measurement includes all elements of the data it seeks to summarise.
Prejudice A negative attitude directed toward people simply because they are members of a specific social group.
Primacy effect The tendency to remember items from the beginning of a list, or earliest information received.
Primary caregiver The person who provides the main, continuous, physical and emotional care of a child. Usually, but not exclusively, the mother.
Privation Occurs when a child has not formed any attachments to a caregiver.
Procedural memory The memory of how to perform specific tasks and actions, such as tying a shoelace or riding a bicycle.
Procedure The way the research runs, the order of events from the perspective of the participants. Also the name of a subsection of the method section of a report detailing this information.
Propaganda The communication of a point of view with the aim of persuading people to adopt this view as their own.
Psychodynamic approach An approach that draws on Freud's psychoanalytic theory and which focuses on the role of motivation and past experiences in the development of personality.
Psychopathology The scientific study of mental disorder.
Racism Prejudice and discrimination against people based on their ethnicity or race.
Realistic conflict theory Sherif's theory of inter-group conflict, which traces the complexion of inter-group behaviour to the nature of goal relations between groups.
Recency effect The tendency to remember the items from the end of a list, most recently heard, or latest information received.
Reconstituted family A family where one or both partners have been previously married and they bring with them children from a previous marriage.
Rehearsal The practice of repeating information in order to extend its duration in STM, or to transfer it to LTM.
Reinforcement/affect theory An application of learning theory to attractions between people – it suggests that we like people who reward us and dislike those who punish us.
Repeated measures The experimental design that uses only one group of participants who participate in both (or all) conditions of the study.

Report The written description and summary of a piece of research, such as an experiment. Sometimes called a laboratory report, or 'write-up'.
Repression Where memories are placed in the unconscious mind away from conscious access in order that the anxiety they would create does not need to be experienced.
Retrieval failure The inability to access something from memory that has previously been learned. The memory is stored but cannot be accessed at that particular time.
Secure attachment A form of attachment that develops when a primary caregiver is sensitive to their child's needs. The child acquires the ability to be independent and is comfortable in social relationships.
Secure attachment style An expectation about social relationships characterised by trust, a lack of concern with being abandoned and a feeling of being valued and well liked.
Semantic coding The coding of information for memory in terms of its meaning.
Separation protest The distress shown when a child is separated from its primary caregiver.
Separation The physical disruption of contact between a child and its primary caregiver.
Serial digit span A list of numbers given to test the capacity of STM. The number of digits recalled in the correct order indicates the capacity of STM.
Sexism Prejudice and discrimination against people based on their sex.
Short-term memory (STM) Memory for immediate events. The STM has limited capacity and limited duration. Memories are lost if not rehearsed or committed to LTM.
Significant difference A difference that is shown by statistical measures to be a true effect of the experimental manipulation of the IV, rather than due to chance factors.
Situational attribution Attributing a person's actions to factors in the situation or environment, as opposed to internal attitudes and motives.
Social exchange theory People assess the benefits received from a relationship and balance that against the costs involved and also against the costs and benefits of alternatives.
Social identity theory Theory of group membership and inter-group relations based on self-categorisation, social comparison and the construction of a shared self-definition in terms of in-group defining properties.
Social influence The exercise of social power by a person or group to change the attitudes or behaviour of others in a particular direction.
Social learning theory (SLT) The view that behaviour can be explained in terms of direct and indirect reinforcement, through imitation, identification, and modelling.
Socialisation The process where an individual learns the customs and practices that characterise and are prevalent in their culture.
Social psychology The scientific discipline that attempts to understand and explain how the thought, feeling, and behaviour of individuals are influenced by the actual, imagined, or implied presence of others.
Stereotype Widely shared and simplified evaluative image of a social group and its members.
'Strange situation' A method of determining the level of anxiety experienced when a child is separated from its caregiver and is placed in the presence of a stranger.
Stress The generic term that incorporates the causes and effects of a person's perceived inability to cope with the perceived demands placed upon them.
Stressors Events or occurrences that cause someone stress.
Superego Part of the personality, according to Freud. The superego works on the morality principle determining a person's sense of right and wrong.
Superordinate goals Goals that each of two groups desires, but that can be achieved only by both groups cooperating.
Sympathetic nervous system A division of the autonomic nervous system that responds to threat by expending energy and preparing the body for fight or flight.
Vicarious Experiencing something as though it were happening to oneself.
Working memory model Explains STM memory in terms of a central executive that co-ordinates the phonological loop (verbal information) and the visuo-spatial scratchpad (visual and spatial information).
'Write-up' See 'report'.

Suggested reading

Abrams, D. and Hogg, M. (1990a) *Social Identity Theory: Constructive and Critical Advances*, London: Harvester Wheatsheaf

Abrams, D. Wetherell, M. Cochrane, S. Hogg, M.A. and Turner, J.C. (1990) 'Knowing what to think by knowing who you are: Self-categorisation and the nature of norm formation, conformity and group polarisation,' *British Journal of Social Psychology*, 29 (Part 2), pp. 97-119

Ainsworth, M.D.S., Blehar, M.C., Waters, E. and Wall, S. (1978), *Patterns of Attachment: a Psychological Study of the Strange Situation,* Hillsdale, NJ, Lawrence Erlbaum Associates Inc.

Allen, H. (1987) *Justice unbalanced: Gender, Psychiatry and the law*, Open University Press

Allport, G.W. (1954) *The Nature of Prejudice*, Reading, MA, Addison-Wesley

Allport, G.W. (1958) *The Nature of Prejudice* (2nd edition), Reading, MA, Addison-Wesley

Altemeyer, B. (1988) *Enemies of freedom,* San Francisco, CA, Jossey-Bass

Altemeyer, B. (1998) 'The other 'authoritarian personality,' in Zanna, M. (ed) *Advances in experimental social psychology*, Vol. 30, pp. 47-92, San Diego, CA, Academic Press

Altemeyer, B. (2003) 'What happens when authoritarians inherit the Earth? A simulation,' *Analyses of Social Issues and Public Policy*, 3, pp. 15-23

Amato, P.R. (1991) 'The 'child of divorce' is a person prototype: bias in the recall of information about children in divorced families,' *Journal of Marriage and the Family*, Vol. 53, pp. 59-70

Aronson, E. (1992) *The Social Animal* (6th edition), New York, NY, Freeman

Aronson, E. (2000) 'Reducing prejudice in the classroom: The Jigsaw strategy,' *Psychology Review*, Vol. 7, No. 2 pp. 2-5

Aronson, E., Wison, T.D. and Akert, R.M. (1999) *Social Psychology* (3rd edition), New York, NY, Addison Wesley Longman

Asch, S.E. (1951) 'Effects of group pressure upon the modification and distortion of judgements,' in Guetzkow, H. (ed), *Groups, leadership and men*, Pittsburgh, Carnegie Press

Bandura, A. (1965) 'Influence of models reinforcement contingencies on the acquisition of initiative responses,' *Journal of Personality and Social Psychology*, 1, 589-595

Banyard, P. and A. Grayson (2000) *Introducing Psychological Research* (2nd Edition), Basingstoke, Palgrave Ltd

Baron, R.A. and Byrne, D. (1999) *Social Psychology* (8th edition), Boston, MA, Allyn and Bacon

Baron, R.S., and Byrne, D. (2000) *Social psychology* (9th edition), Boston, MA, Allyn and Bacon

Baron and Richardson, D.R. (1994) *Human Aggression* (2nd edition), New York, NY, Plenum

Bassett, J., Pearcey, S., Dabbs, J.M., (2001) 'Jealousy and partner preference among butch and femme lesbians,' *Psychology, Evolution and Gender*, Vol. 3, No. 2, pp. 155-165 (11)

Baumeister, R.F. (2001) 'Violent pride,' *Scientific American*, April, pp. 82-87

Bee, H. (1994) *Lifespan Development*, New York, NY, HarperCollins

Bell, J. (1999) *Doing Your Research Project* (3rd Edition), Buckingham, Open University Press

Bellur, R. (1995) 'Interpersonal attraction revisited: Cross-cultural concepts of love,' *Psychology Review*, 1, pp. 24-26

Bentley, E. (2000) 'Prejudice: An evolutionary attitude?' *Psychology Review*, Vol. 7, No. 2, pp. 18-19

Bentley, E. (2002), Letting off steam, Exploring aggression, Psychology Review, Vol. 8, No. 3, pp. 14-17

Berkowitz, L. (1964) 'Aggressive cues in aggressive behaviour and hostility catharsis,' *Psychological Review*, 71, pp. 104-122

Berkowitz, L. (1974) 'Some determinants of impulsive aggression: The role of mediated associations with reinforcements of aggression,' *Psychological Review*, 81, pp. 165-176

Berkowitz, L. and LePage, A. (1967) 'Weapons as aggressive-eliciting stimuli,' *Journal of Personality and Social Psychology*, 7, pp. 202-207

Blais, M.R. Sabourin, S., Boucher, C. and Vallerand, R.J. (1990) 'Toward a motivational model of couple happiness,' *Journal of Personality and Social Psychology*, 59, pp. 1021-31

Bowlby, J. (1953) *Childcare and the growth of love*, Harmondsworth, Penguin

Bradby, H. (ed.) (1996) *Defining violence*, Aldershot, Avebury

Breakwell, G. M., Hammons, S. and Fife-Shaw, C. (1995) *Research Methods in Psychology*, Sage, London

Brehm, S.S. and Kassin, S.M. (1996) *Social Psychology* (3rd edition), New York, NY, Houghton Mufflin

Bretherton, I. (1985), 'Attachment theory: Retrospect and prospect,' in Bretherton, I. and Walters, E. (eds) 'Growing points of attachment theory and research', *Child Development Monographs*, 50, Nos. 1-2

Brewer, M.B. and Brown, R.J. (1998) 'Intergroup relations,' in Gilbert, D.T., Gilbert, S.T., Fisk, S.T. and Lindzey, G. (eds) *The handbook of social psychology* (4th edition, Vol.2), New York, NY, McGraw-Hill

Broverman, I.K., Vogel. S.R., Broverman, D.M., Clarkson, F.E. and Rosencrantz, P.S. (1972) 'Sex role stereotypes: a current appraisal,' *Journal of Social Issues*, 28, pp. 59-78

Brown, R.J. (1995) *Prejudice: its social psychology*, Oxford, Blackwell

Browne,K. and Pennell, A. (1998) 'The effects of video violence on young offenders,' *Research Findings*, No. 65, London, Home Office Research and Statistics Directorate, HMSO

Burns, J. (1992), 'Mad or just plain bad: Gender and the work of forensic clinical psychologists,' in Usher, J.M. and Nicholson, P. (eds) *Gender issues in clinical psychology*, London, Routledge

Burton, L. J. (2002) *An Interactive Approach to Writing Essays and Research Reports in Psychology*, Milton, Queensland, John Wiley and Sons

Bushman, B. J. and Baumeister, R.F. (1998) 'Threatened egotism, narcissism, self-esteem, and direct and displaced aggression: does self-love or self-hate lead to violence?' *Journal of Personality and Social Psychology*, 75, pp. 219-29

Bushman, B. J. Baumeister, R. F. and Stack, A. D. (1999) 'Catharsis, aggressive and persuasive influence: self-fulfilling or self-defeating prophecies?' *Journal of Personality and Social Psychology*, 76, pp. 367-76

Buss, D.M. (1988) 'Love acts: The evolutionary biology of love, in Sternberg, R.J. and Barnes, M.L. (eds) *The psychology of love*, New Haven, CT, Yale University Press

Buss, D.M., Abbott, M. *et al* (1990) 'International preferences in selecting mates,' *Journal of Cross-cultural Psychology*, 21, pp. 5-47

Buunk, B.P., Dijkstra, P., Fetchenhauer, D., Kenrick, D.T. (2002) 'Age and Gender Differences in Mate Selection Criteria for Various Involvement Levels,' *Personal Relationships*, Vol. 9, No. 3, pp. 271-278 (08)

Byrne, D. (1971) *The attraction paradigm*, New York, NY, Academic Press

Calvert-Smith, D. (2001) 'CPS accepts charge of 'institutional racism,' Special report: race issues in the UK, (July 26, 2001), http://www.guardian.co.uk/racism/Story/0,2763,527962,00.html

Campbell, A. (1999) 'Staying alive: Evolution, culture, and women's intrasexual aggression,' *Behavioural and Brain Sciences*, 22, pp. 203-252

Carlson, E.A. and Stroufe, L.A. (1995) 'Contribution of attachment theory to developmental psychopathology,' in Cicchetti, D. and Conen, D.J, (eds) *Developmental psychopathology: Volume 1. Theory and methods*, New York, NY, Wiley

Catalano, R. Novaco, R. and McConnell, W. (1997) 'A model of the net effect of job loss on violence,' *Journal of Personality and Social Psychology*, 72, pp.1440-1447

Chalmers, A. F. (1985) *What is this thing called Science?* Milton Keynes, Open University Press

Clark, R.D. III (1990) 'Minority influence: The role of argument refutation of the majority position and social support for the minority position,' *European Journal of Social Psychology*, 20, pp. 489-497

Clore, G.L. (1976) 'Interpersonal attraction: An overview,' in Thilbaut, J.W., Spence, J.T. and Carson, R.C. (eds.) *Contemporary topics in social psychology*, Morristown, NJ, General Learning Press

Cochrane, R. (1983) *The Social Creation of Mental Illness*, London, Longman

Cochrane, R. (1996) 'Marriage and madness,' *Psychology Review*, 3, pp. 2-5

Cohen-Kettenis, P.T. and van Goozen, S.H.M. (1997) 'Sex reassignment of adolescent transsexuals: a follow-up study,' *Journal of the American Academy of Child and Adolescent Psychiatry*, 36, pp. 263-71

Coie and Koepple (1990) in Woodhead, M. *et al* (eds) (1998) *Making sense of social development,* London, Routledge

Collins, S.C. and Kneale, P.E. (2001) *Study Skills for Psychology Students: A Practical Guide*, Trowbridge, Redwood Books

Coolican, H. (1996) *Introduction to Research Methods and Statistics in Psychology* (2nd edition), London, Hodder and Stoughton

Craik, F.I.M. and Lockhart, R.S. (1972) 'Levels of processing: A framework for memory research,' *Journal of Verbal Learning and Verbal Behaviour*, 11, pp. 671-684.

Craik, F.I.M. and Tulving, E. (1975) 'Depth of processing and the retention of words in episodic memory,' *Journal of Experimental Psychology*, 104, pp. 268-294

Cramer, D. (1995) 'Special issue on personal relationships,' *The Psychologist*, Vol. 8, pp. 58-59

Crisp, R.J. (2002) 'Social categorisation: Blurring the boundaries,' *The Psychologist*, Vol. 15, No. 12, pp. 612-615

Crisp, R.J., Hewstone, M. and Rubin, M. (2001) 'Does multiple categorisation reduce intergroup bias?' *Personality and Social Psychology Bulletin*, 27, pp. 76-89

Curtis, A. (2002) 'Terrorism,' *Psychology Review*, Vol. 19, No. 1

Darwin, C. (1859) *The origin of species by means of natural selection*, London, John Murray

Deaux, K. Dane, F.C. and Wrightsman, L.S. (1993) *Social Psychology in the '90s*. (6th edition), Pacific Grove, CA, Brooks-Cole

Divine, J, Bishop (2004) 'Bigotry is not bred in school,' *The Sunday Times – Scotland*, February 1

Dollard, J., Doob, L.W., Miller, N.E., Mower, O.H. and Sears, R.R. (1939) *Frustration and aggression*, New Haven, CT, Yale University Press
Douglas, N., Warwick, I., Whitty, G., Aggleton, P., Kemp, S., (1999) 'Homophobic bullying in secondary schools in England and Wales – teachers' experiences,' *Health Education*, Vol. 99, No. 2, pp. 53-60 (8)
Dowling, E., Barnes, G. (2000) (as cited in Dowling, E.) 'The changing family,' *The Psychologist*, Vol.15, No.10, pp. 4-5
Duck, S. (1988) *Relating to others*, Milton Keynes, Open University Press
Duck, S. (1992) *Human Relationships* (2nd edition), London, Sage
Duck, S. (1999) *Relating to Other,* (2nd edition), Milton Keynes, Open University Press
Duck, S. (1995) 'Repelling the study of attraction,' *The Psychologist*, 8, pp. 60-3
Eiser, J.R. (1986) *Social Psychology: Attitudes, Cognition and Social Behaviour*, Cambridge, Cambridge University Press
Feeney, J.A. (1994) 'Attachment style, communication patterns and satisfaction across the life cycle of marriage,' *Personal Relationships*, 1, pp. 338-48
Feeney, J.A. and Noller, P. (1990) 'Attachment style as a predictor of adult romantic relationships,' *Journal of Personality and Social Psychology*, 58, pp. 281-91
Fehr, B. (1996) *Friendship processes*, Thousand Oaks, CA, Sage
Feldman, S. (2003) 'Enforcing Social Conformity: A Theory of Authoritarianism,' *Political Psychology*, Vol. 24, No.1, pp. 41-74
Feyerabend, P. (1986) *Against Method*, London, Verso
Fincham, F. (1997) 'Understanding marriage. From fish scales to milliseconds,' *The Psychologist*, 10, pp. 543-547
Fisher, R. A. and Yates, F. (1953) *Statistical Tables for Biological, Agricultural and Medical Research*, Edinburgh, Oliver and Boyd Ltd
Foster, K., (2003) 'Fury at gay propaganda in schools,' *The Scottish Daily Mail*, 31 December 2003
Freud, S. (1920 [1975]) *Beyond the pleasure Principle*, New York, NY, Norton
Freud, S. (1963) *Two Short Accounts of Psychoanalysis*, Harmondsworth, Pelican
Gaertner, S.L., Mann, J., Marrell, A., Dovidio, J.F. (1989) 'Reducing in-group bias: the benefits of recategorisation,' *Journal of Personality and Social Psychology*, 57, pp. 239-249
Gaertner, S.L., Rust M.C., Dovidio, J.F., Bachman, B.A. and Anastasio, P.A. 'The contact hypothesis: the role of a common in-group identity on reducing inter-group bias,' *Small Groups Research*, 25 (2), pp. 224-249
Gamson, W.B., Fireman, B. and Rytina, S. (1982), *Encounters with unjust authority*, Homewood, IL, Dorsey Press
Gladue, B. (1991) 'Aggressive behavioural characteristics, hormones, and sexual orientation in men and women,' *Aggressive Behaviour*, 17, pp. 313-26
Gladue, B.A. Boechler, M. and McColl, K.D. (1989), Hormonal response to competition in human males, Aggressive Behaviour, 15, 409-22
Glick, R.A. and Roose, S.P. (eds) (1993) *Rage, power, and aggression*, New Haven, CT, Yale University Press
Goodwin, R. (1995) 'Personal relationships across cultures,' *The Psychologist*, 8, pp. 73-75
Griffit, W.B. and Veitch, R. (1971) 'Hot and crowded: influence of population density and temperature on interpersonal affective behaviour,' *Journal of Personality and Social Psychology*, 17, pp. 92-8
Gross, R, (2002) 'Partnering,' *Psychology Review*, Vol. 9, No. 1, pp. 26 –27
Gross, R. (2003) 'The Strange Situation: Study of attachments in 1-year-olds', *Psychology Review*, Vol. 9, No. 3, pp. 24-25
Gross, R.D., McIlveen, R., Coolican, H., Clamp, A., and Russell, J. (2000), *Psychology: a New Introduction for A2,* London, Hodder and Stoughton
Grossmann, K., Grossmann, K.E., Spangler, S. Suess, G. and Unzner, L. (1985) 'Maternal sensitivity and newborn orientation responses as related to quality of attachment in Northern Germany,' *Monographs of the Society for Research in Child Development*, 50 (1-2 Serial No. 209)
Harris, N.B. (1992) 'Sex, race and experiences of aggression,' *Aggressive Behaviour*, 18, pp. 201-17
Harris, P. (2002) *Designing and Reporting Experiments in Psychology* (2nd Edition), Maidenhead, Open University Press
Harrower, J. (1999) 'Why do children kill? Applying psychology to serious crime,' *Psychology Review*, Vol. 6, No. 2, pp. 22-25
Hazan, C. and Shaver, P. (1987) 'Romantic love conceptualised as an attachment process,' *Journal of Personality and Social Psychology*, 59, pp. 511-24
Hetherington, E.M., Cox, M. and Cox, R. (1982) 'Effects of divorce on parents and children,' in Lamb, M. (ed) *Nontraditional Families*, Hillsdale, NJ, Erlbaum
Hetherington, E.M. (1989) 'Coping with family transitions: Winners, losers and survivors,' *Child Development*, 60

Hetherington, E.M. (1991a) 'The role of individual differences and family relationships in children's coping with divorce and remarriage,' in Cowen, P.A. and Hetherington, M. (eds) *Family transitions*, Hillsdale, NJ, Erlbaum
Hetherington, E.M. (1991b) 'Presidential address: Families, lies, and videotapes,' *Journal of Research on Adolescence*, I, pp. 323-348
Hewstone, M. (2003) 'The contact hypothesis, Intergroup contact Panacea for prejudice?' *The Psychologist*, Vol. 16, No. 7, pp. 352-355
Hill, C.T., Rubin, Z. and Peplau, L.A. (1976) 'Break-ups before marriage: the end of 103 affairs,' *Journal of Social Issues*, 32 (1), pp. 147-68
Hogg, M.A. and Vaughan, G.M. (1995) *Social Psychology: An introduction*, Hemel Hempstead, Prentice Hall/Harvester Wheatsheaf
Hollin, C.R. (1990) 'Social skills training with delinquents: a look at the evidence and some recommendations for practice,' *British Journal of Social Work*, 20, pp. 483-93
Holmes, T.H. and Rahe, R. H. (1967) 'The social readjustment rating scale,' *Journal of Psychosomatic Research*, 11, pp. 213-218.
Homan, G.C. (1961) *Social behaviour: Its elementary forms*, New York, NY, Harcourt, Bruce and World
Hoyle, F. and Wickramasinghe, C. (1999) 'Towards an understanding of the nature of racial prejudice,' *Journal of Scientific Exploration*, Vol. 13, No. 4, pp. 681-684
Jones, J.M. (1996) *The psychology of racism and prejudice*, New York, NY, McGraw-Hill
Keat, R. and Urry, J. (1982) *Social Theory as Science*, London, Routledge and Kegan Paul Ltd
Kelley, H.H., Berscheid, E., Christensen, A., Harvey, J.H., Hustin, T.L., Levinger, G., McClintock, E., Peplau, L.A. and Peterson, D.R. (1983) *Close Relationships*, New York, NY, Freeman
Kernis *et al* (1989) 'Stability and level of self-esteem as predictors of anger arousal and hostility,' *Journal of personality and Social Psychology*, 56, pp. 1013-1022
Kiecolt-Glaser, J. K., Marucha, P.T., Malarkey, W. B., Mercado, A. M. and Glaser, R. (1995) 'Slowing of wound healing by psychological stress,' *The Lancet*, 346, pp. 1194-1196
Kitzinger, C. and Coyle, A. *et al* (1995) 'Lesbian and gay couples: Speaking of difference,' *The Psychologist*, 8, pp. 64-69
Knafo, A. (2003) 'Authoritarians, the Next Generations: Values and Bullying Among Adolescent Children of Authoritarian Fathers,' *Analyses of Social Issues and Public Policy*, Vol. 3, No.1, pp. 199-204
Koluchova, J. (1976) 'The further development of twins after severe and prolonged deprivation: A second report,' *Journal of Child Psychology and Psychiatry*, 17, pp. 181-188
Krebs, D. and Blackman, R. (1988) *Psychology: A First Encounter*, New York, NY, Harcourt Brace Jovanovich
Kushner, H. (1996) 'Suicide bombers: business as usual,' *Studies in Conflict and Terrorism*, Vol. 19, pp. 329-38
La Piere, R.T. (1934) 'Attitudes versus actions,' *Social Forces*, 13, pp. 230-237
Latane, B. and Darley, J.M. (1968) 'Group inhibitions of bystander intervention in emergencies,' *Journal of Personality and Social Psychology*, 10, pp. 215-221
Levitt, M.J. (1991) 'Attachment and close relationships: A life-span perspective,' in Gewirtz, J.L. and Kurtines, W.M. (eds) *Intersections with attachment*, Hillsdale, NJ, Erlbaum
Levy, J. (1989) 'Lateral dominance and aesthetic preference,' *Neuropsychologia*, 14, pp. 431-445
Loew, (1967) 'Acquisition of a hostile attitude and its relationship to aggressive behaviour,' *Journal of Personality and Social Psychology*, 5, pp. 335-341
Lorenz, K., (1950) 'The comparative method in studying innate behaviour patterns,' *Symposium of the Society of Experimental Biology*, 4, pp. 2221-2268
Macpherson of Cluny, Sir W. (1999) *The Stephen Lawrence Inquiry: Report of an Inquiry* by Sir William Macpherson of Cluny, London, HMSO
McDougall, W. (1908) *An Introduction to Social Psychology*, London, Metheun
McNeill, P. (1985) *Research Methods*, London, Tavistock Publications
Milgram, S. (1963) 'Behavioural study of obedience,' *Journal of Abnormal Psychology*, 67, pp. 371-378
Miller, S. (1975) *Experimental Design and Statistics*, London, Methuen
Moghaddam, F.M., Taylor, D.M., and Wright, S.C. (1993) *Social psychology in cross-cultural perspectives*, New York, NY, Freeman and Company
Moscovici, S. Lage, E. and Naffrechoux, M. (1969) 'Influence of a consistent minority on the responses of a majority in a colour perception task,' *Sociometry*, 32, pp. 365-380
Moser, C.A. and Kalton, G. (1983) *Survey Methods in Social Investigation*, Aldershot, Gower Publishing Company
Mugny, G. and Papatamou, S. (1980) 'When rigidity does not fail: Individualisation and psychologisation as resistances to the diffusion of minority innovation,' *European Journal of Social Psychology*, 10, pp. 43-62
Malim, T. and Birch, A. (1998) *Introductory Psychology*, Houndsmills, Macmillan

Myers, L.B. and Brewin, C.R. (1994) 'Recall of early experiences and the repressive coping style,' *Journal of Abnormal Psychology*, 103, pp. 288-292
Newton-Smith, W. H. (1986) *The Rationality of Science*, London, Routledge and Kegan Paul
O'Conner, T. (2004) *Experimental and Quasi-Experimental Research Design*, at http://faculty.ncwc.edu/toconnor/308/308lect06.htm
Office of National Statistics (1997) *Labour Force Survey*, Spring (data made available by DfEE)
Orne, M.T. (1962) 'On the social psychology of the psychological experiment: With particular reference to demand characteristics and their implications,' *American Psychologist*, 17, pp. 776-783
Orne, M.T. and Holland, C.C. (1968) 'On the ecological validity of laboratory deceptions,' *International Journal of Psychiatry,* 6 (4), pp. 282-293
Orne, M. T. and Scheibe, K. E. (1964) 'The contribution of non-deprivation factors in the production of sensory deprivation effects: the psychology of the 'panic button',' *Journal of Abnormal and Social Psychology*, 68, pp. 3-12
Osama Bin Laden (February 1998) at http://www.understandingprejudice.org/apa/english/
Oswald, D.B. and Clark, E.M. (2003) 'Best friends forever? High school best friendships and the transition to college,' *Personal Relationships*, 10, pp. 187-196
Owen, F. and Jones, R. (1990) *Statistics*, London, Pitman
Peplau, L.A. (1982) 'Research on homosexual couples: An overview,' *Journal of Homosexuality*, 8, pp. 3-8
Peplau, L.A. (1991) 'Lesbian and gay relationships,' in Gonsiorek, J.C. and Weinrich, J.D. (eds) *Homosexuality: Research Implications for Public Policy*, London, Sage
Peterson, L.R. and Peterson, M.J. (1959) 'Short-term retention of individual items,' *Journal of Experimental Psychology*, 58, pp. 193-198
Petty and Cacioppo (1981) (as cited in) Malim, T. and Birch, A. (1998) *Introductory Psychology*, Houndsmills, Macmillan
Piliavin, I.M., Rodin, J. and Piliavin, J.A. (1969) 'Good Samaritanism: An underground phenomenon?' *Journal of Personality and Social Psychology*, 13, pp. 289-299
Popper, K.R. (1959) *The Logic of Scientific Discovery*, Hutchinson, London
Popper, K.R. (1972) *Conjectures and Refutations: The Growth of Scientific Knowledge*, London. Routledge and Kegan Paul
Prior, P.M. and Hayes B.C. (2003) 'The relationship between marital status and health: An Empirical Investigation of Differences in Bed Occupancy Within Health and Social Care Facilities in Britain, 1921-1991,' *Journal of Family Issues*, Vol. 24, No.1, January 2003, pp. 124-148
Prunier, G. (1995) *The Rwanda Crisis (1959-1994): History of a genocide*, London, Hurst and Co.
Quattrone, G.A. (1982) 'Overattribution and unit formation: when behaviour engulfs the person,' *Journal of Personality and Social Psychology*, Vol. 36, pp. 247-56
Rasch, W. (1996) 'Psychological dimensions of political terrorism in the Federal Republic of Germany,' *International Journal of Law and Psychiatry*, Vol. 2, pp. 79-85
Raye, R.H. Mahan, J. and Arthur, R. (1970) 'Prediction of near-future health-change from subject' preceding life changes,' *Journal of Psychosomatic Research*, 14, pp. 401-406
Reaves, C.C. (1992) *Quantitative Research for the Behavioural Sciences*, New York, NY, Wiley
Reis, H.T. (1986) 'Relationships,' in Manstead, A.S.R. and Hewstone, M. *et al* (eds) *The Blackwell Encyclopedia of social psychology*, Oxford, Blackwell
Rhodewalt, F., Madrian, J.C. and Cheney, S. (1998) 'Narcissism, self-knowledge, organization, and emotional reactivity: the effects of daily experiences on self-esteem and affect,' *Personality and Social Psychology Bulletin*, 24, pp. 75-86
Riggio, H.R. (2004) 'Parental marital conflict and divorce, parent-child relationships, social support, and relationship anxiety in young adulthood,' *Personal Relationships*, 11, pp. 99-114
Robson, C. (1973) *Experimental Design and Statistics in Psychology*, London, Penguin
Rodgers and Price (1998) (as cited in) Dowling, E., 'The changing family,' *The Psychologist*, Vol.15, No.10, pp. 4-5
Roethlisberger, F.J. and Dickson, W.J. (1939) *Management and the Worker*, Cambridge, MA, Harvard University Press
Rosenhan, D.L. (1973) 'On being sane in insane places,' *Science*, 179, pp. 250-258
Rosenkoetter, L.I., Rosenkoetter, S.E., Ozretich, R.A. and Acock, A.C. (2004) 'Mitigating the harmful effects of violent television,' *Applied Developmental Psychology*, 25, pp. 25-47
Rosenthal, R. and Jacobson, L. (1968) *Pygmalion in the classroom*, New York, NY, Holt, Rhinehart and Winston
Ross, N. (1999) 'The banned played on,' *The Guardian*, March 25
Sayer, A. (1984) *Method in Social Science*, Melbourne, Victoria, Hutchinson and Co. (Publishers)
Schaffer, H.R. and Emerson, P.E. (1964) 'The development of social attachments in infancy,' *Monographs of the Society for Research in Child Development*, Vol. 29, No. 3

Searle, A. (1999) *Introducing Research and Data in Psychology: A guide to Methods and Analysis*, London, Psychology Press
Shepard, C., Giles, H., and LePoire, B.A. (2001) 'Communication accommodation theory,' in Robinson, W.P. and Giles, H. (eds) *The new handbook of language and social psychology*, Chichester, John Wiley
Sherif, M., Harvey, O.J., and Sherif, C. (1961) *Inter-group conflict and cooperation: The Robber's Cave experiment,* Norman, OK, University of Oklahoma, Institute of Inter-group Relationships
Shettel-Neuber, J., Bryson, J.B. and Young, L.E. (1978) 'Physical attractiveness of the 'other person' and jealousy,' *Personality and Social Psychology Bulletin*, 4, pp. 612-15
Silke, A. (2002) *Understanding Terrorism*, Vol. 9, No. 1, pp. 17-19
Singh, D. (1993) 'Adaptive significance of female physical attractiveness: Role of waist-to-hip ratio,' *Journal of Personality and Social Psychology*, 65, pp. 293-307
Sjoberg, G. and Nett, R. (1968) *A Methodology for Social Research*, London, Harper and Row
Smith, C.A., Stillman, S., (May 2002) 'What do Women Want? The Effects of Gender and Sexual Orientation on the Desirability of Physical Attributes in the Personal Ads of Women,' *Sex Roles*, Vol. 46, No. 9-10, pp. 337-342(6)
Sperling, G. (1960) 'The information available in brief visual presentations,' *Psychological Monographs*, 74 (489), pp. 1-29
Soliz, J. Harwood, J. (November 2003) 'Perceptions of Communication in a Family Relationship and the Reduction of Intergroup Prejudice,' *Journal of Applied Communication Research*, Vol. 31, No.4, pp. 320-345
Strangor, C. (ed) (2000) *Stereotypes and prejudice: Essential readings*, Philadelphia, Psychology Press
Sutton, J. (1998) 'Stepfamilies and children's development,' *The Psychologist*, Vol. 12, No. 3, pp. 120
Tajfel, H. (1981) *Human groups and social categories: studies in social psychology*, Cambridge, Cambridge University Press
Tajfel, H. and Turner, J.C. (1979) 'An integrative theory of inter-group conflict,' in Austin, W.G. and Worchel, S. (eds) *The Social Psychology of inter-group relationships*, Monterey, CA, Brooks/Cole
Takahashi, K. (1990) 'Are the key assumptions of the 'strange situation' universal?' *Human Development,* 33, pp. 23-30
Thibaut, J.W. and Kelley, H.H. (1959) *The Social psychology of Groups*, Wiley
Thigpen, C.H. and Cleckley, H. (1954) 'A case of multiple personality,' *Journal of Personality and Social Psychology*, 46, pp. 561-574
Turner, J.C. (1991) *Social influence*, Milton Keynes, Open University Press
Van Goozen *et al* (1995) 'Gender differences in behaviour: activating effects of cross-sex hormones,' *Psychoneurondocrindology*, 20, pp. 343-63
Van Ijzendoorn, M.H. and Kroonenberg, P.M. (1988) 'Cross-cultural patterns of attachment: A meta-analysis of the Strange Situation,' *Child Development*, 59, pp. 147-156
Waddington, D., Jones, K. and Critcher, C. (1987) 'Flashpoints of public disorder,' in Gaskell, G. and Benewick, R. (eds) *The Crowd in Contemporary Britain*, London, Sage
Walster, E., Aronson, V., Abrahan, D. and Rottman, L., 'Importance of physical attraction in dating behaviour,' *Journal of Personality and Social Psychology*, 5, pp. 508-516
Ward, D. (2003) 'Culture Class,' *The Guardian* (January 14), in
http://education.guardian.co.uk/egweekly/story/0,5500,873800,00.html
Watson, J.B. and Rayner, R. (1920) 'Conditioned emotional reactions,' *Journal of Experimental Psychology*, 3, pp. 1-14
Wyke, S. and Ford, G. (1992) 'Competing explanations for associations between marital status and health,' *Social Science and Medicine*, 34, pp. 523-532
Zarate, M., Garcia, B., Garza, A.A., Hitlan, R.T. (2004) 'Cultural threat and perceived realistic group conflict as dual predictors of prejudice,' *Journal of Experimental Social Psychology*, Vol. 40, Issue 1, January, pp. 99-105
Zimbardo, P.G. (1979) *Psychology and Life* (Tenth Edition), Glenview, IL, Scott Foresman

Useful websites

Acton, G.S. (1999) 'Great Ideas in Personality: Intelligence,' http://www.personalityresearch.org/intelligence.html
BPS (2004) 'The Research Digest', http://www.bps.org.uk
Keegan, G. (2003) 'Research methods and the correlation: What is a psychology research investigation all about?' http://www.gerardkeegan.co.uk/resource/research1.htm
Rudner, L and Schafer, W.D. (1999) 'How to write a scholarly research report,' *ERIC/AE digest*, http://www.ericfacility.net/databases/ERIC_Digests/ed435712.html
Sturt, G. (1999) 'Gary Sturt's Web Site,' http://www.garysturt.free-online.co.uk/contacts.htm

www.s-cool.co.uk A useful website for all sorts of psychological information, including stress. Follow the links for AS level, pick 'psychology' and there you will find a link to 'stress'.
www.bbc.co.uk A great website for all sorts of interesting, fun and informative topics relating to psychology. From the homepage follow the browse section link to 'science and nature – human mind and body'. Updated regularly to include current BBC programme information relating to psychology.
www.s-cool.co.uk A useful website for all sorts of psychological information, including attachment. Follow the links for AS level, pick 'psychology' and there you will find a link to 'attachment'.
www.ChildTrauma.org The Child Trauma Academy is a not-for-profit organisation based in Houston, Texas. The mission of the Academy is to help improve the lives of traumatised and maltreated children and their families.

Websites offering help and information relating to parenting issues can be found at:
www.home-start.org.uk
www.surestart.gov.uk
www.connexions.gov.uk
www.nfpi.org
www.children1st.org.uk/parentline/

Statistical information relating to families and family life can be found at www.homeoffice.gov.uk.
http://www.homeoffice.gov.uk/rds/immigration1 for government statistics on immigration in the UK.
http://www.asylumscotland.org.uk/media_myths.php for facts on asylum seekers in the UK from the asylum seekers consortium.
http://www.rcn.org.uk/publications/pdf/heretostay-irns.pdf for statistics from the Royal College of Nursing.
http://www.Scotland.gov.uk/stats for government crime statistics in Scotland.
http://myweb.lsbu.ac.uk/~stafflag/lawsection28.html#Scotland for information on Clause 28.
http://www.eoc.org.uk for information on the relative situation of men and women in Great Britain.
http://www.cre.gov.uk for information on racial equality in Great Britain.
http://www.statistics.gov.uk for information on social trends in Great Britain.

Other:
www.mind-map.com A website with great information on mind-mapping.
www.s-cool.co.uk A useful website for all sorts of psychological information, including memory. Follow the links for AS level, pick 'psychology' and there you will find a link to 'memory'.
www.school.discovery.com Has some fun and brain-boosting games and quizzes. Follow the link to 'brainboosters'.
http://www.holah.karoo.net for summaries of many of the key studies you will be studying on the Higher Psychology course, e.g. Samuel and Bryant (1984), Bandura, Ross and Ross (1961), Hodges and Tizard (1989), Freud (1909), Gould (1982), Hraba and Grant (1970), Rosenhan (1973), Thigpen and Cleckley (1954), Schacter and Singer (1962), Dement and Kleitman (1957), Sperry (1968), Raine (1997), Milgram (1963), Zimbardo (1973), Piliavin (1960) and Tajfel (1970).
http://www.garysturt.free-online.co.uk/keystud2.htm for details of key studies in psychology. This site has examples of the type of questions you may be asked on the research studies in the higher Psychology examination.
http://psychclassics.yorku.ca/topic.htm#psychoanalysis for classic studies on the history of psychology. This may be of interest to those who are keen to further their knowledge of the development of the following areas in psychology: behaviourism; cognition; evolutionary theory; intelligence testing; neuropsychology; personality; statistics and methodology; psychoanalysis and psychotherapy; social psychology; and women and psychology.
http://socialpsychology.org/social.htm for information on a variety of social psychology topics including stereotyping, prejudice and discrimination, social influence, self and social identity, group behaviour, prosocial behaviour and aggression.
http://www.psy.pdx.edu/PsiCafe/KeyTheorists/Ainsworth.htm for information on Ainsworth and the strange situation. This site clearly describes the 'strange situation' study and allows you to work out your own attachment type.
http://www.lapas.org for information on fatherhood. This site looks at contemporary issues facing fathers today.
http://www.mothersandmore.org/Features/Maushart_interview.htm for information on motherhood. This site tackles the myths and misinformation surrounding motherhood.
http://www.hhs.oregonstate.edu/hdfs/acock/tv/ for the entire curriculum used by Rosenkoetter *et al* 1 in their investigation into mitigating the harmful effects of violent television
http://www.bps.org.uk
http://www.apa.org/
http://www.bps.org.uk/index.cfm

http://www.holah.karoo.net/practicalquestions.htm/as.htm
http://www.psychology.org
http://www.sociology.org.uk/methpo8.htm
http://www.s-cool.co.uk/
http://www.sosig.ac.uk/roads/subject-listing/World-cat/resdes.html/

References

Ainsworth M.D.S. (1964) 'Patterns of attachment behaviour shown by the infant in interaction with his mother,' *Merrill-Palmer Quarterly*, Vol. 10, pp. 51-58

Ainsworth, M.D.S. (1967) *Infancy in Uganda: Childcare and the Growth of Love*, Baltimore, MD, John Hopkins University Press

Ainsworth, M.D.S and Bell, S.M (1970). 'Attachment, exploration and separation: Illustrated by the behavior of one-year-olds in a strange situation,' *Child Development*, 41, pp. 49-67

Ainsworth, M.D.S., Blehar, M.C., Waters, E. and Wall, S. (1978) *Patterns of Attachment: A Psychological Study of the Strange Situation*, Hillsdale, New Jersey, NJ, Erlbaum

American Psychiatric Association (1987) *Diagnostic and Statistical Manual of Mental Disorders*, Washington, DC, American Psychiatric Association

Anderson, L.P. (1991) 'Acculturative stress: A theory of relevance to black Americans,' *Clinical Psychology Review*, Vol.11, pp. 685-702

Atkinson, R.C. and Shiffrin, R.M. (1968). 'Human memory: A proposed system and its control processes,' in K.W. Spence and Spence, J.T. (eds), *The Psychology of Learning and Motivation* (Vol. 2), London, Academic Press

Baddeley, A.D. (1999) *Essentials of Human Memory*, Hove, Psychology Press

Baddeley, A.D. (1997) *Human Memory: Theory and Practice (revised edition)*, Hove, Psychology Press

Baddeley, A.D. (1986) *Working Memory*, Oxford, Clarendon Press

Baddeley, A.D., Grant, S., Wright, E. and Thomson, N. (1975) 'Imagery and visual working memory,' in Rabbitt, P.M.A. and Dornic, S. (eds) *Attention and Performance*, Vol. V, London, Academic Press

Baddeley, A.D. and Hitch, G.J. (1977) 'Recency re-examined,' in Dornic, S. (ed) *Attention and Performance*, Hillsdale, New Jersey, NJ, Erlbaum

Baddeley, A.D. and Hitch, G.J. (1974) 'Working memory,' in Bower, G.H. (ed) *The Psychology of Learning and Motivation*, Vol. 8, London, Academic Press

Baddeley, A.D., Thomson, N. and Buchanan, M. (1975) 'Word length and the structure of short-term memory,' *Journal of Verbal Language and Verbal Behaviour*, Vol. 14, pp. 575-589

Bandura, A. (1965) 'Influence of model's reinforcement contingencies on the acquisition of imitative responses,' *Journal of Personality and Social Psychology*, Vol.1, pp. 589-595

Bandura, A., Ross, D. and Ross, S.A. (1961) 'Transmission of aggression through imitation of aggressive models,' *Journal of Abnormal and Social Psychology*, 63, pp. 575-582

Barefoot, J.C., Dodge, K.A., Peterson, B.F., Dahlstrom, W.G. and Williams, R.B. Jr (1989) 'The Cook-Medley hostility scale: Item content and ability to predict survival,' *Psychosomatic Medicine*, Vol.51, pp. 46-57

Baumrind, D. (1967) 'Child care practices anteceding three patterns of preschool behaviour,' *Genetic Psychology Monographs*, Vol. 75, pp. 43-88

Baumrind, D. (1996) 'The discipline controversy revisited,' *Family Relations*, Vol. 45, No. 4, pp. 405-414

Beardsley, T. (1997) 'The machinery of thought,' *Scientific American*, August, pp. 58-63

Beck, A.T. (1976) *Cognitive Therapy and the Emotional Disorders*, New York, NY, International Universities Press

Benton, D. and Cook, R. (1991) 'Vitamins and mineral supplements improve intelligence scores and concentration,' 12 (11), pp. 1151-1158

Berk, L.S., Tan, S.A., Fry, W.F., Napier, B.J., Lee, J.W., Hubbard, R.W., Lewis, J.E. and Eby, W.C. (1989) 'Neuroendocrine and stress hormone changes during mirthful laughter,' *American Journal of the Medical Sciences*, Vol. 298(6), pp. 390-396

Bifulco, A., Harris, T. and Brown, G.W. (1992) 'Mourning or early inadequate care? Re-examining the relationship of maternal loss in childhood with adult depression and anxiety,' *Development and Psychopathology*, Vol. 4, pp. 433-449

Binet, A. and Simon, T. (1905) 'Méthodes nouvelles pour le diagnostique du niveau intellectuel des anormaux,' *L'Année Psychologique*, 11, pp. 245-336

Blum, J.E., Jarvik, L.F. and Clark, E.T. (1970) 'Rate of change on selective tests of intelligence: a twenty-year longitudinal study,' *Journal of Gerontology*, 25, pp. 171-176

Bouchard, T.J. Jr, Lykken, D.T., McGue, M., Segal, N.L. and Tellegen, A. (1981) 'Sources of human psychological differences: The Minnesota study of twins reared apart,' *Science*, 250, No. 4778, pp. 223-227

Bower, G.H. (1972) 'Mental imagery and associative learning,' in Gregg, L. (ed), *Cognition in Learning and Memory*, New York, NY, Wiley

Bower, G.H. (1981) 'Mood and memory,' *American Psychologist*, Vol. 32, pp.129-148

Bowlby, J. (1969) *Attachment and Loss, Vol. 1 Attachment*, London, Hogarth Press

Bowlby, J. (1973) *Attachment and Loss, Vol. 2 Separation: Anxiety and Anger*, New York, NY, Basic Books

Bowlby, J. (1953) *Child Care and the Growth of Love*, Harmondsworth, Penguin
Bowlby, J. (1944) 'Forty-four juvenile thieves, their characters and home lives,' *International Journal of Psychoanalysis*, Vol. 25, pp.107-127
Bowlby, J. (1951) *Maternal Care and Mental Health*, Geneva, World Health Organisation
Brown, G.W. and Harris, T.O. (1978) *Social Origins of Depression*, London, Tavistock
Brown, J.A. (1958) 'Some tests of the decay theory of immediate memory,' *Quarterly Journal of Experimental Psychology*, Vol. 10, pp. 12-21
Browne, K. (1989) 'The naturalistic context of family violence and child abuse,' in Archer, J. and Browne, K. (eds) *Human Aggression: Naturalistic Approaches*, London, Routledge
Burton, L. J. (2002) *An Interactive Approach to Writing Essays and Research Reports in Psychology*, Milton, Queensland, John Wiley and Sons
Bushnell, I.W.R., Sai, F., and Mullin, J.Y. (1989) 'Neonatal recognition of the mother's face,' *British Journal of Developmental Psychology*, Vol. 7, pp. 3-15
Buzan, T. and Buzan, B. (1993) *The Mind Map Book*, London, BBC Worldwide Ltd
Carlson, V., Cicchetti, D., Barnett, D. and Braunwald, K. (1989) 'Disorganised/disoriented attachment relationships in maltreated infants,' *Developmental Psychology*, Vol. 25 pp. 525-531
Castle, D., Scott, K., Wessley, S. and Murray, R.M. (1993) 'Does social deprivation during gestation and early life predispose to schizophrenia?' *Social Psychiatry and Psychiatric Epidemiology* 25, pp. 210-215
Cattell, R.B. (1963) 'Theory of fluid and crystallised intelligence: a critical experiment,' *Journal of Educational Psychology* 54, pp. 1-22
Cohen, S., Tyrell, D.A.J. and Smith, A.P. (1991) 'Psychological stress and susceptibility to the common cold,' *The New England Journal of Medicine*, Vol. 325, pp. 600-612
Conrad, R. (1964) 'Acoustic confusions in immediate memory,' *British Journal of Psychology*, Vol. 55, pp. 75-84
Coolican, H. (1996) *Introduction to Research Methods and Statistics in Psychology* (2nd edition), London, Hodder and Stoughton
Coolican, H. (2004) *Research Methods and Statistics in Psychology* (4th Edition), London, Hodder and Stoughton
Coopersmith, S. (1967) The Antecedents of Self-Esteem, San Fransisco, CA, Freeman
Cossu, G, Rossini, F. and Marshall, J.C. (1992) 'When reading is acquired but phonemic awareness is not: A study of literacy in Down's syndrome,' *Cognition* 46, pp. 129-138
Craik, F.I.M. and Lockhart, R.S. (1972) 'Levels of processing: A framework for memory research,' *Journal of Verbal Learning and Verbal Behaviour*, Vol. 11, pp. 671-684
Craik, F.M. and Tulving, E. (1975) 'Depth of processing and the retention of words in episodic memory,' *Journal of Experimental Psychology*, Vol. 104, pp. 268-294
Crow, T. (1985) 'The two syndrome concept. Origins and current status,' *Schizophrenia Bulletin*, 9, pp. 471-486
Curtiss, S. (1977) *Genie: A Psycholinguistic Study of a Modern-day 'Wild Child,'* London, Academic Press
Darwin, C. (1872) *Expressions of Emotion in Man and Animals*, London, John Murray
Darwin, C. (1859) *The Origin of Species*, London, Collins
DeLongis, A., Coyne, J.C., Dakof, G., Folkman, S. and Lazarus, R.S. (1982) 'Relationship of daily hassles, uplifts and major life events to health status,' *Health Psychology*, Vol.1, No. 2, pp.119-136
Dennis, W. (1973) *Children of the Crèche*, New York, NY, Appleton-Century-Crofts
Devine, P.G. (1989) 'Stereotypes and prejudice: Their automatic and controlled components,' *Journal of Personality and Social Psychology*, 56, pp. 5-18
Dollard, J. and Miller, N.E. (1950) *Personality and Psychotherapy: An Analysis in terms of Learning, Thinking and Culture*, New York, NY, McGraw-Hill
Ebbinghaus, H. (1885) *Memory*, New York, NY, Teacher's College Press
Egeland, J.A., Gerhard, D.S., Pauls, D.L., Sussex, J.N. and Kidd, K.K. (1987) 'Bipolar affective disorders linked to DNA markers on chromosome II,' *Nature*, 325, pp. 783-787
Ellis, A. (1962) Reason and Emotion in Psychotherapy, New York, NY, Life Stuart
Erikson, E. (1963) *Childhood and Society*, New York, NY, Norton
Eysenck, H.J. (1967) *The Biological Basis of Personality*, Springfield, IL, Charles C. Thomas
Fernando, S. (1991) *Mental Health, Race and Culture*, London, Macmillan, in association with MIND Publications
Fiske, S.T. (1989) 'Examining the role of intent: Toward understanding its role in stereotyping and prejudice,' in J.S. Uleman and Bargh, J.A. (eds), *Unintended thought*, New York, NY, Guilford Press
Fleischman, E.A. and Parker, J.F. Jr (1962) 'Factors in the retention and relearning of perceptual motor skills,' *Journal of Experimental Psychology*, Vol. 64, pp. 215-226
Flynn, J.R. (1992) 'Searching for justice: The discovery of IQ gains over time,' *American Psychologist*, 54, pp. 5-20
Foster, J. J. and Parker, I. (1995) *Carrying out Investigations in Psychology*, Guildford and King's Lynn, British Psychology Society

Fox, N. (1977) 'Attachment of Kibbutz infants to mother and metapelet,' *Child Development*, Vol. 48, pp. 1228-1239
Frankenhauser, M. (1983) 'The sympathetic-adrenal and pituitary-adrenal response to challenge: Comparison between the sexes,' in Dembroski, T.M., Schmidt, T.D. and Blumchen, G. (eds) *Biobehavioural bases of coronary heart disease*, Basel, Karger
Frankenhauser, M., Dunne, E. and Lundberg, U. (1976) 'Sex differences in sympathetic-adrenal medullary reactions induced by different stressors,' *Psychopharmacology*, Vol. 47, pp.1-5
Frankenhauser, M., Lundberg, U. and Chesney, M. (1991) *Women, Work and Health: Stress and Opportunities*, New York, NY, Plenum
Freud, S. (1915-1918) *Introductory Lectures on Psychoanalysis*, London, Hogarth Press
Freud, S. (1921) 'Group psychology and the analysis of the ego,' in Strachey, J. (ed) *Standard Edition of the Complete Psychological Works of Sigmund Freud*, Vol. 1, London, Hogarth Press
Freud, S. (1923) 'The ego and the id,' in Strachey, J. (ed) *Standard Edition of the Complete Psychological Works of Sigmund Freud*, Vol. 19, London, Hogarth Press
Freud, S. (1933) *New Introductory Lectures on Psychoanalysis*, New York, NY, Norton
Freud, S. (1936) *The Ego and the Mechanisms of Defence*, London, Chatto and Windus
Freud, S. (1938) *The Basic Writings of Sigmund Freud*, New York, NY, Modern Library
Freud, S. and Breuer, J. (1895 [1991]) 'Studies on hysteria,' in *Penguin Freud Library*, Vol. 3, London, Penguin
Friedman, M. and Rosenman, R.H. (1974) *Type A Behaviour and Your Heart*, New York, NY, Knopf
Freud, S. (1974) *Obedience to Authority*, New York, Harper and Row
Gardner, H. (1983) *Frames of Mind: The theory of multiple intelligence*, New York, NY, Basic Books
Geiselman, R.E., Fisher, R.P., MacKinnon, D.P. and Holland, H.L. (1985) 'Eyewitness memory enhancement in police interview: Cognitive retrieval mnemonics versus hypnosis,' *Journal of Applied Psychology*, Vol. 70, pp. 401-412
Goldfarb, W. (1944) 'The effects of early institutional care on adolescent personality,' *Journal of Experiential Education*, 12, pp. 106-129
Gould, S.J. (1981) *The mismeasure of man*, Harmondsworth, Penguin
Guilford, J.P. (1967) *The Nature of Human Intelligence*, New York, NY, McGraw-Hill
Glanzer, M. and Cunitz, A.R. (1966) 'Two storage mechanisms in free recall,' *Journal of Verbal Learning and Verbal Behaviour*, Vol. 5, pp. 351-360
Godden, D. and Baddeley, A.D. (1975) 'Context-dependent memory in two natural environments: on land and under water,' *British Journal of Psychology*, Vol. 66, pp. 325-331
Goodwin, D.W., Powell, B., Bremer, D., Hoine, H. and Stern, J. (1969) 'Alcohol and recall: State dependent effects in man,' *Science*, Vol. 163, pp. 1358
Grasha, A.F. (1983) *Practical Applications of Psychology* (2nd edition), Boston, MA, Little, Brown and Company
Grossman, K.E. and Grossman, K. (1991) 'Attachment quality as an organiser of emotional and behavioural responses in a longitudinal perspective,' in C.M. Parkes, Stevenson-Hinde, J. and Marris, P. (eds) *Attachment across the life cycle*, London, Tavistock/Routledge
Halgin, R.P. and Whitbourne, S.K. (1993) *Abnormal Psychology: The human experience of psychological disorders*, Fort Worth, TX, Harcourt Brace Jovanovich
Harrell, R.F., Woodyard, E. and Gates, A.I. (1955) *The effects of mother's diet on the intelligence of offspring*, New York, NY, Public Teachers' College, Columbia University
Harlow, H.F. and Zimmerman, R.R. (1959) 'Affectional responses in the infant monkey,' *Science*, Vol. 130, pp. 421-432
Harris, J. (1998) *The Nurture Assumption*, New York, NY, The Free Press
Harris, P. (2002) *Designing and Reporting Experiments in Psychology* (2nd Edition), Maidenhead, Berkshire, Open University Press
Hazan, C. and Shaver, P.R. (1987) 'Romantic love conceptualised as an attachment process,' *Journal of Personality and Social Psychology*, Vol. 52, pp. 511-524
Herman, L. and Hogben, L. (1932) 'The intellectual resemblance of twins,' *Proceedings of the Royal Society of Edinburgh*, 53, pp. 105-129
Hernstein, R.J. and Murray, C. (1994) *The Bell Curve: Intelligence and Class Structure in American Life*, New York, NY, The Free Press
Hetherington, E.M., Bridges, M. and Insabella, G.M. (1998) 'What matters? What does not? Five perspectives on the association between marital transitions and children's adjustment,' *American Psychologist*, Vol. 53 pp. 167-184
Hetherington, E.M. and Stanley-Hagan, M. (1999) 'The adjustment of children with divorced parents: A risk and resiliency perspective,' *Journal of Child Psychology and Psychiatry*, Vol. 40, No. 1, pp. 129-140
Hitch, G. and Baddeley, A.D. (1976) 'Verbal reasoning and working memory,' *Quarterly Journal of Experimental Psychology*, Vol. 28, pp. 603-621

Hodges, J. and Tizard, B. (1989) 'Social and family relationships of ex-institutional adolescents,' *Journal of Child Psychology and Psychiatry*, Vol. 30, No. 1, pp. 77-97
Hogan, H. (1978) 'IQ self-estimates of males and females,' *Journal of Social Psychology*, 106, pp. 137-138
Holmes, T.H. and Rahe, R.H. (1967) 'The social readjustment rating scale,' *Journal of Psychosomatic Research*, Vol.11, pp. 213-218
Horn, J.M. (1983) 'The Texas Adoption Project: Adopted children and their intellectual resemblance to biological and adoptive parents,' *Child Development*, 54, pp. 266-275
Howe, M.J.A. (1997) *IQ in Question: The truth about intelligence*, London, Sage Publications
Kendler, K.S. (1992) 'The genetic epidemiology of phobias in women: the inter-relationships of agoraphobia, social phobias, situational phobia and simple phobia,' *Archives of General Psychiatry*, 49, pp. 273-281
Koluchova, J. (1972, 1976) 'Severe deprivation in twins: A case study,' *Journal of Child Psychology and Psychiatry*, 13, pp. 107-114
Koluchova, J. (1976) 'A report on the further development of twins after severe and prolonged deprivation,' in Clarke, A.M. and Clarke, A.D.B. (eds) *Early Experience: Myth and Evidence*, London, Open Books
Laing, R.D. (1965) *The Divided Self: An Existential Study into Sanity and Madness*, Harmondworth, Penguin
Lamb, M.E. (1977) 'The development of mother-infant and father-infant attachments in the second year of life,' *Developmental Psychology*, Vol. 13, pp. 637-648
Lamb, M.E. (1981) 'The development of the father-infant relationships' in Lamb, M.E. (ed) *The Role of the Father in Child Development*, New York, NY, Wiley
Lazarus, R.S. (1966) *Psychological Stress and the Coping Process*, New York, NY, McGraw-Hill
Lewis, M., Feiring, C., McGuffoy, C. and Jaskir, J. (1984) 'Predicting psychopathology in six-year-olds from early social relations,' *Child Development*, Vol. 55, pp123-136
Loftus, E.F. (1993) 'The reality of repressed memories,' *American Psychologist*, Vol. 48, pp. 518-537
Loftus, E.F. and Palmer, J. (1974) 'Reconstruction of automobile destruction: An example of the interaction between language and memory,' *Journal of Verbal Learning and Verbal Behaviour*, Vol. 13, pp. 585-589
Lynn, R. (1986) 'The rise of national intelligence: Evidence from Britain, Japan and the USA,' *Personality and Individual Differences*, 7(1), pp. 29-32
Newman, H.H., Freeman, F.M. and Holzinger, K.J. (1937) *Twins: A study in heredity and environment*, Chicago, IL, University of Chicago Press
Pavlov, I. (1927) *Conditioned Reflexes*, London, Oxford University Press
Peterson, L.R. and Peterson, M.J. (1959) 'Short term retention of individual items,' *Journal of Experimental Psychology*, Vol. 58, pp. 193-198
Piaget, J. (1952) *Origins of Intelligence in Children*, New York, NY, International Universities Press
Maccoby, E.E. (1980) *Social Development: Psychological Growth and the Parent-child Relationship*, San Diego, CA, Harcourt Brace Jovanovich
MacRae, C.N., Bodenhausen, G.V., Milne, A.B., and Jetten, J. (1994) 'Out of mind but back in sight: stereotypes on the rebound,' *Journal of Personality and Social Psychology*, 67(5), 808-817
Main, M. and Solomon, J (1986) 'Discovery of a disorganised disoriented attachment pattern,' in T.B. Brazelton and Yogman, M.W. (eds) *Affective Development in Infancy*, Norwood, NJ, Ablex
Maquet, P. (2000) 'Sleep on it!' *Nature Neuroscience*, Vol. 3, No. 12, pp. 1235-1236
Maslow, A.H. (1959) 'Cognition of being in the peak experiences,' *Journal of Genetic Psychology*, 94, pp. 43-66
Maslow, A.H. (1970) *The Further Reaches of Human Nature*, New York, NY, Viking
Maurer, D. and Maurer, C. (1989) *The World of the Newborn*, London, Viking
McKenna, S.P. and Glendon, A.I. (1985) 'Occupational first aid training: decay in cardiopulmonary resuscitation (CPR) skills,' *Journal of Occupational Psychology*, Vol. 58, pp.109-117
Meichenbaum, D. (1985) *Stress Inoculation Training*, New York, NY, Pergamon
Miller, G.A. (1956) 'The magical number seven, plus or minus two: some limits on our capacity for processing information,' *Psychological Review*, Vol. 63, pp. 81-97
Milner, B. (1966) 'Amnesia following operation on the temporal lobes,' in Whitty, C.W.M. and Zangwill, O.L. (eds) *Amnesia*, London, Butterworth
Milgram, S. (1974) Obedience to Authority, New York, NY, Harper and Row
Orne, M.T. (1962) 'On the social psychology of the psychological experiment: With particular reference to demand characteristics and their implications,' *American Psychologist*, 17, pp. 776-83
Pederson, N.L., Plomin, R., Nesselrode, J.R. and McClearn, G.E. (1992) 'A quantitative genetic analysis of cognitive abilities during the second half of the life span,' *Psychological Science*, 3(6), pp. 346-353
Piaget, J. (1953) *Play, dreams and imitation in childhood*, London, Routledge and Kegan Paul
Ratcliffe-Crain, J. and Baum, A. (1990) 'Individual differences and health: Gender, coping, and stress,' in Friedman, H.S. (ed) *Personality and Disease*, New York, NY, Wiley

Robertson, J. and Bowlby, J. (1952) 'Responses of young children to separation from their mothers,' *Courier Centre International de l'Enfance*, Vol. 2, pp. 131-142
Robertson, J. and Robertson, J. (1971) 'Young child in brief separation,' *Psychoanalytic Study of the Child*, Vol. 26, pp. 264-315
Robson, C. (1994) *Experiment, Design and Statistics in Psychology* (3rd Edition), London, Penguin
Rogers, C.R. (1961) *On becoming a person*, Boston, MA, Houghton Mifflin
Rogers, C. (1959) 'A theory of therapy, personality and interpersonal relationships, as developed in the client-centred framework,'in Koch, S. (ed) *Psychology: A Study of a Science*. Volume 3, New York, NY, McGraw-Hill
Rosenhan, D.L. (1973) 'On being sane in insane places,' *Science*, 179, pp. 250-258 and pp. 365-369
Rosenhan, D.L. and Seligman, M.E.P. (1995) *Abnormal Psychology*. 3rd Edition, New York, NY, Norton
Rosenthal, R. and Jacobsen, L. (1968) *Pygmalion in the classroom*, New York, NY, Holt, Rinehart and Winston
Rudner, L and Schafer, W.D. (1999) 'How to write a scholarly research report,' *ERIC/AE digest*, http://www.ericfacility.net/databases/ERIC_Digests/ed435712.html
Rushton, J.P. (1995) *Race, Evolution and Behaviour*, New Brunswick, N.J, Transaction Publishers
Rutter, M. (1976) 'Parent-child separation: psychological effects on the child,' in Clarke, A.M. and Clarke, A.D.B. (eds) *Early Experience: Myth and Evidence*, London, Open Books
Rutter, M. (1981) *Maternal Deprivation Reassessed* (2nd Edition), Harmondsworth, Penguin
Sameroff, A.J., Seifer, R., Baldwin, A. and Baldwin, C. (1993) 'Stability of intelligence from pre-school to adolescence: The influence of social and family risk factors,' *Child Development*, 64, pp. 80-97
Scarr, S. and Weinberg, R.A. (1976) 'IQ test performances of black children adopted by white families,' *American Psychologist*, 31, pp. 726-739
Schaffer, H.R. (1996) *Social Development*, Oxford, Blackwell
Schaffer, H.R. (1998*) Making Decisions about Children*, Oxford, Blackwell
Schaffer, H.R. and Emerson, R.E. (1964) 'The development of social attachments in infancy,' *Monographs of the Society for Research in Child Development*, Vol. 29, No. 3, serial no. 94
Schiff, M. and Lewontin, R. (1986) *Education and Class: The Irreverence of IQ Genetic Studies*, Oxford: Clarendon Press
Selye, H. (1956) *The Stress of Life*, New York, NY, McGraw-Hill
Shallice, T. and Warrington, E.K. (1970) 'Independent functioning of verbal memory stores: A neurophysiological study,' *Quarterly Journal of Experimental Psychology*, 22, pp. 261-73
Shallice, T. (1967) *Paper presented at NATO symposium on short-term memory*, Cambridge, England
Shields, J. (1962) *Monozygotic Twins Brought Up Apart and Brought Up Together*, London, Oxford University Press
Skeels, H. (1966) 'Adult status of children with contrasting early life experiences: a follow up study,' *Monographs of Society for Research of Child Development*, 31 (3) (whole issue)
Skinner, B.F. (1938) *The Behaviour of Organisms*, New York, NY, Appleton-Century-Crofts
Skinner, B.F. (1948) *Walden Two*, New York, NY, Macmillan
Skinner, B.F. (1953) *Science and Human Behaviour*, New York, NY, Macmillan
Skinner, B.F. (1974) *About Behaviourism*, New York, NY, Knopf
Spearman, C.E. (1904) 'General Intelligence objectively determined and measured,' *American Journal of Psychology*, 15, pp. : 201-293
Smith, S.M. (1979) 'Remembering in and out of context,' *Journal of Experimental Psychology, Human Learning and Memory*, Vol. 5, pp. 360-371
Steinem, G. (1983) *Outrageous Acts and Everyday Rebellions*, New York, NY, New American Library
Sternberg, R.J. (1977) *Intelligence, Information Processing and Analogical Reasoning: The componential analysis of human abilities*, Hillsdale, N.J, Lawrence Erlbaum
Stoney, C.M., Matthews, K.A., McDonald, R.H. and Johnson, C.A. (1990) 'Sex differences in acute stress response: lipid, lipoprotein, cardiovascular and neuroendocrine adjustments,' *Psychophysiology*, Vol. 12, pp. 52-61
Swanson, V., Power, K.G. and Simpson, R.J. (1998) 'Occupational stress and family life: A comparison of male and female doctors,' *Journal of Occupational and Organisational Psychology*, Vol. 71, pp. 237-260
Takahashi, K. (1990) 'Are the key assumptions of the Strange Situation procedure universal? A view from Japanese research,' *Human Development*, Vol. 33, pp. 23-30
Thurstone, L.L. (1938) *Primary Mental Abilities*, Chicago, IL, University of Chicago Press
Tobin, J.J., Wu, D.Y.H. and Davison, D.H. (1989) *Preschool in Three Cultures: Japan, China and the United States*, New Haven, CT, Yale University Press
Tronick, E.Z., Morrelli, G.A. and Ivey, P.K. (1992) 'The Efe forager infant and toddler's pattern of social relationships: multiple and simultaneous,' *Developmental Psychology*, Vol. 28, pp. 568-577
Tulving, E. (1974) 'Cue-dependent forgetting,' *American Scientist*, Vol. 62, pp. 74-82
Ucros, C.G. (1989) 'Mood state-dependent memory. A meta-analysis,' *Cognition and Emotion*, Vol. 3, pp. 139-167

Vernon, P.E. (1971) *The Structure of Human Abilities*, London, Methuen
Walters, J. and Gardiner, H. (1986) 'The crystallising experience: discovering an intellectual gift,' in Sternberg, R.J. and Davidson, J.E. (eds) *Conception of Giftedness*, New York, NY, Cambridge University Press
Watson, J.B. and Rayner, R. (1920) 'Conditioned emotional responses,' *Journal of Experimental Psychology*, 3, pp. 1-14
Waugh, N.C. and Norman, D.A. (1965) 'Primary memory,' *Psychological Review*, Vol. 72, pp. 89-104
Zajonc, R.B. and Markus, G.B. (1975) 'Birth order and intellectual development,' *Psychological Review*, 82, pp. 74-88

Index

Subject index

Name index